9

Love & Lies

LOVE and LIES by MUSAWO

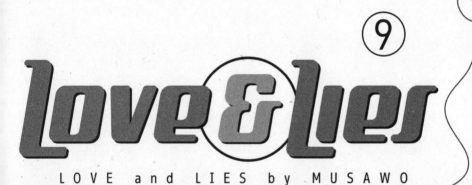

CONTENTS

Chapter 32: The Day the Lies Began

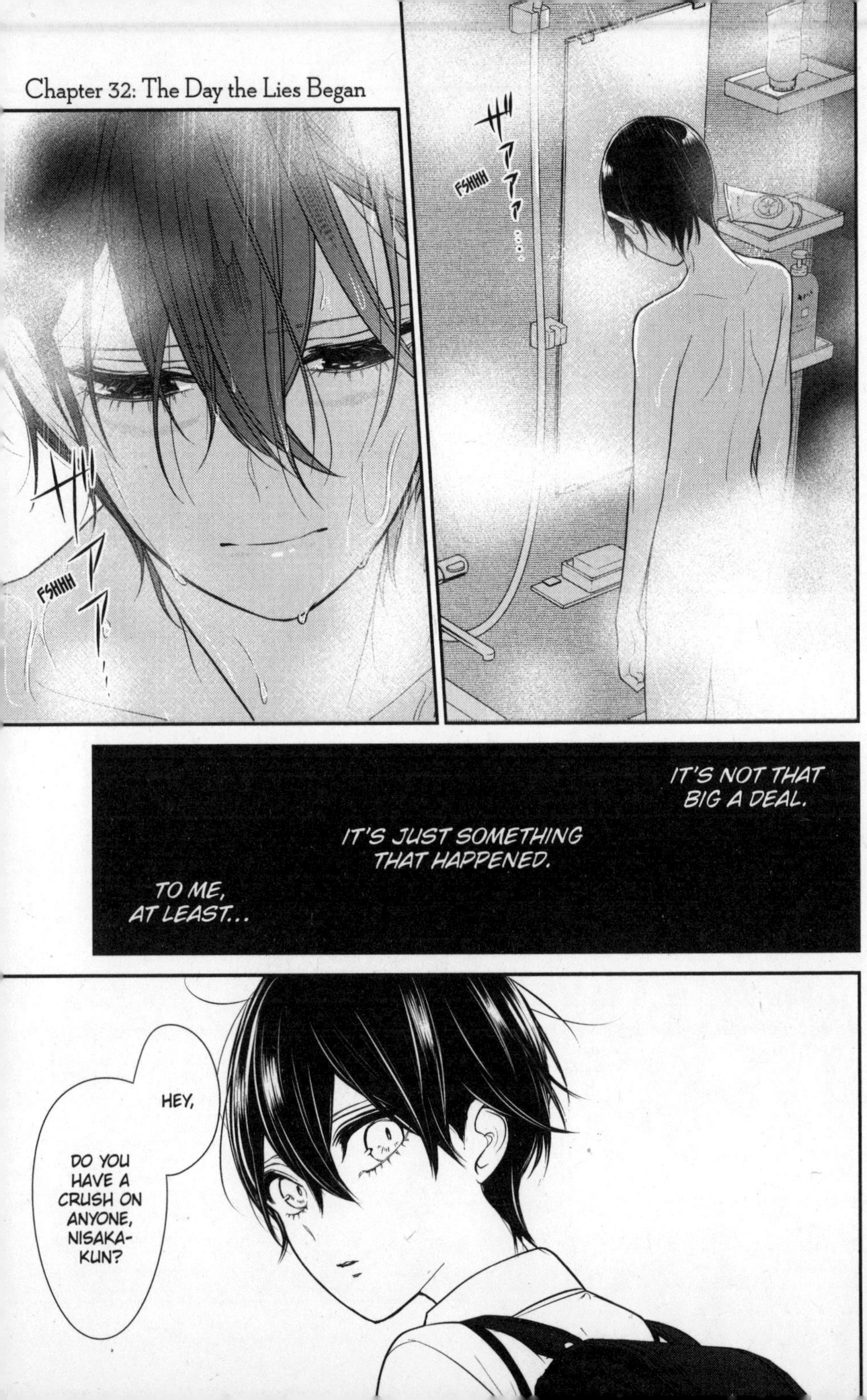
ザァァァ…
FSHHH
ザァァ!
FSHHH
IT'S NOT THAT BIG A DEAL.
IT'S JUST SOMETHING THAT HAPPENED.
TO ME, AT LEAST...
HEY,
DO YOU HAVE A CRUSH ON ANYONE, NISAKA-KUN?

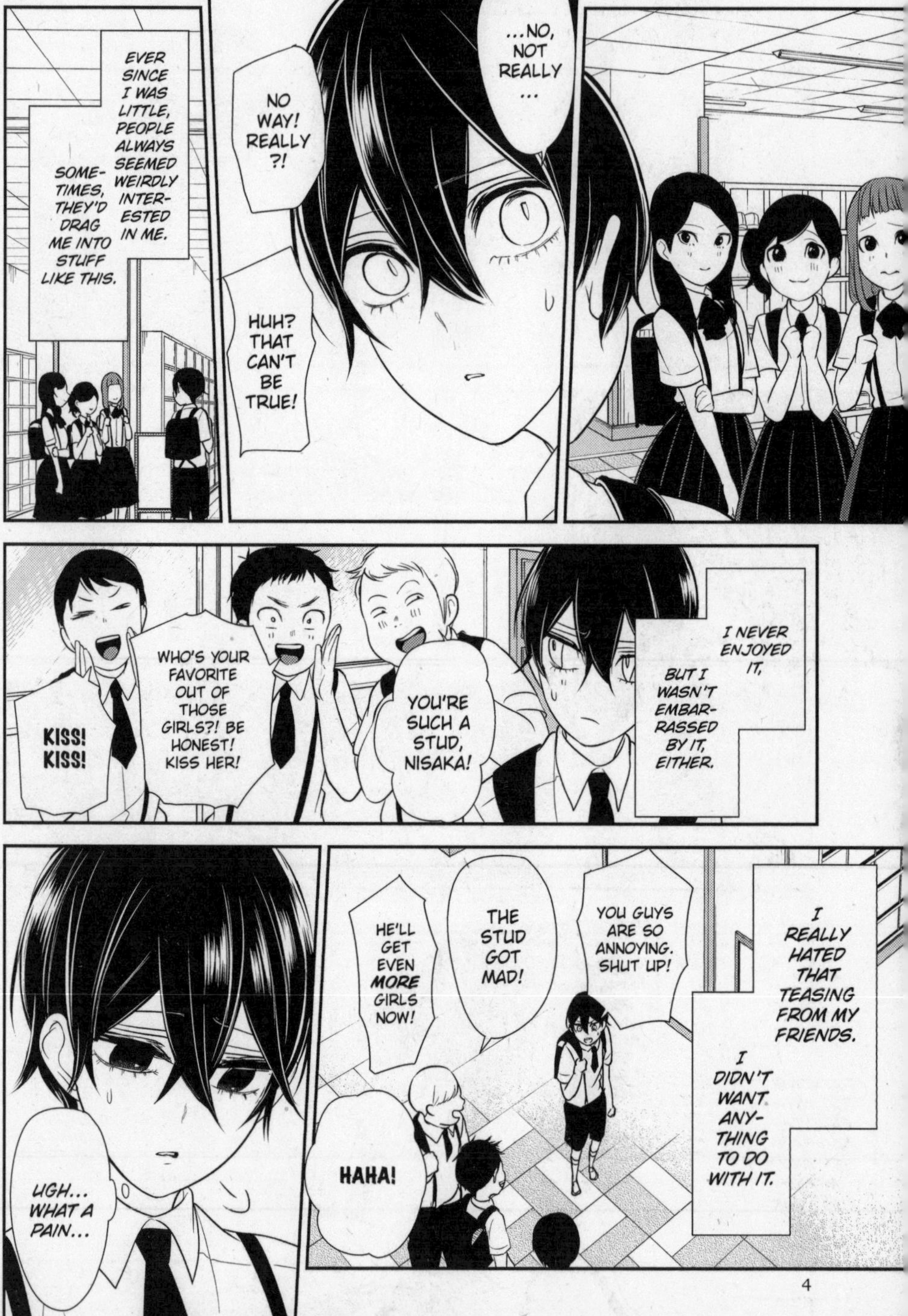
...NO, NOT REALLY...
NO WAY! REALLY?!
HUH? THAT CAN'T BE TRUE!
EVER SINCE I WAS LITTLE, PEOPLE ALWAYS SEEMED WEIRDLY INTERESTED IN ME.
SOMETIMES, THEY'D DRAG ME INTO STUFF LIKE THIS.
I NEVER ENJOYED IT,
BUT I WASN'T EMBARRASSED BY IT, EITHER.
YOU'RE SUCH A STUD, NISAKA!
WHO'S YOUR FAVORITE OUT OF THOSE GIRLS?! BE HONEST! KISS HER!
KISS! KISS!
I REALLY HATED THAT TEASING FROM MY FRIENDS.
I DIDN'T WANT ANYTHING TO DO WITH IT.
YOU GUYS ARE SO ANNOYING. SHUT UP!
THE STUD GOT MAD!
HE'LL GET EVEN *MORE* GIRLS NOW!
HAHA!
UGH... WHAT A PAIN...

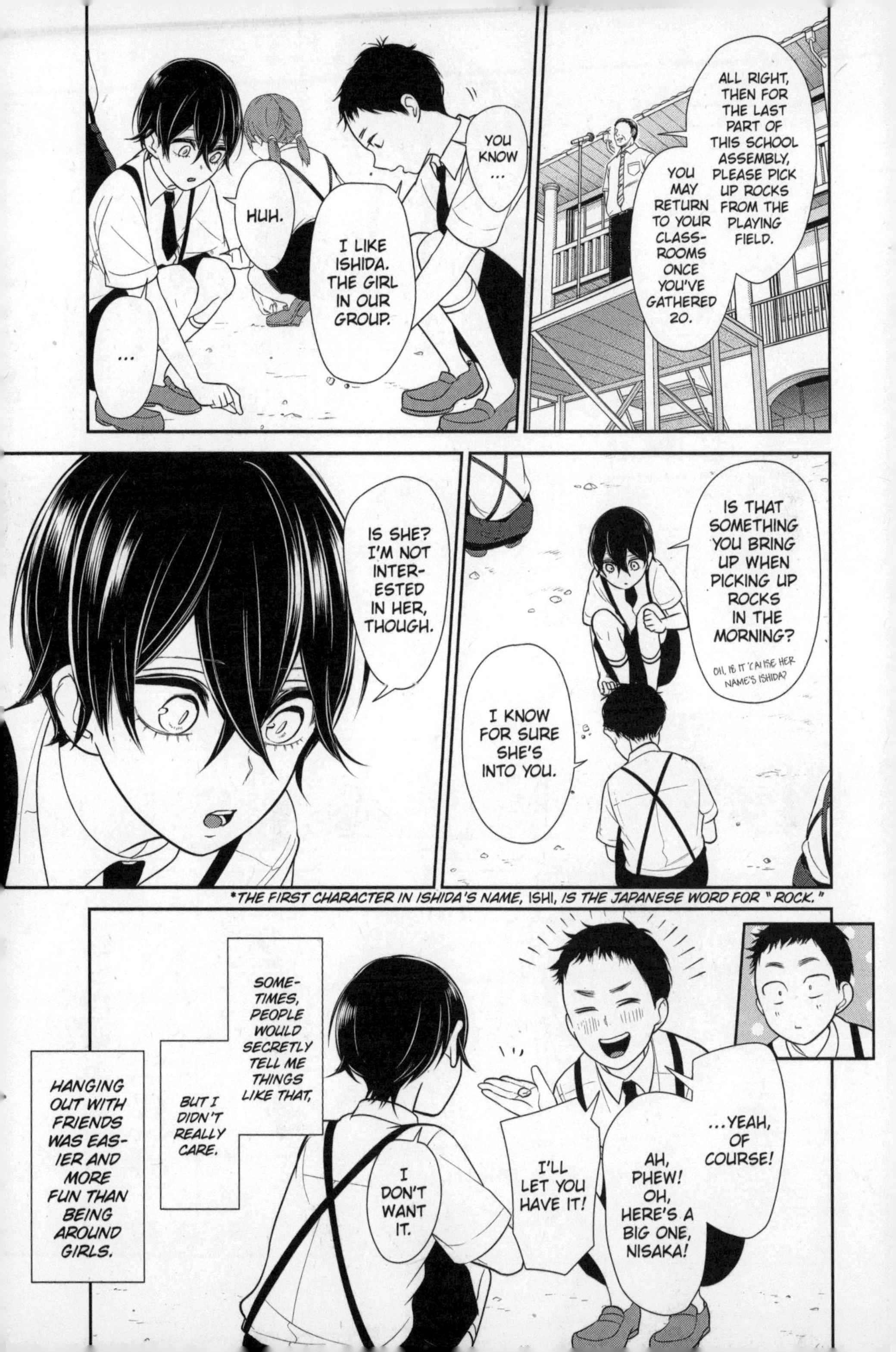
ALL RIGHT, THEN FOR THE LAST PART OF THIS SCHOOL ASSEMBLY, PLEASE PICK UP ROCKS FROM THE PLAYING FIELD.
YOU MAY RETURN TO YOUR CLASS-ROOMS ONCE YOU'VE GATHERED 20.
YOU KNOW ...
I LIKE ISHIDA. THE GIRL IN OUR GROUP.
HUH.
...
IS THAT SOMETHING YOU BRING UP WHEN PICKING UP ROCKS IN THE MORNING?
OH, IS IT 'CAUSE HER NAME'S ISHIDA?
I KNOW FOR SURE SHE'S INTO YOU.
IS SHE? I'M NOT INTER-ESTED IN HER, THOUGH.
*THE FIRST CHARACTER IN ISHIDA'S NAME, ISHI, IS THE JAPANESE WORD FOR "ROCK."
...YEAH, OF COURSE!
AH, PHEW! OH, HERE'S A BIG ONE, NISAKA!
I'LL LET YOU HAVE IT!
SOME-TIMES, PEOPLE WOULD SECRETLY TELL ME THINGS LIKE THAT,
I DON'T WANT IT.
BUT I DIDN'T REALLY CARE.
HANGING OUT WITH FRIENDS WAS EAS-IER AND MORE FUN THAN BEING AROUND GIRLS.

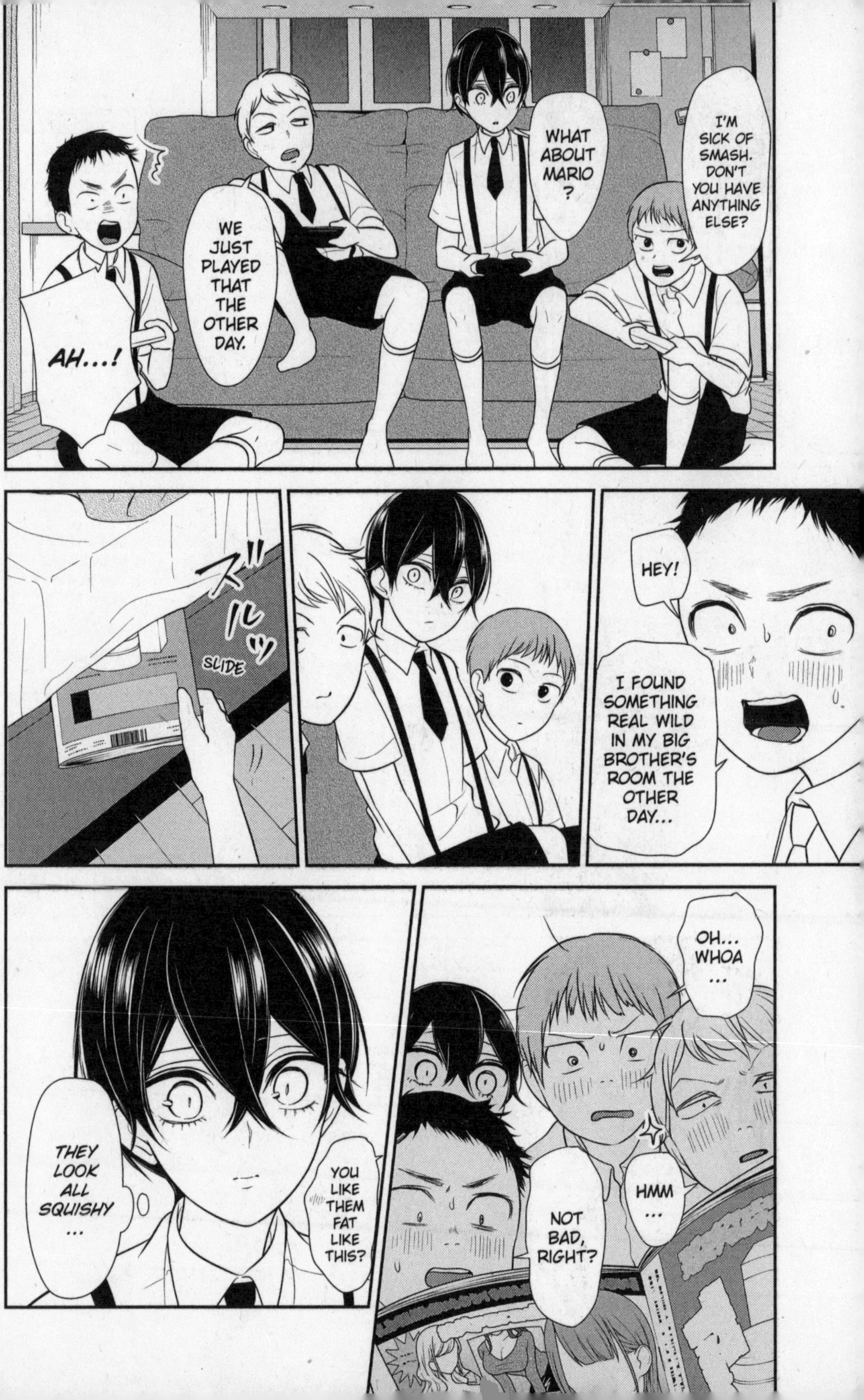
I'M SICK OF SMASH. DON'T YOU HAVE ANYTHING ELSE?
WHAT ABOUT MARIO?
WE JUST PLAYED THAT THE OTHER DAY.
AH...!
HEY!
I FOUND SOMETHING REAL WILD IN MY BIG BROTHER'S ROOM THE OTHER DAY...
ズルッ
SLIDE
OH... WHOA ...
HMM ...
NOT BAD, RIGHT?
YOU LIKE THEM FAT LIKE THIS?
THEY LOOK ALL SQUISHY ...

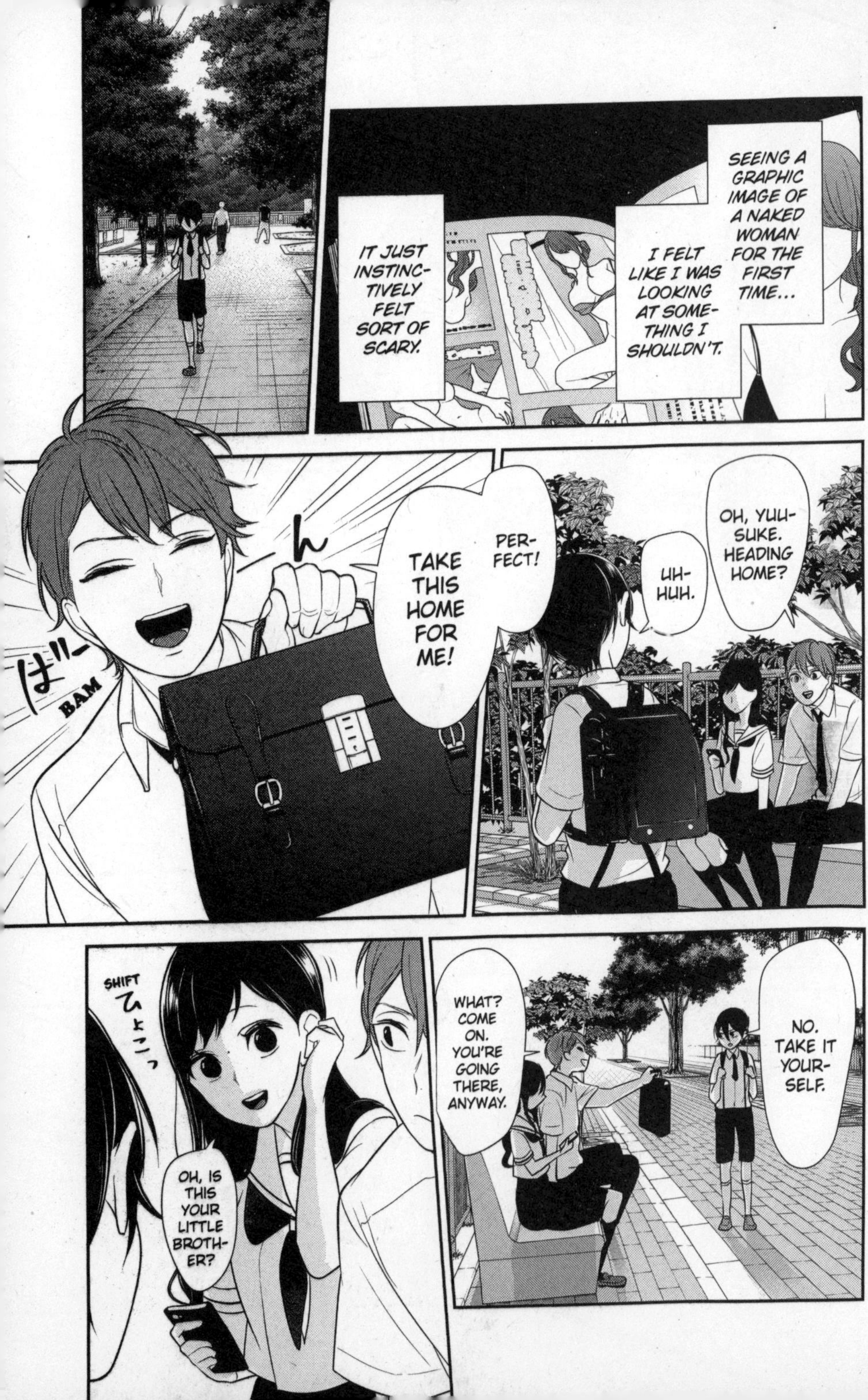
SEEING A GRAPHIC IMAGE OF A NAKED WOMAN FOR THE FIRST TIME...
I FELT LIKE I WAS LOOKING AT SOME-THING I SHOULDN'T.
IT JUST INSTINC-TIVELY FELT SORT OF SCARY.
OH, YUU-SUKE. HEADING HOME?
UH-HUH.
PER-FECT!
TAKE THIS HOME FOR ME!
ん
ばーん
BAM
NO. TAKE IT YOUR-SELF.
WHAT? COME ON. YOU'RE GOING THERE, ANYWAY.
SHIFT
ひょこっ
OH, IS THIS YOUR LITTLE BROTH-ER?

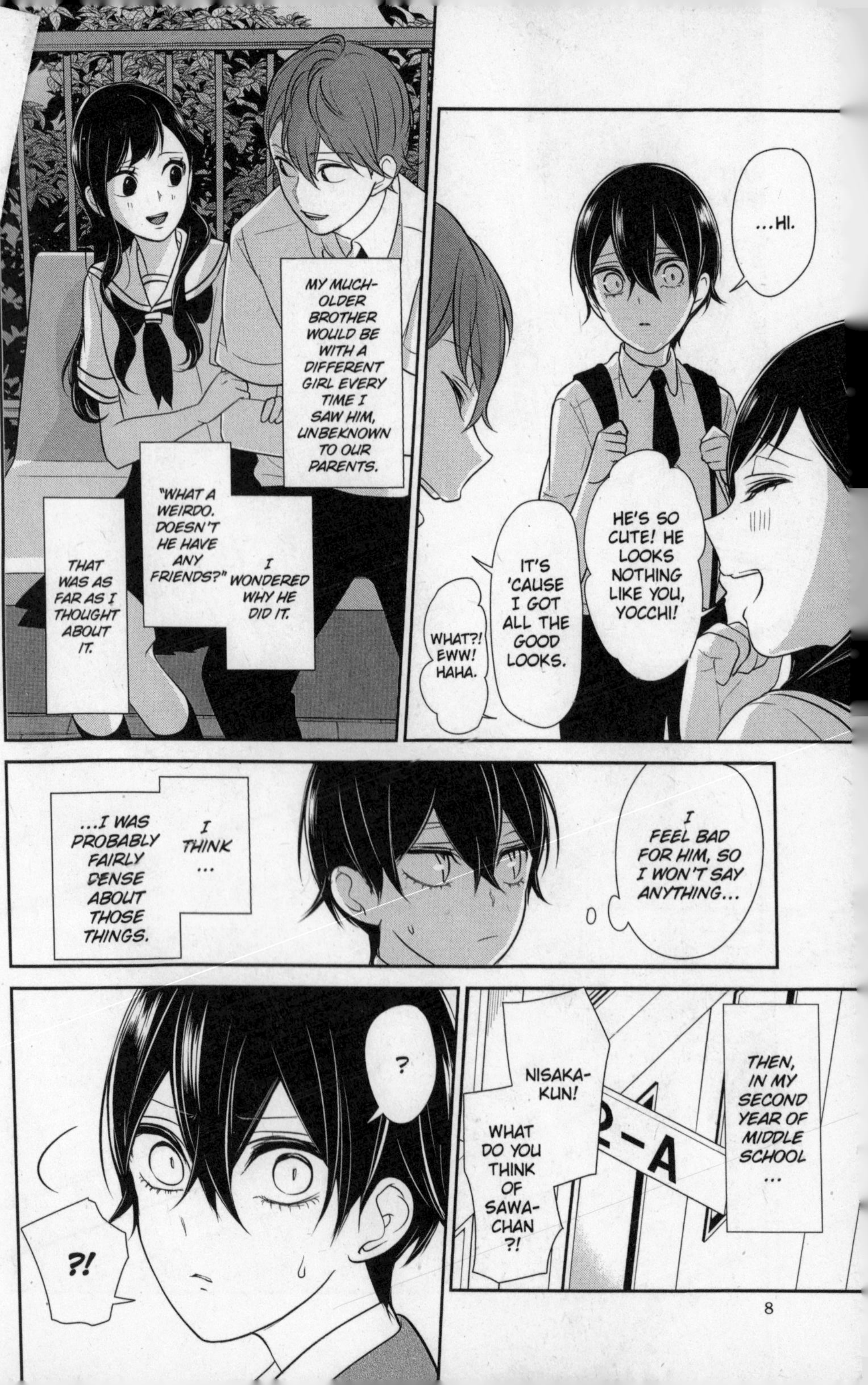
...HI.
HE'S SO CUTE! HE LOOKS NOTHING LIKE YOU, YOCCHI!
IT'S 'CAUSE I GOT ALL THE GOOD LOOKS.
WHAT?! EWW! HAHA.
MY MUCH-OLDER BROTHER WOULD BE WITH A DIFFERENT GIRL EVERY TIME I SAW HIM, UNBEKNOWN TO OUR PARENTS.
"WHAT A WEIRDO. DOESN'T HE HAVE ANY FRIENDS?"
I WONDERED WHY HE DID IT.
THAT WAS AS FAR AS I THOUGHT ABOUT IT.
I FEEL BAD FOR HIM, SO I WON'T SAY ANYTHING...
I THINK...
...I WAS PROBABLY FAIRLY DENSE ABOUT THOSE THINGS.
THEN, IN MY SECOND YEAR OF MIDDLE SCHOOL...
2-A
NISAKA-KUN!
WHAT DO YOU THINK OF SAWA-CHAN?!
?
?!

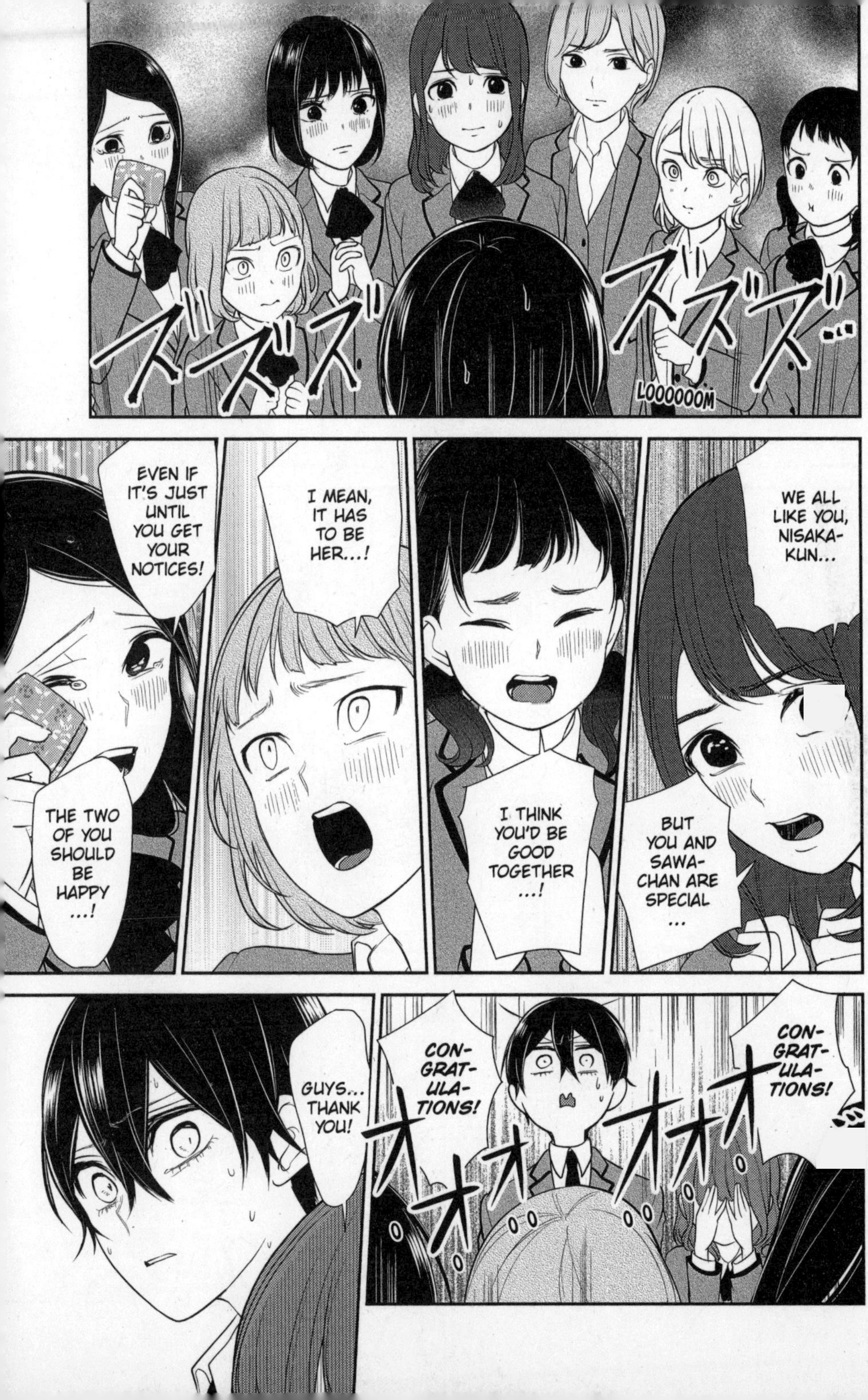
ズズズ..
LOOOOOOM
ズズズ
WE ALL LIKE YOU, NISAKA-KUN...
BUT YOU AND SAWA-CHAN ARE SPECIAL ...
I THINK YOU'D BE GOOD TOGETHER ...!
I MEAN, IT HAS TO BE HER...!
EVEN IF IT'S JUST UNTIL YOU GET YOUR NOTICES!
THE TWO OF YOU SHOULD BE HAPPY ...!
CON-GRAT-ULA-TIONS!
オオオオオオ
CON-GRAT-ULA-TIONS!
GUYS... THANK YOU!

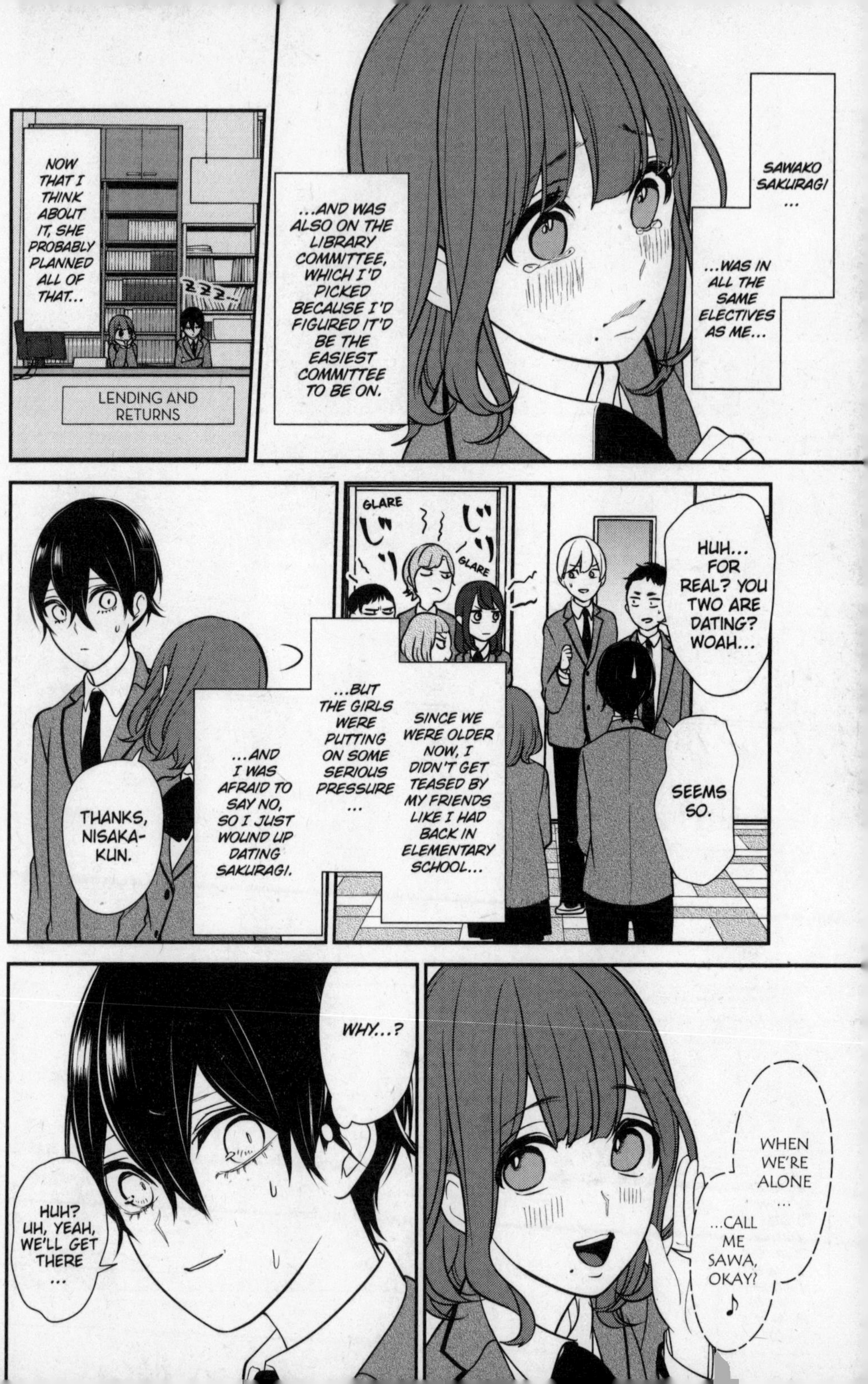
SAWAKO SAKURAGI ...
...WAS IN ALL THE SAME ELECTIVES AS ME...
...AND WAS ALSO ON THE LIBRARY COMMITTEE, WHICH I'D PICKED BECAUSE I'D FIGURED IT'D BE THE EASIEST COMMITTEE TO BE ON.
NOW THAT I THINK ABOUT IT, SHE PROBABLY PLANNED ALL OF THAT...
ZZZ...
LENDING AND RETURNS
HUH... FOR REAL? YOU TWO ARE DATING? WOAH...
SEEMS SO.
GLARE
じり
じり
GLARE
SINCE WE WERE OLDER NOW, I DIDN'T GET TEASED BY MY FRIENDS LIKE I HAD BACK IN ELEMENTARY SCHOOL...
...BUT THE GIRLS WERE PUTTING ON SOME SERIOUS PRESSURE...
...AND I WAS AFRAID TO SAY NO, SO I JUST WOUND UP DATING SAKURAGI.
THANKS, NISAKA-KUN.
WHEN WE'RE ALONE ... ...CALL ME SAWA, OKAY? ♪
WHY...?
HUH? UH, YEAH, WE'LL GET THERE ...

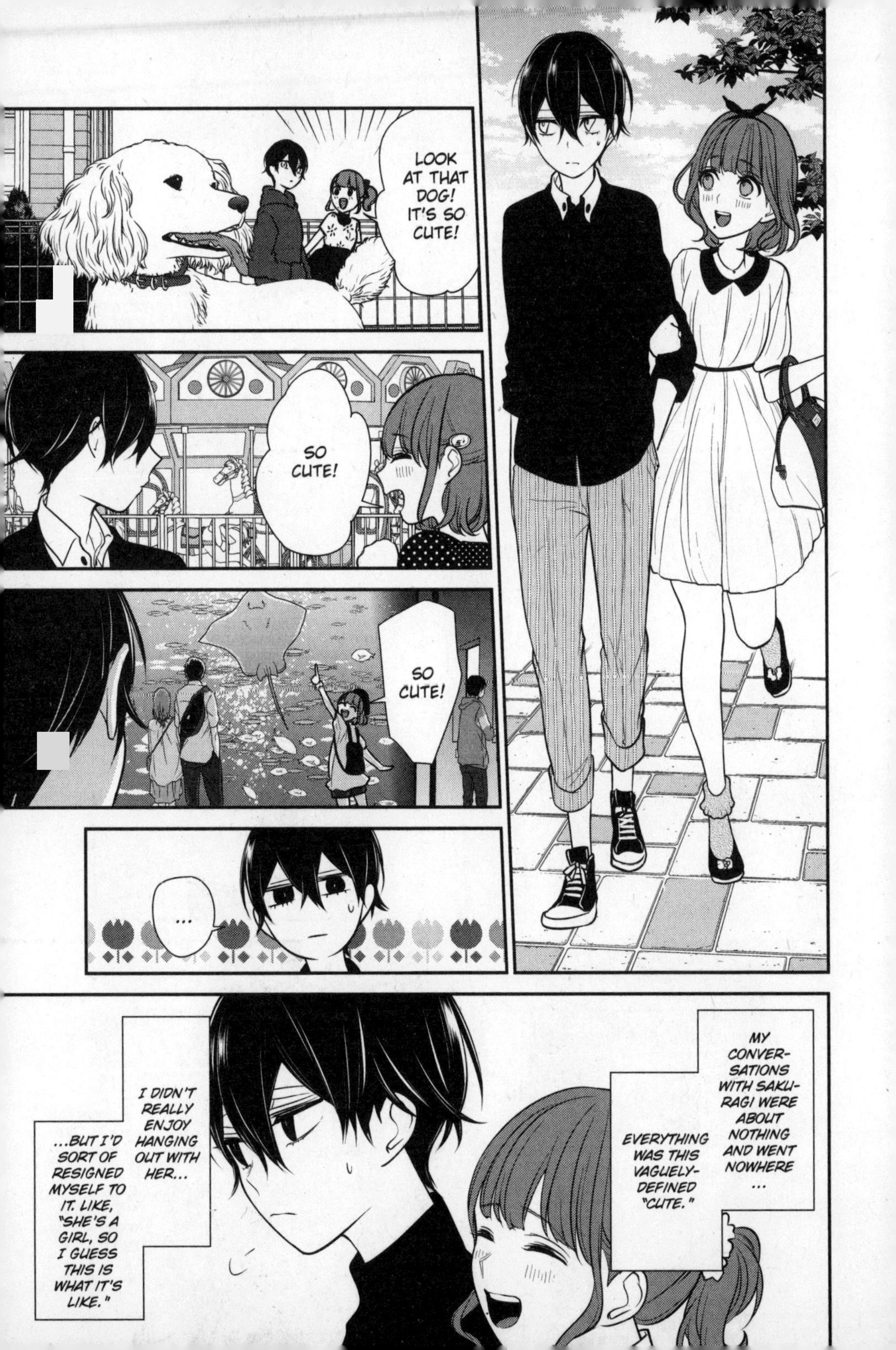
LOOK AT THAT DOG! IT'S SO CUTE!
SO CUTE!
SO CUTE!
...
MY CONVERSATIONS WITH SAKURAGI WERE ABOUT NOTHING AND WENT NOWHERE...
EVERYTHING WAS THIS VAGUELY-DEFINED "CUTE."
I DIDN'T REALLY ENJOY HANGING OUT WITH HER...
...BUT I'D SORT OF RESIGNED MYSELF TO IT. LIKE, "SHE'S A GIRL, SO I GUESS THIS IS WHAT IT'S LIKE."

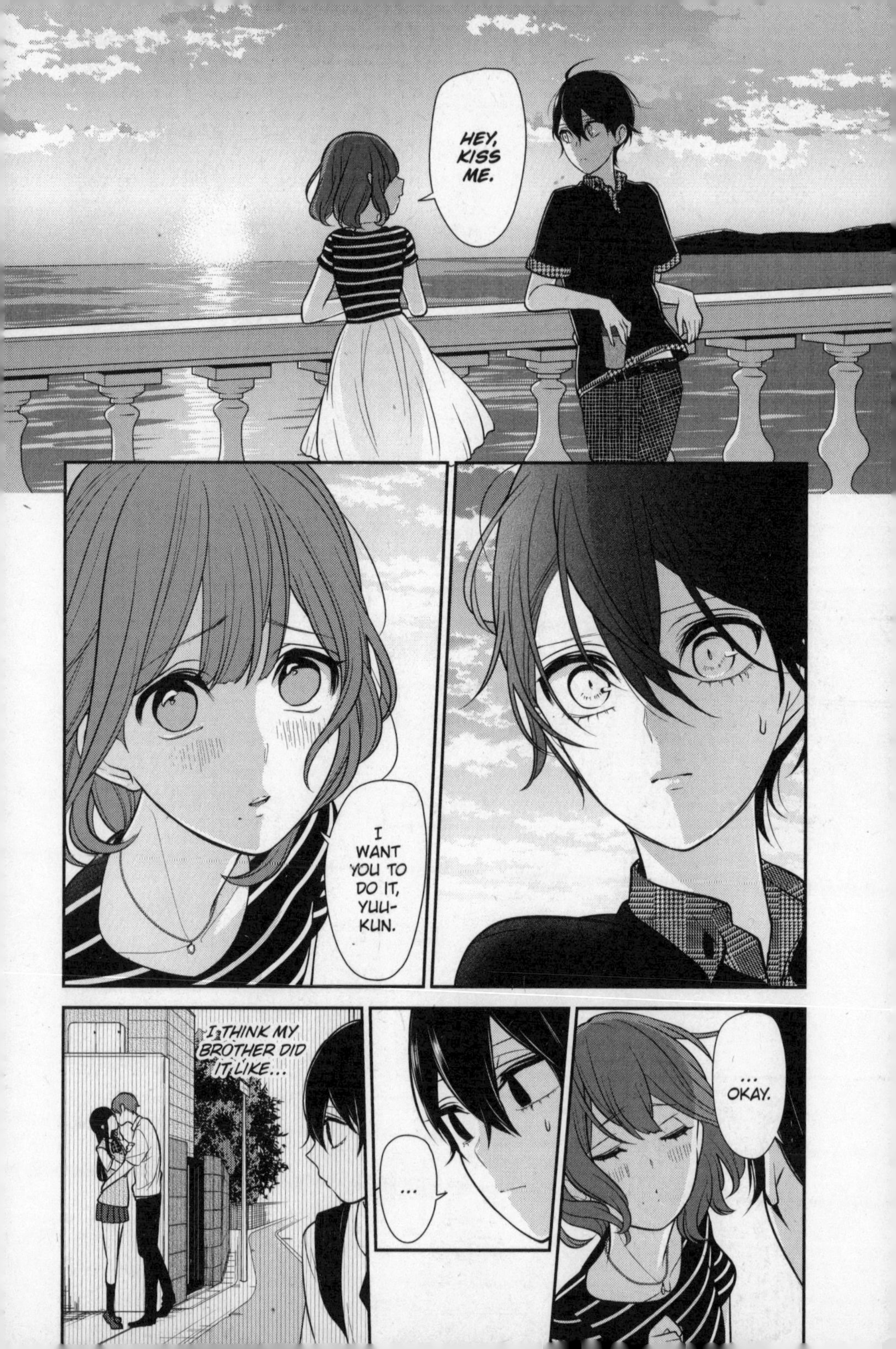
HEY, KISS ME.
I WANT YOU TO DO IT, YUU-KUN.
... OKAY.
...
I THINK MY BROTHER DID IT LIKE...

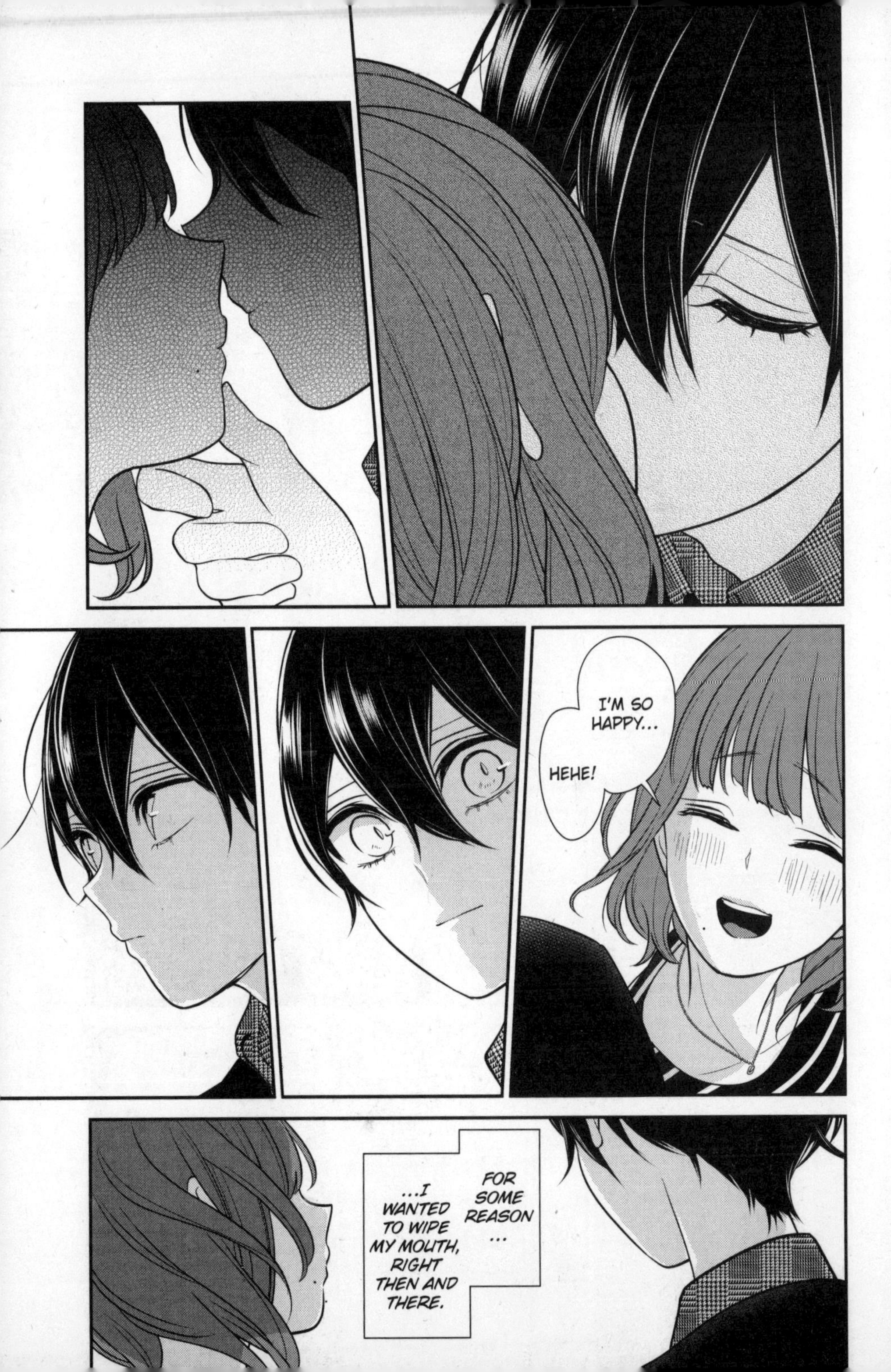
I'M SO HAPPY...
HEHE!
FOR SOME REASON ...
...I WANTED TO WIPE MY MOUTH, RIGHT THEN AND THERE.

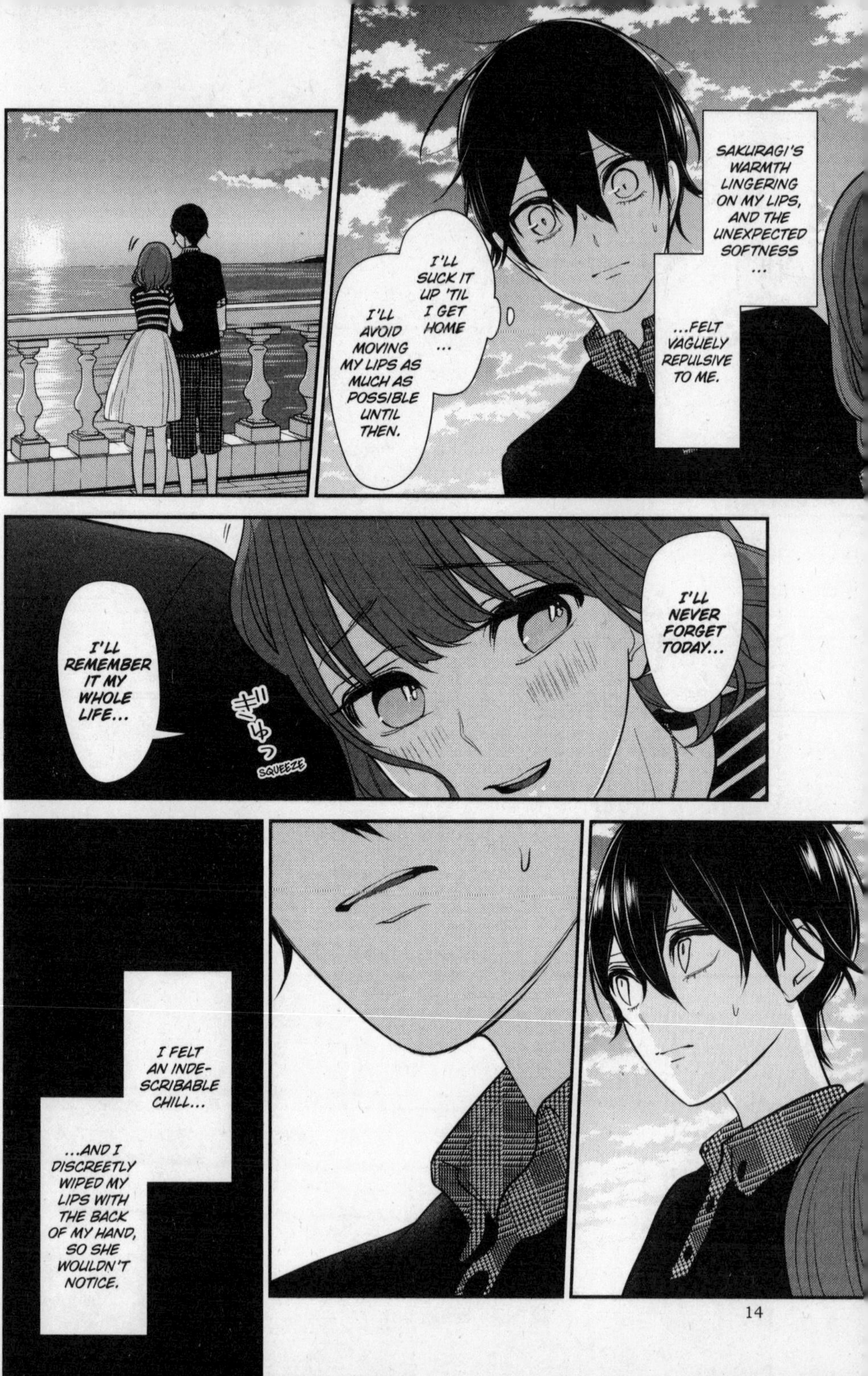
SAKURAGI'S WARMTH LINGERING ON MY LIPS, AND THE UNEXPECTED SOFTNESS...
...FELT VAGUELY REPULSIVE TO ME.
I'LL SUCK IT UP 'TIL I GET HOME... I'LL AVOID MOVING MY LIPS AS MUCH AS POSSIBLE UNTIL THEN.
I'LL NEVER FORGET TODAY...
ぎゅっ SQUEEZE
I'LL REMEMBER IT MY WHOLE LIFE...
I FELT AN INDE-SCRIBABLE CHILL...
...AND I DISCREETLY WIPED MY LIPS WITH THE BACK OF MY HAND, SO SHE WOULDN'T NOTICE.

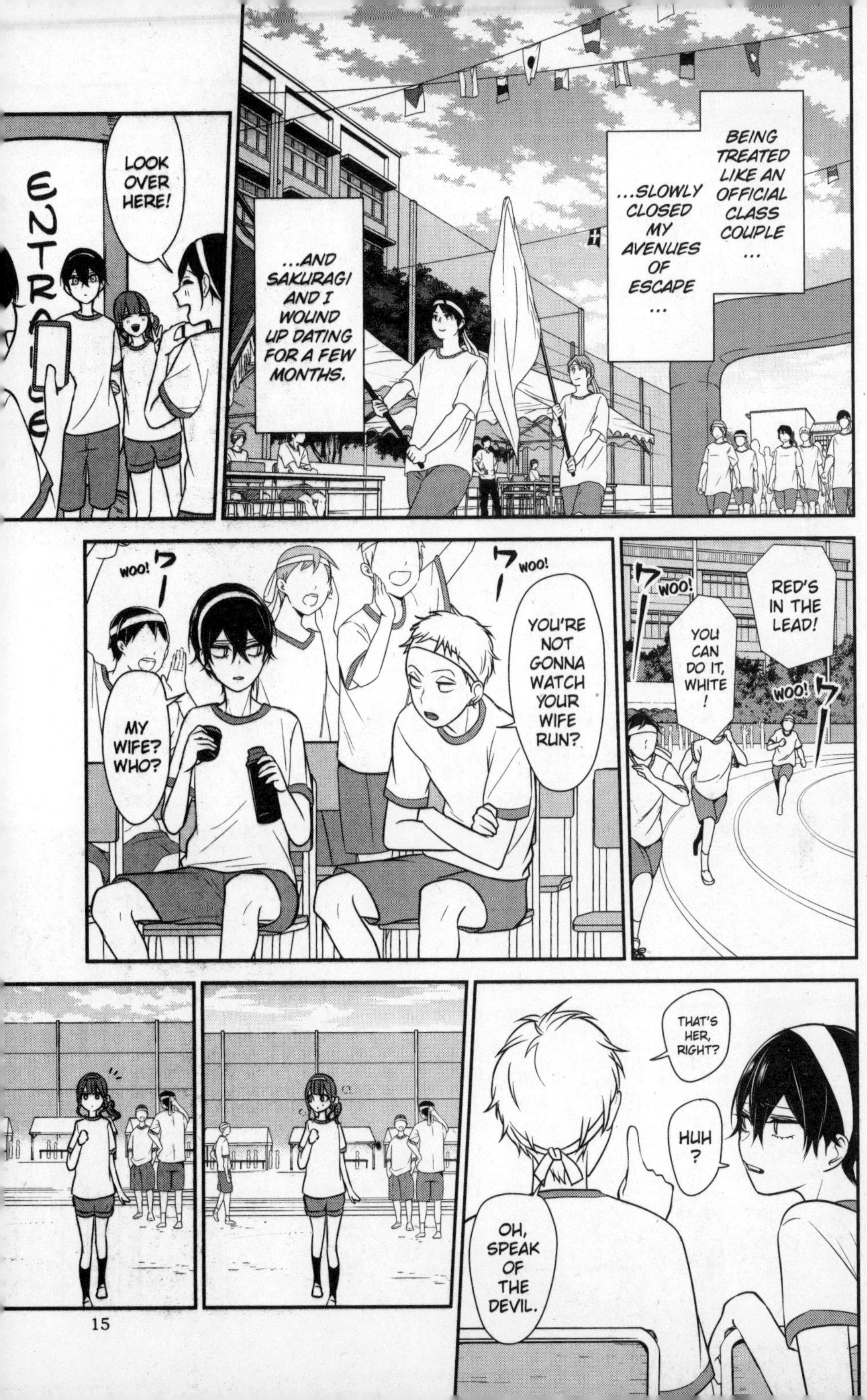

BEING TREATED LIKE AN OFFICIAL CLASS COUPLE...
...SLOWLY CLOSED MY AVENUES OF ESCAPE...
...AND SAKURAGI AND I WOUND UP DATING FOR A FEW MONTHS.
LOOK OVER HERE!
RED'S IN THE LEAD!
WOO!
YOU CAN DO IT, WHITE!
WOO!
WOO!
YOU'RE NOT GONNA WATCH YOUR WIFE RUN?
WOO!
MY WIFE? WHO?
THAT'S HER, RIGHT?
HUH?
OH, SPEAK OF THE DEVIL.

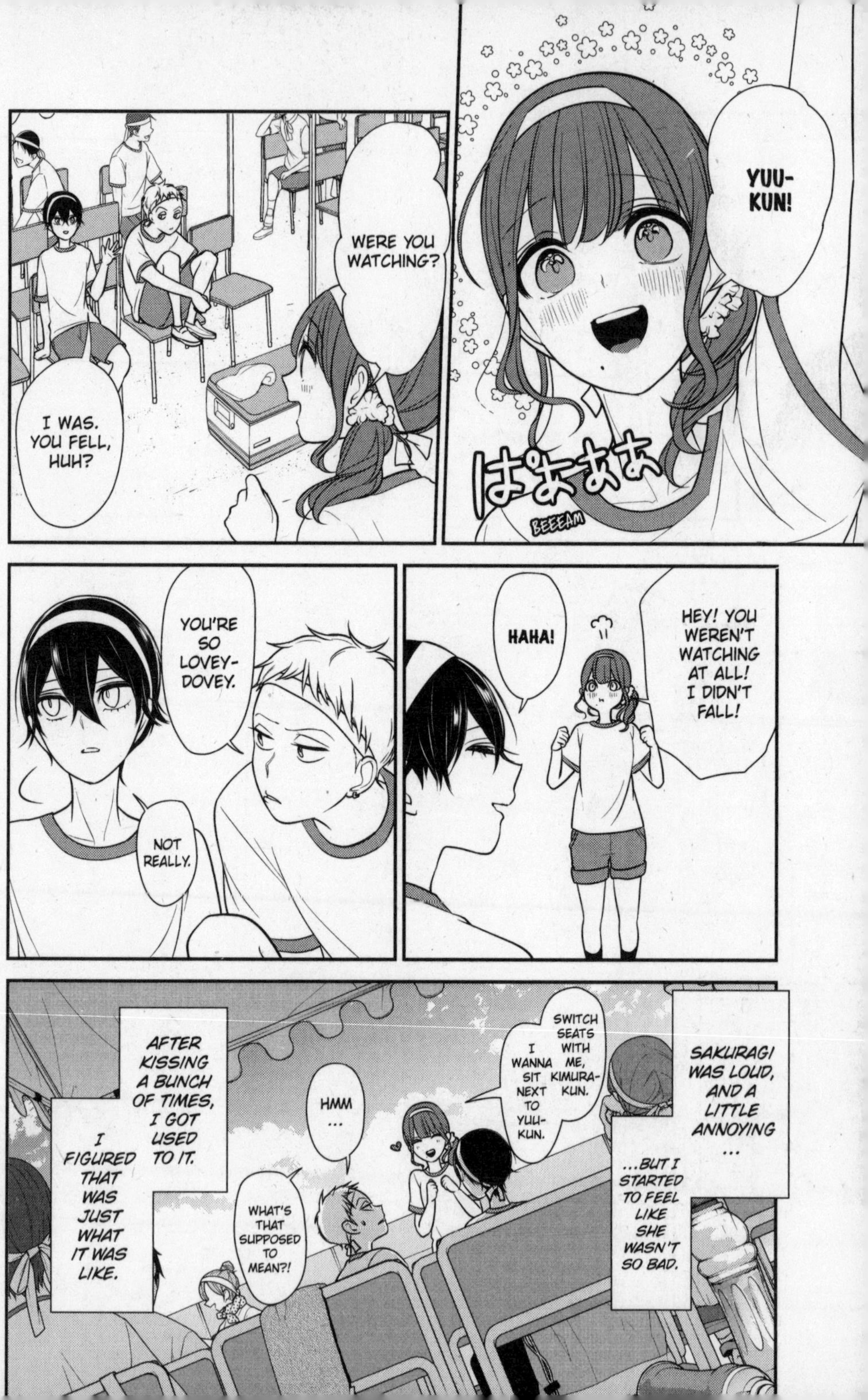
YUU-KUN!
ぱあああ
BEEEAM
WERE YOU WATCHING?
I WAS. YOU FELL, HUH?
HEY! YOU WEREN'T WATCHING AT ALL! I DIDN'T FALL!
HAHA!
YOU'RE SO LOVEY-DOVEY.
NOT REALLY.
SAKURAGI WAS LOUD, AND A LITTLE ANNOYING...
...BUT I STARTED TO FEEL LIKE SHE WASN'T SO BAD.
SWITCH SEATS WITH ME, KIMURA-KUN.
I WANNA SIT NEXT TO YUU-KUN.
HMM...
WHAT'S THAT SUPPOSED TO MEAN?!
AFTER KISSING A BUNCH OF TIMES, I GOT USED TO IT.
I FIGURED THAT WAS JUST WHAT IT WAS LIKE.

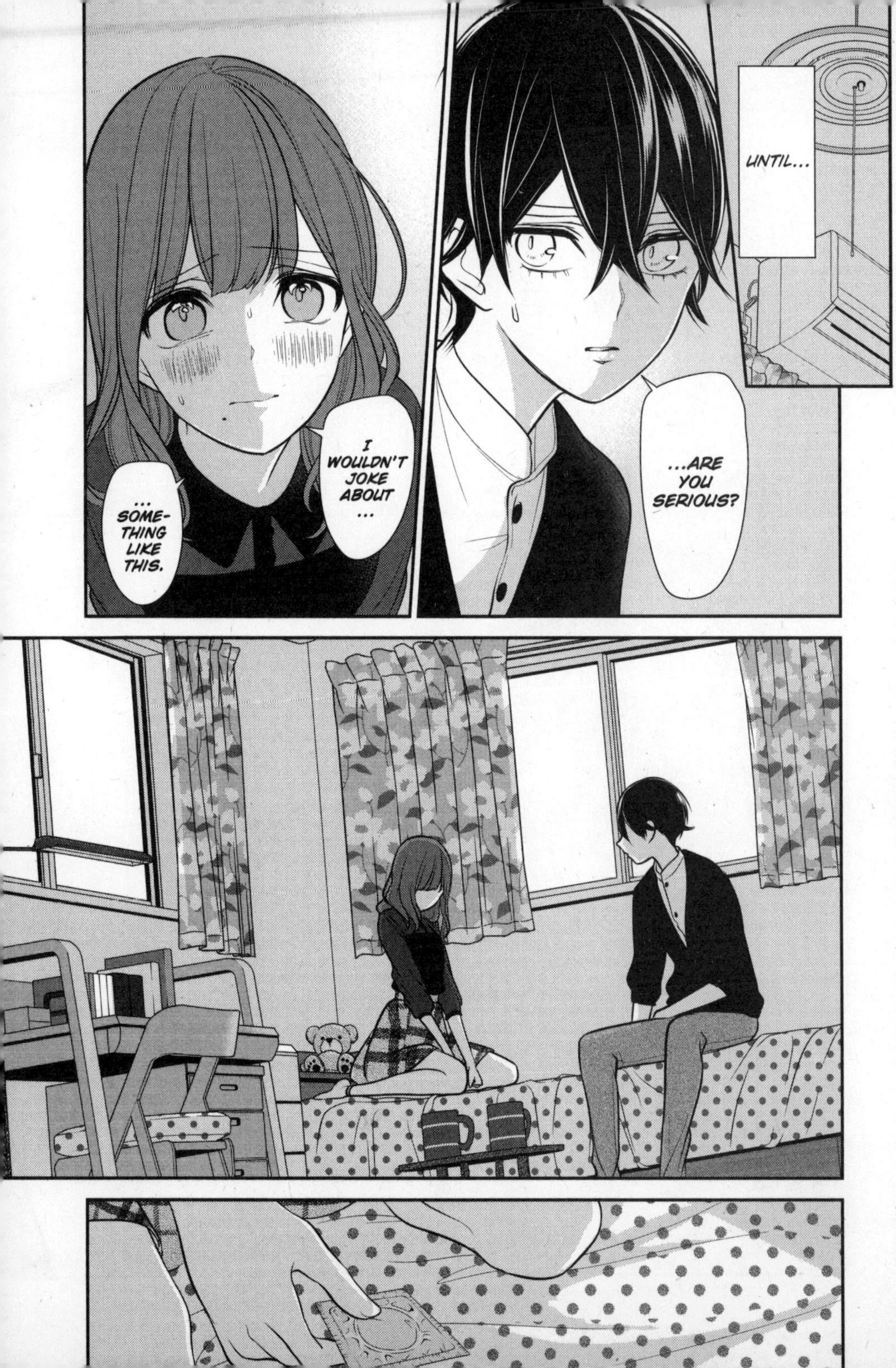
UNTIL...
...ARE YOU SERIOUS?
I WOULDN'T JOKE ABOUT ...
... SOME-THING LIKE THIS.

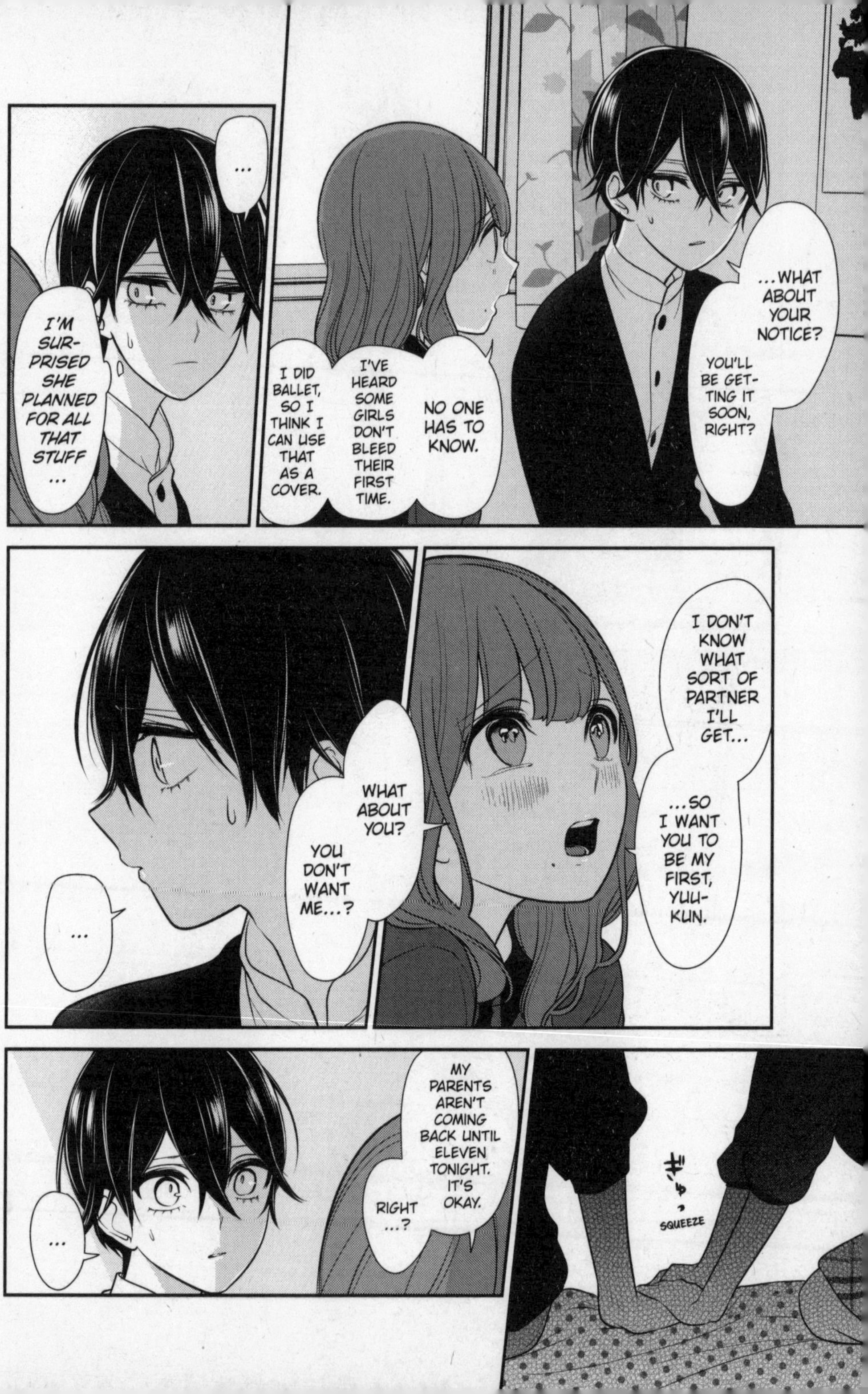
...WHAT ABOUT YOUR NOTICE?
YOU'LL BE GETTING IT SOON, RIGHT?
NO ONE HAS TO KNOW.
I'VE HEARD SOME GIRLS DON'T BLEED THEIR FIRST TIME.
I DID BALLET, SO I THINK I CAN USE THAT AS A COVER.
...
I'M SUR-PRISED SHE PLANNED FOR ALL THAT STUFF...
I DON'T KNOW WHAT SORT OF PARTNER I'LL GET...
...SO I WANT YOU TO BE MY FIRST, YUU-KUN.
WHAT ABOUT YOU?
YOU DON'T WANT ME...?
...
ぎゅっ
SQUEEZE
MY PARENTS AREN'T COMING BACK UNTIL ELEVEN TONIGHT. IT'S OKAY.
RIGHT...?
...

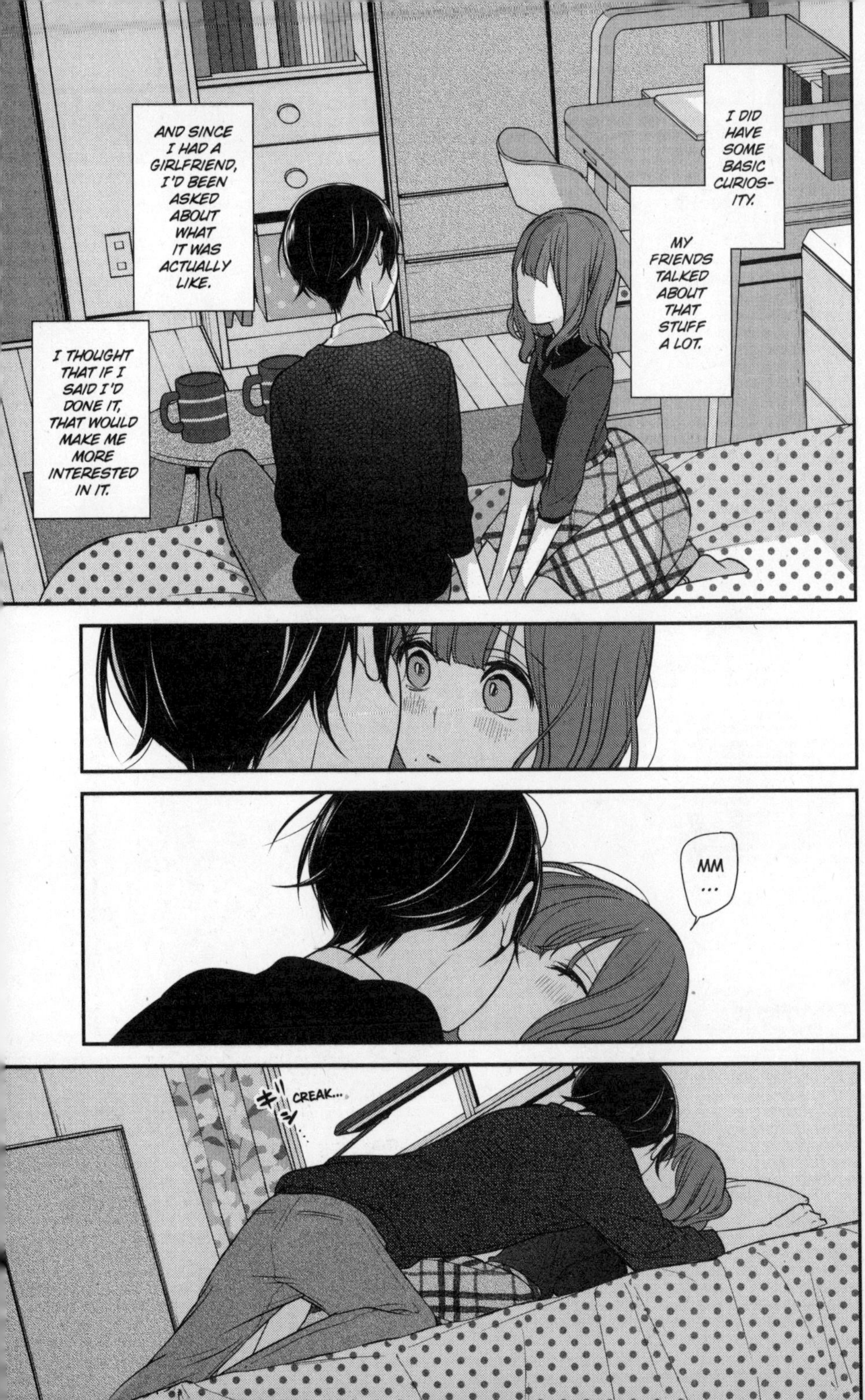
I DID HAVE SOME BASIC CURIOSITY.
MY FRIENDS TALKED ABOUT THAT STUFF A LOT.
AND SINCE I HAD A GIRLFRIEND, I'D BEEN ASKED ABOUT WHAT IT WAS ACTUALLY LIKE.
I THOUGHT THAT IF I SAID I'D DONE IT, THAT WOULD MAKE ME MORE INTERESTED IN IT.
MM...
CREAK...

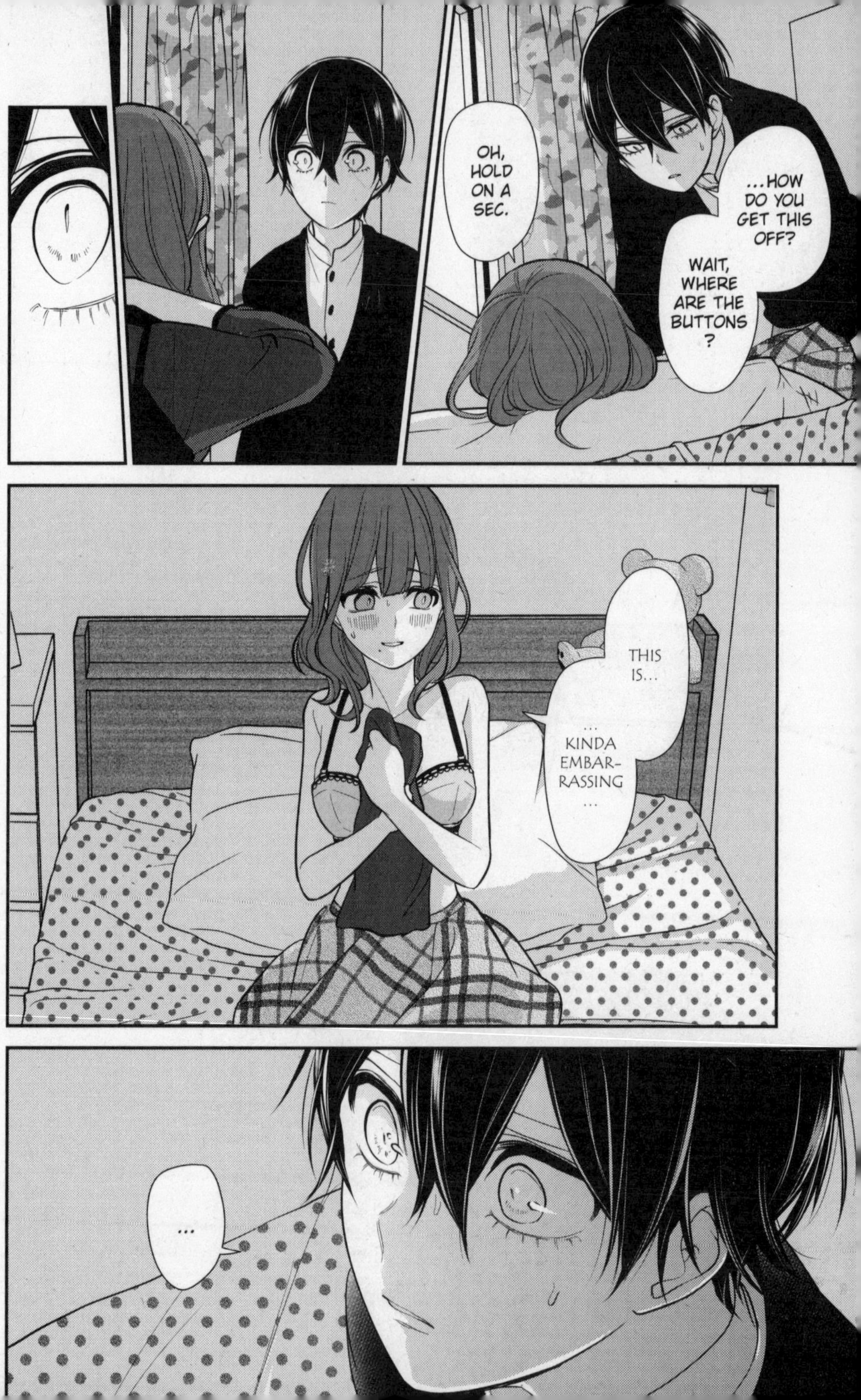
...HOW DO YOU GET THIS OFF?
WAIT, WHERE ARE THE BUTTONS?
OH, HOLD ON A SEC.
THIS IS...
... KINDA EMBARRASSING ...
...

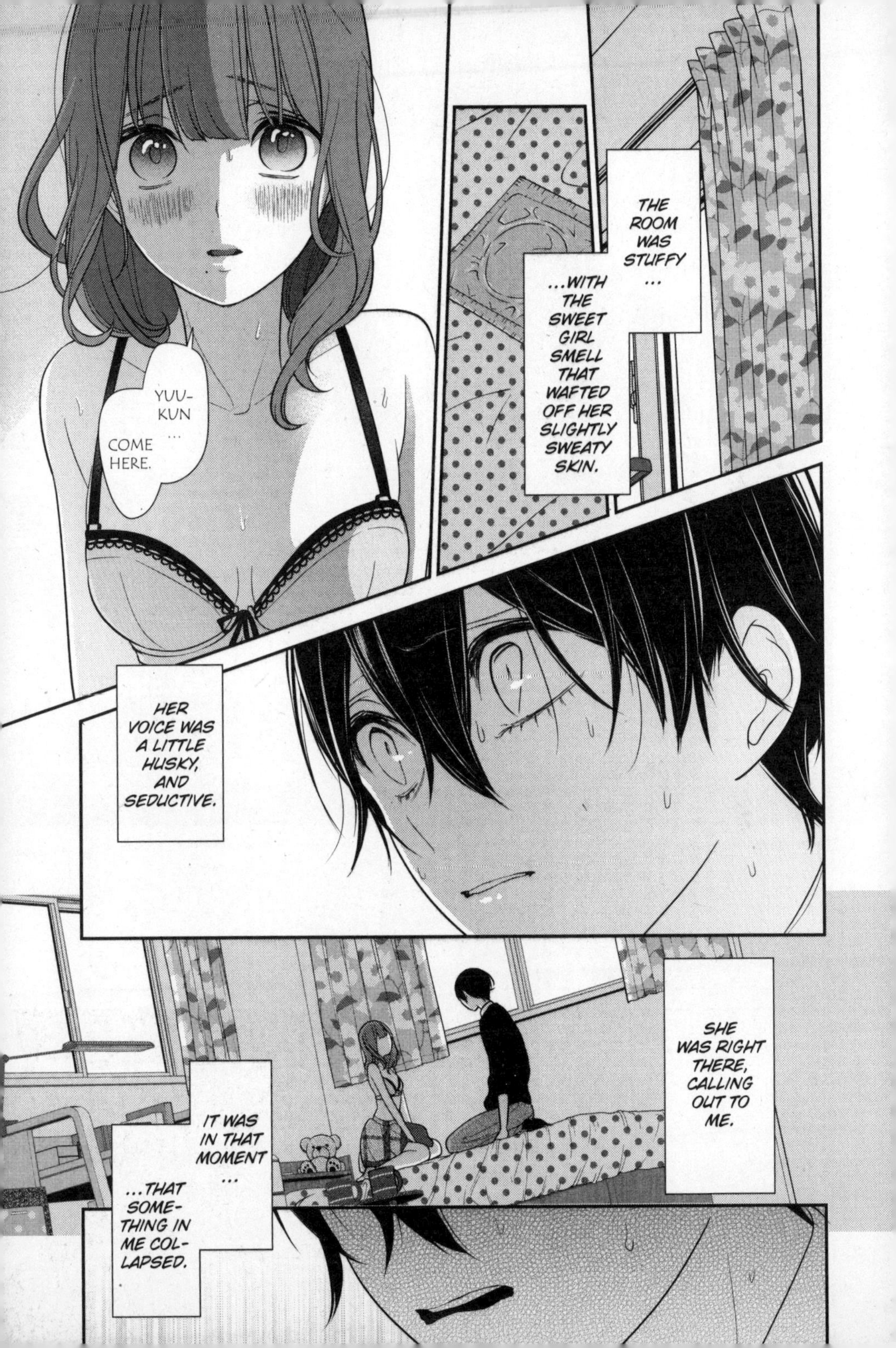
THE ROOM WAS STUFFY ...
...WITH THE SWEET GIRL SMELL THAT WAFTED OFF HER SLIGHTLY SWEATY SKIN.
YUU-KUN ... COME HERE.
HER VOICE WAS A LITTLE HUSKY, AND SEDUCTIVE.
SHE WAS RIGHT THERE, CALLING OUT TO ME.
IT WAS IN THAT MOMENT ...
...THAT SOME-THING IN ME COL-LAPSED.

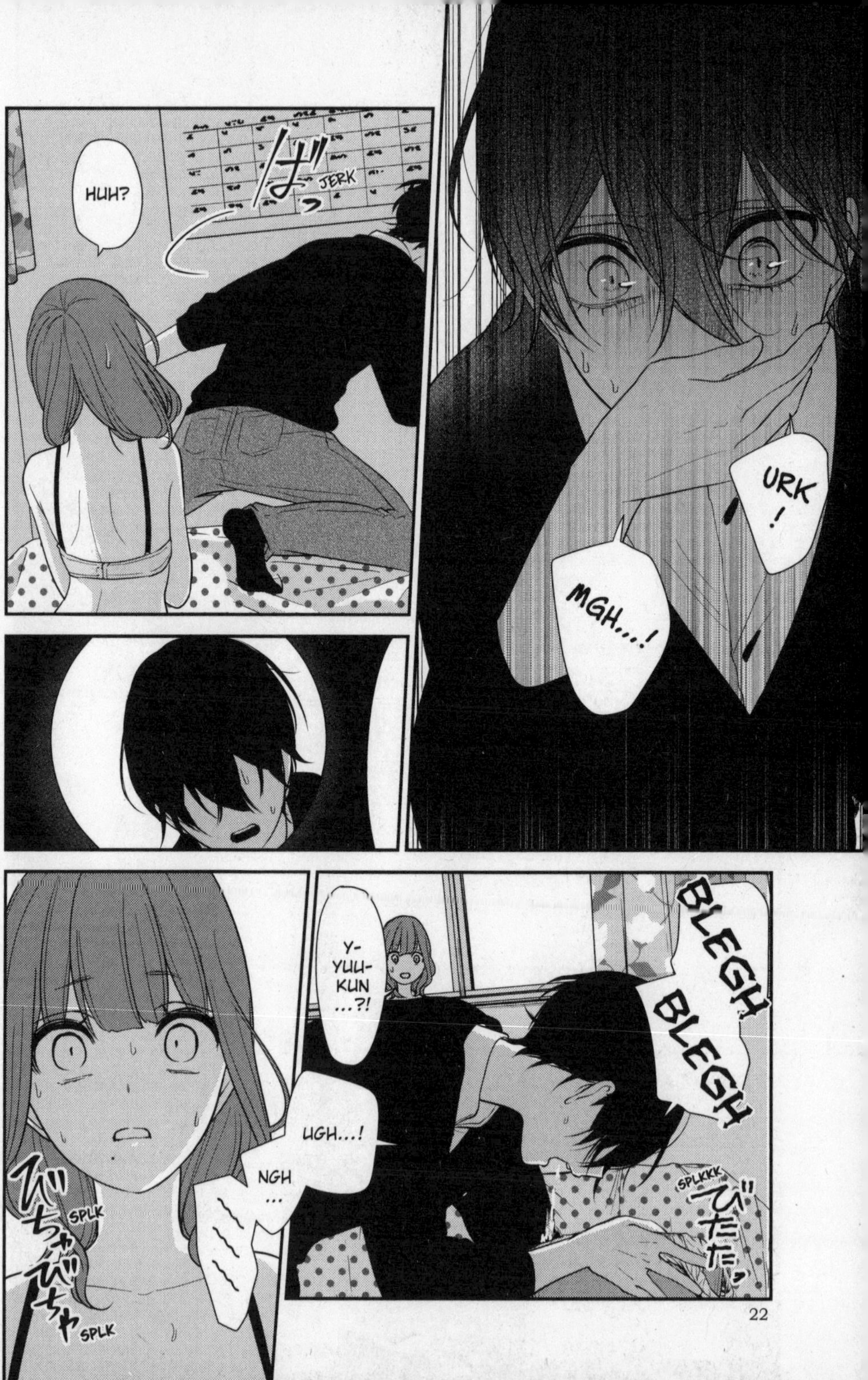
URK!
MGH...!
HUH?
ばっ
JERK
BLEGH
BLEGH
BLEGH
Y-YUU-KUN...?!
びたたっ
SPLKKK
UGH...!
NGH...
びちゃびちゃ
SPLK
SPLK

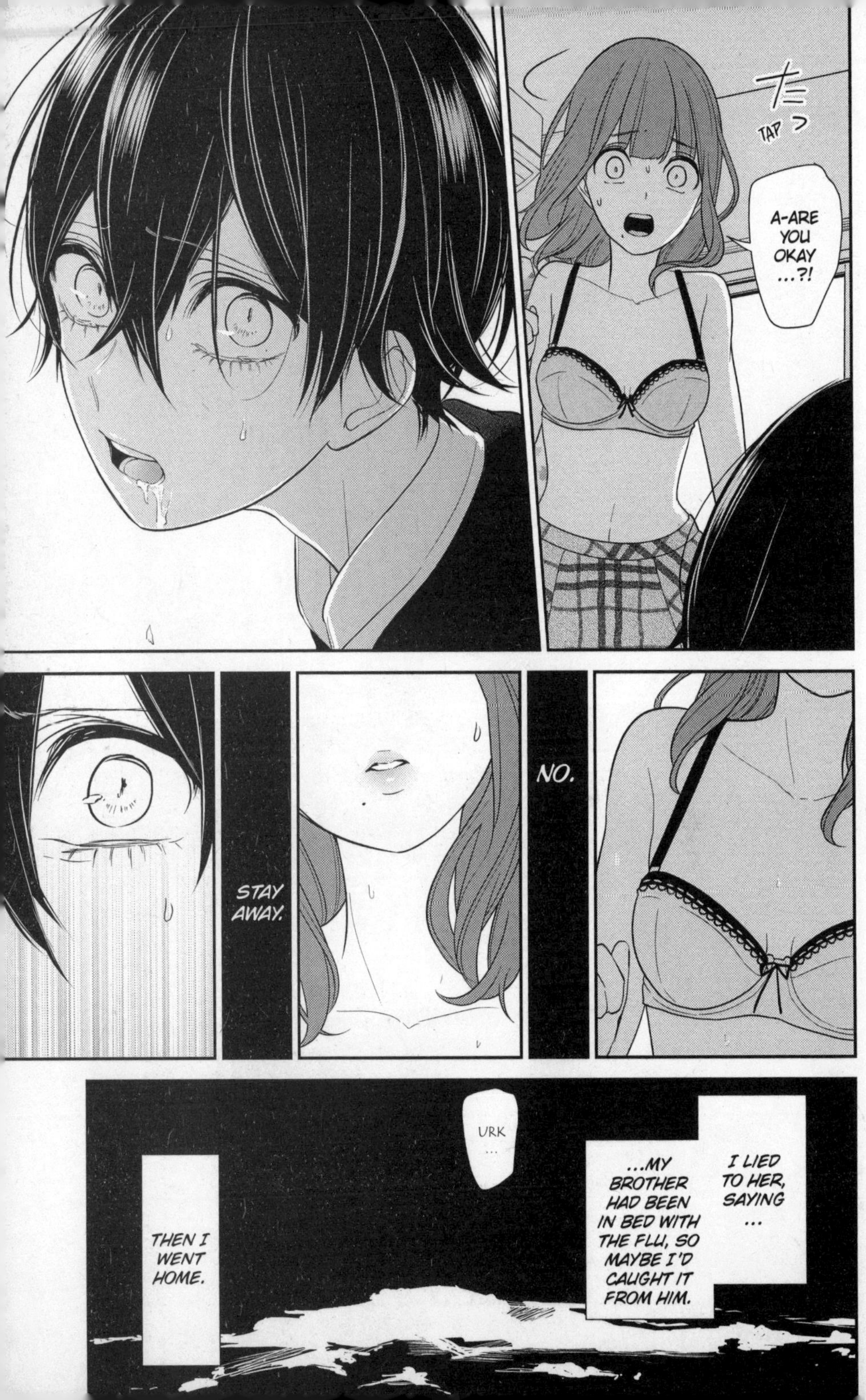
TAP
A-ARE YOU OKAY ...?!
NO.
STAY AWAY.
I LIED TO HER, SAYING ...
...MY BROTHER HAD BEEN IN BED WITH THE FLU, SO MAYBE I'D CAUGHT IT FROM HIM.
URK ...
THEN I WENT HOME.

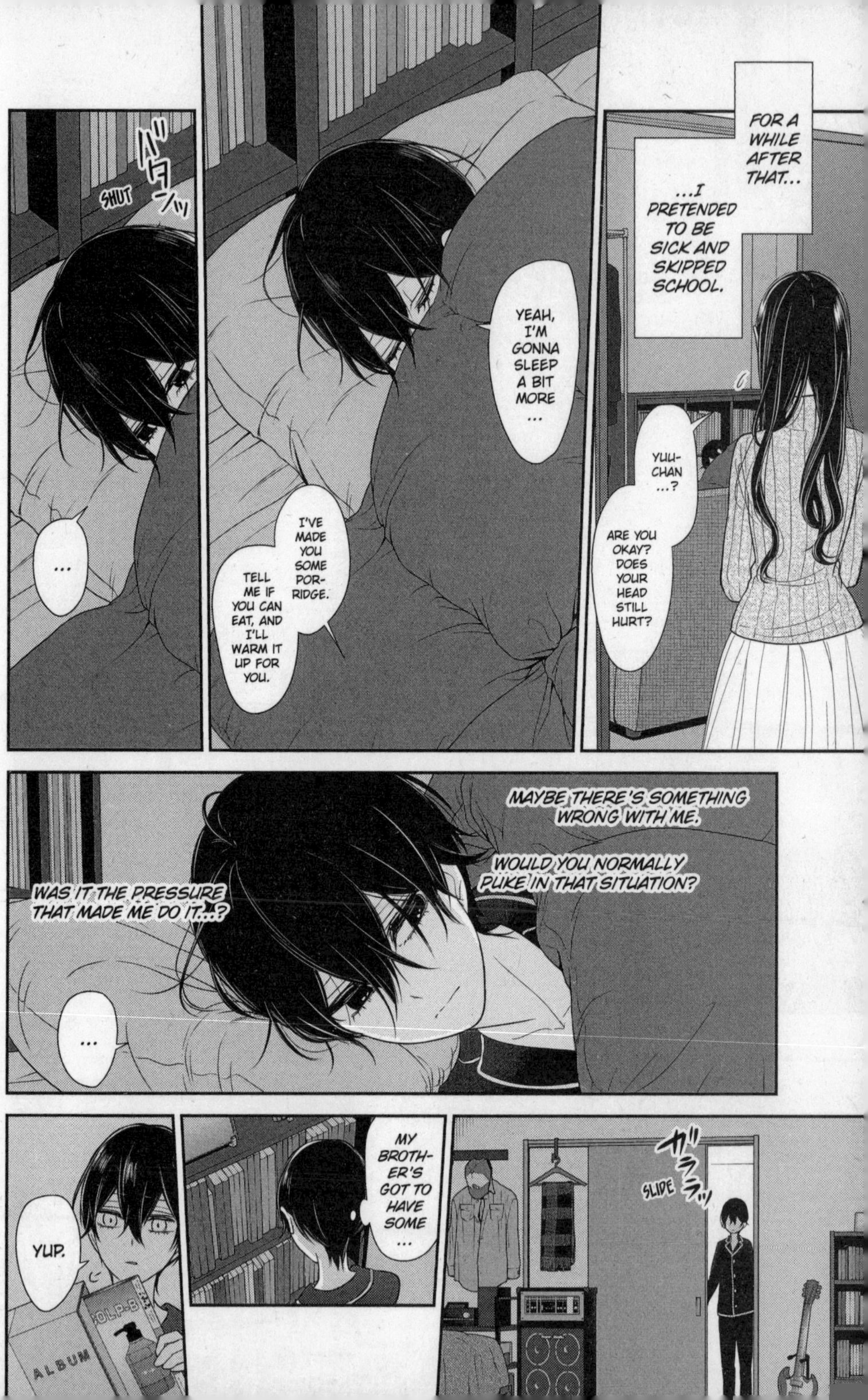
FOR A WHILE AFTER THAT...
...I PRETENDED TO BE SICK AND SKIPPED SCHOOL.
YUU-CHAN ...?
ARE YOU OKAY? DOES YOUR HEAD STILL HURT?
YEAH, I'M GONNA SLEEP A BIT MORE ...
I'VE MADE YOU SOME PORRIDGE.
TELL ME IF YOU CAN EAT, AND I'LL WARM IT UP FOR YOU.
SHUT
...
MAYBE THERE'S SOMETHING WRONG WITH ME.
WOULD YOU NORMALLY PUKE IN THAT SITUATION?
WAS IT THE PRESSURE THAT MADE ME DO IT...?
...
SLIDE
MY BROTHER'S GOT TO HAVE SOME ...
YUP.
ALBUM

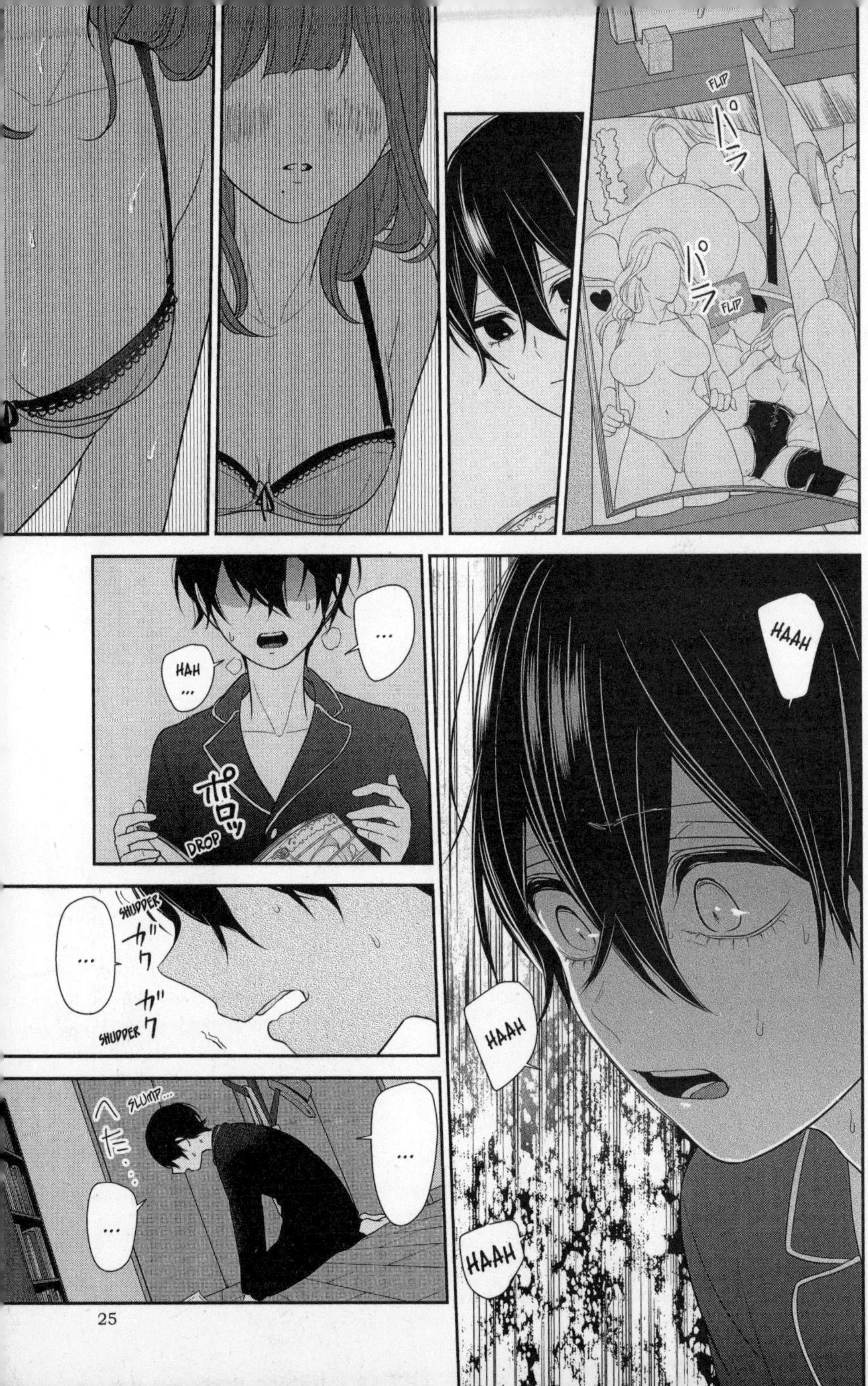
パラ
FLIP
パラ
FLIP
HAAH
HAAH
HAAH
...
HAH ...
ポロッ
DROP
ガク
SHUDDER
ガク
SHUDDER
...
...
へた...
SLUMP...
...

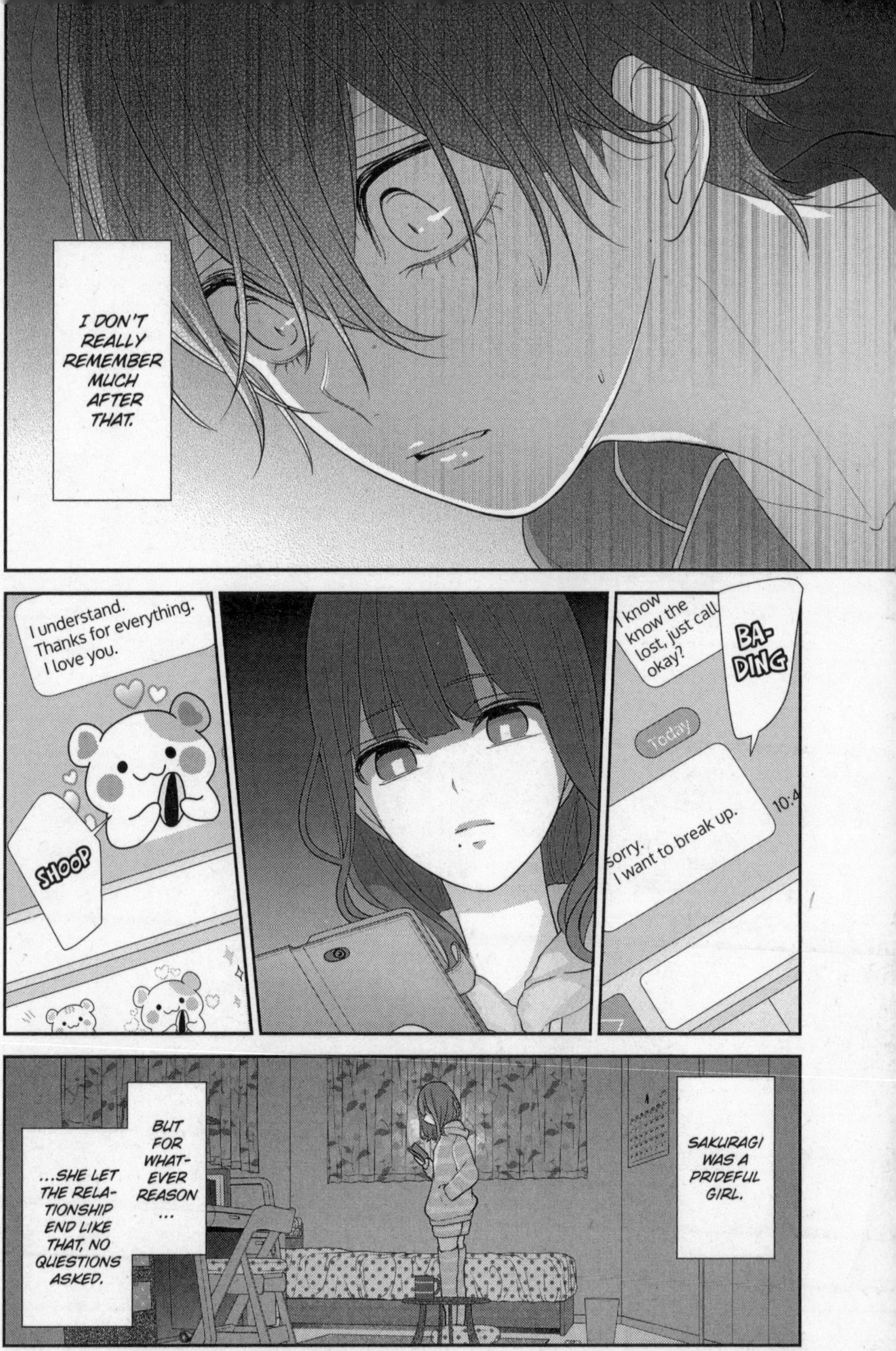
I DON'T REALLY REMEMBER MUCH AFTER THAT.
I know
know the
lost, just call
okay?
BA-DING
Today
10:4
sorry.
I want to break up.
I understand.
Thanks for everything.
I love you.
SHOOP
SAKURAGI WAS A PRIDEFUL GIRL.
BUT FOR WHATEVER REASON...
...SHE LET THE RELATIONSHIP END LIKE THAT, NO QUESTIONS ASKED.

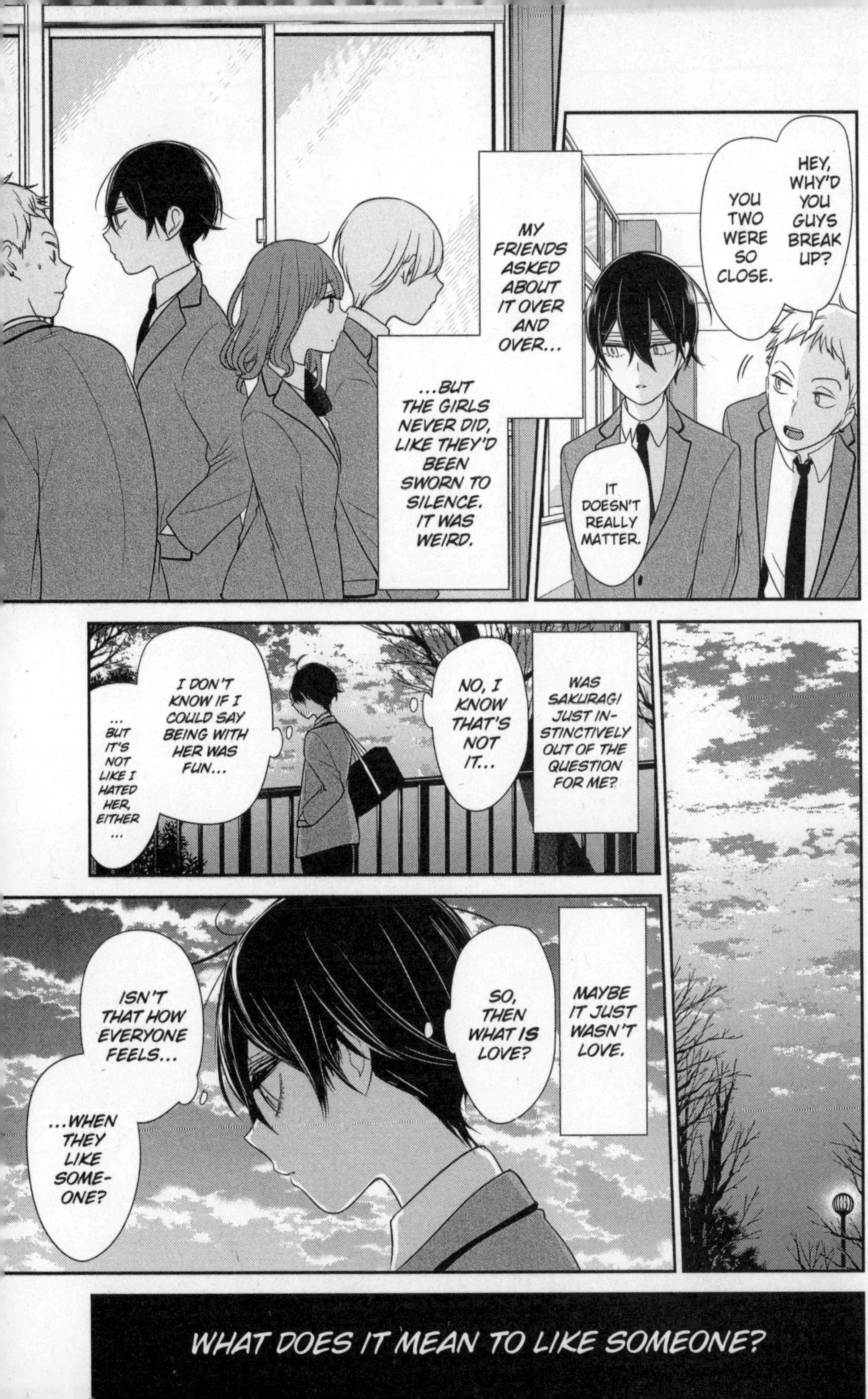
HEY, WHY'D YOU GUYS BREAK UP?
YOU TWO WERE SO CLOSE.
IT DOESN'T REALLY MATTER.
MY FRIENDS ASKED ABOUT IT OVER AND OVER...
...BUT THE GIRLS NEVER DID, LIKE THEY'D BEEN SWORN TO SILENCE. IT WAS WEIRD.
WAS SAKURAGI JUST IN-STINCTIVELY OUT OF THE QUESTION FOR ME?
NO, I KNOW THAT'S NOT IT...
I DON'T KNOW IF I COULD SAY BEING WITH HER WAS FUN...
...BUT IT'S NOT LIKE I HATED HER, EITHER...
MAYBE IT JUST WASN'T LOVE.
SO, THEN WHAT IS LOVE?
ISN'T THAT HOW EVERYONE FEELS...
...WHEN THEY LIKE SOME-ONE?
WHAT DOES IT MEAN TO LIKE SOMEONE?

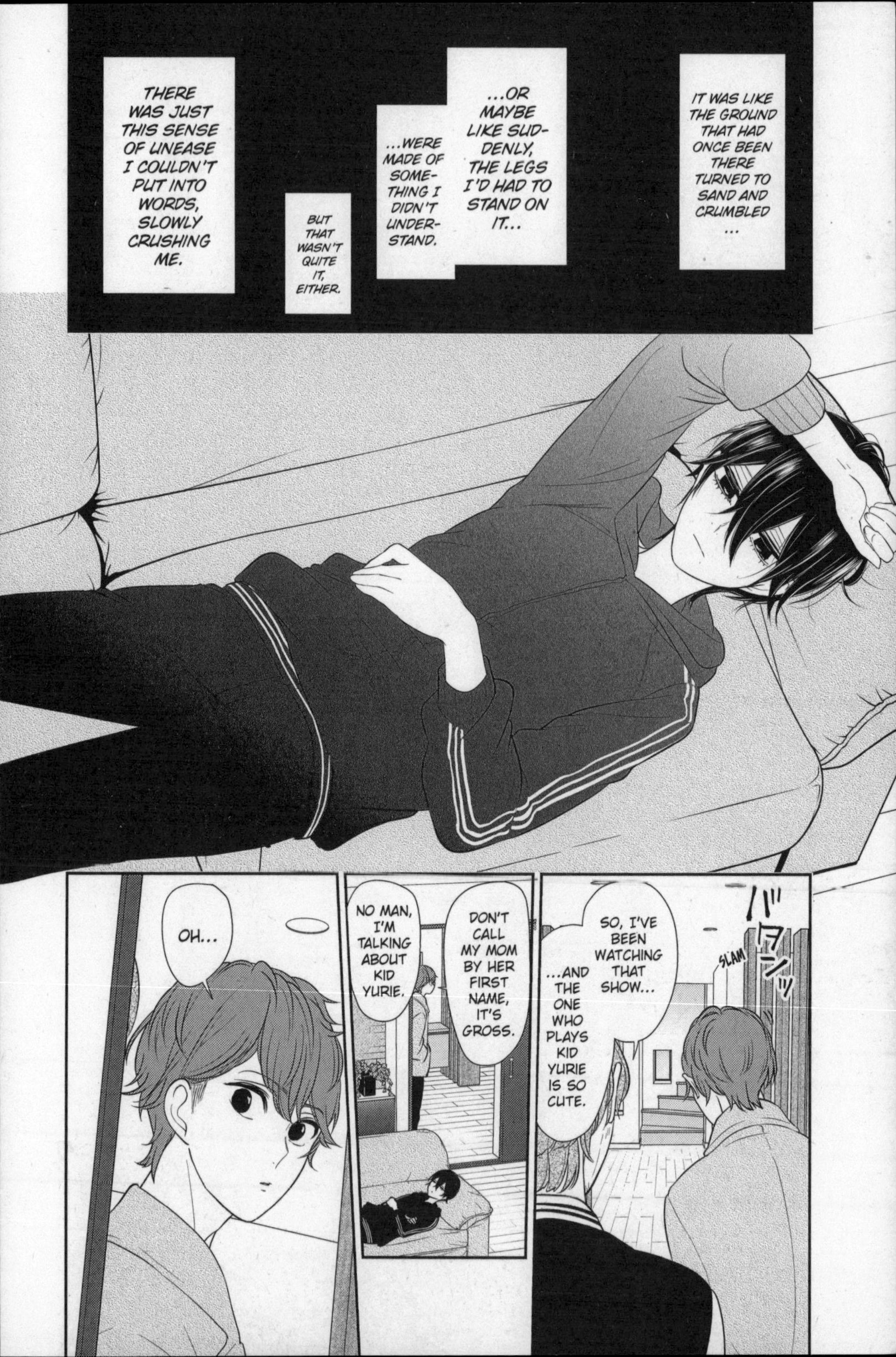
IT WAS LIKE THE GROUND THAT HAD ONCE BEEN THERE TURNED TO SAND AND CRUMBLED...
...OR MAYBE LIKE SUDDENLY, THE LEGS I'D HAD TO STAND ON IT...
...WERE MADE OF SOMETHING I DIDN'T UNDERSTAND.
BUT THAT WASN'T QUITE IT, EITHER.
THERE WAS JUST THIS SENSE OF UNEASE I COULDN'T PUT INTO WORDS, SLOWLY CRUSHING ME.
バタンッ
SLAM
SO, I'VE BEEN WATCHING THAT SHOW...
...AND THE ONE WHO PLAYS KID YURIE IS SO CUTE.
DON'T CALL MY MOM BY HER FIRST NAME, IT'S GROSS.
NO MAN, I'M TALKING ABOUT KID YURIE.
OH...

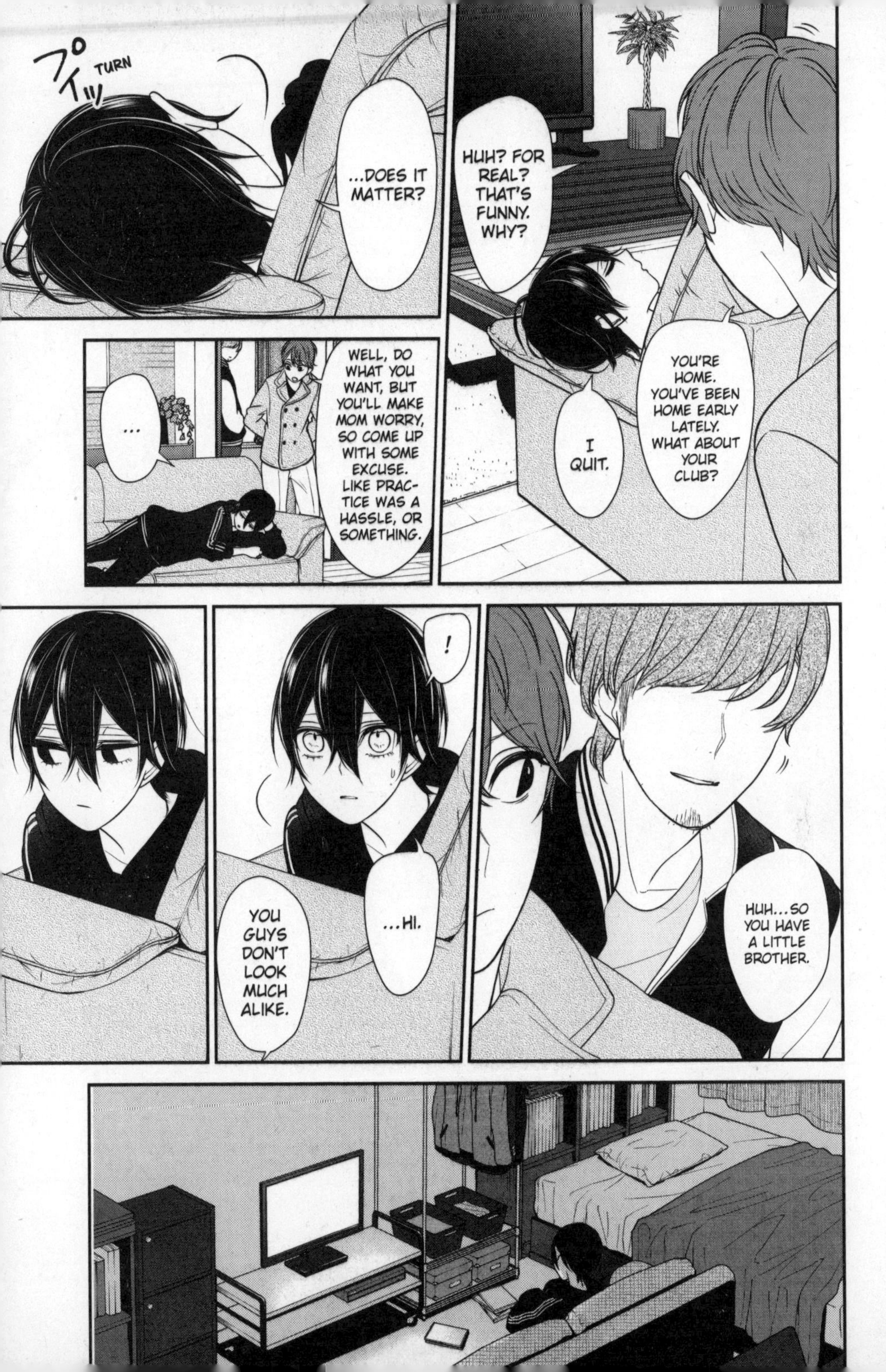
YOU'RE HOME. YOU'VE BEEN HOME EARLY LATELY. WHAT ABOUT YOUR CLUB?
I QUIT.
HUH? FOR REAL? THAT'S FUNNY. WHY?
プイッ
TURN
...DOES IT MATTER?
WELL, DO WHAT YOU WANT, BUT YOU'LL MAKE MOM WORRY, SO COME UP WITH SOME EXCUSE. LIKE PRACTICE WAS A HASSLE, OR SOMETHING.
...
HUH...SO YOU HAVE A LITTLE BROTHER.
!
...HI.
YOU GUYS DON'T LOOK MUCH ALIKE.

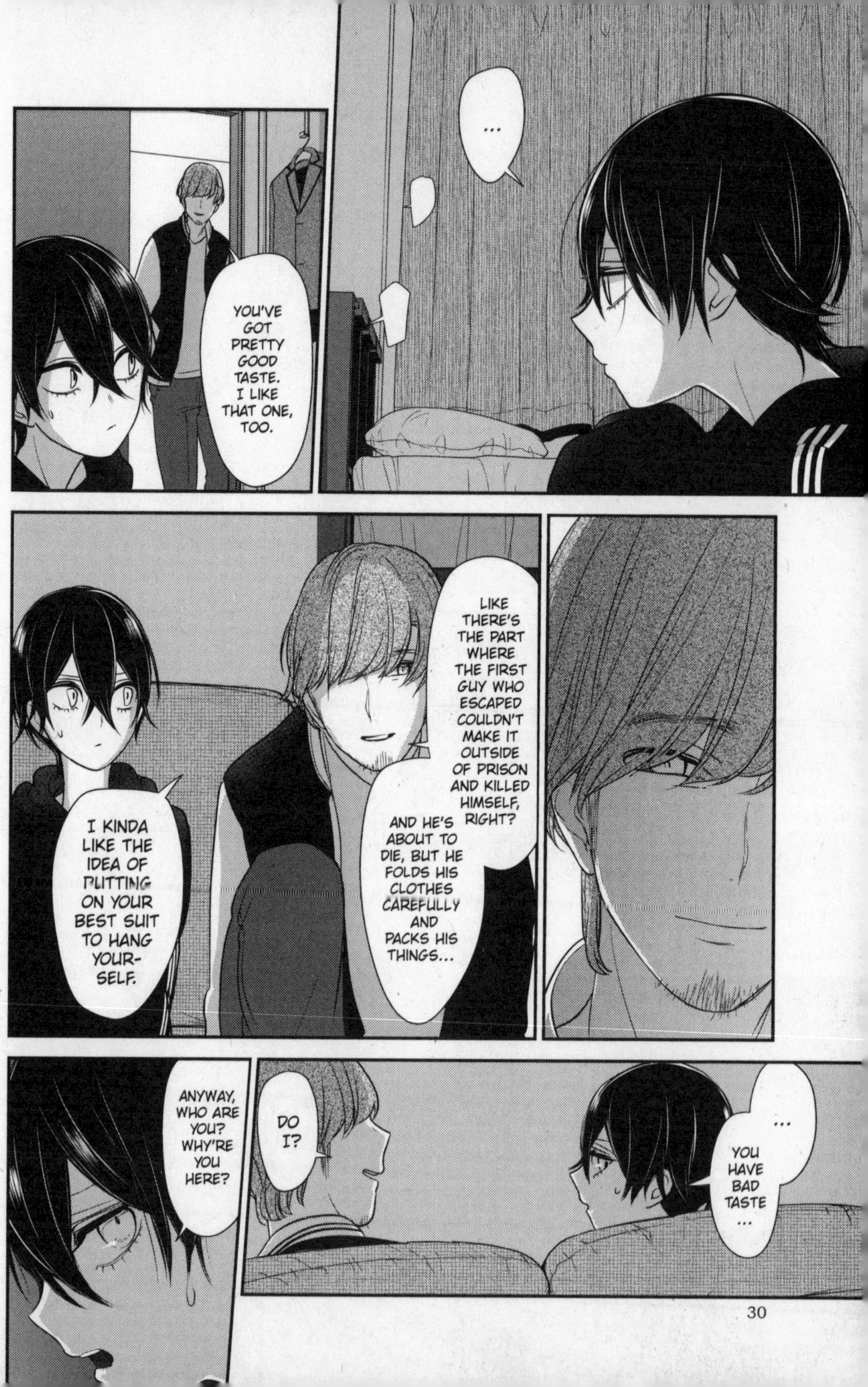
...
YOU'VE GOT PRETTY GOOD TASTE. I LIKE THAT ONE, TOO.
LIKE THERE'S THE PART WHERE THE FIRST GUY WHO ESCAPED COULDN'T MAKE IT OUTSIDE OF PRISON AND KILLED HIMSELF, RIGHT?
AND HE'S ABOUT TO DIE, BUT HE FOLDS HIS CLOTHES CAREFULLY AND PACKS HIS THINGS...
I KINDA LIKE THE IDEA OF PUTTING ON YOUR BEST SUIT TO HANG YOUR-SELF.
...
YOU HAVE BAD TASTE...
DO I?
ANYWAY, WHO ARE YOU? WHY'RE YOU HERE?

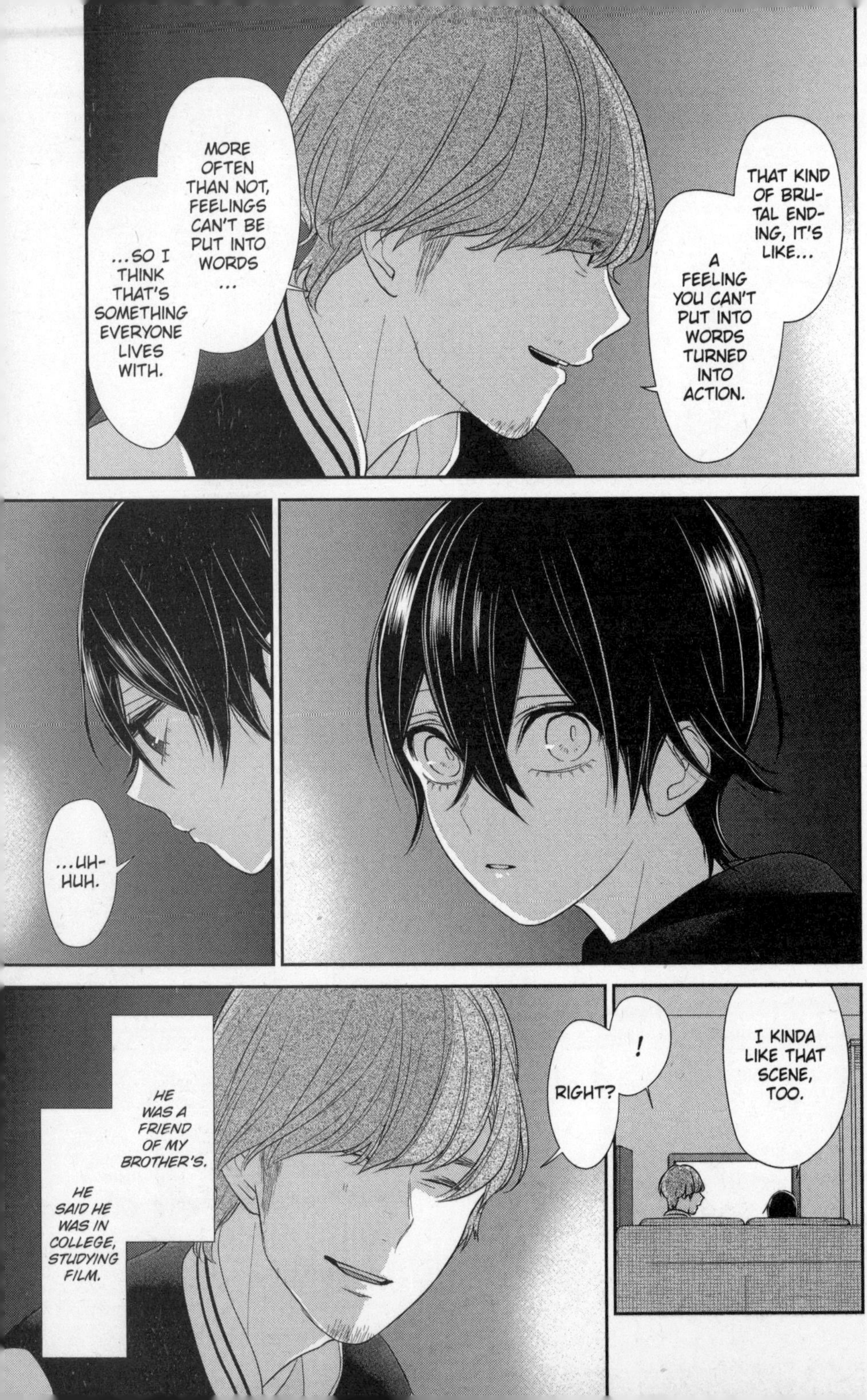

THAT KIND OF BRUTAL ENDING, IT'S LIKE...
A FEELING YOU CAN'T PUT INTO WORDS TURNED INTO ACTION.
MORE OFTEN THAN NOT, FEELINGS CAN'T BE PUT INTO WORDS...
...SO I THINK THAT'S SOMETHING EVERYONE LIVES WITH.
...UH-HUH.
I KINDA LIKE THAT SCENE, TOO.
!
RIGHT?
HE WAS A FRIEND OF MY BROTHER'S.
HE SAID HE WAS IN COLLEGE, STUDYING FILM.

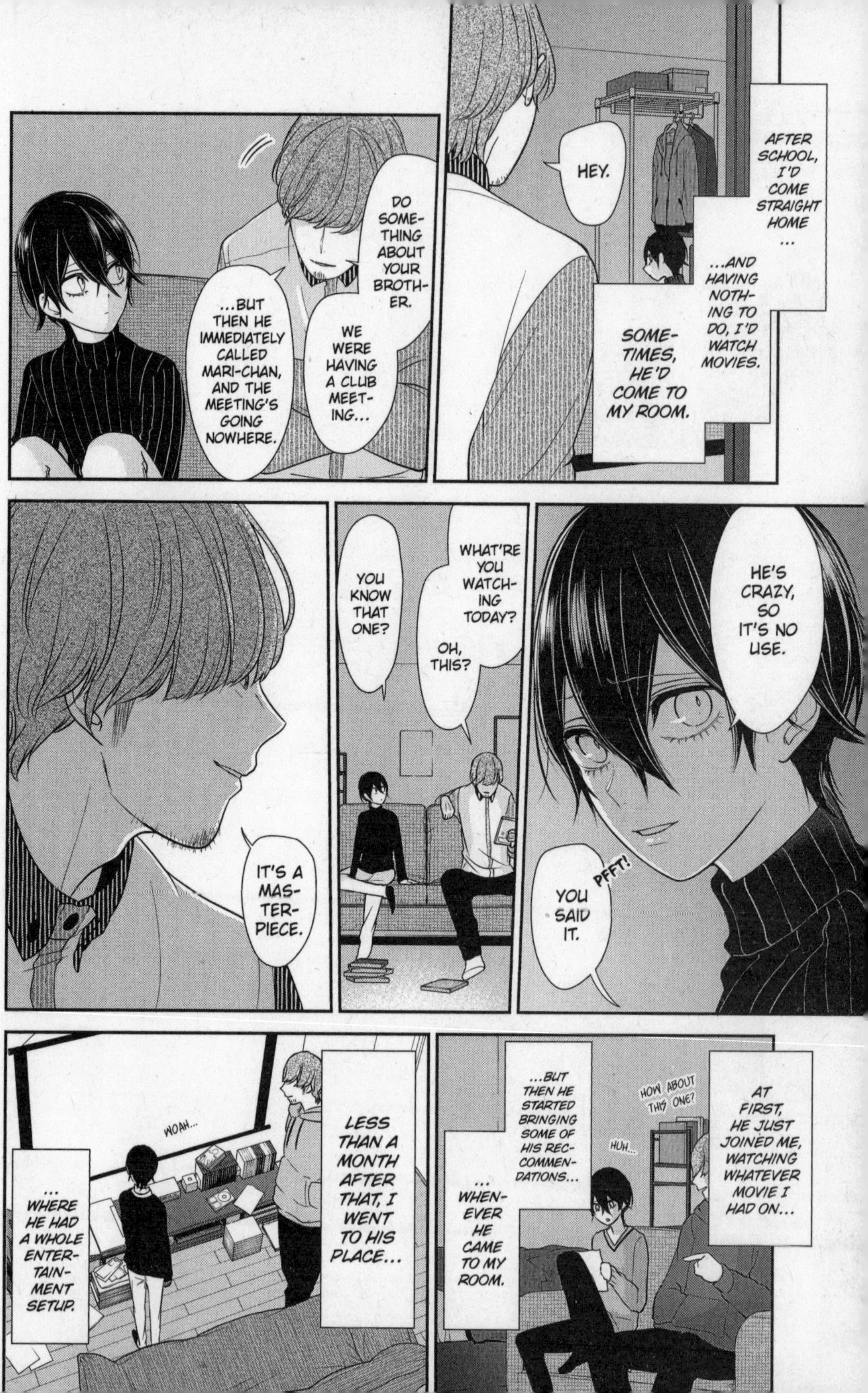
AFTER SCHOOL, I'D COME STRAIGHT HOME...
...AND HAVING NOTHING TO DO, I'D WATCH MOVIES.
HEY.
SOMETIMES, HE'D COME TO MY ROOM.
DO SOMETHING ABOUT YOUR BROTHER.
WE WERE HAVING A CLUB MEETING...
...BUT THEN HE IMMEDIATELY CALLED MARI-CHAN, AND THE MEETING'S GOING NOWHERE.
HE'S CRAZY, SO IT'S NO USE.
PFFT!
YOU SAID IT.
WHAT'RE YOU WATCHING TODAY?
OH, THIS?
YOU KNOW THAT ONE?
IT'S A MASTERPIECE.
AT FIRST, HE JUST JOINED ME, WATCHING WHATEVER MOVIE I HAD ON...
HOW ABOUT THIS ONE?
...BUT THEN HE STARTED BRINGING SOME OF HIS RECOMMENDATIONS...
HUH...
...WHENEVER HE CAME TO MY ROOM.
LESS THAN A MONTH AFTER THAT, I WENT TO HIS PLACE...
WOAH...
...WHERE HE HAD A WHOLE ENTERTAINMENT SETUP.

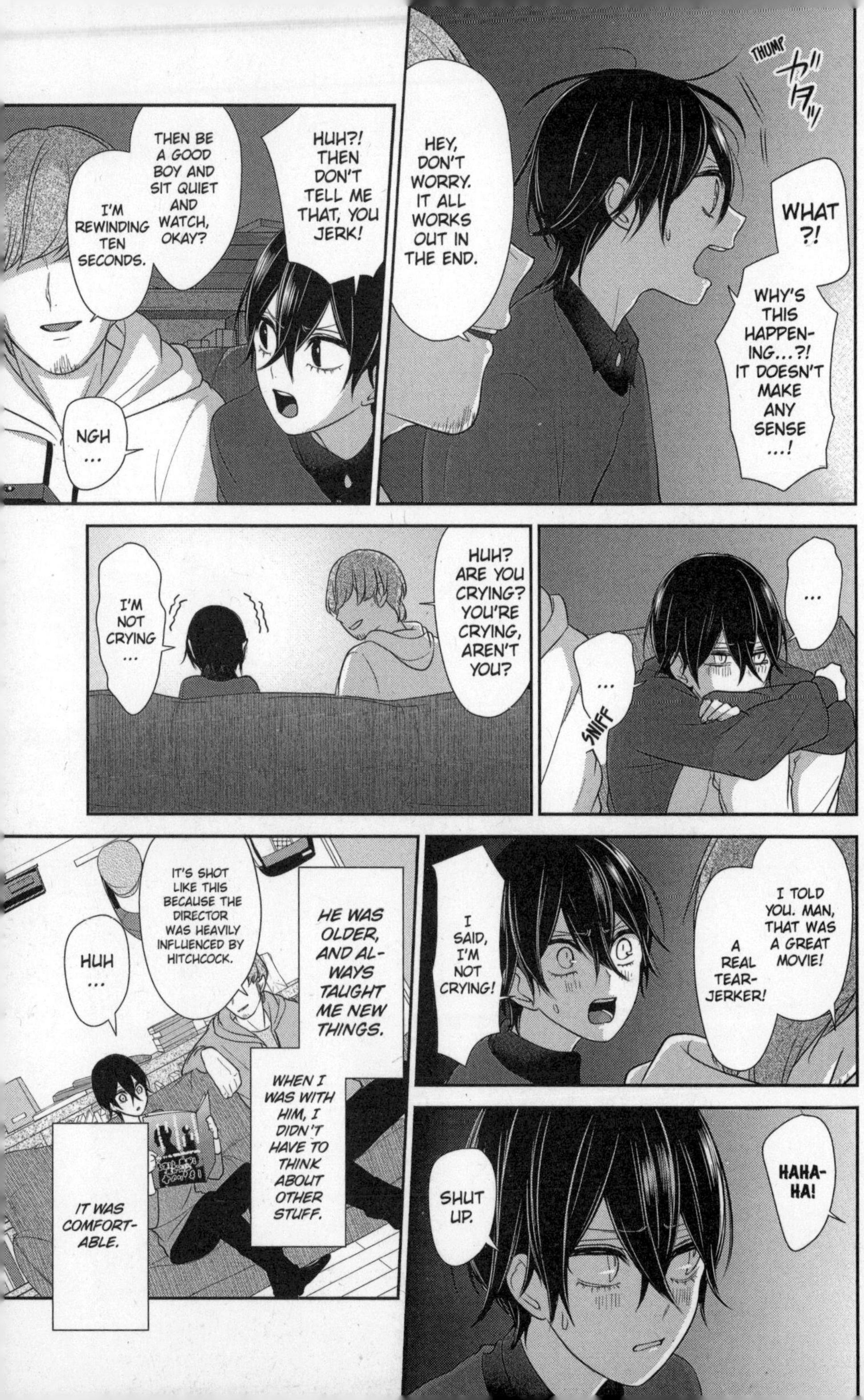
THUMP
ガタッ
WHAT?!
WHY'S THIS HAPPENING...?! IT DOESN'T MAKE ANY SENSE...!
HEY, DON'T WORRY. IT ALL WORKS OUT IN THE END.
HUH?! THEN DON'T TELL ME THAT, YOU JERK!
THEN BE A GOOD BOY AND SIT QUIET AND WATCH, OKAY?
I'M REWINDING TEN SECONDS.
NGH...
...
...
SNIFF
HUH? ARE YOU CRYING? YOU'RE CRYING, AREN'T YOU?
I'M NOT CRYING...
I TOLD YOU. MAN, THAT WAS A GREAT MOVIE!
A REAL TEAR-JERKER!
I SAID, I'M NOT CRYING!
HAHA-HA!
SHUT UP.
HE WAS OLDER, AND AL-WAYS TAUGHT ME NEW THINGS.
IT'S SHOT LIKE THIS BECAUSE THE DIRECTOR WAS HEAVILY INFLUENCED BY HITCHCOCK.
HUH...
WHEN I WAS WITH HIM, I DIDN'T HAVE TO THINK ABOUT OTHER STUFF.
IT WAS COMFORT-ABLE.

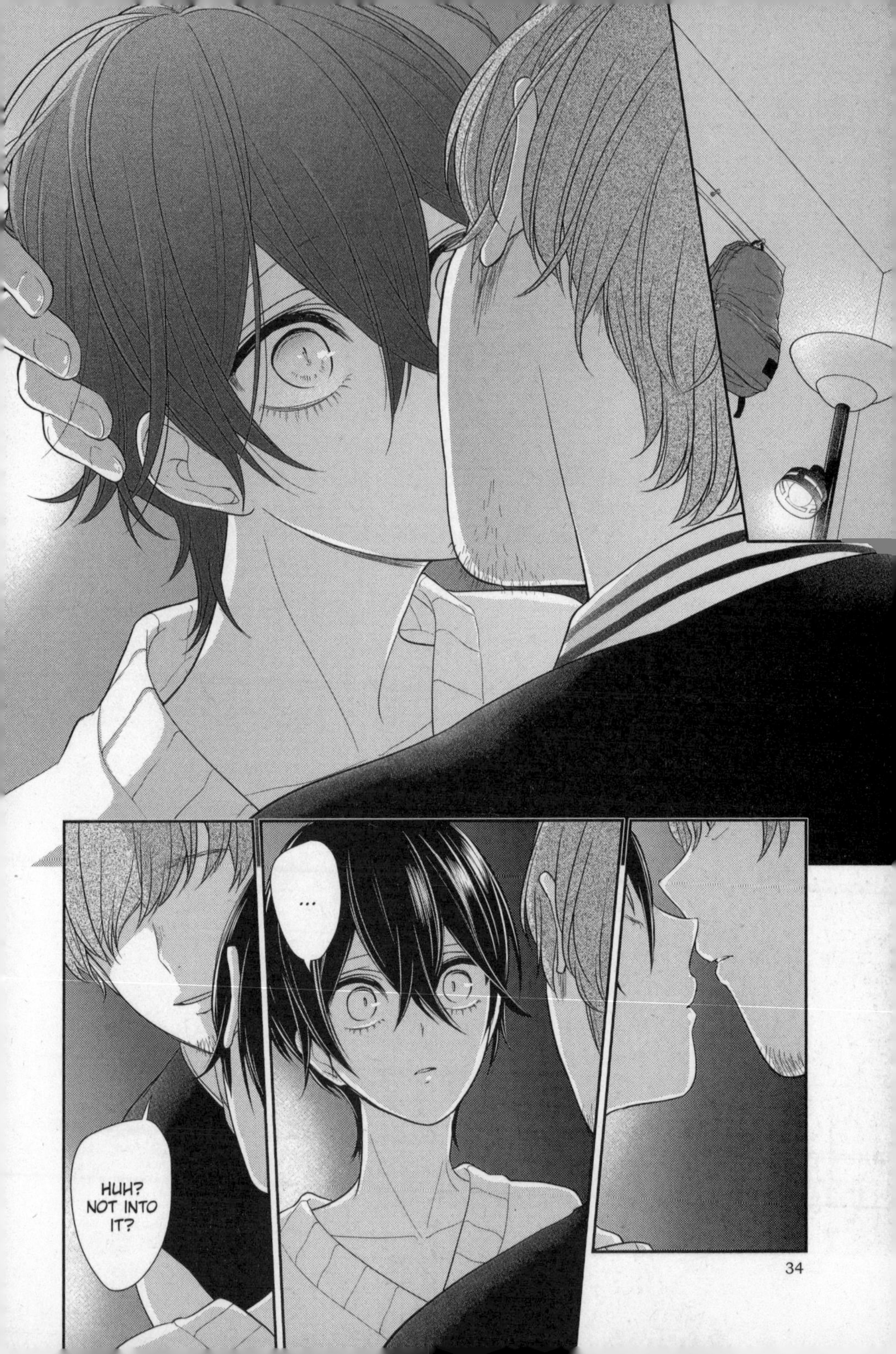
...
HUH? NOT INTO IT?

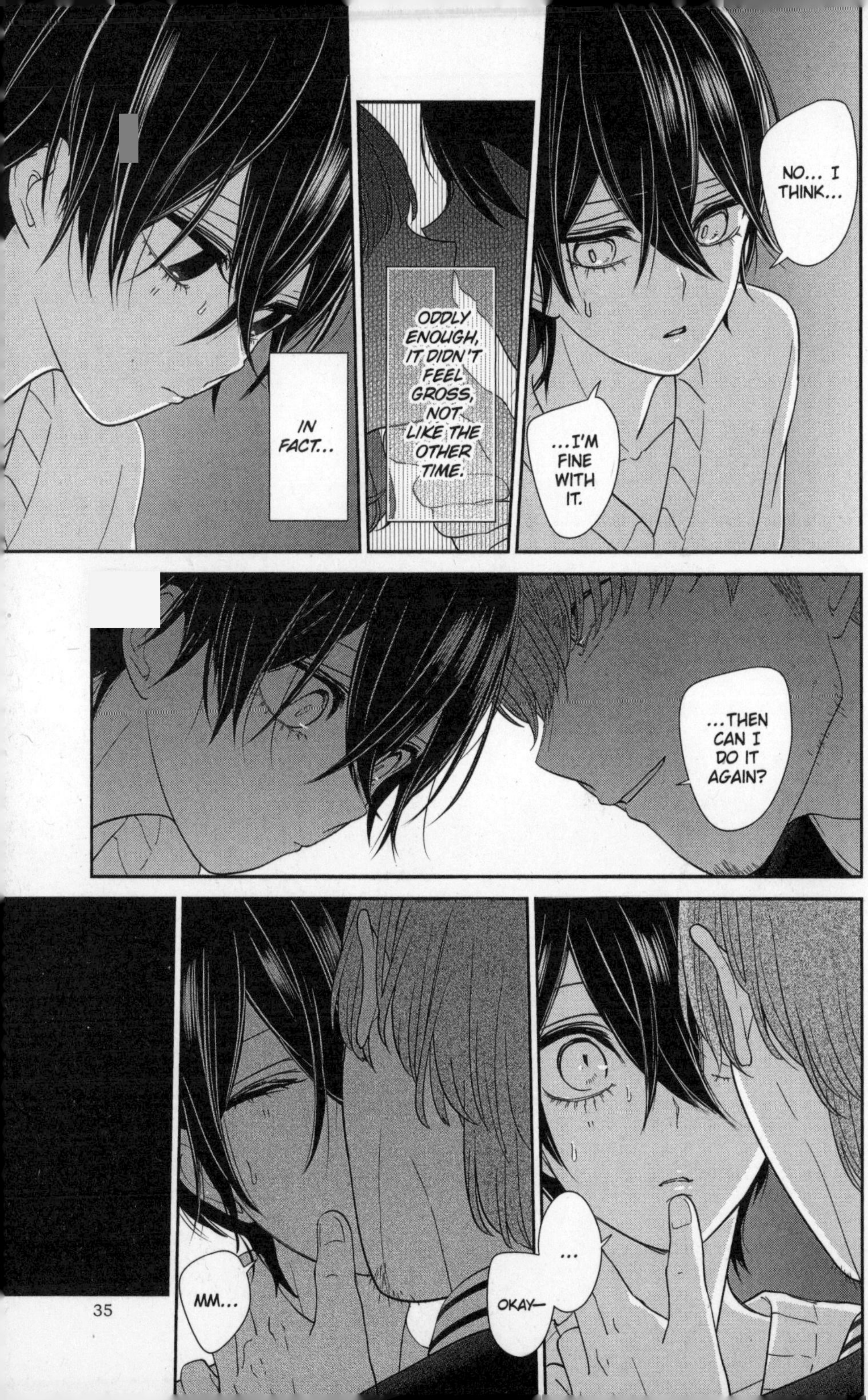
NO... I THINK...
...I'M FINE WITH IT.
ODDLY ENOUGH, IT DIDN'T FEEL GROSS, NOT LIKE THE OTHER TIME.
IN FACT...
...THEN CAN I DO IT AGAIN?
...
OKAY—
MM...

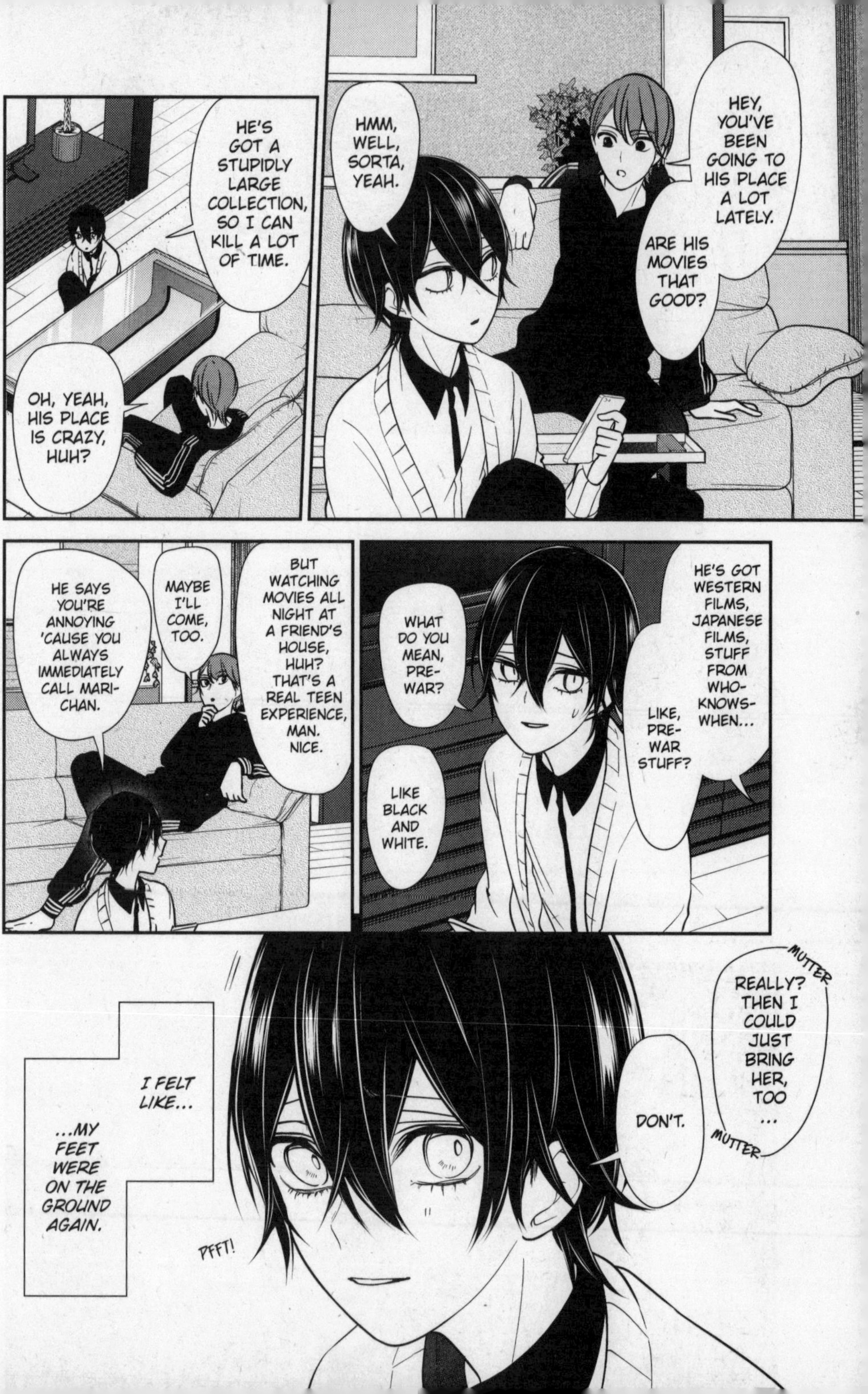
HEY, YOU'VE BEEN GOING TO HIS PLACE A LOT LATELY.
ARE HIS MOVIES THAT GOOD?
HMM, WELL, SORTA, YEAH.
HE'S GOT A STUPIDLY LARGE COLLECTION, SO I CAN KILL A LOT OF TIME.
OH, YEAH, HIS PLACE IS CRAZY, HUH?
HE'S GOT WESTERN FILMS, JAPANESE FILMS, STUFF FROM WHO-KNOWS-WHEN...
LIKE, PRE-WAR STUFF?
WHAT DO YOU MEAN, PRE-WAR?
LIKE BLACK AND WHITE.
BUT WATCHING MOVIES ALL NIGHT AT A FRIEND'S HOUSE, HUH? THAT'S A REAL TEEN EXPERIENCE, MAN. NICE.
MAYBE I'LL COME, TOO.
HE SAYS YOU'RE ANNOYING 'CAUSE YOU ALWAYS IMMEDIATELY CALL MARI-CHAN.
MUTTER
REALLY? THEN I COULD JUST BRING HER, TOO...
MUTTER
DON'T.
PFFT!
I FELT LIKE...
...MY FEET WERE ON THE GROUND AGAIN.

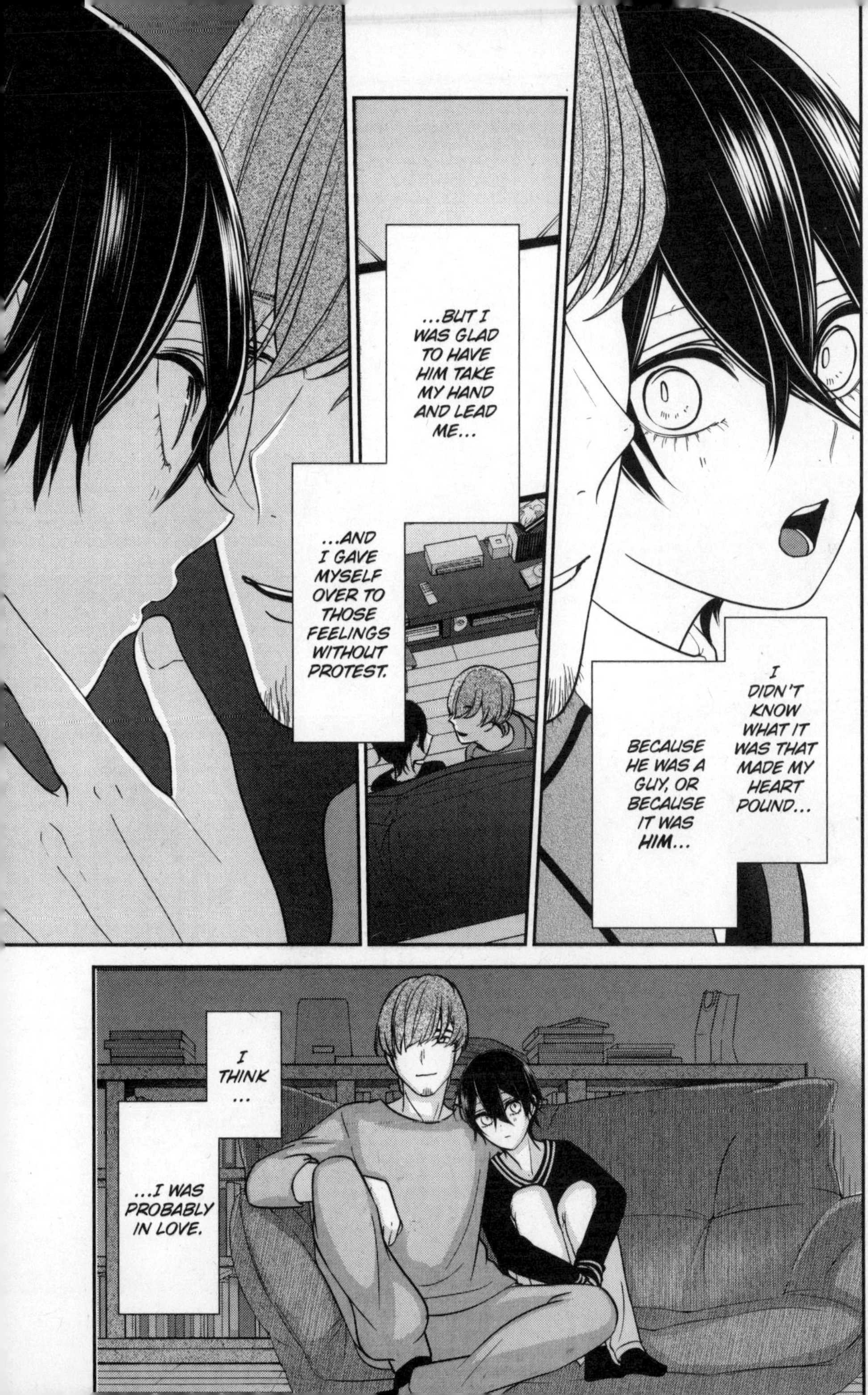
I DIDN'T KNOW WHAT IT WAS THAT MADE MY HEART POUND...
BECAUSE HE WAS A GUY, OR BECAUSE IT WAS HIM...
...BUT I WAS GLAD TO HAVE HIM TAKE MY HAND AND LEAD ME...
...AND I GAVE MYSELF OVER TO THOSE FEELINGS WITHOUT PROTEST.
I THINK...
...I WAS PROBABLY IN LOVE.

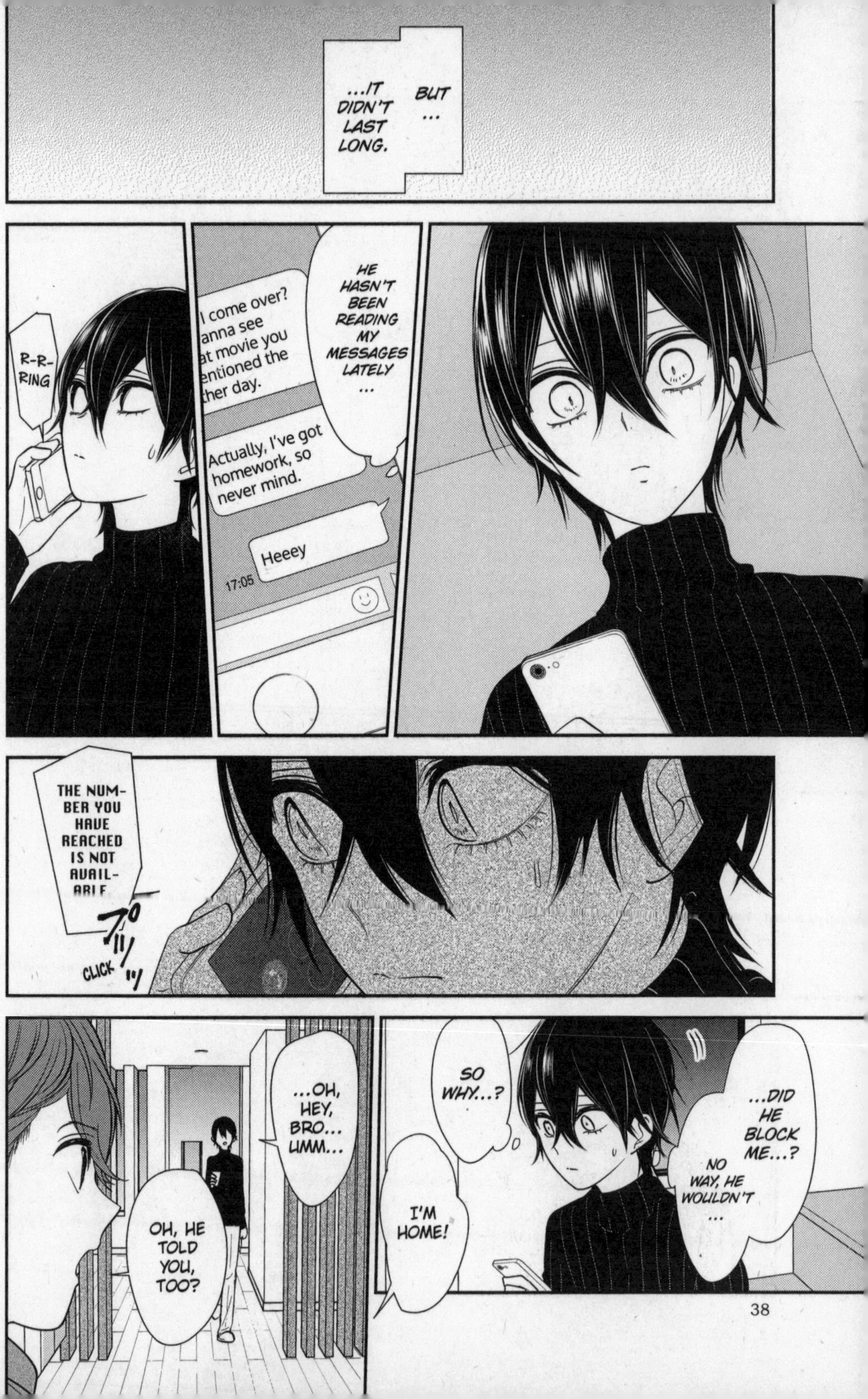
BUT...
...IT DIDN'T LAST LONG.
HE HASN'T BEEN READING MY MESSAGES LATELY...
I come over?
anna see
at movie you
entioned the
ther day.
Actually, I've got homework, so never mind.
Heeey
17:05
R-R-RING
THE NUM-BER YOU HAVE REACHED IS NOT AVAIL-ABLE
CLICK
...DID HE BLOCK ME...?
NO WAY, HE WOULDN'T...
SO WHY...?
I'M HOME!
...OH, HEY, BRO... UMM...
OH, HE TOLD YOU, TOO?

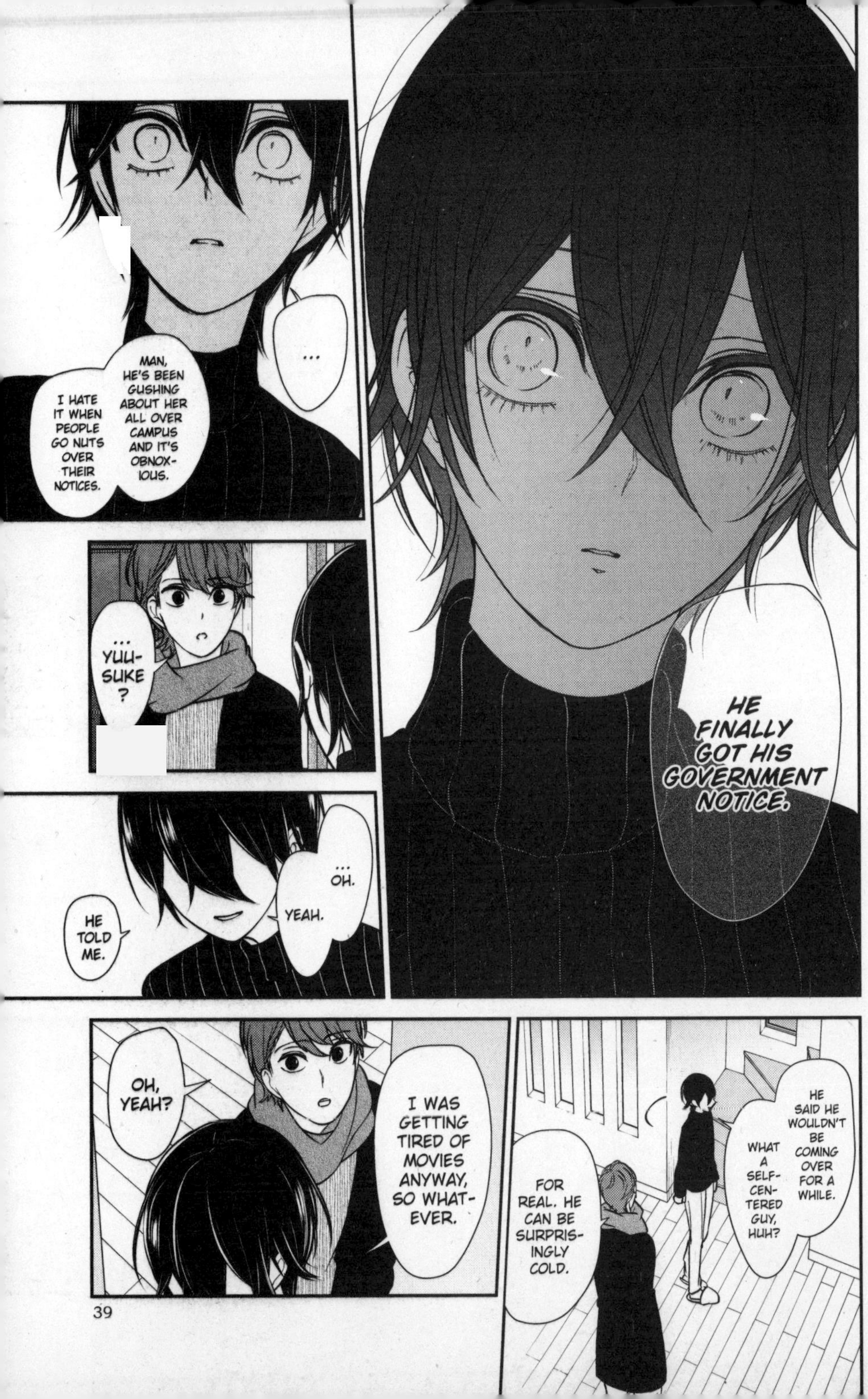
HE FINALLY GOT HIS GOVERNMENT NOTICE.
...
MAN, HE'S BEEN GUSHING ABOUT HER ALL OVER CAMPUS AND IT'S OBNOX-IOUS.
I HATE IT WHEN PEOPLE GO NUTS OVER THEIR NOTICES.
... YUU-SUKE ?
... OH.
YEAH.
HE TOLD ME.
HE SAID HE WOULDN'T BE COMING OVER FOR A WHILE.
WHAT A SELF-CEN-TERED GUY, HUH?
FOR REAL. HE CAN BE SURPRIS-INGLY COLD.
I WAS GETTING TIRED OF MOVIES ANYWAY, SO WHAT-EVER.
OH, YEAH?

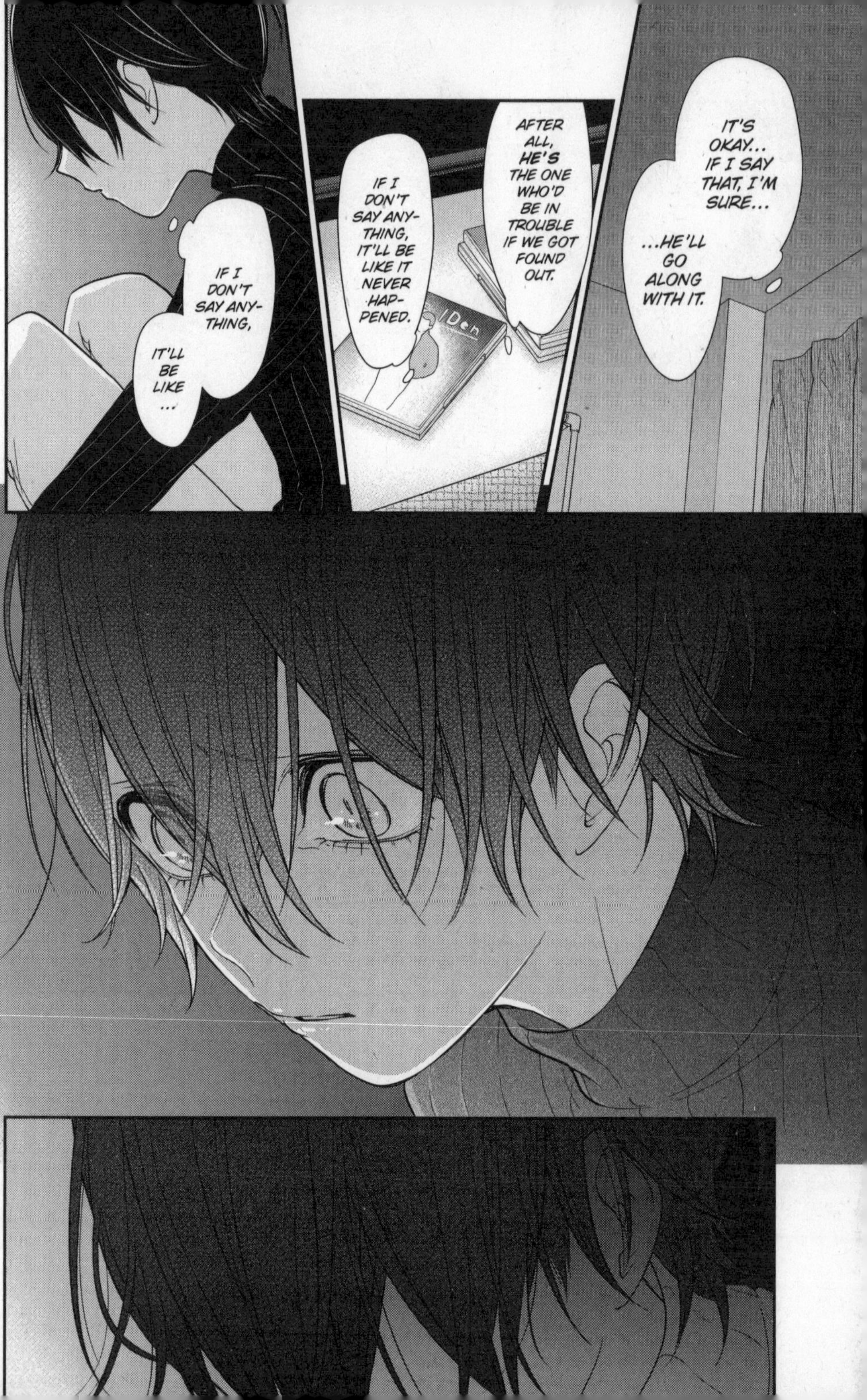
IT'S OKAY... IF I SAY THAT, I'M SURE...
...HE'LL GO ALONG WITH IT.
AFTER ALL, HE'S THE ONE WHO'D BE IN TROUBLE IF WE GOT FOUND OUT.
IF I DON'T SAY ANYTHING, IT'LL BE LIKE IT NEVER HAPPENED.
IF I DON'T SAY ANYTHING,
IT'LL BE LIKE...

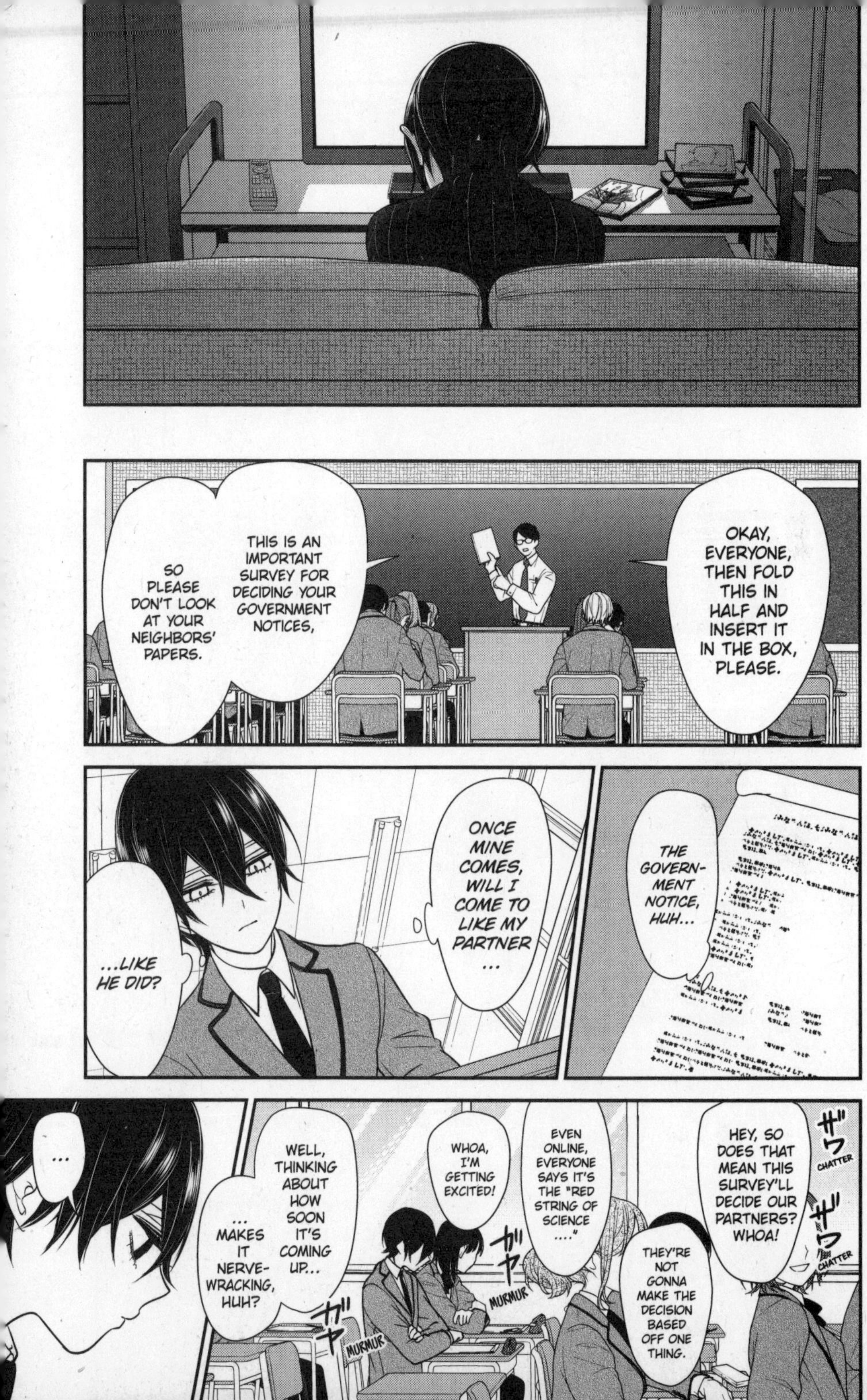
OKAY, EVERYONE, THEN FOLD THIS IN HALF AND INSERT IT IN THE BOX, PLEASE.
THIS IS AN IMPORTANT SURVEY FOR DECIDING YOUR GOVERNMENT NOTICES,
SO PLEASE DON'T LOOK AT YOUR NEIGHBORS' PAPERS.
THE GOVERNMENT NOTICE, HUH...
ONCE MINE COMES, WILL I COME TO LIKE MY PARTNER ...
...LIKE HE DID?
ザワ CHATTER
HEY, SO DOES THAT MEAN THIS SURVEY'LL DECIDE OUR PARTNERS? WHOA!
ザワ CHATTER
THEY'RE NOT GONNA MAKE THE DECISION BASED OFF ONE THING.
EVEN ONLINE, EVERYONE SAYS IT'S THE "RED STRING OF SCIENCE ...."
WHOA, I'M GETTING EXCITED!
ガヤ MURMUR
WELL, THINKING ABOUT HOW SOON IT'S COMING UP...
... MAKES IT NERVE-WRACKING, HUH?
ガヤ MURMUR
...

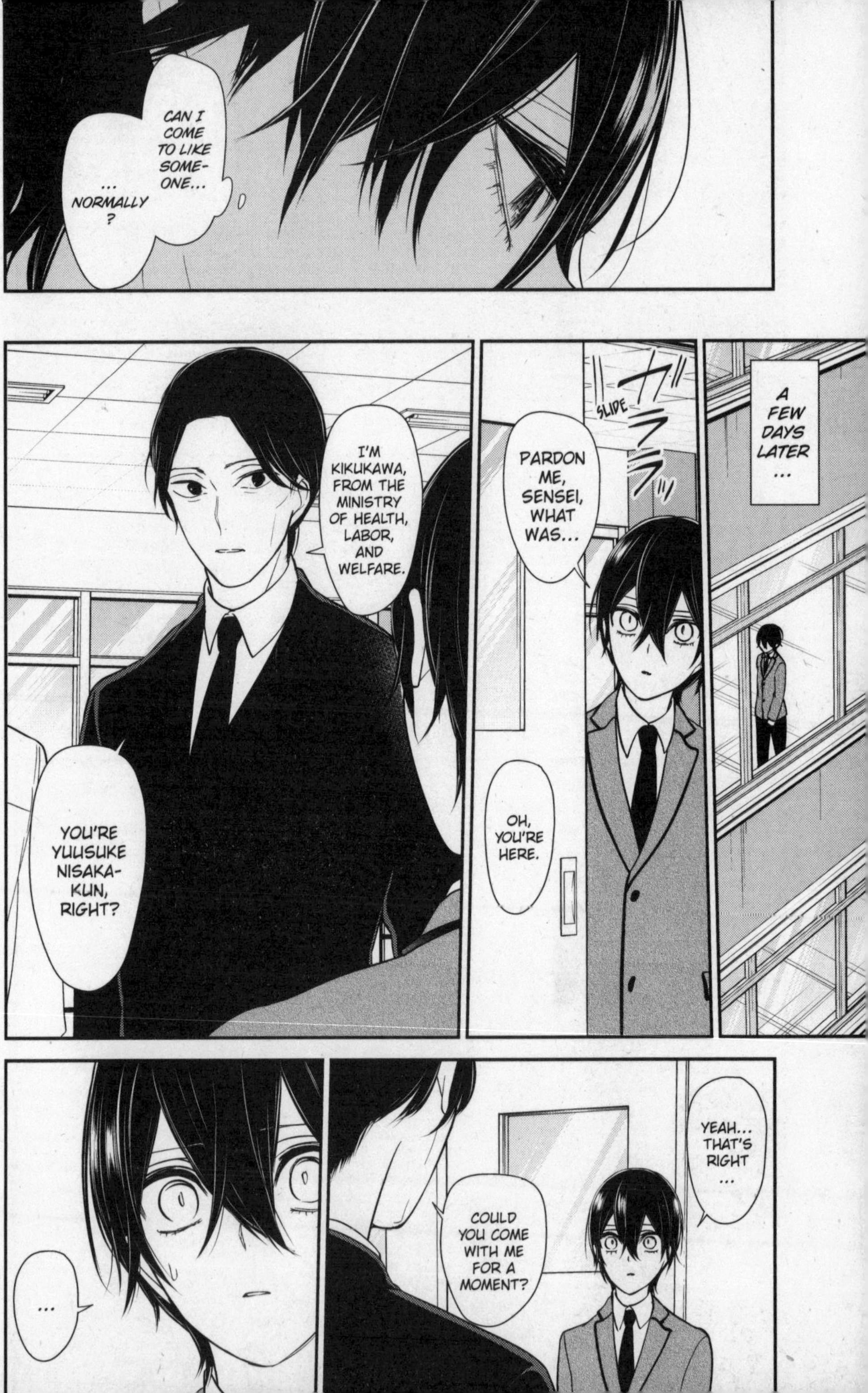
CAN I COME TO LIKE SOME-ONE...
... NORMALLY ?
A FEW DAYS LATER ...
SLIDE
PARDON ME, SENSEI, WHAT WAS...
OH, YOU'RE HERE.
I'M KIKUKAWA, FROM THE MINISTRY OF HEALTH, LABOR, AND WELFARE.
YOU'RE YUUSUKE NISAKA-KUN, RIGHT?
YEAH... THAT'S RIGHT ...
COULD YOU COME WITH ME FOR A MOMENT?
...

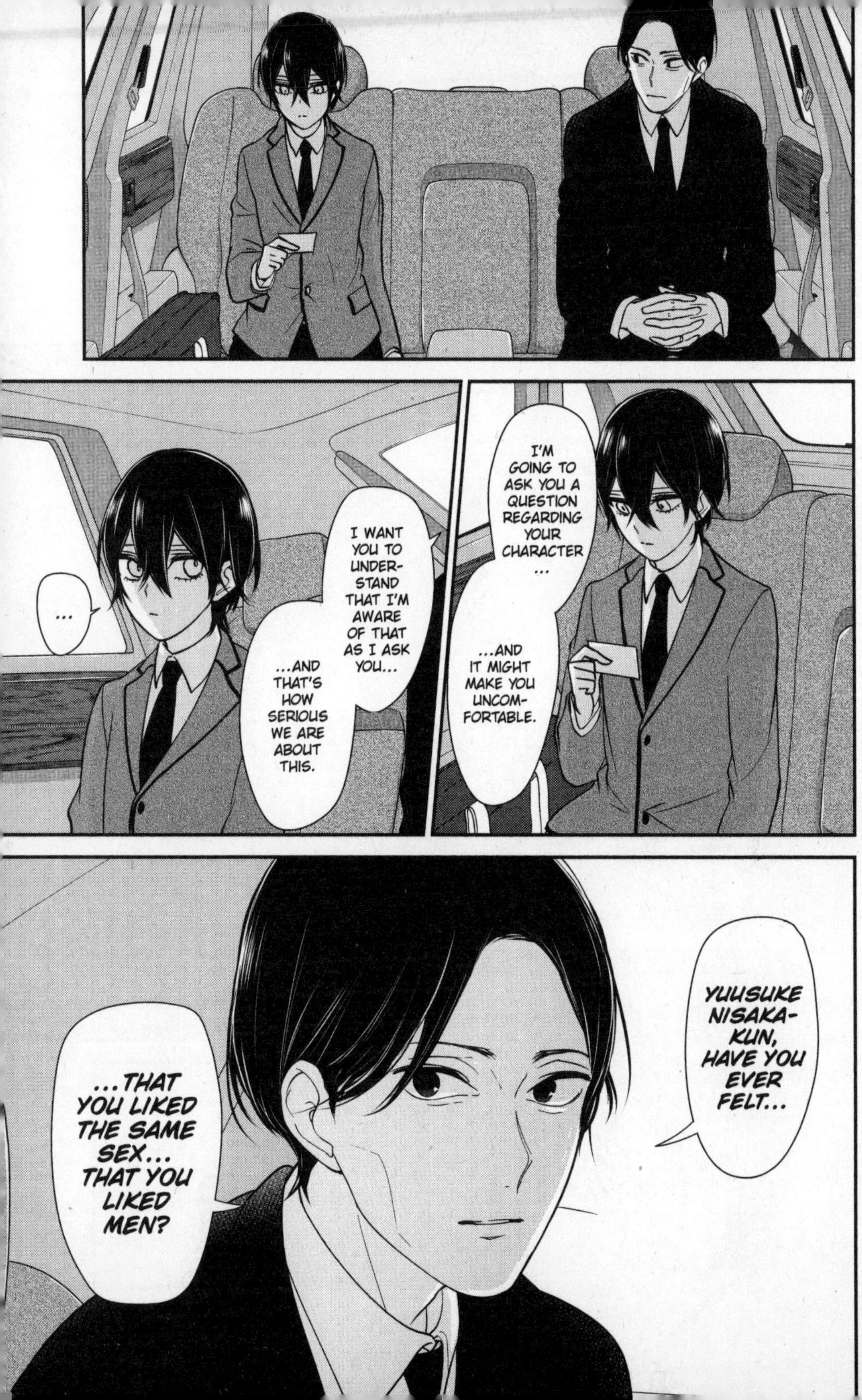
I'M GOING TO ASK YOU A QUESTION REGARDING YOUR CHARACTER...
...AND IT MIGHT MAKE YOU UNCOMFORTABLE.
I WANT YOU TO UNDERSTAND THAT I'M AWARE OF THAT AS I ASK YOU...
...AND THAT'S HOW SERIOUS WE ARE ABOUT THIS.
...
YUUSUKE NISAKA-KUN, HAVE YOU EVER FELT...
...THAT YOU LIKED THE SAME SEX... THAT YOU LIKED MEN?

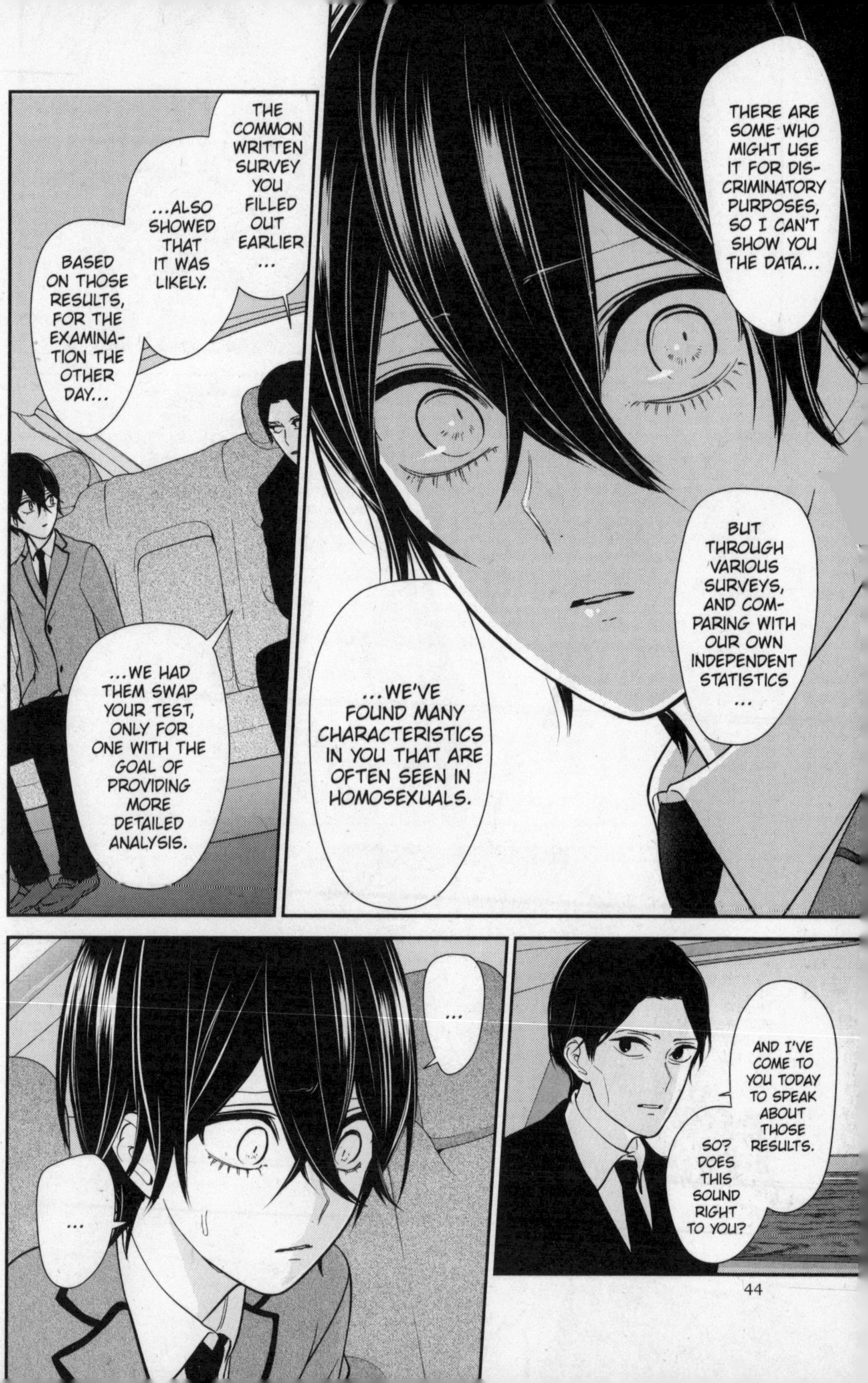

THERE ARE SOME WHO MIGHT USE IT FOR DISCRIMINATORY PURPOSES, SO I CAN'T SHOW YOU THE DATA...
BUT THROUGH VARIOUS SURVEYS, AND COMPARING WITH OUR OWN INDEPENDENT STATISTICS ...
...WE'VE FOUND MANY CHARACTERISTICS IN YOU THAT ARE OFTEN SEEN IN HOMOSEXUALS.
THE COMMON WRITTEN SURVEY YOU FILLED OUT EARLIER ...
...ALSO SHOWED THAT IT WAS LIKELY.
BASED ON THOSE RESULTS, FOR THE EXAMINATION THE OTHER DAY...
...WE HAD THEM SWAP YOUR TEST, ONLY FOR ONE WITH THE GOAL OF PROVIDING MORE DETAILED ANALYSIS.
AND I'VE COME TO YOU TODAY TO SPEAK ABOUT THOSE RESULTS.
SO? DOES THIS SOUND RIGHT TO YOU?
...
...

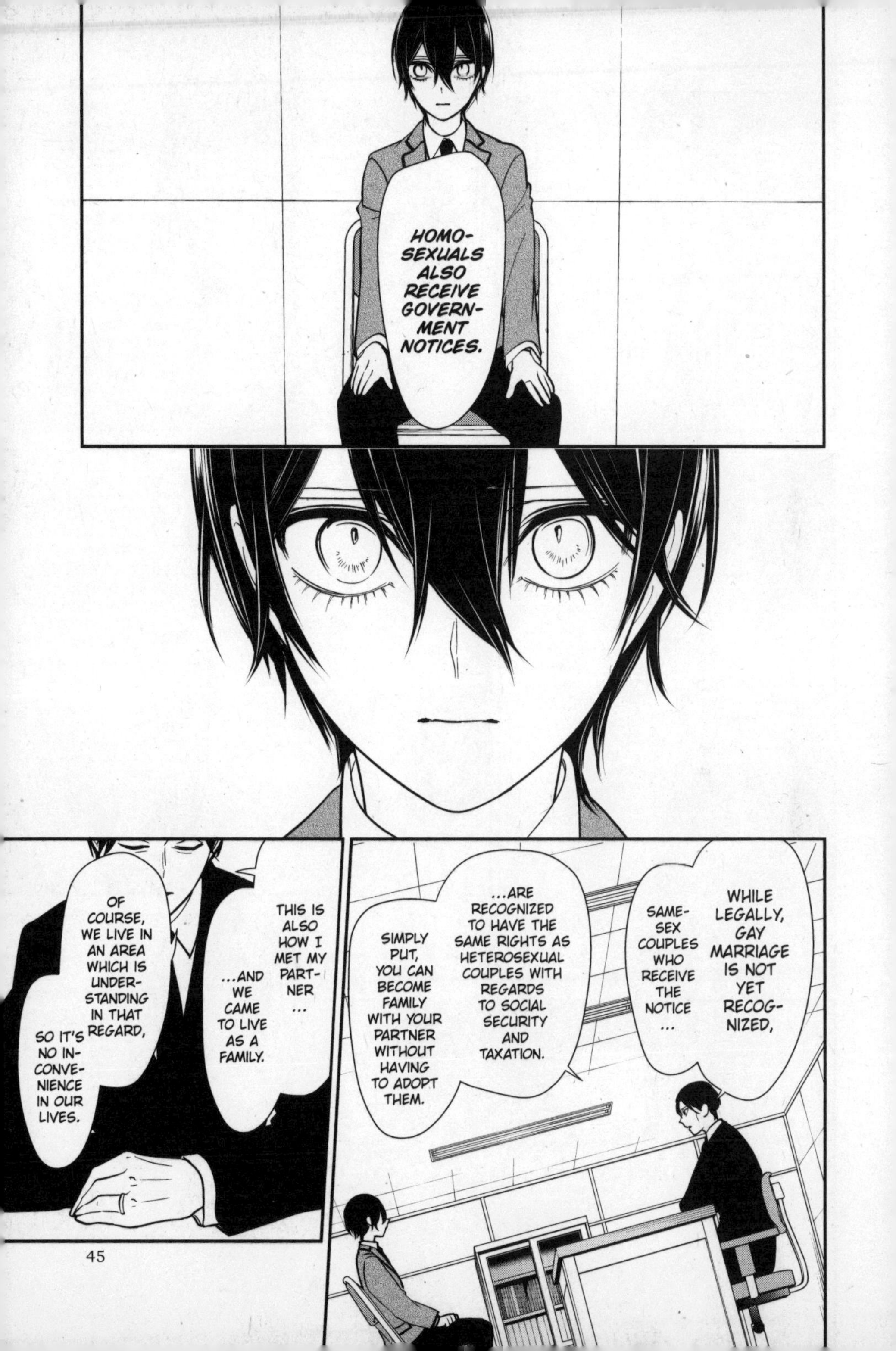
HOMO-SEXUALS ALSO RECEIVE GOVERN-MENT NOTICES.
WHILE LEGALLY, GAY MARRIAGE IS NOT YET RECOG-NIZED,
SAME-SEX COUPLES WHO RECEIVE THE NOTICE ...
...ARE RECOGNIZED TO HAVE THE SAME RIGHTS AS HETEROSEXUAL COUPLES WITH REGARDS TO SOCIAL SECURITY AND TAXATION.
SIMPLY PUT, YOU CAN BECOME FAMILY WITH YOUR PARTNER WITHOUT HAVING TO ADOPT THEM.
THIS IS ALSO HOW I MET MY PART-NER ...
...AND WE CAME TO LIVE AS A FAMILY.
OF COURSE, WE LIVE IN AN AREA WHICH IS UNDER-STANDING IN THAT REGARD,
SO IT'S NO IN-CONVE-NIENCE IN OUR LIVES.

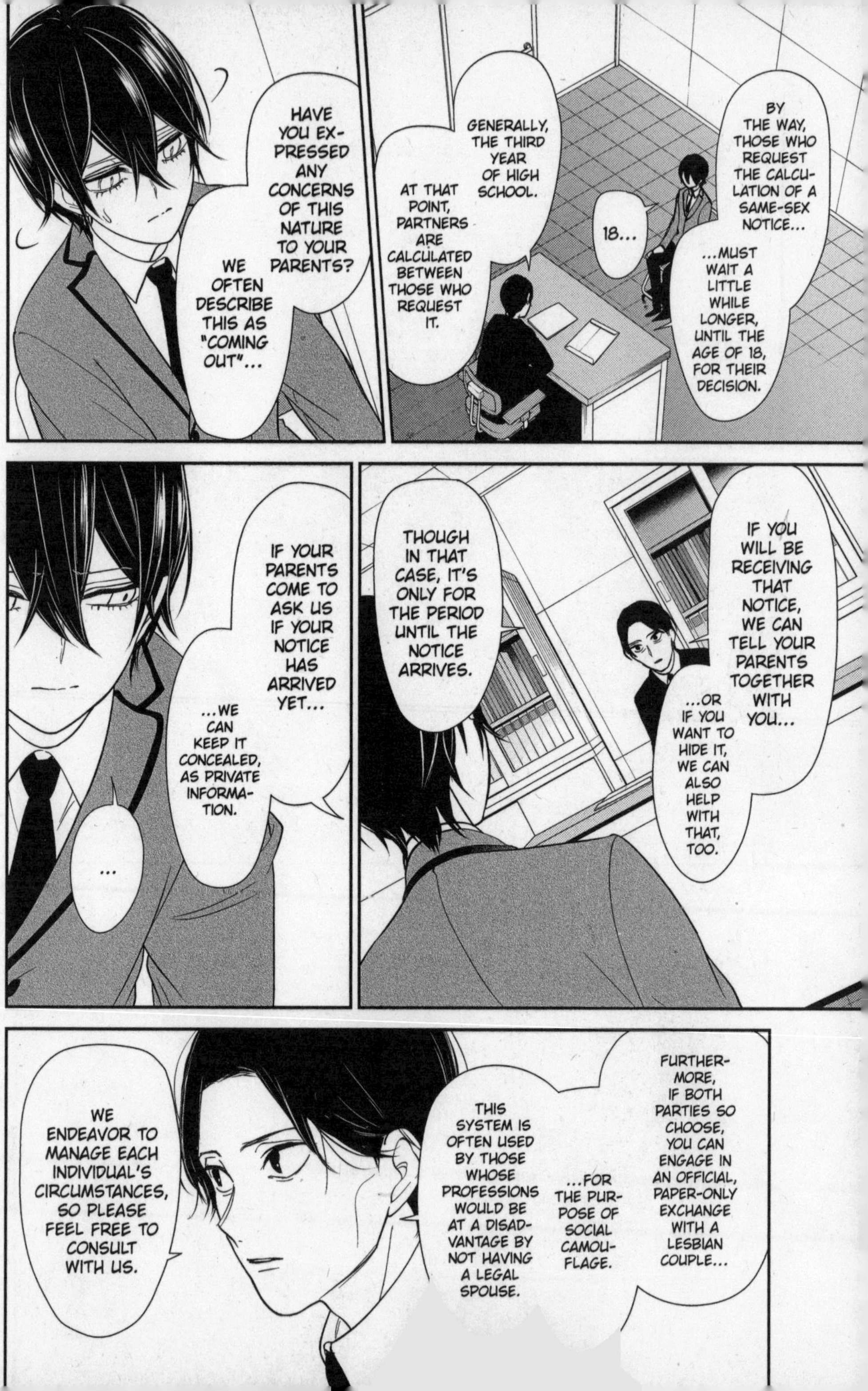
BY THE WAY, THOSE WHO REQUEST THE CALCULATION OF A SAME-SEX NOTICE...
...MUST WAIT A LITTLE WHILE LONGER, UNTIL THE AGE OF 18, FOR THEIR DECISION.
18...
GENERALLY, THE THIRD YEAR OF HIGH SCHOOL.
AT THAT POINT, PARTNERS ARE CALCULATED BETWEEN THOSE WHO REQUEST IT.
HAVE YOU EXPRESSED ANY CONCERNS OF THIS NATURE TO YOUR PARENTS?
WE OFTEN DESCRIBE THIS AS "COMING OUT"...
IF YOU WILL BE RECEIVING THAT NOTICE, WE CAN TELL YOUR PARENTS TOGETHER WITH YOU...
...OR IF YOU WANT TO HIDE IT, WE CAN ALSO HELP WITH THAT, TOO.
THOUGH IN THAT CASE, IT'S ONLY FOR THE PERIOD UNTIL THE NOTICE ARRIVES.
IF YOUR PARENTS COME TO ASK US IF YOUR NOTICE HAS ARRIVED YET...
...WE CAN KEEP IT CONCEALED, AS PRIVATE INFORMATION.
...
FURTHERMORE, IF BOTH PARTIES SO CHOOSE, YOU CAN ENGAGE IN AN OFFICIAL, PAPER-ONLY EXCHANGE WITH A LESBIAN COUPLE...
...FOR THE PURPOSE OF SOCIAL CAMOUFLAGE.
THIS SYSTEM IS OFTEN USED BY THOSE WHOSE PROFESSIONS WOULD BE AT A DISADVANTAGE BY NOT HAVING A LEGAL SPOUSE.
WE ENDEAVOR TO MANAGE EACH INDIVIDUAL'S CIRCUMSTANCES, SO PLEASE FEEL FREE TO CONSULT WITH US.

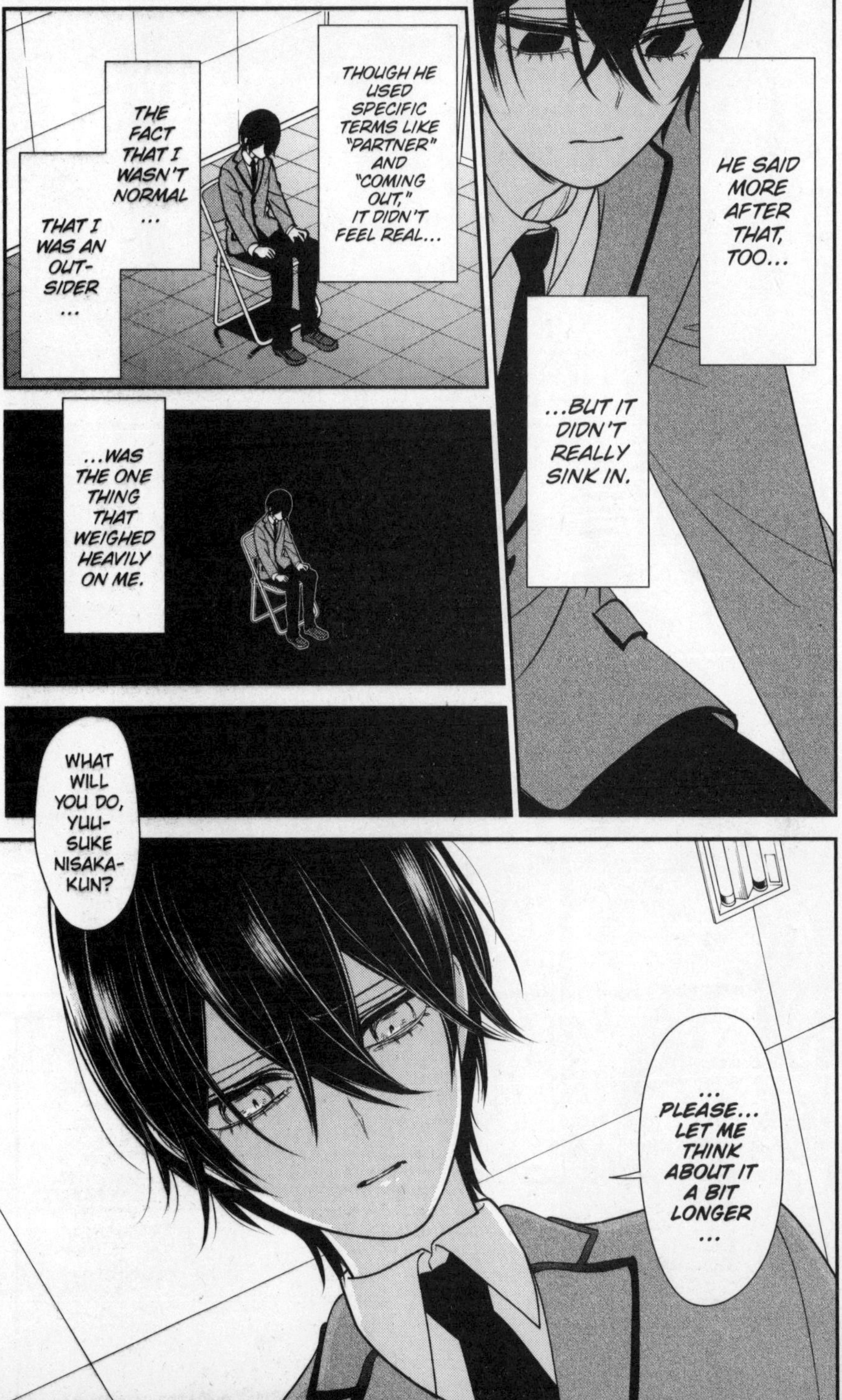
HE SAID MORE AFTER THAT, TOO...
...BUT IT DIDN'T REALLY SINK IN.
THOUGH HE USED SPECIFIC TERMS LIKE "PARTNER" AND "COMING OUT," IT DIDN'T FEEL REAL...
THE FACT THAT I WASN'T NORMAL...
THAT I WAS AN OUT-SIDER...
...WAS THE ONE THING THAT WEIGHED HEAVILY ON ME.
WHAT WILL YOU DO, YUU-SUKE NISAKA-KUN?
...PLEASE... LET ME THINK ABOUT IT A BIT LONGER...

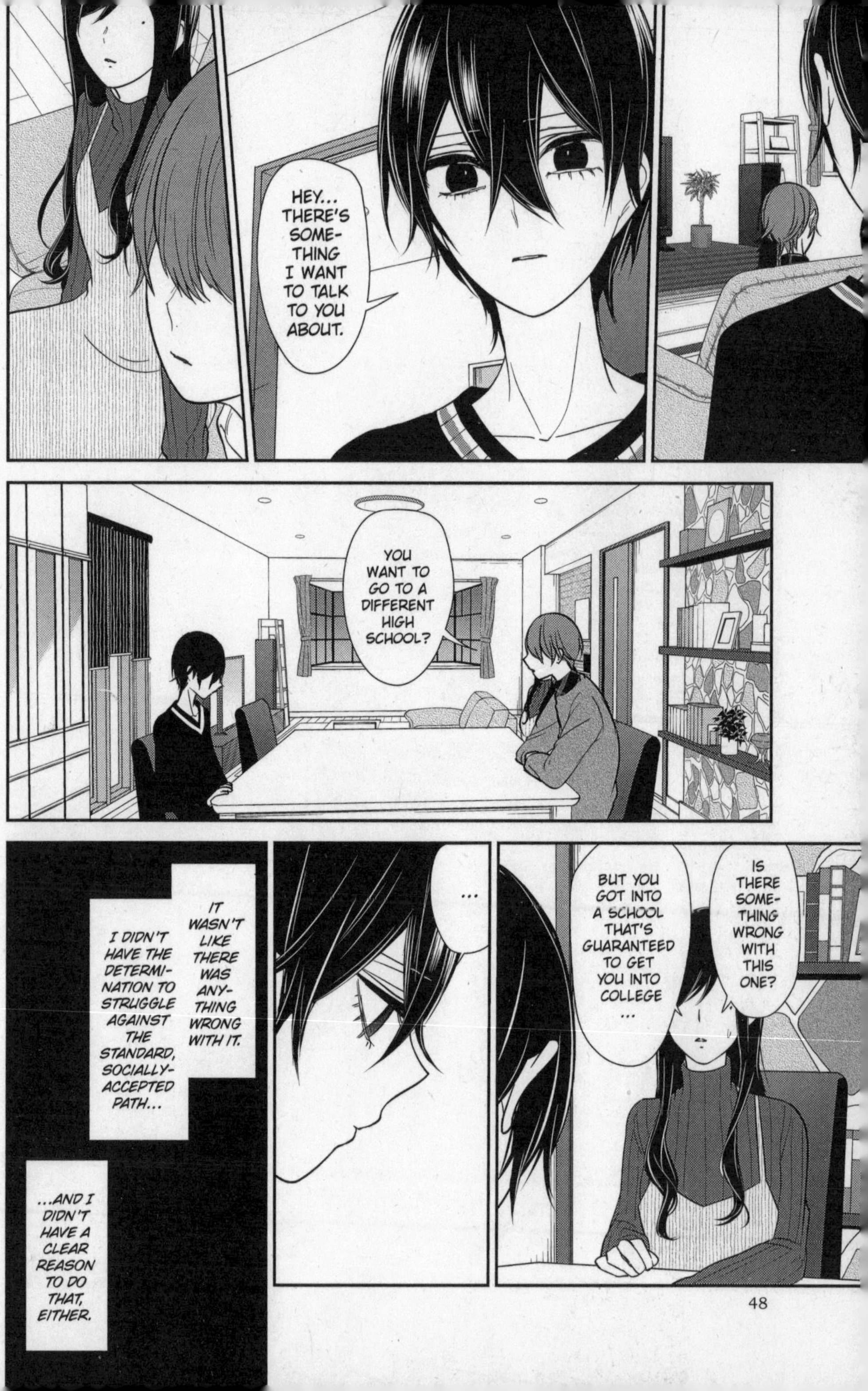
HEY... THERE'S SOMETHING I WANT TO TALK TO YOU ABOUT.
YOU WANT TO GO TO A DIFFERENT HIGH SCHOOL?
IS THERE SOMETHING WRONG WITH THIS ONE?
BUT YOU GOT INTO A SCHOOL THAT'S GUARANTEED TO GET YOU INTO COLLEGE...
...
IT WASN'T LIKE THERE WAS ANYTHING WRONG WITH IT.
I DIDN'T HAVE THE DETERMINATION TO STRUGGLE AGAINST THE STANDARD, SOCIALLY-ACCEPTED PATH...
...AND I DIDN'T HAVE A CLEAR REASON TO DO THAT, EITHER.

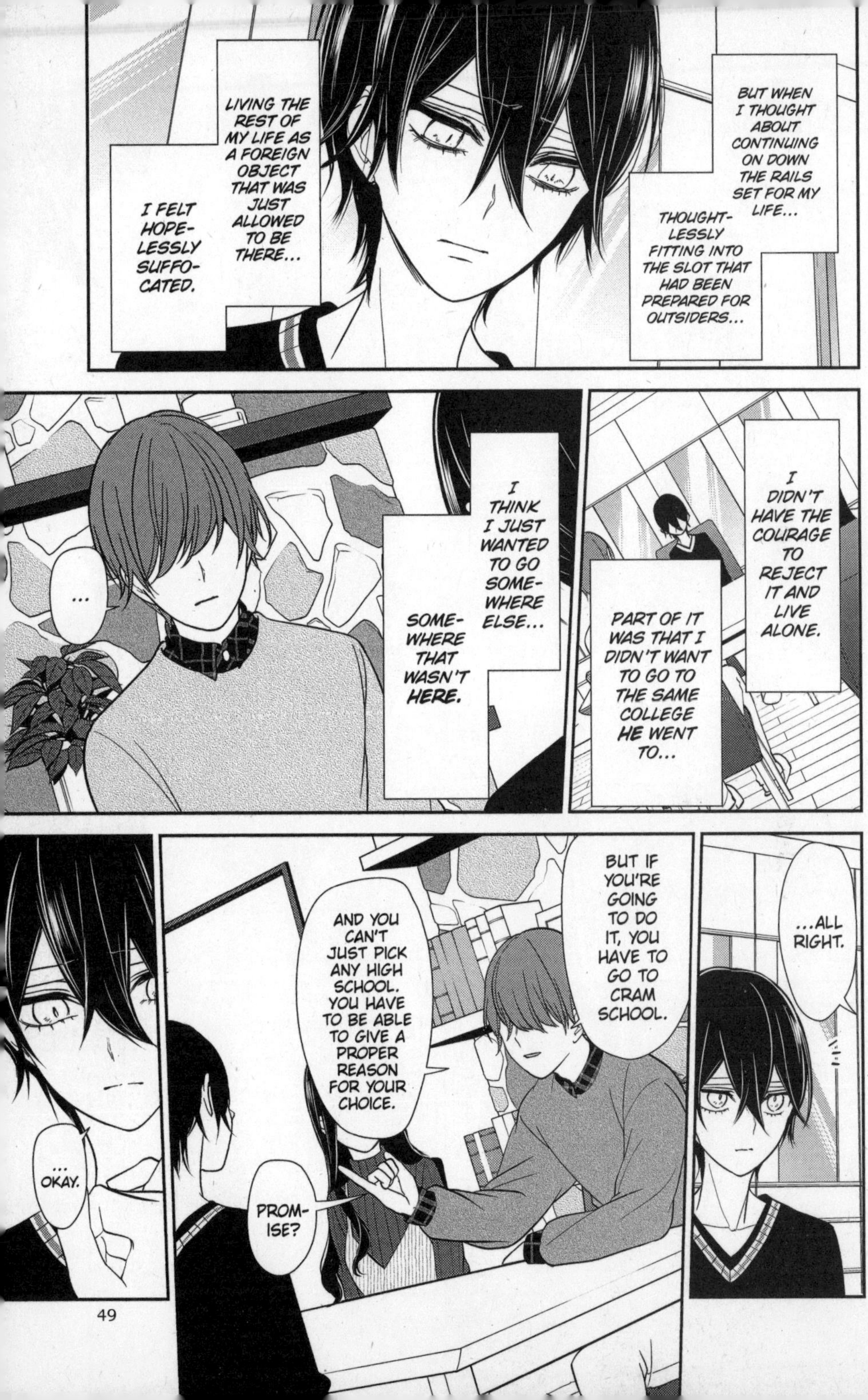

BUT WHEN I THOUGHT ABOUT CONTINUING ON DOWN THE RAILS SET FOR MY LIFE...
THOUGHTLESSLY FITTING INTO THE SLOT THAT HAD BEEN PREPARED FOR OUTSIDERS...
LIVING THE REST OF MY LIFE AS A FOREIGN OBJECT THAT WAS JUST ALLOWED TO BE THERE...
I FELT HOPELESSLY SUFFOCATED.
I DIDN'T HAVE THE COURAGE TO REJECT IT AND LIVE ALONE.
PART OF IT WAS THAT I DIDN'T WANT TO GO TO THE SAME COLLEGE HE WENT TO...
I THINK I JUST WANTED TO GO SOMEWHERE ELSE...
SOMEWHERE THAT WASN'T HERE.
...
...ALL RIGHT.
BUT IF YOU'RE GOING TO DO IT, YOU HAVE TO GO TO CRAM SCHOOL.
AND YOU CAN'T JUST PICK ANY HIGH SCHOOL. YOU HAVE TO BE ABLE TO GIVE A PROPER REASON FOR YOUR CHOICE.
PROMISE?
...OKAY.

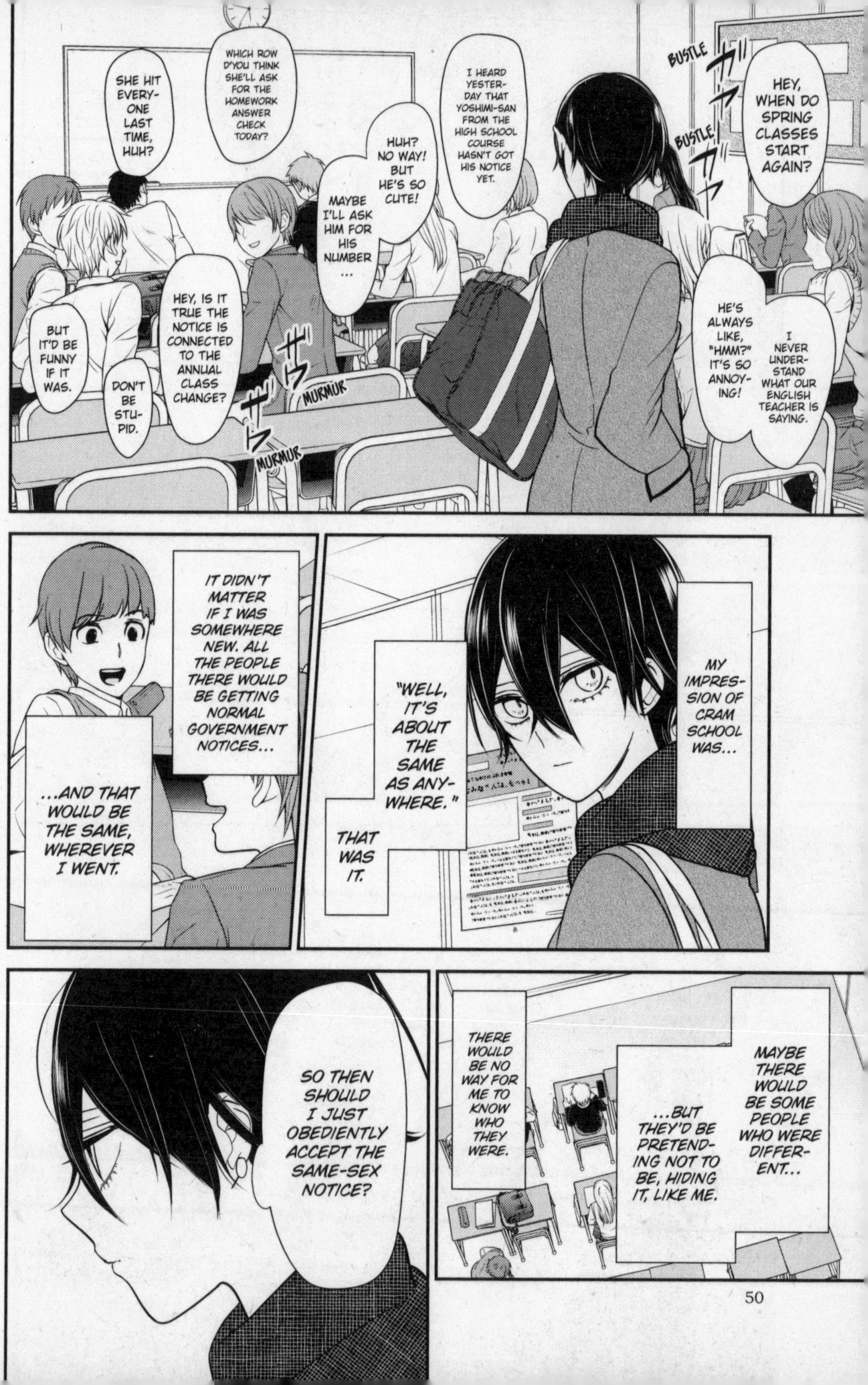
HEY, WHEN DO SPRING CLASSES START AGAIN?
BUSTLE
BUSTLE
I HEARD YESTERDAY THAT YOSHIMI-SAN FROM THE HIGH SCHOOL COURSE HASN'T GOT HIS NOTICE YET.
WHICH ROW D'YOU THINK SHE'LL ASK FOR THE HOMEWORK ANSWER CHECK TODAY?
SHE HIT EVERYONE LAST TIME, HUH?
HUH? NO WAY! BUT HE'S SO CUTE!
MAYBE I'LL ASK HIM FOR HIS NUMBER...
I NEVER UNDERSTAND WHAT OUR ENGLISH TEACHER IS SAYING.
HE'S ALWAYS LIKE, "HMM?" IT'S SO ANNOYING!
HEY, IS IT TRUE THE NOTICE IS CONNECTED TO THE ANNUAL CLASS CHANGE?
BUT IT'D BE FUNNY IF IT WAS.
DON'T BE STUPID.
MURMUR
MURMUR
MY IMPRESSION OF CRAM SCHOOL WAS...
"WELL, IT'S ABOUT THE SAME AS ANYWHERE."
THAT WAS IT.
IT DIDN'T MATTER IF I WAS SOMEWHERE NEW. ALL THE PEOPLE THERE WOULD BE GETTING NORMAL GOVERNMENT NOTICES...
...AND THAT WOULD BE THE SAME, WHEREVER I WENT.
MAYBE THERE WOULD BE SOME PEOPLE WHO WERE DIFFERENT...
...BUT THEY'D BE PRETENDING NOT TO BE, HIDING IT, LIKE ME.
THERE WOULD BE NO WAY FOR ME TO KNOW WHO THEY WERE.
SO THEN SHOULD I JUST OBEDIENTLY ACCEPT THE SAME-SEX NOTICE?

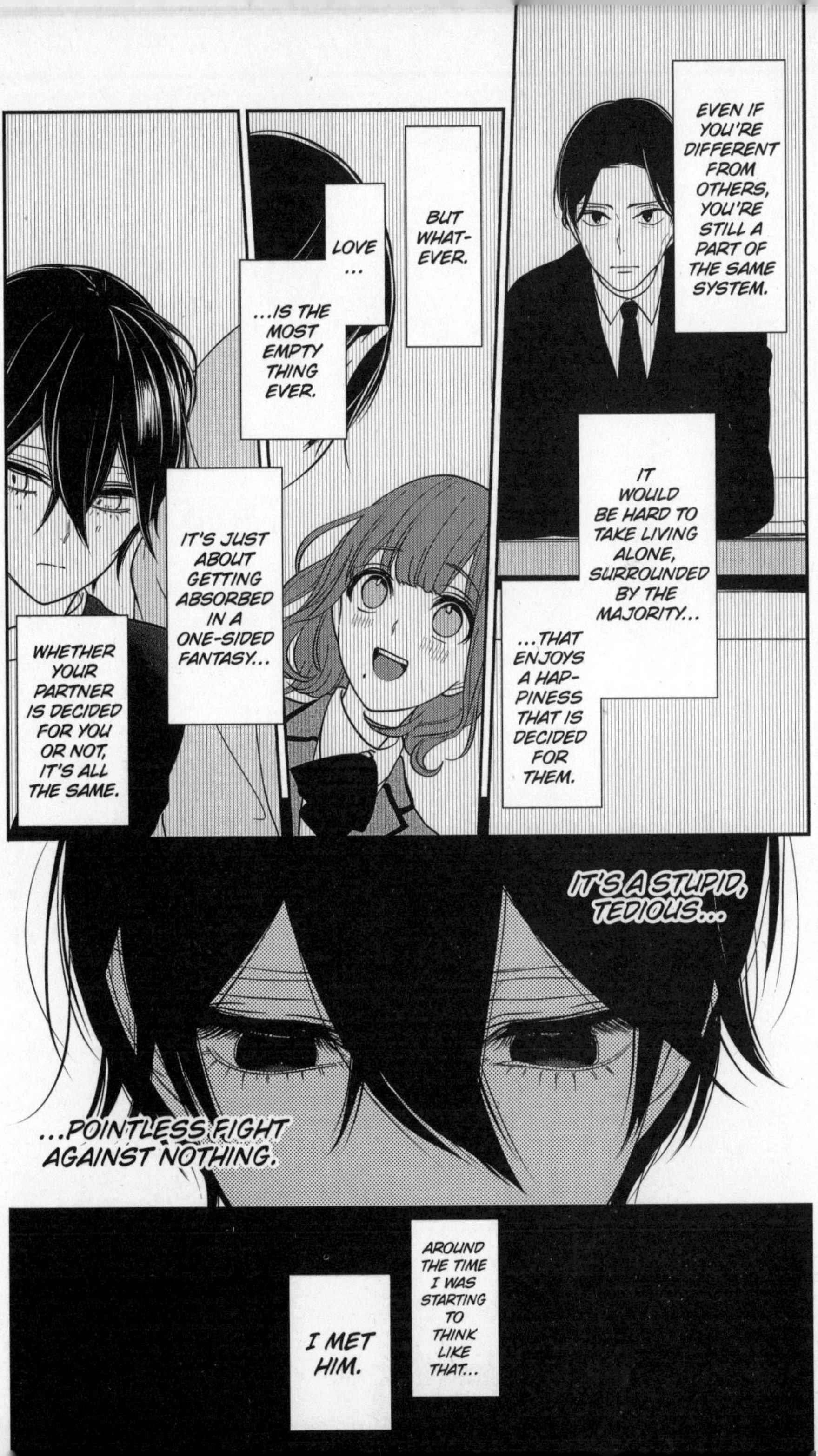
EVEN IF YOU'RE DIFFERENT FROM OTHERS, YOU'RE STILL A PART OF THE SAME SYSTEM.
IT WOULD BE HARD TO TAKE LIVING ALONE, SURROUNDED BY THE MAJORITY...
...THAT ENJOYS A HAPPINESS THAT IS DECIDED FOR THEM.
BUT WHAT-EVER.
LOVE...
...IS THE MOST EMPTY THING EVER.
IT'S JUST ABOUT GETTING ABSORBED IN A ONE-SIDED FANTASY...
WHETHER YOUR PARTNER IS DECIDED FOR YOU OR NOT, IT'S ALL THE SAME.
IT'S A STUPID, TEDIOUS...
...POINTLESS FIGHT AGAINST NOTHING.
AROUND THE TIME I WAS STARTING TO THINK LIKE THAT...
I MET HIM.

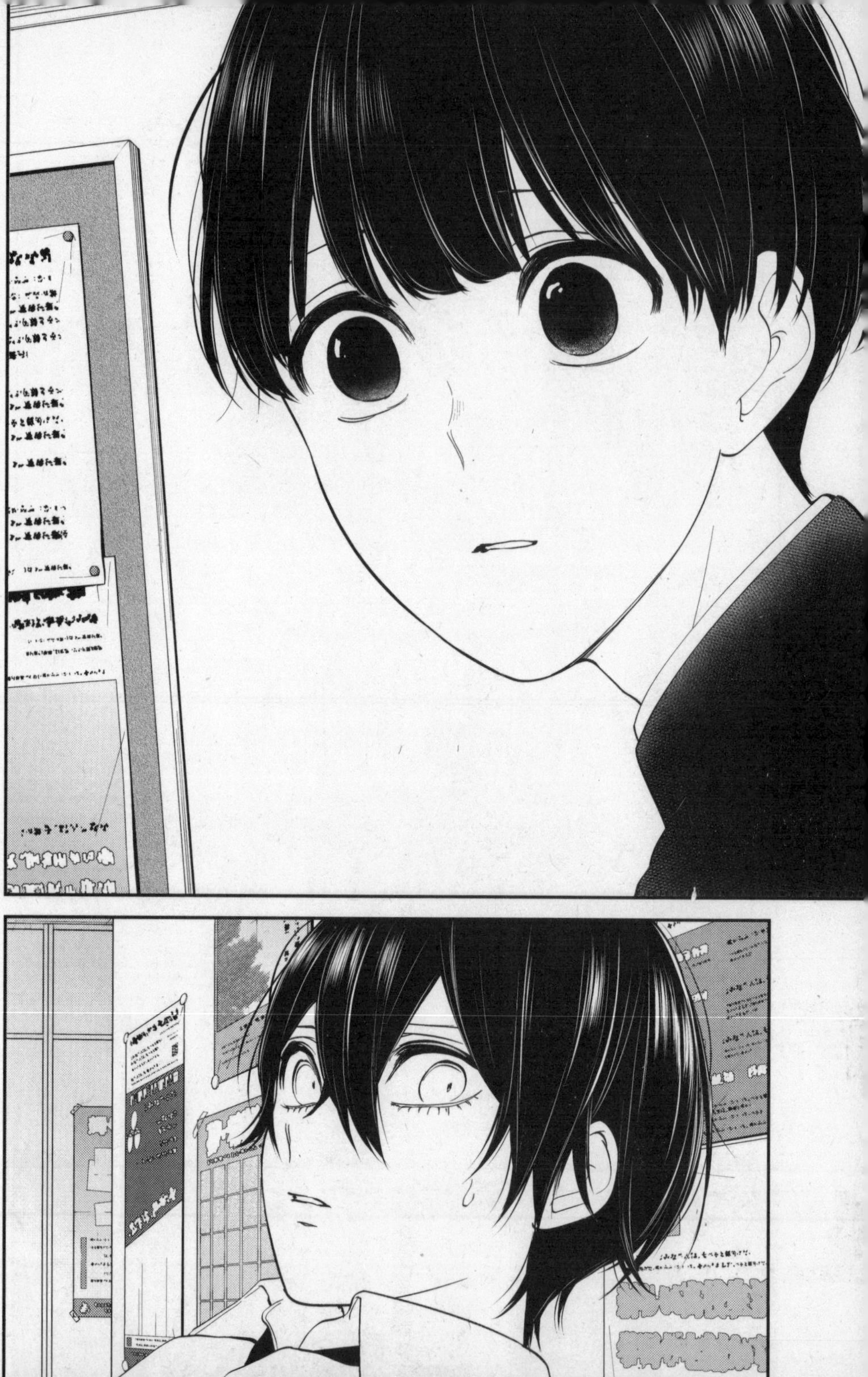

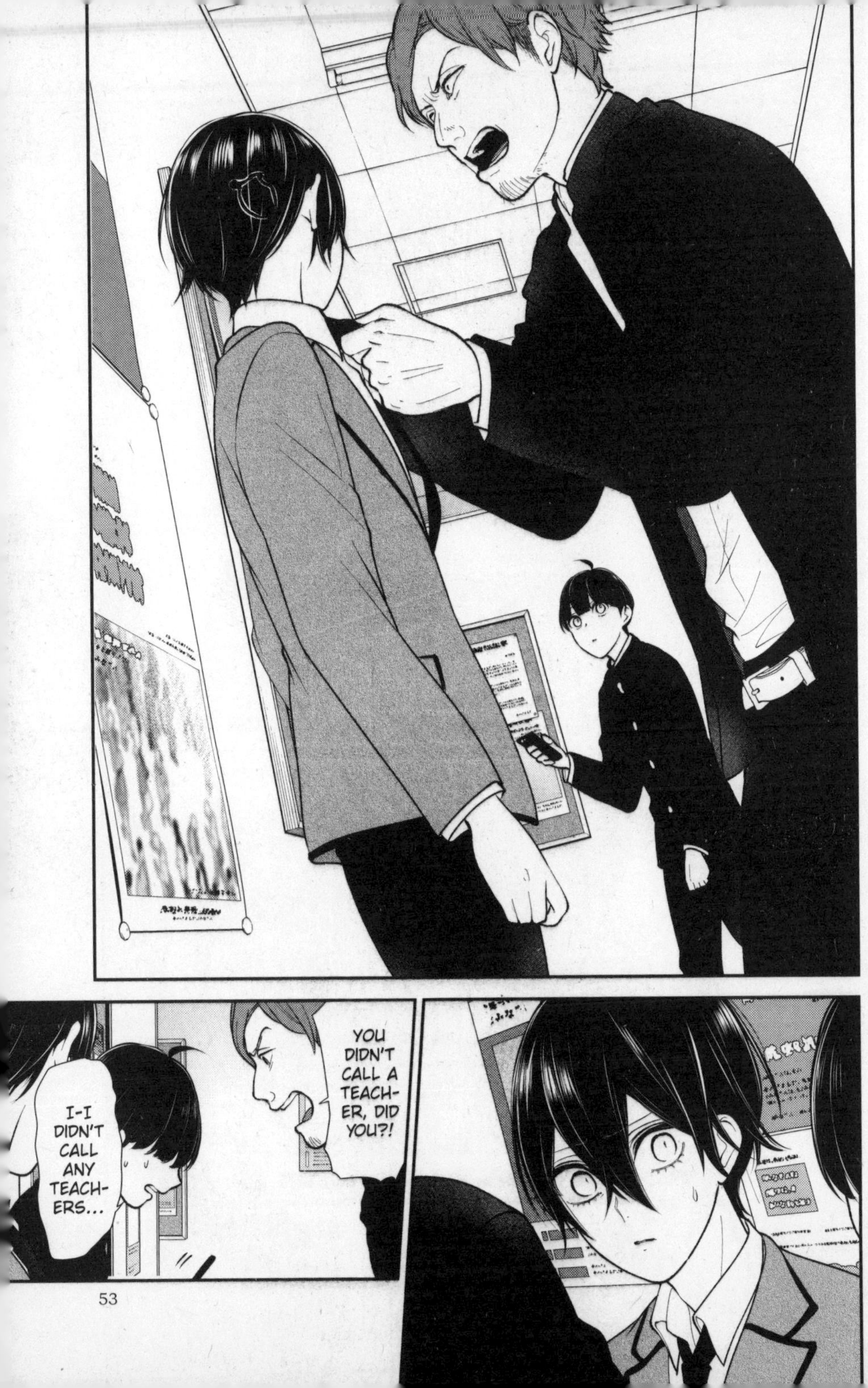
YOU DIDN'T CALL A TEACHER, DID YOU?!
I-I DIDN'T CALL ANY TEACHERS...

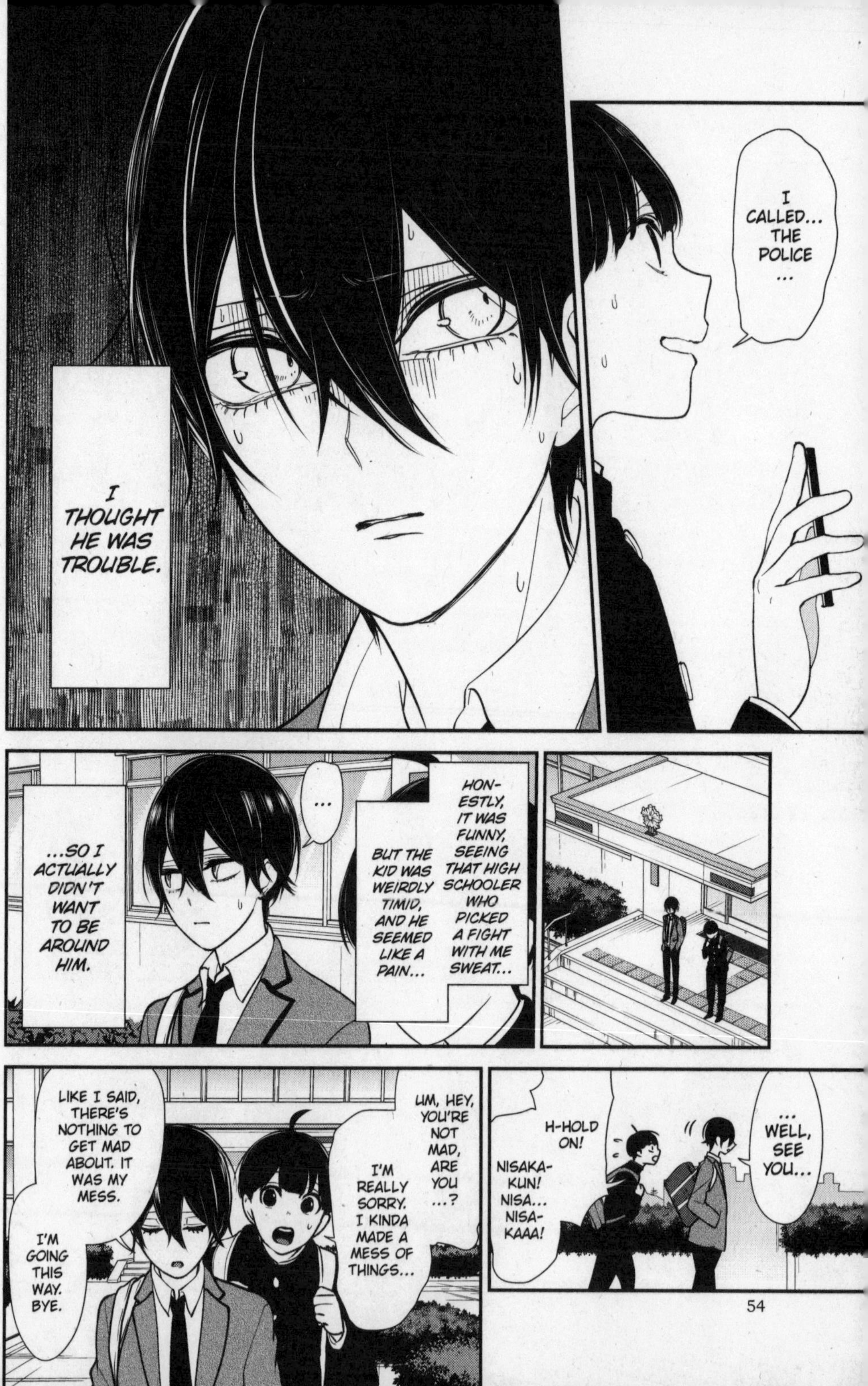
I CALLED... THE POLICE ...
I THOUGHT HE WAS TROUBLE.
HONESTLY, IT WAS FUNNY, SEEING THAT HIGH SCHOOLER WHO PICKED A FIGHT WITH ME SWEAT...
...
BUT THE KID WAS WEIRDLY TIMID, AND HE SEEMED LIKE A PAIN...
...SO I ACTUALLY DIDN'T WANT TO BE AROUND HIM.
... WELL, SEE YOU...
H-HOLD ON!
NISAKA-KUN! NISA... NISA-KAAA!
UM, HEY, YOU'RE NOT MAD, ARE YOU ...?
I'M REALLY SORRY. I KINDA MADE A MESS OF THINGS...
LIKE I SAID, THERE'S NOTHING TO GET MAD ABOUT. IT WAS MY MESS.
I'M GOING THIS WAY. BYE.

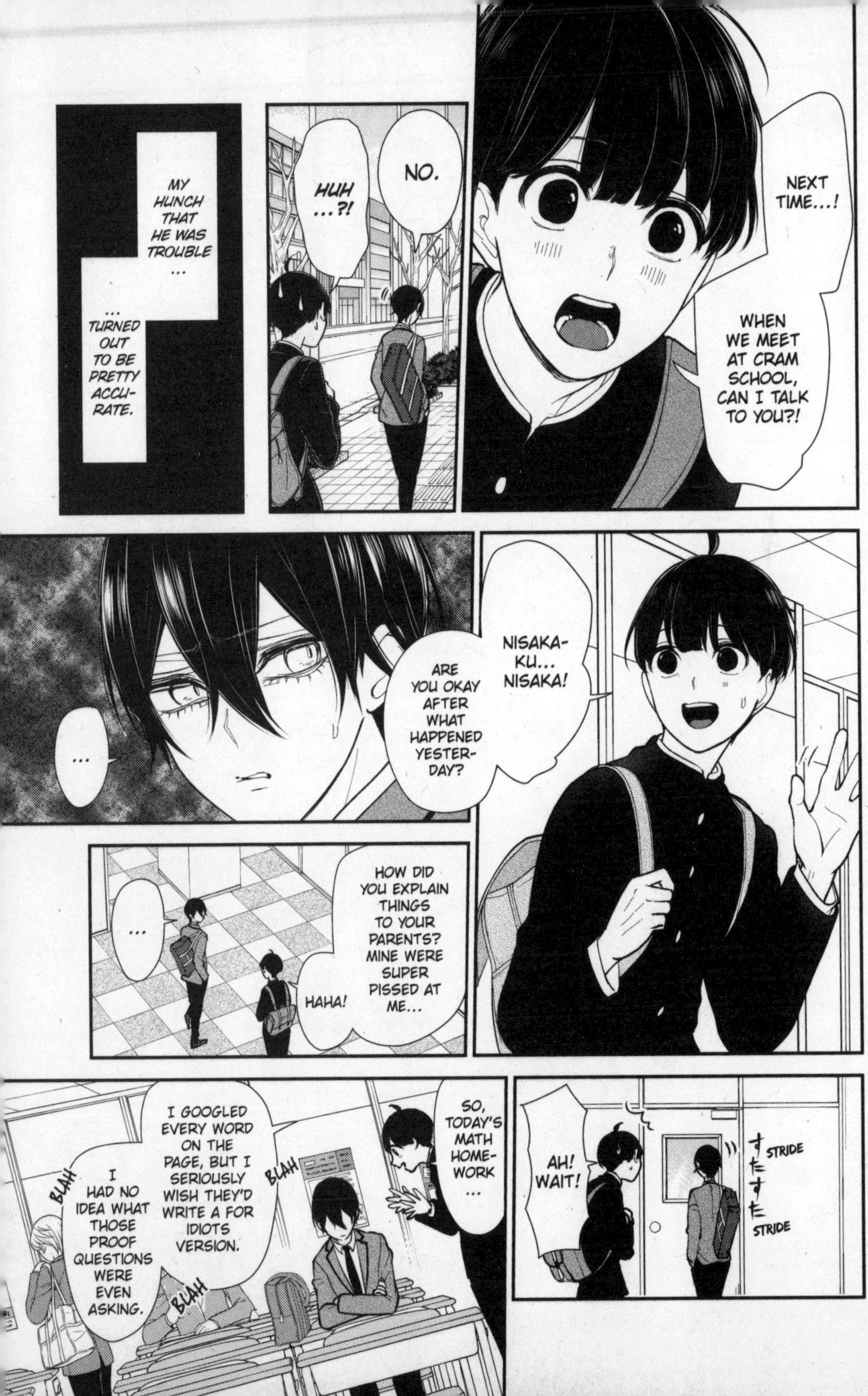
NEXT TIME...!
WHEN WE MEET AT CRAM SCHOOL, CAN I TALK TO YOU?!
NO.
HUH ...?!
MY HUNCH THAT HE WAS TROUBLE ...
... TURNED OUT TO BE PRETTY ACCURATE.
NISAKA-KU... NISAKA!
ARE YOU OKAY AFTER WHAT HAPPENED YESTER-DAY?
...
HOW DID YOU EXPLAIN THINGS TO YOUR PARENTS? MINE WERE SUPER PISSED AT ME...
HAHA!
...
AH! WAIT!
すたすた
STRIDE
STRIDE
SO, TODAY'S MATH HOME-WORK ...
BLAH
I GOOGLED EVERY WORD ON THE PAGE, BUT I SERIOUSLY WISH THEY'D WRITE A FOR IDIOTS VERSION.
BLAH
I HAD NO IDEA WHAT THOSE PROOF QUESTIONS WERE EVEN ASKING.
BLAH

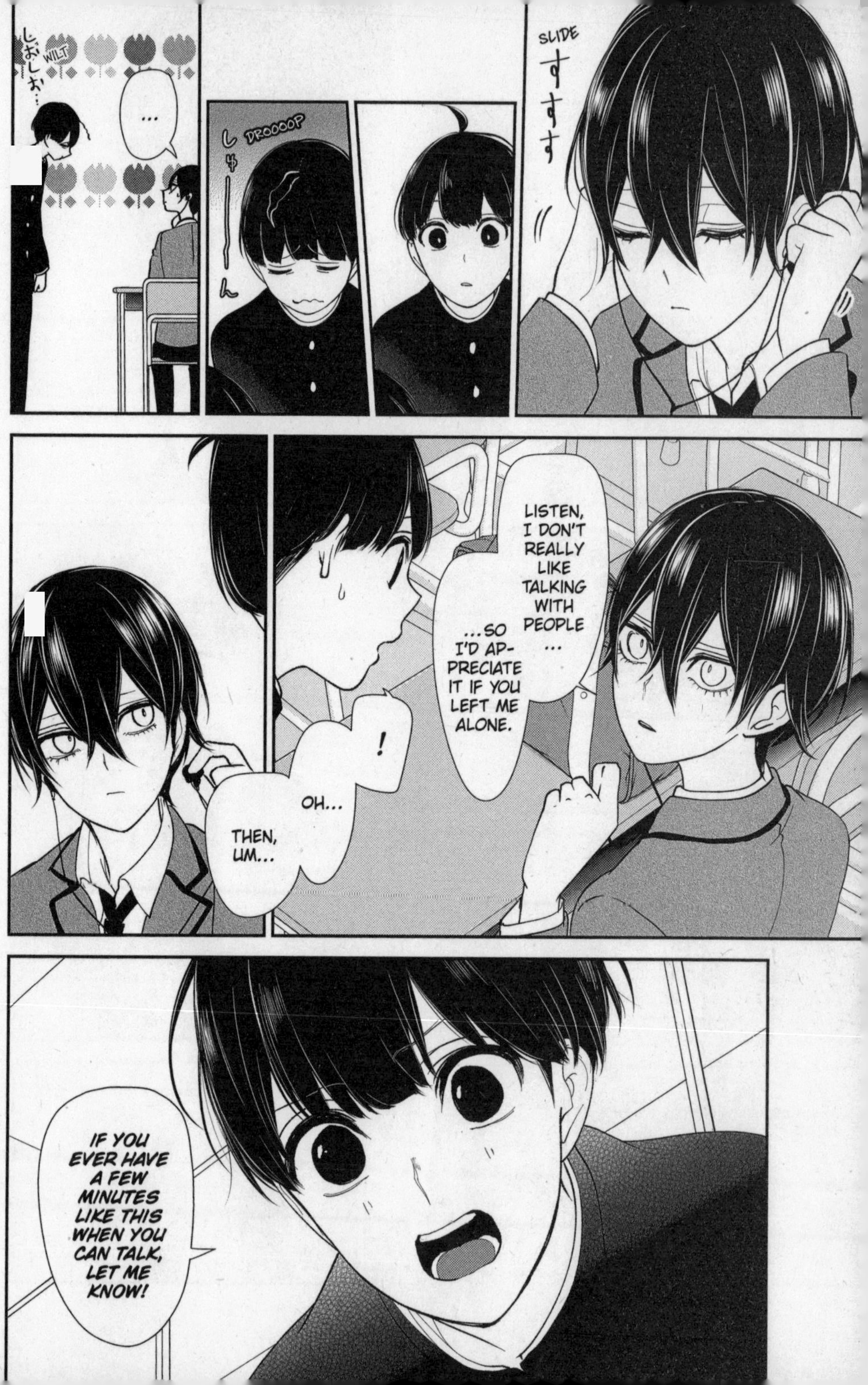
SLIDE
すすす
DROOOOP
しゅーーん
WILT
しおしお…
...
LISTEN, I DON'T REALLY LIKE TALKING WITH PEOPLE...
...SO I'D APPRECIATE IT IF YOU LEFT ME ALONE.
!
OH...
THEN, UM...
IF YOU EVER HAVE A FEW MINUTES LIKE THIS WHEN YOU CAN TALK, LET ME KNOW!

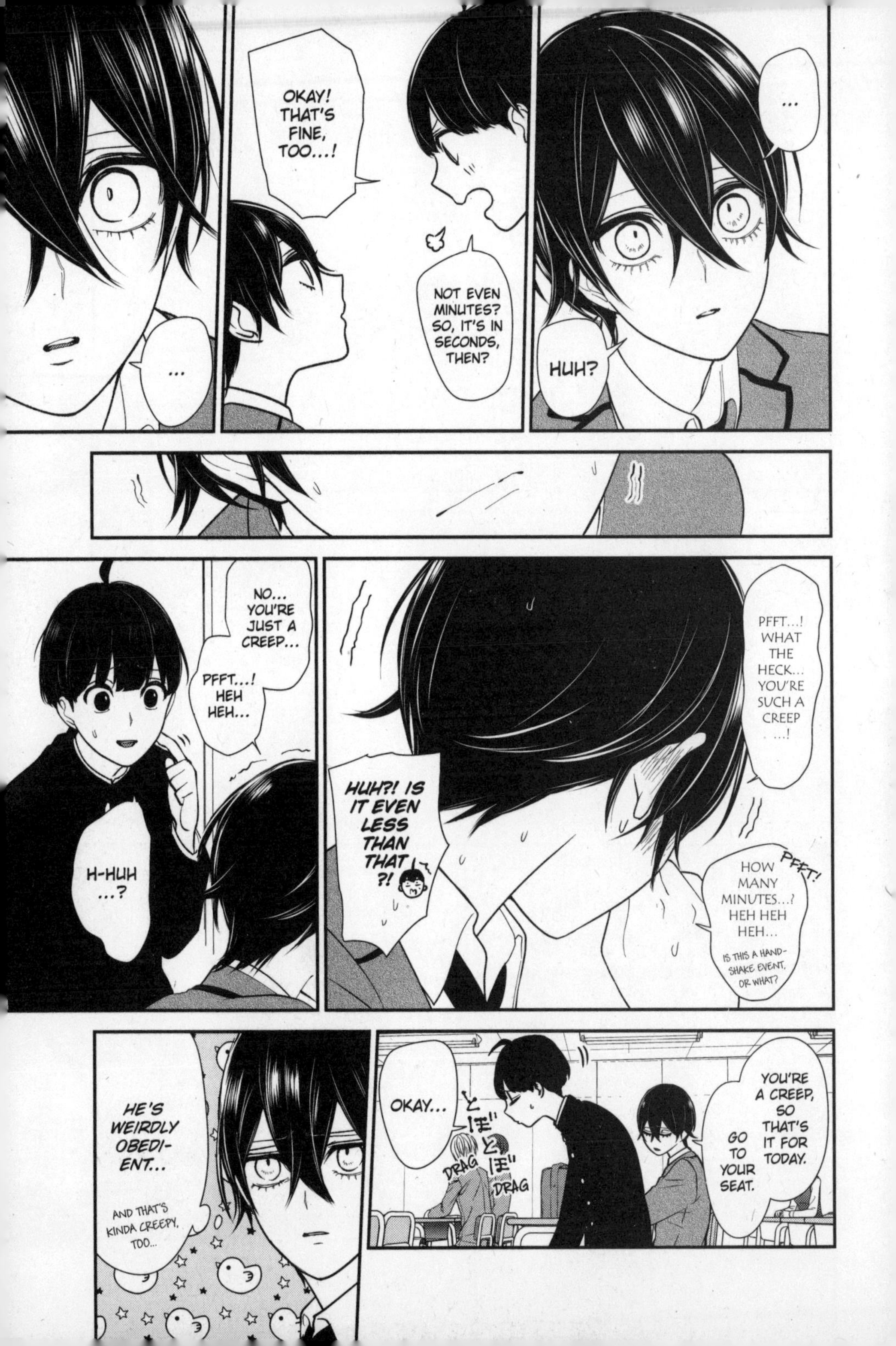
...
HUH?
OKAY! THAT'S FINE, TOO...!
NOT EVEN MINUTES? SO, IT'S IN SECONDS, THEN?
...
PFFT...! WHAT THE HECK... YOU'RE SUCH A CREEP ...!
HUH?! IS IT EVEN LESS THAN THAT ?!
PFFT!
HOW MANY MINUTES...? HEH HEH HEH...
IS THIS A HAND-SHAKE EVENT, OR WHAT?
NO... YOU'RE JUST A CREEP...
PFFT...! HEH HEH...
H-HUH ...?
YOU'RE A CREEP, SO THAT'S IT FOR TODAY.
GO TO YOUR SEAT.
OKAY...
DRAG
DRAG
HE'S WEIRDLY OBEDI- ENT...
AND THAT'S KINDA CREEPY, TOO...

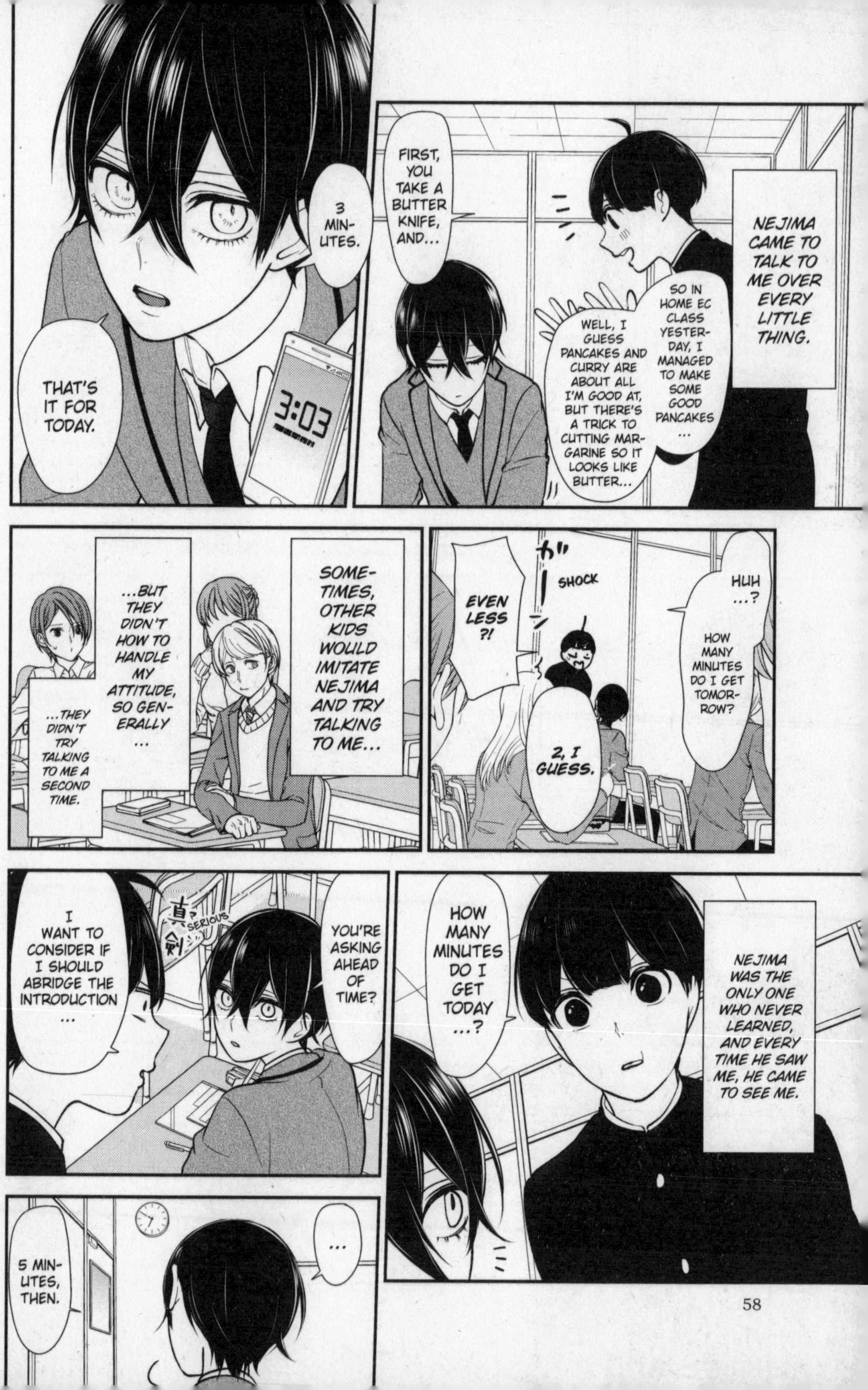
NEJIMA CAME TO TALK TO ME OVER EVERY LITTLE THING.
SO IN HOME EC CLASS YESTER-DAY, I MANAGED TO MAKE SOME GOOD PANCAKES ...
WELL, I GUESS PANCAKES AND CURRY ARE ABOUT ALL I'M GOOD AT, BUT THERE'S A TRICK TO CUTTING MAR-GARINE SO IT LOOKS LIKE BUTTER...
FIRST, YOU TAKE A BUTTER KNIFE, AND...
3 MIN-UTES.
3:03
THAT'S IT FOR TODAY.
HUH ...?
HOW MANY MINUTES DO I GET TOMOR-ROW?
2, I GUESS.
SHOCK
EVEN LESS ?!
SOME-TIMES, OTHER KIDS WOULD IMITATE NEJIMA AND TRY TALKING TO ME...
...BUT THEY DIDN'T HOW TO HANDLE MY ATTITUDE, SO GEN-ERALLY ...
...THEY DIDN'T TRY TALKING TO ME A SECOND TIME.
NEJIMA WAS THE ONLY ONE WHO NEVER LEARNED, AND EVERY TIME HE SAW ME, HE CAME TO SEE ME.
HOW MANY MINUTES DO I GET TODAY ...?
YOU'RE ASKING AHEAD OF TIME?
SERIOUS
I WANT TO CONSIDER IF I SHOULD ABRIDGE THE INTRODUCTION ...
...
5 MIN-UTES, THEN.

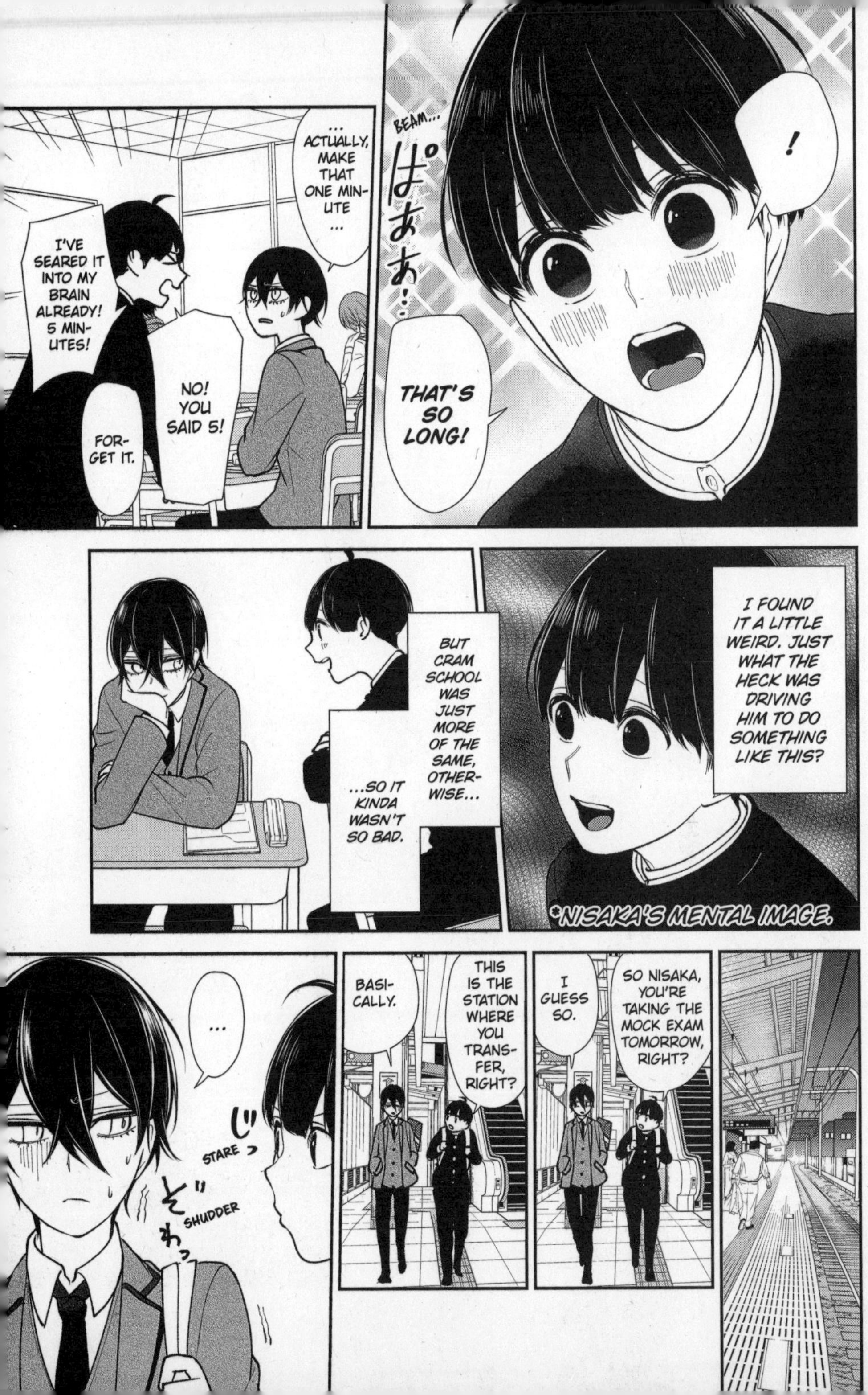
!
BEAM...
ぱぁぁ!
THAT'S SO LONG!
...ACTUALLY, MAKE THAT ONE MIN-UTE...
NO! YOU SAID 5!
I'VE SEARED IT INTO MY BRAIN ALREADY! 5 MIN-UTES!
FOR-GET IT.
I FOUND IT A LITTLE WEIRD. JUST WHAT THE HECK WAS DRIVING HIM TO DO SOMETHING LIKE THIS?
*NISAKA'S MENTAL IMAGE.
BUT CRAM SCHOOL WAS JUST MORE OF THE SAME, OTHER-WISE...
...SO IT KINDA WASN'T SO BAD.
SO NISAKA, YOU'RE TAKING THE MOCK EXAM TOMORROW, RIGHT?
I GUESS SO.
THIS IS THE STATION WHERE YOU TRANS-FER, RIGHT?
BASI-CALLY.
...
じ
STARE
ぞわっ
SHUDDER

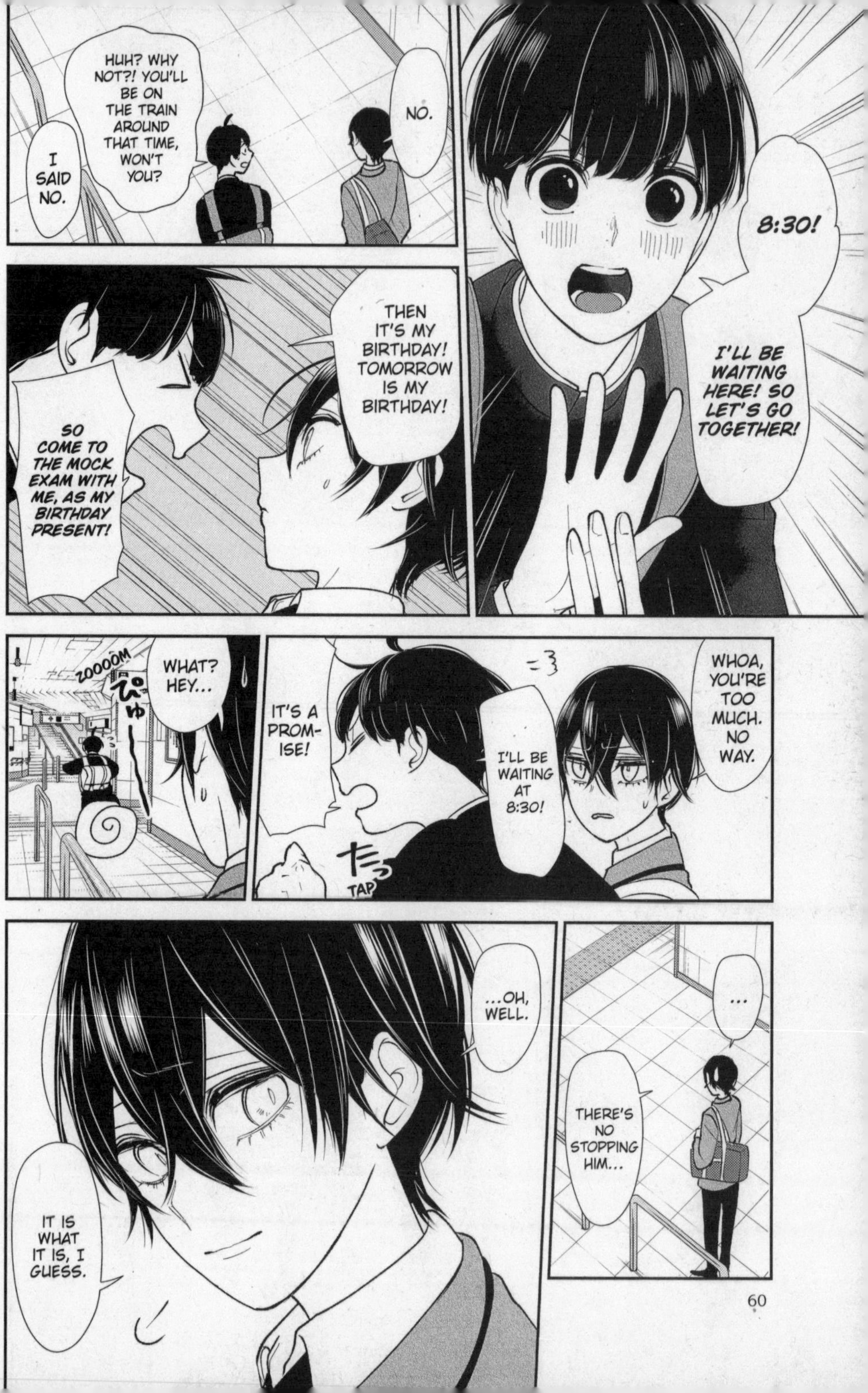
8:30!
I'LL BE WAITING HERE! SO LET'S GO TOGETHER!
NO.
HUH? WHY NOT?! YOU'LL BE ON THE TRAIN AROUND THAT TIME, WON'T YOU?
I SAID NO.
THEN IT'S MY BIRTHDAY! TOMORROW IS MY BIRTHDAY!
SO COME TO THE MOCK EXAM WITH ME, AS MY BIRTHDAY PRESENT!
WHOA, YOU'RE TOO MUCH. NO WAY.
I'LL BE WAITING AT 8:30!
IT'S A PROMISE!
TAP
WHAT? HEY...
ZOOOOM
...
THERE'S NO STOPPING HIM...
...OH, WELL.
IT IS WHAT IT IS, I GUESS.

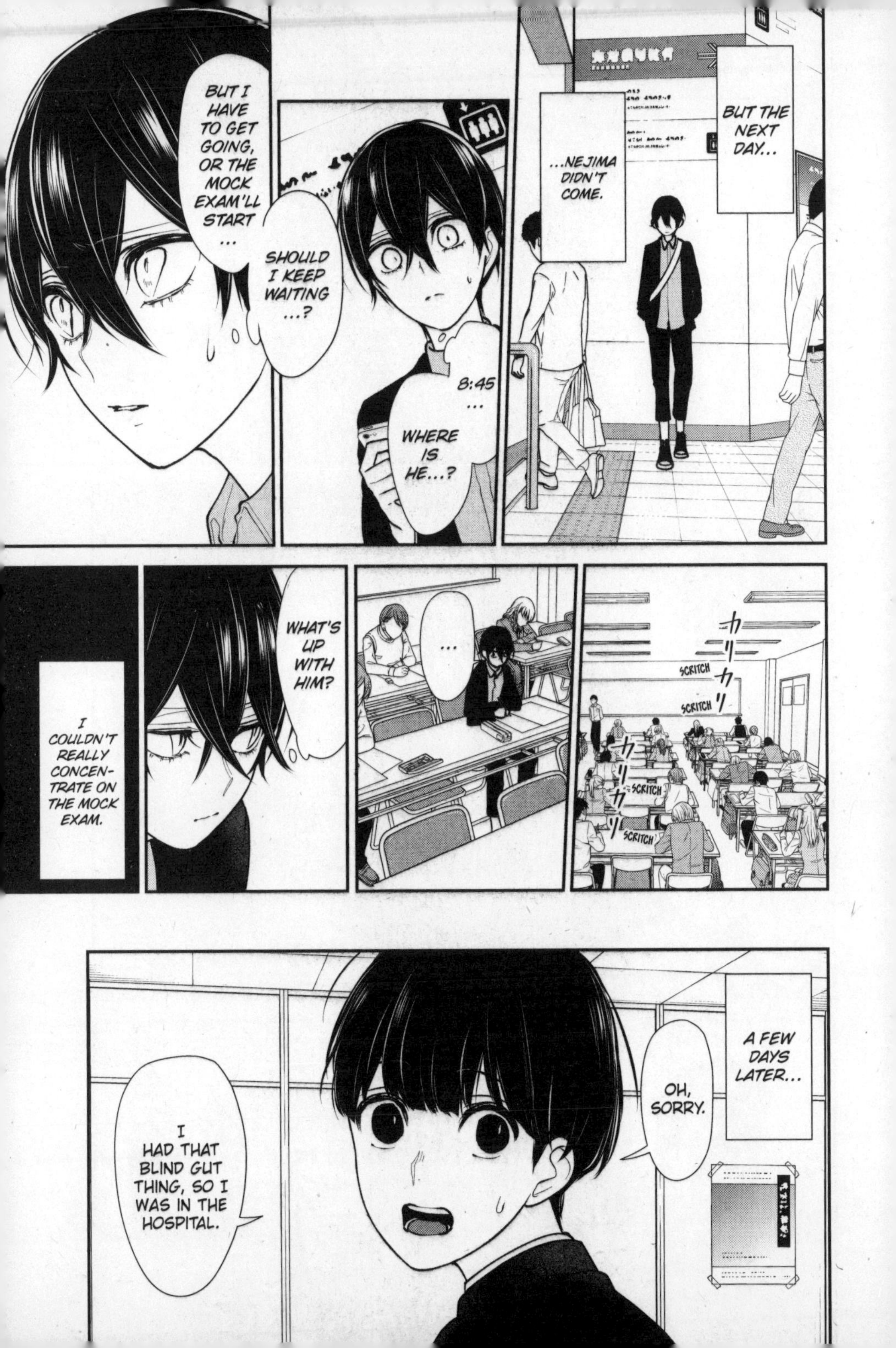
BUT THE NEXT DAY...
...NEJIMA DIDN'T COME.
8:45 ... WHERE IS HE...?
SHOULD I KEEP WAITING ...?
BUT I HAVE TO GET GOING, OR THE MOCK EXAM'LL START ...
カリカリ
SCRITCH
SCRITCH
カリカリ
SCRITCH
SCRITCH
...
WHAT'S UP WITH HIM?
I COULDN'T REALLY CONCENTRATE ON THE MOCK EXAM.
A FEW DAYS LATER...
OH, SORRY.
I HAD THAT BLIND GUT THING, SO I WAS IN THE HOSPITAL.

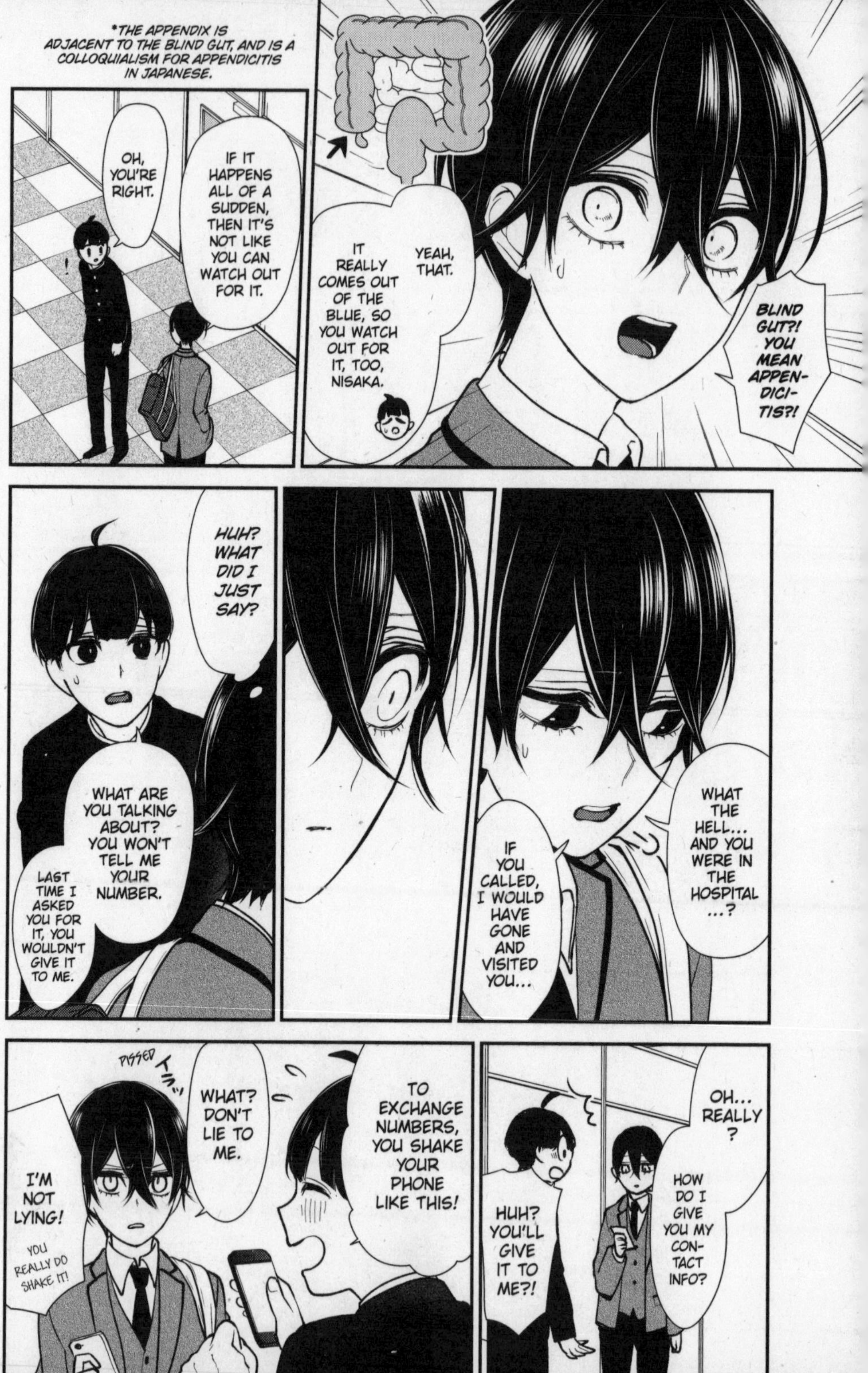
BLIND GUT?! YOU MEAN APPENDICITIS?!
YEAH, THAT.
IT REALLY COMES OUT OF THE BLUE, SO YOU WATCH OUT FOR IT, TOO, NISAKA.
*THE APPENDIX IS ADJACENT TO THE BLIND GUT, AND IS A COLLOQUIALISM FOR APPENDICITIS IN JAPANESE.
IF IT HAPPENS ALL OF A SUDDEN, THEN IT'S NOT LIKE YOU CAN WATCH OUT FOR IT.
OH, YOU'RE RIGHT.
WHAT THE HELL... AND YOU WERE IN THE HOSPITAL...?
IF YOU CALLED, I WOULD HAVE GONE AND VISITED YOU...
HUH? WHAT DID I JUST SAY?
WHAT ARE YOU TALKING ABOUT? YOU WON'T TELL ME YOUR NUMBER.
LAST TIME I ASKED YOU FOR IT, YOU WOULDN'T GIVE IT TO ME.
OH... REALLY?
HOW DO I GIVE YOU MY CONTACT INFO?
HUH? YOU'LL GIVE IT TO ME?!
TO EXCHANGE NUMBERS, YOU SHAKE YOUR PHONE LIKE THIS!
WHAT? DON'T LIE TO ME.
PISSED
I'M NOT LYING!
YOU REALLY DO SHAKE IT!

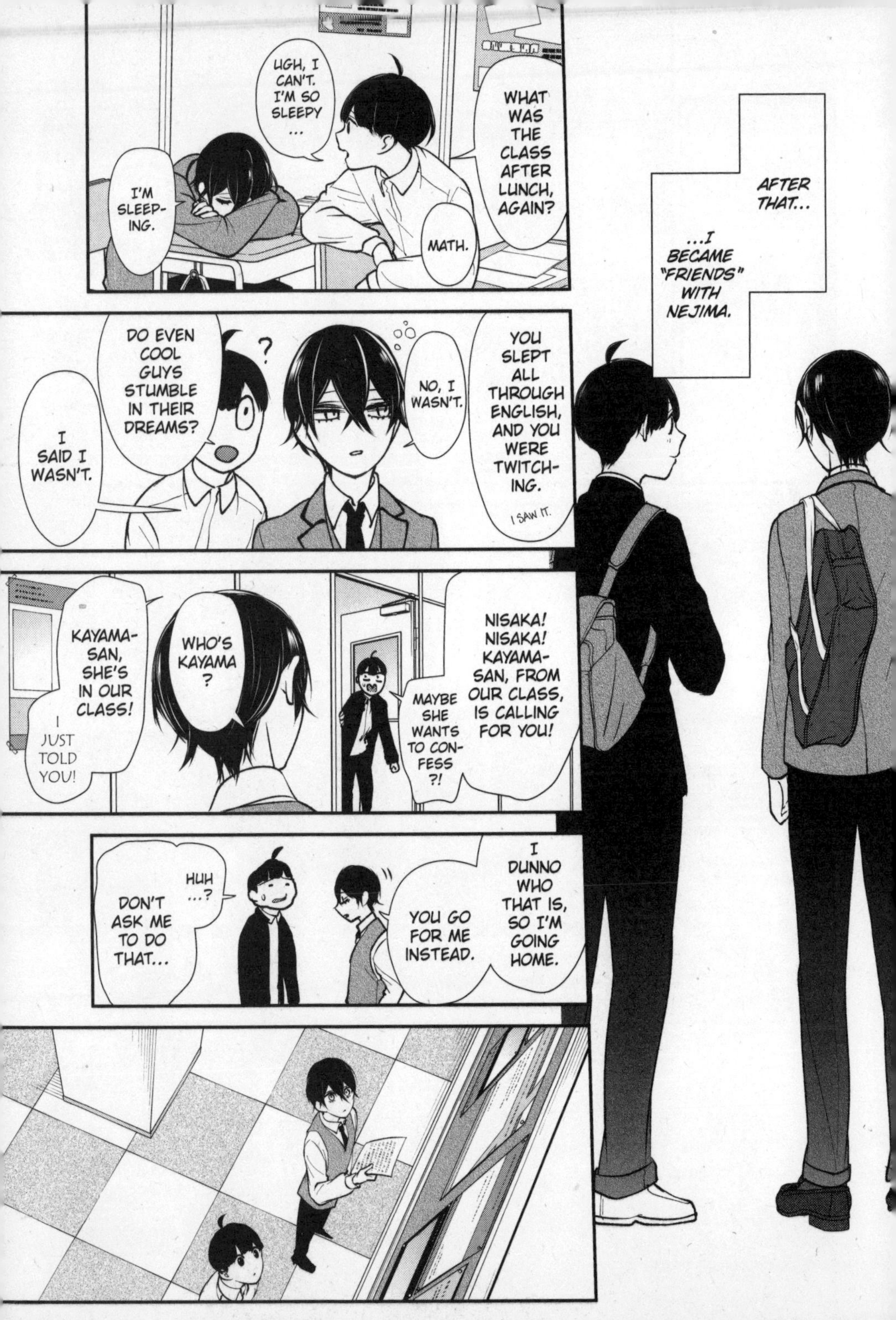
AFTER THAT...
...I BECAME "FRIENDS" WITH NEJIMA.
WHAT WAS THE CLASS AFTER LUNCH, AGAIN?
MATH.
UGH, I CAN'T. I'M SO SLEEPY...
I'M SLEEPING.
YOU SLEPT ALL THROUGH ENGLISH, AND YOU WERE TWITCHING.
I SAW IT.
NO, I WASN'T.
DO EVEN COOL GUYS STUMBLE IN THEIR DREAMS?
I SAID I WASN'T.
NISAKA! NISAKA! KAYAMA-SAN, FROM OUR CLASS, IS CALLING FOR YOU!
MAYBE SHE WANTS TO CONFESS?!
WHO'S KAYAMA?
KAYAMA-SAN, SHE'S IN OUR CLASS!
I JUST TOLD YOU!
I DUNNO WHO THAT IS, SO I'M GOING HOME.
YOU GO FOR ME INSTEAD.
HUH...?
DON'T ASK ME TO DO THAT...

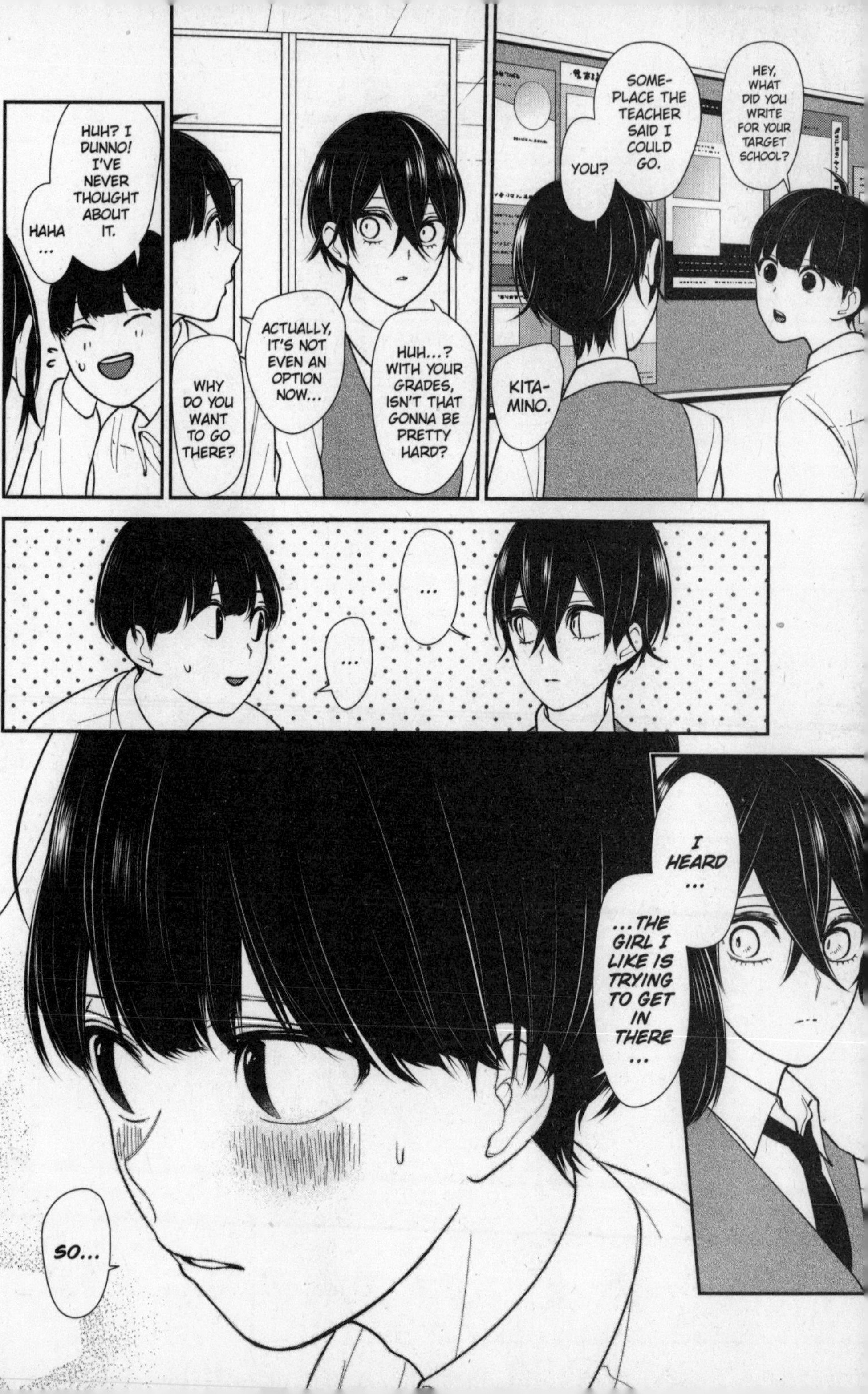
HEY, WHAT DID YOU WRITE FOR YOUR TARGET SCHOOL?
SOME-PLACE THE TEACHER SAID I COULD GO.
YOU?
KITA-MINO.
HUH...? WITH YOUR GRADES, ISN'T THAT GONNA BE PRETTY HARD?
ACTUALLY, IT'S NOT EVEN AN OPTION NOW...
WHY DO YOU WANT TO GO THERE?
HUH? I DUNNO! I'VE NEVER THOUGHT ABOUT IT.
HAHA...
...
...
I HEARD...
...THE GIRL I LIKE IS TRYING TO GET IN THERE...
SO...

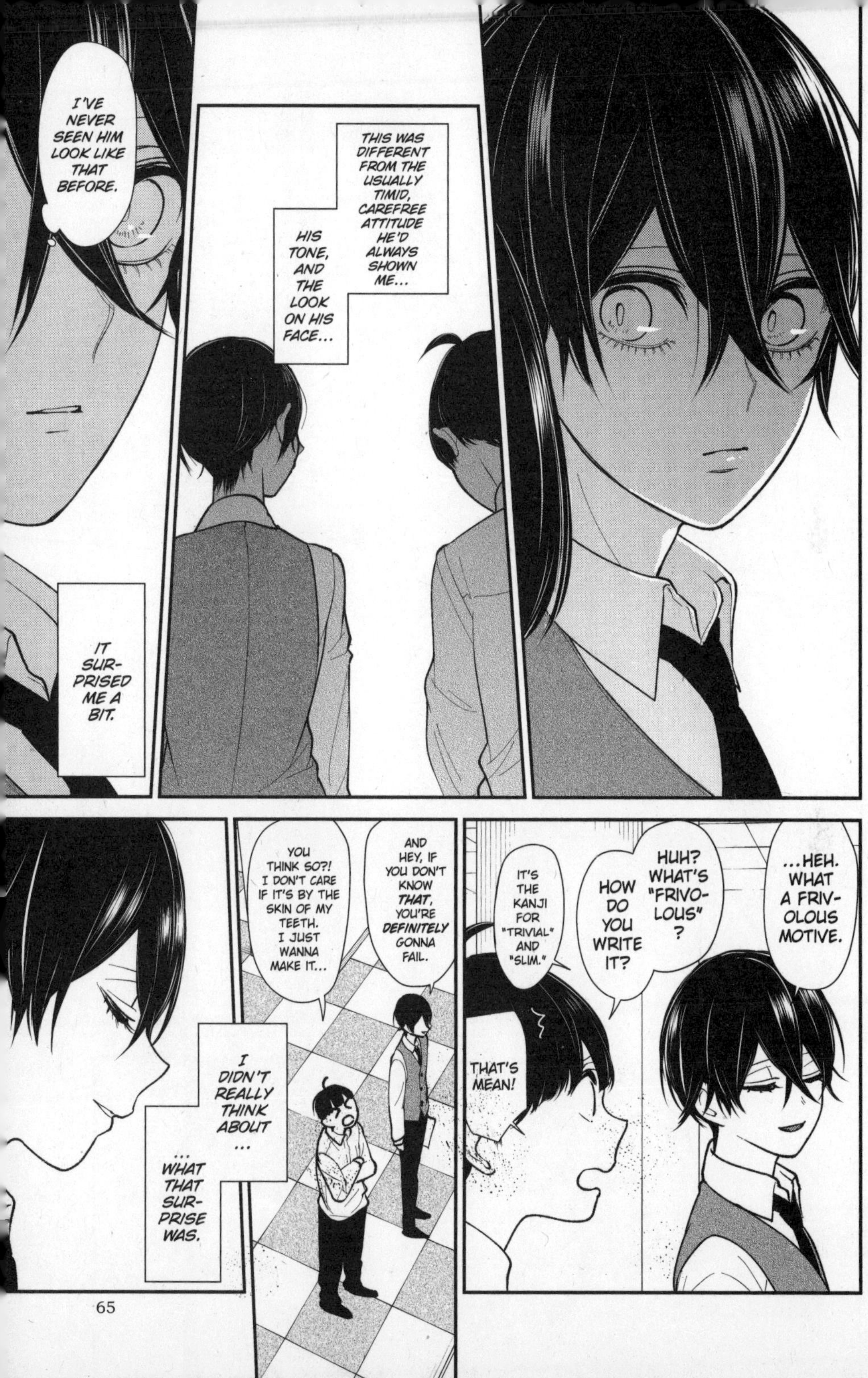
THIS WAS DIFFERENT FROM THE USUALLY TIMID, CAREFREE ATTITUDE HE'D ALWAYS SHOWN ME...
HIS TONE, AND THE LOOK ON HIS FACE...
I'VE NEVER SEEN HIM LOOK LIKE THAT BEFORE.
IT SUR-PRISED ME A BIT.
...HEH. WHAT A FRIVO-OLOUS MOTIVE.
HUH? WHAT'S "FRIVO-LOUS"?
HOW DO YOU WRITE IT?
IT'S THE KANJI FOR "TRIVIAL" AND "SLIM."
THAT'S MEAN!
AND HEY, IF YOU DON'T KNOW *THAT*, YOU'RE *DEFINITELY* GONNA FAIL.
YOU THINK SO?! I DON'T CARE IF IT'S BY THE SKIN OF MY TEETH. I JUST WANNA MAKE IT...
I DIDN'T REALLY THINK ABOUT...
...WHAT THAT SUR-PRISE WAS.

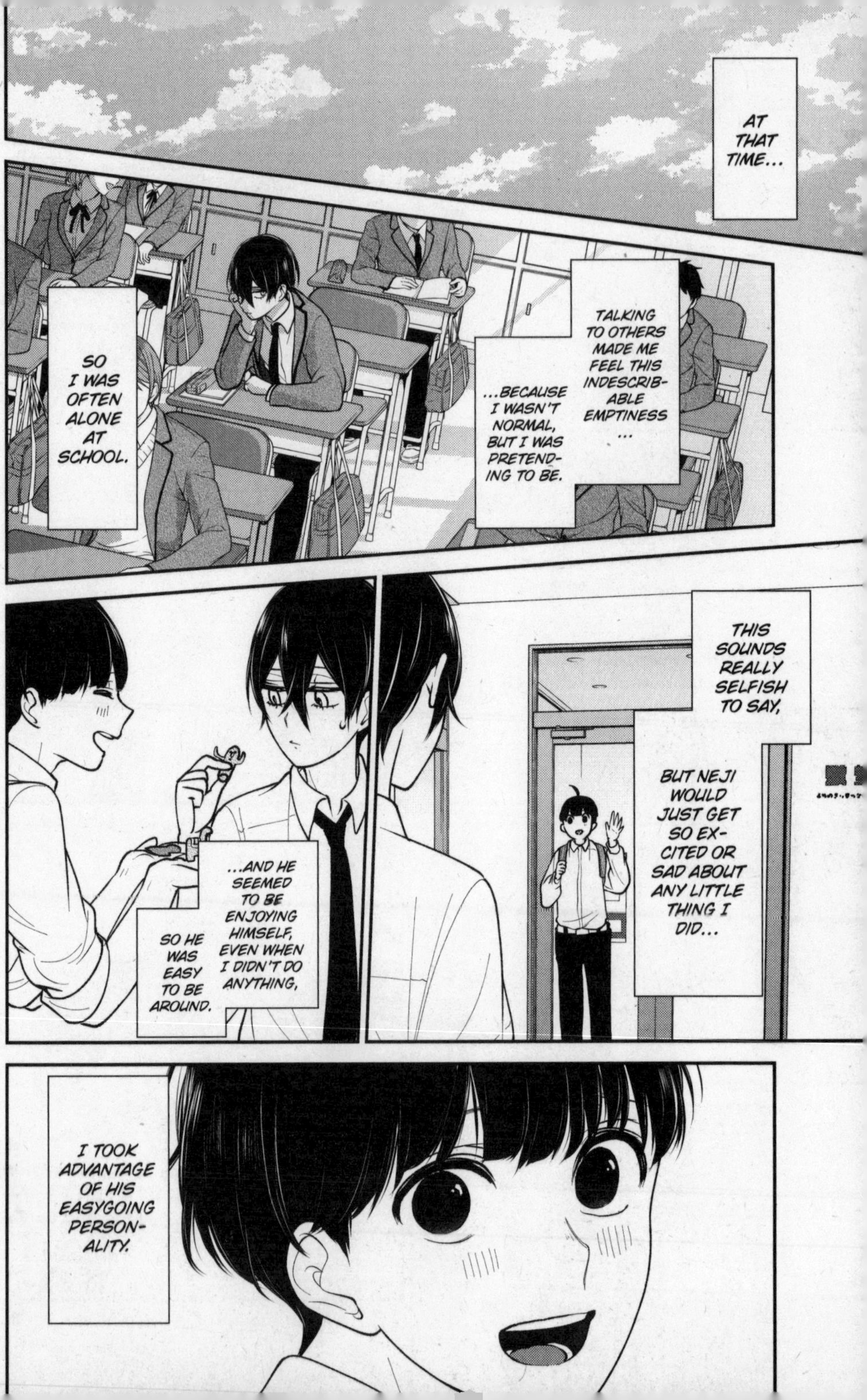
AT THAT TIME...
TALKING TO OTHERS MADE ME FEEL THIS INDESCRIBABLE EMPTINESS...
...BECAUSE I WASN'T NORMAL, BUT I WAS PRETENDING TO BE.
SO I WAS OFTEN ALONE AT SCHOOL.
THIS SOUNDS REALLY SELFISH TO SAY,
BUT NEJI WOULD JUST GET SO EXCITED OR SAD ABOUT ANY LITTLE THING I DID...
...AND HE SEEMED TO BE ENJOYING HIMSELF, EVEN WHEN I DIDN'T DO ANYTHING,
SO HE WAS EASY TO BE AROUND.
I TOOK ADVANTAGE OF HIS EASYGOING PERSONALITY.

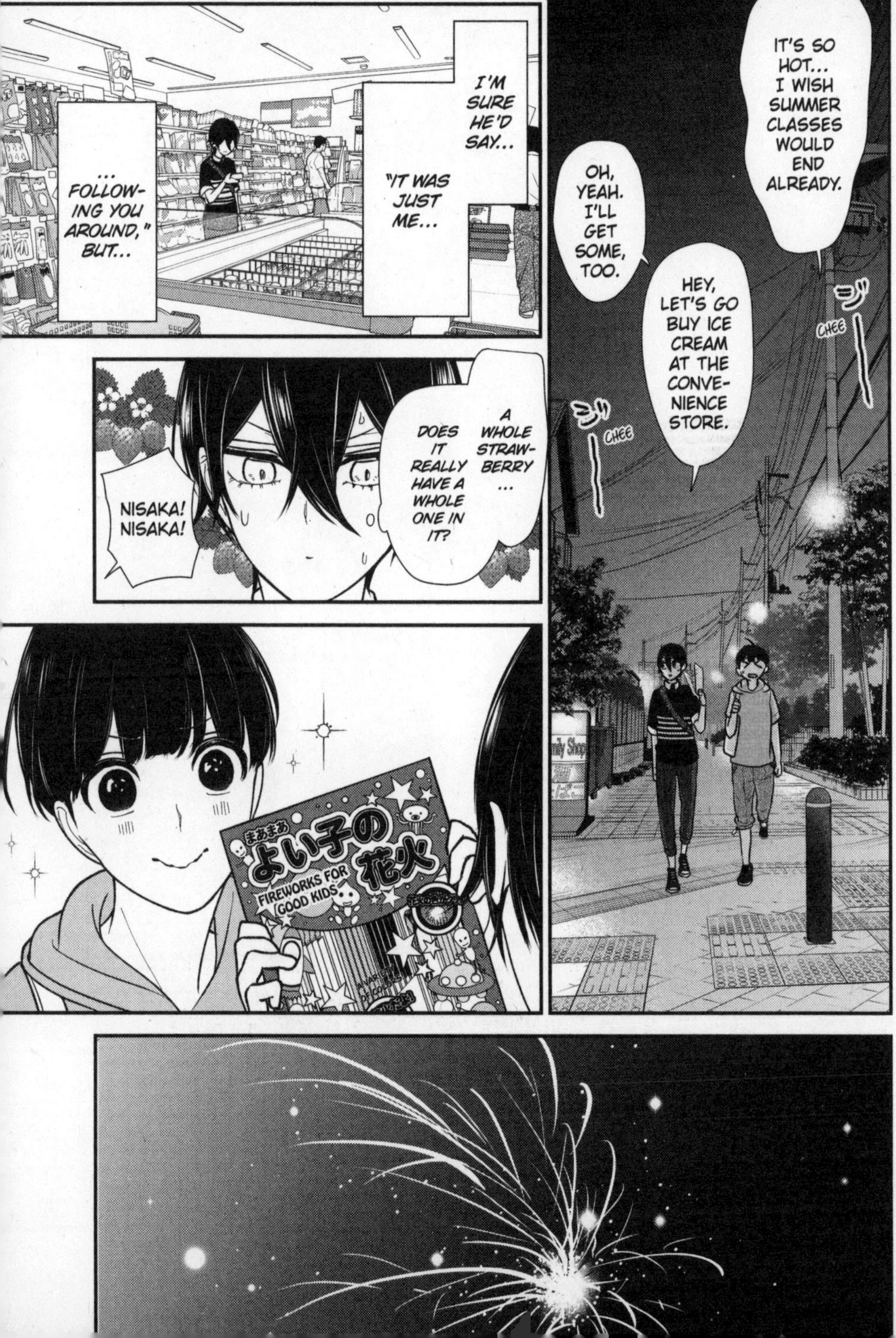
IT'S SO HOT... I WISH SUMMER CLASSES WOULD END ALREADY.
CHEE
HEY, LET'S GO BUY ICE CREAM AT THE CONVENIENCE STORE.
OH, YEAH. I'LL GET SOME, TOO.
CHEE
I'M SURE HE'D SAY...
"IT WAS JUST ME...
...FOLLOWING YOU AROUND," BUT...
A WHOLE STRAWBERRY...
DOES IT REALLY HAVE A WHOLE ONE IN IT?
NISAKA! NISAKA!
まあまあ
よい子の花火
FIREWORKS FOR GOOD KIDS

*NEJI IS REFERRING TO THE POPULAR BOYBAND KANJANI8. STYLIZED AS KANJANI∞, THE 8 IN THEIR NAME IS TURNED TO LOOK LIKE AN INFINITY SYMBOL.

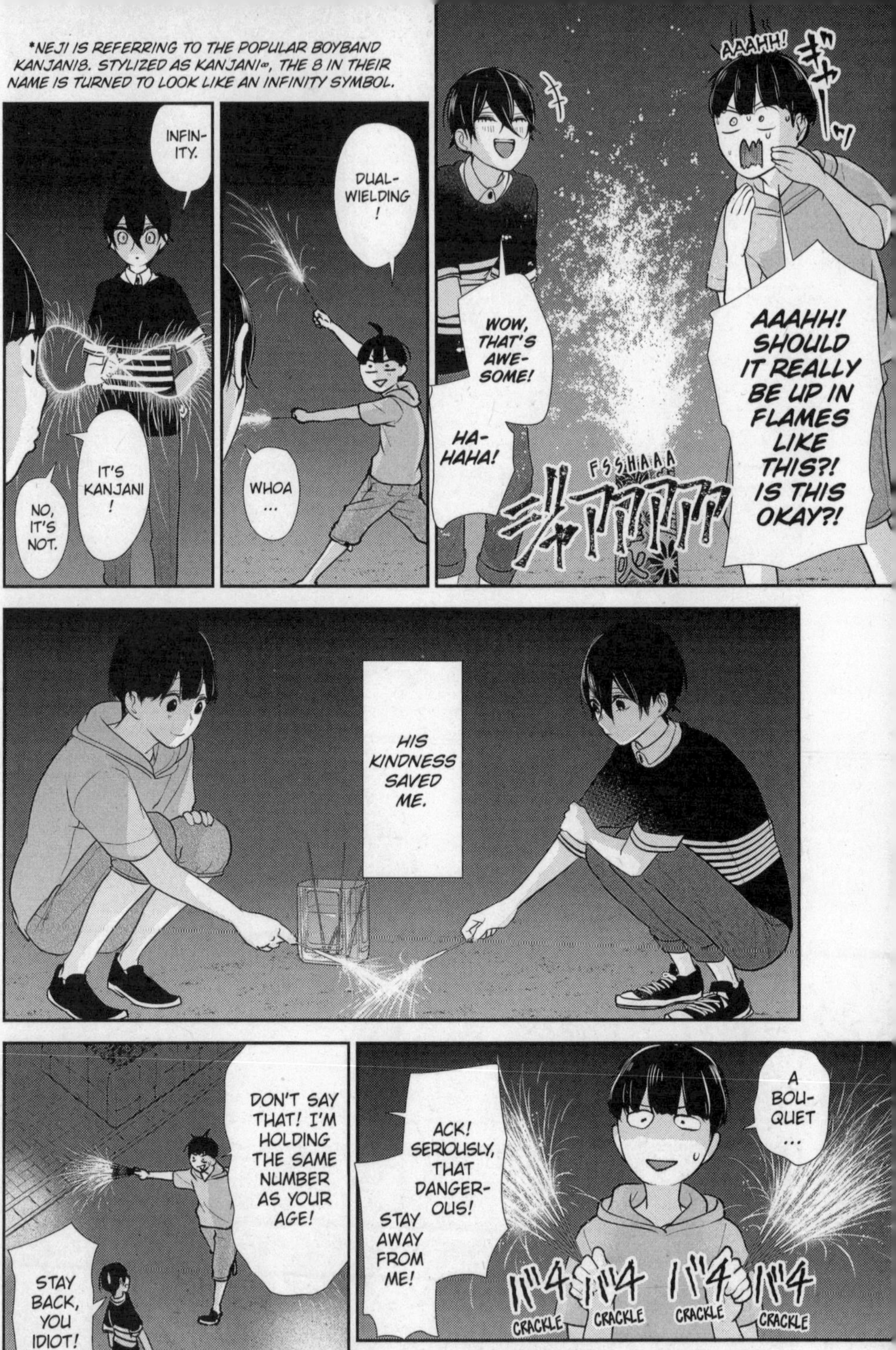
AAAHH!
AAAHH! SHOULD IT REALLY BE UP IN FLAMES LIKE THIS?! IS THIS OKAY?!
WOW, THAT'S AWE-SOME!
HA-HAHA!
FSSHAAA
シャアアアア
DUAL-WIELDING!
WHOA...
INFIN-ITY.
IT'S KANJANI!
NO, IT'S NOT.
HIS KINDNESS SAVED ME.
A BOU-QUET...
ACK! SERIOUSLY, THAT DANGER-OUS!
STAY AWAY FROM ME!
CRACKLE
CRACKLE
CRACKLE
CRACKLE
DON'T SAY THAT! I'M HOLDING THE SAME NUMBER AS YOUR AGE!
STAY BACK, YOU IDIOT!

*DON'T TRY THIS AT HOME, KIDS.

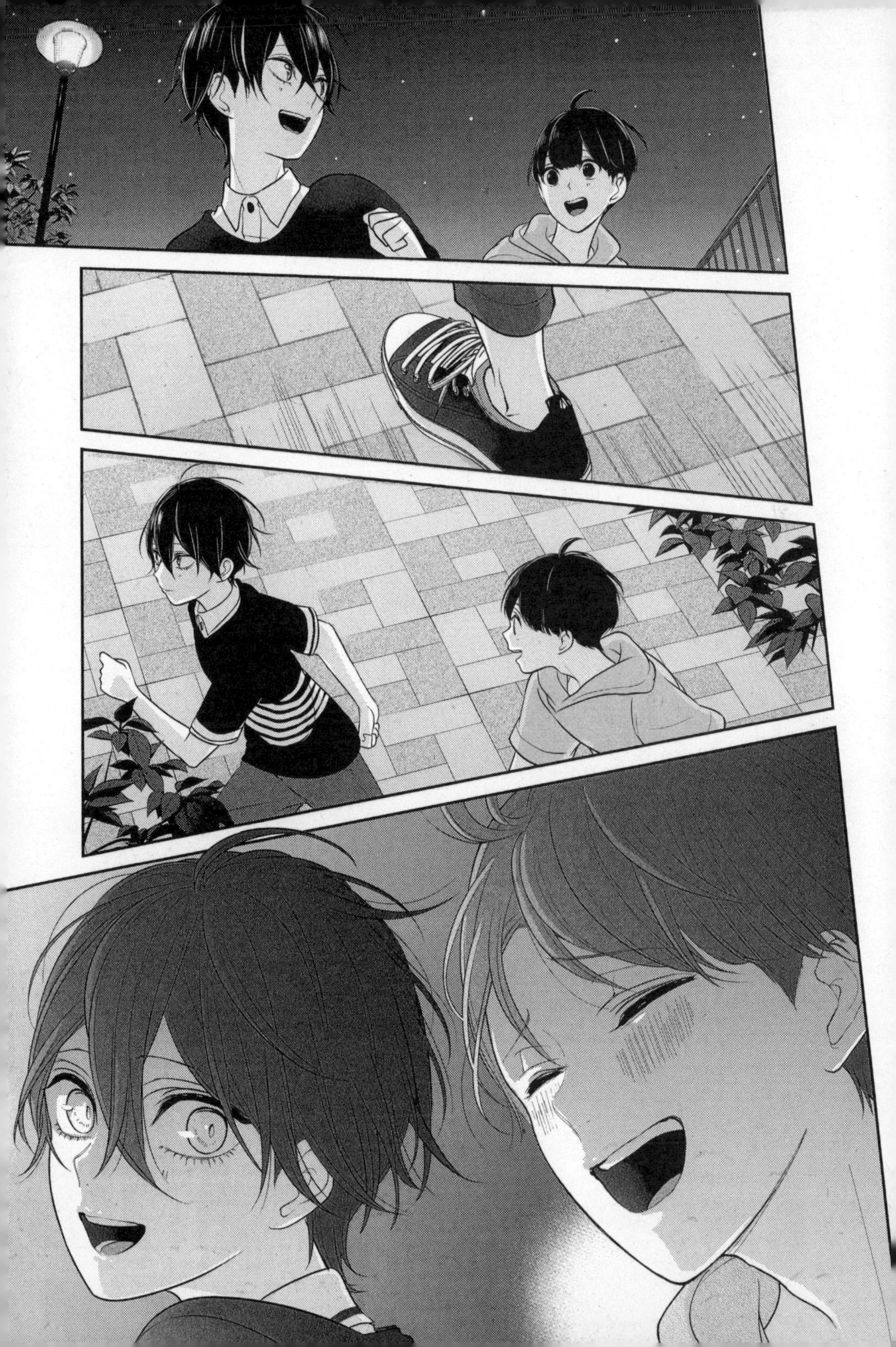

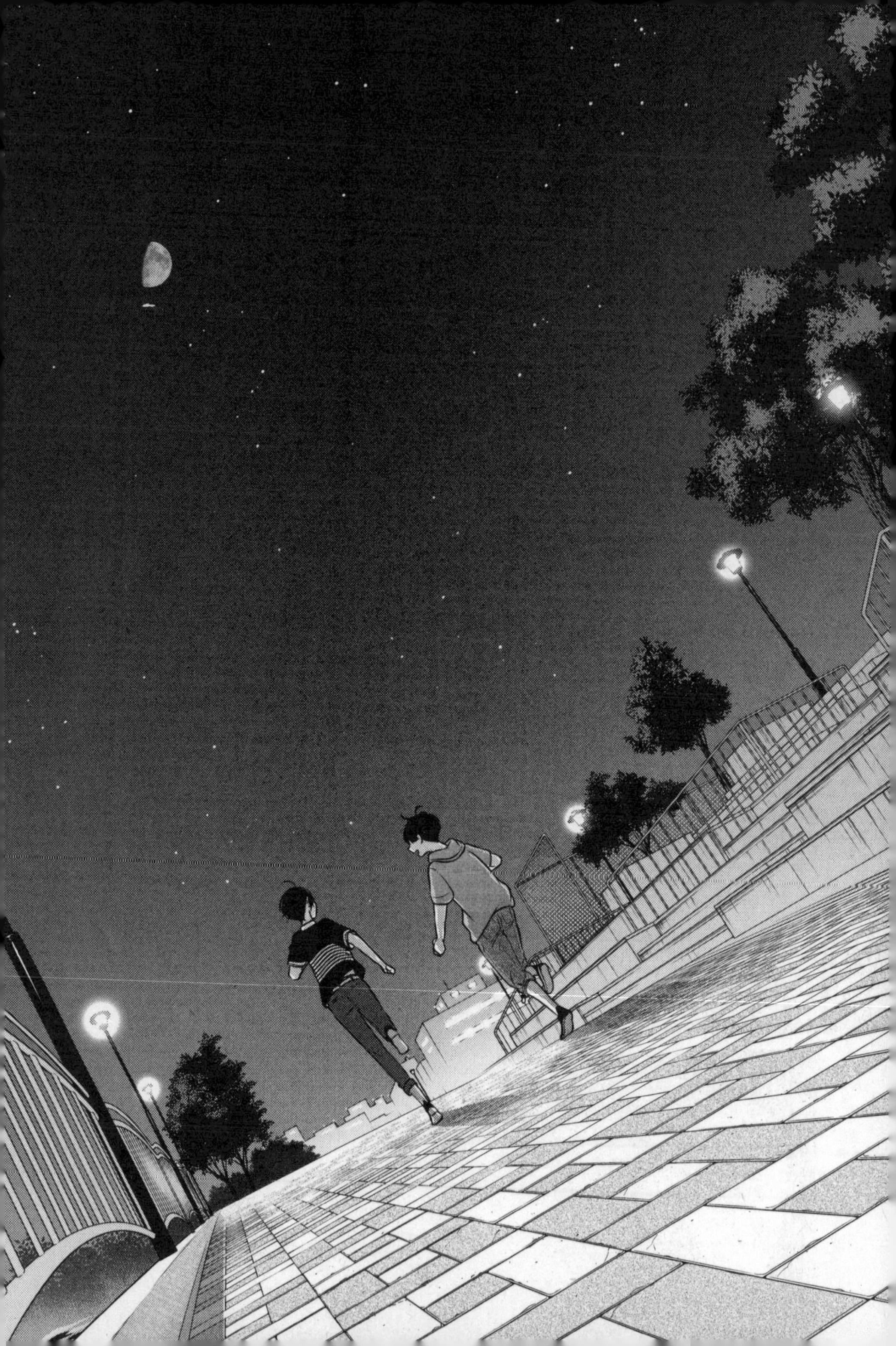

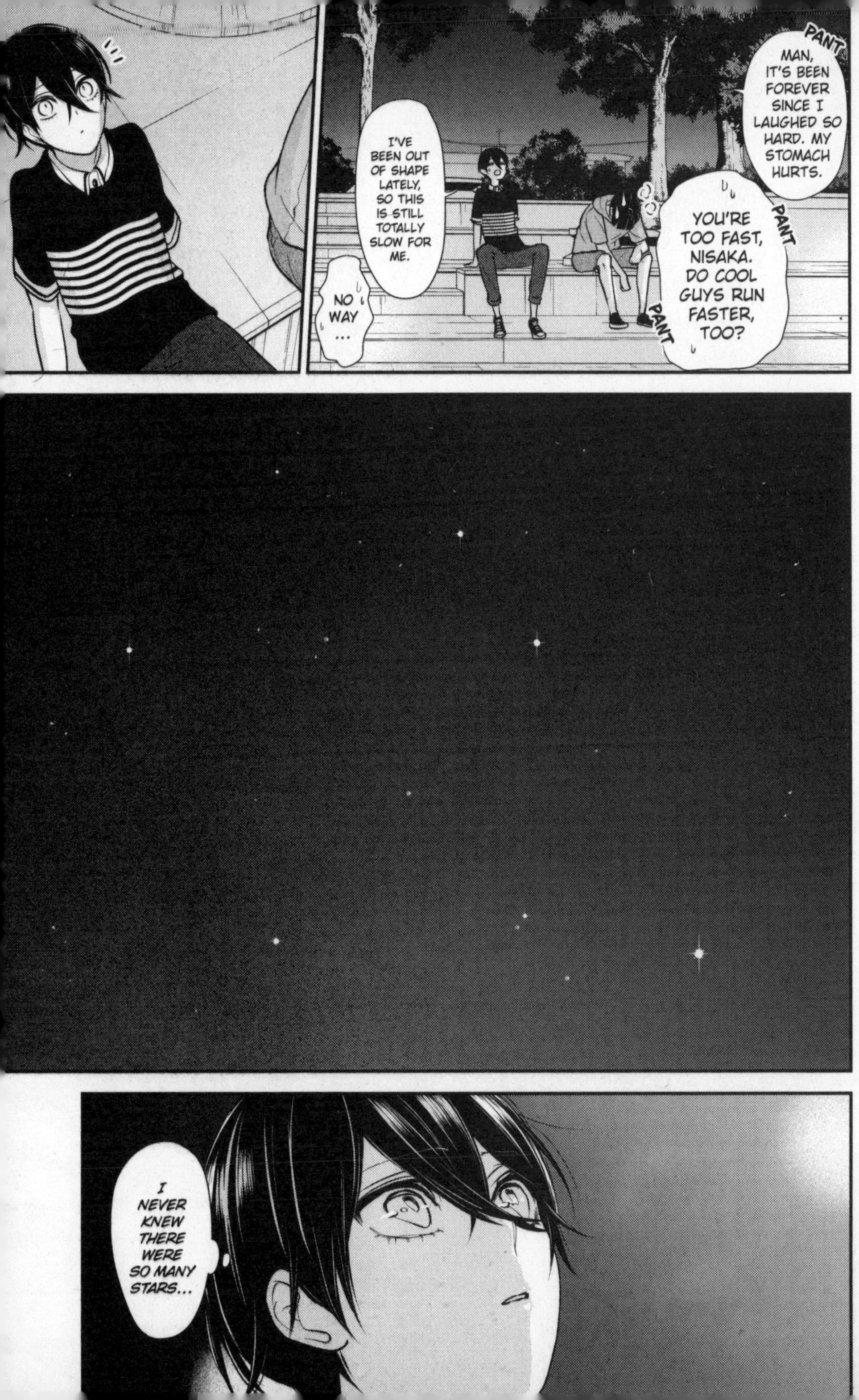
PANT
MAN, IT'S BEEN FOREVER SINCE I LAUGHED SO HARD. MY STOMACH HURTS.
PANT
YOU'RE TOO FAST, NISAKA. DO COOL GUYS RUN FASTER, TOO?
PANT
I'VE BEEN OUT OF SHAPE LATELY, SO THIS IS STILL TOTALLY SLOW FOR ME.
NO WAY...
I NEVER KNEW THERE WERE SO MANY STARS...

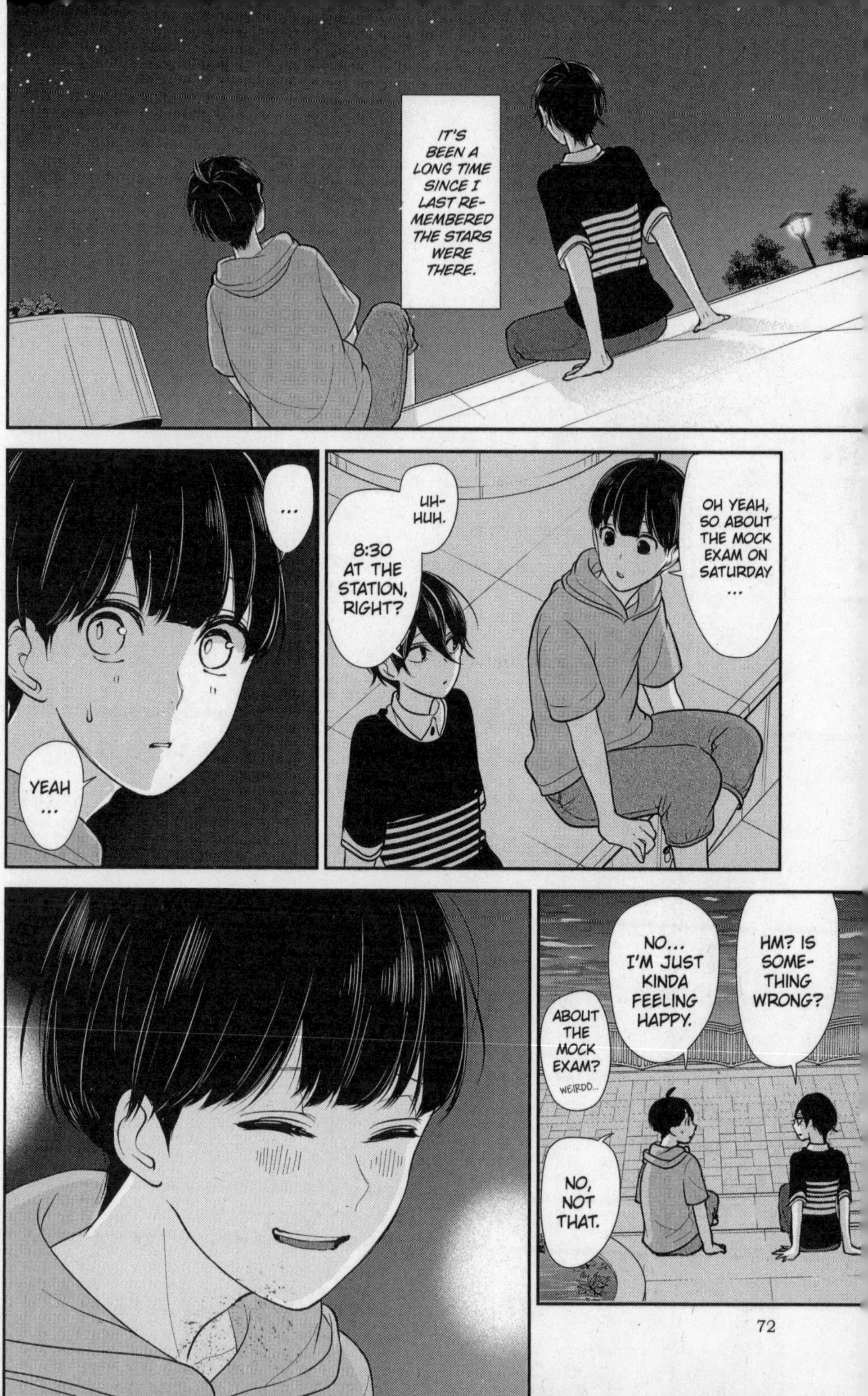
IT'S BEEN A LONG TIME SINCE I LAST RE-MEMBERED THE STARS WERE THERE.
OH YEAH, SO ABOUT THE MOCK EXAM ON SATURDAY ...
UH-HUH.
8:30 AT THE STATION, RIGHT?
...
YEAH ...
HM? IS SOME-THING WRONG?
NO... I'M JUST KINDA FEELING HAPPY.
ABOUT THE MOCK EXAM?
WEIRDO...
NO, NOT THAT.

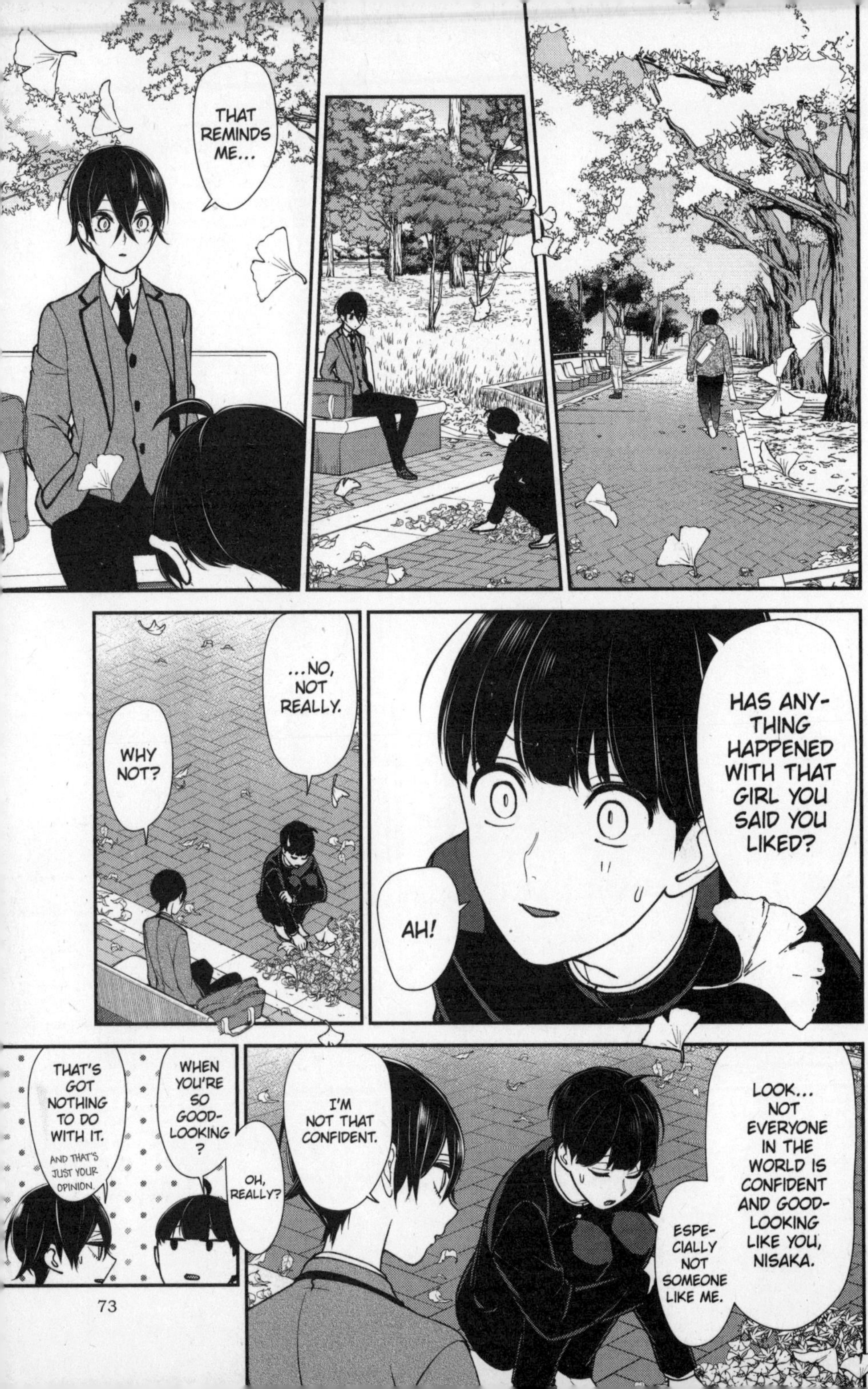
THAT REMINDS ME...
HAS ANY-THING HAPPENED WITH THAT GIRL YOU SAID YOU LIKED?
AH!
...NO, NOT REALLY.
WHY NOT?
LOOK... NOT EVERYONE IN THE WORLD IS CONFIDENT AND GOOD-LOOKING LIKE YOU, NISAKA.
ESPE-CIALLY NOT SOMEONE LIKE ME.
I'M NOT THAT CONFIDENT.
WHEN YOU'RE SO GOOD-LOOKING?
OH, REALLY?
THAT'S GOT NOTHING TO DO WITH IT.
AND THAT'S JUST YOUR OPINION.

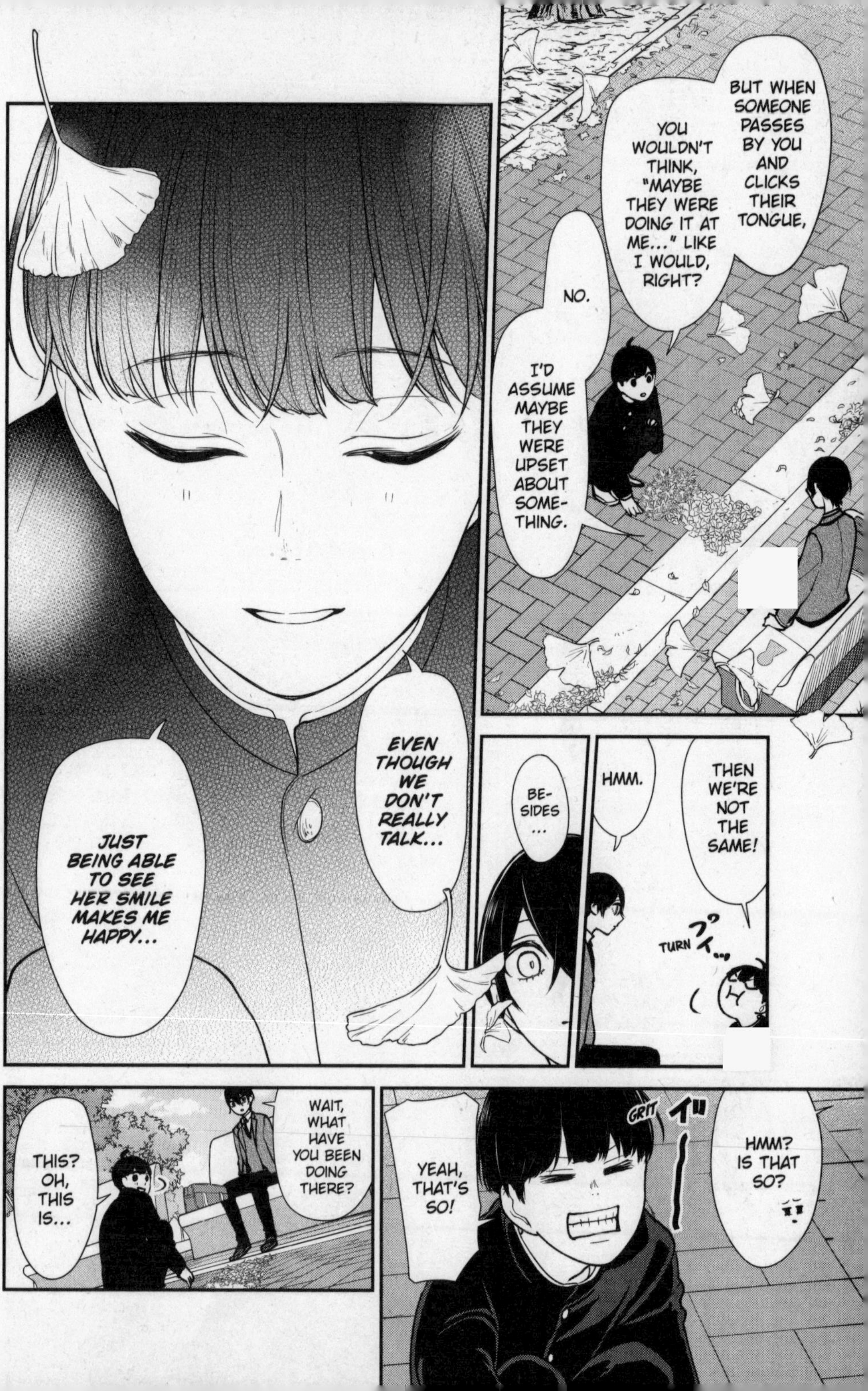

BUT WHEN SOMEONE PASSES BY YOU AND CLICKS THEIR TONGUE,
YOU WOULDN'T THINK, "MAYBE THEY WERE DOING IT AT ME..." LIKE I WOULD, RIGHT?
NO.
I'D ASSUME MAYBE THEY WERE UPSET ABOUT SOMETHING.
THEN WE'RE NOT THE SAME!
TURN
HMM.
BESIDES...
EVEN THOUGH WE DON'T REALLY TALK...
JUST BEING ABLE TO SEE HER SMILE MAKES ME HAPPY...
HMM? IS THAT SO?
GRIT
YEAH, THAT'S SO!
WAIT, WHAT HAVE YOU BEEN DOING THERE?
THIS? OH, THIS IS...

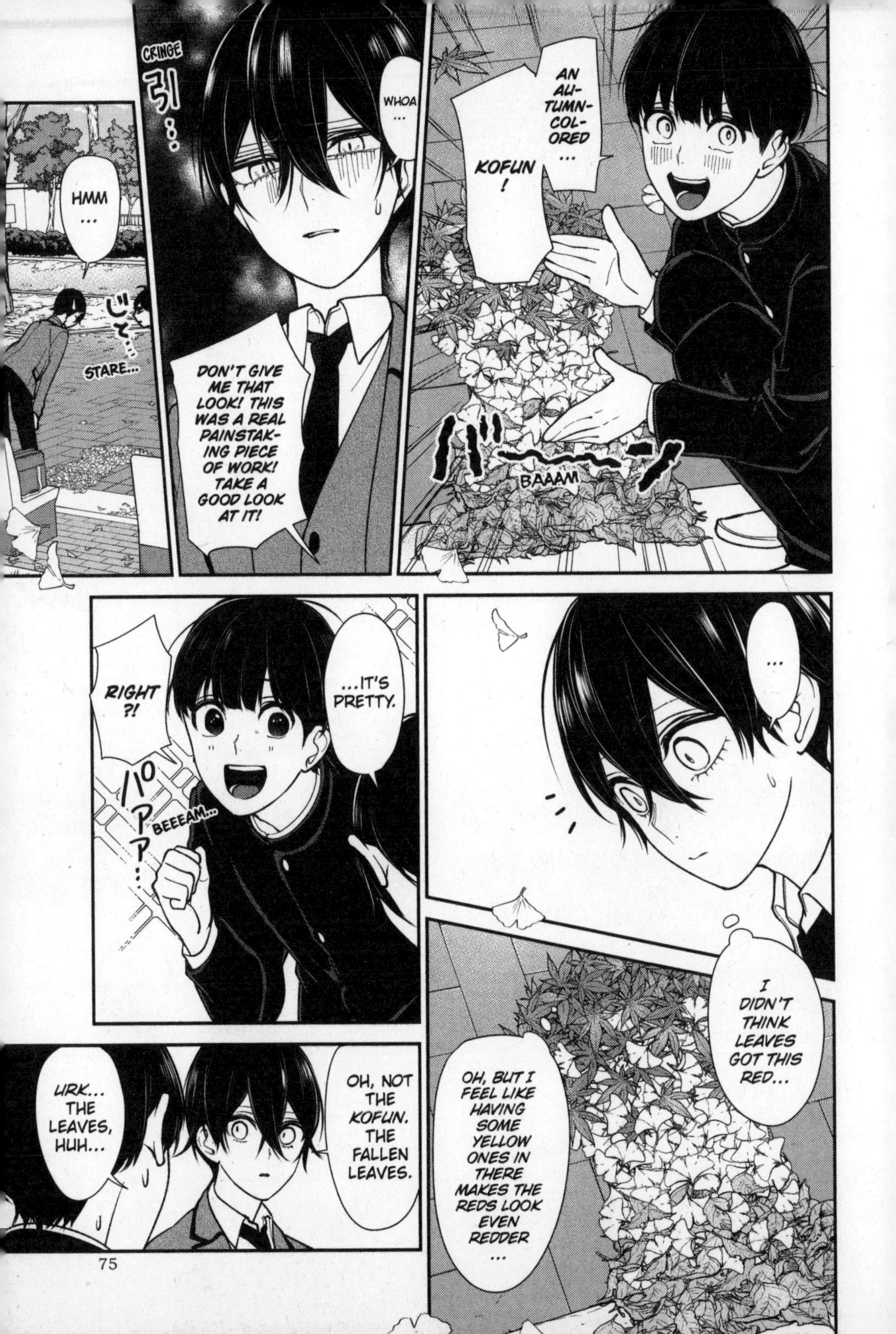

AN AUTUMN-COLORED ...
KOFUN !
BAAAM
WHOA ...
CRINGE
DON'T GIVE ME THAT LOOK! THIS WAS A REAL PAINSTAKING PIECE OF WORK! TAKE A GOOD LOOK AT IT!
HMM ...
STARE...
...
...IT'S PRETTY.
RIGHT ?!
BEEEAM...
I DIDN'T THINK LEAVES GOT THIS RED...
OH, BUT I FEEL LIKE HAVING SOME YELLOW ONES IN THERE MAKES THE REDS LOOK EVEN REDDER ...
OH, NOT THE KOFUN. THE FALLEN LEAVES.
URK... THE LEAVES, HUH...

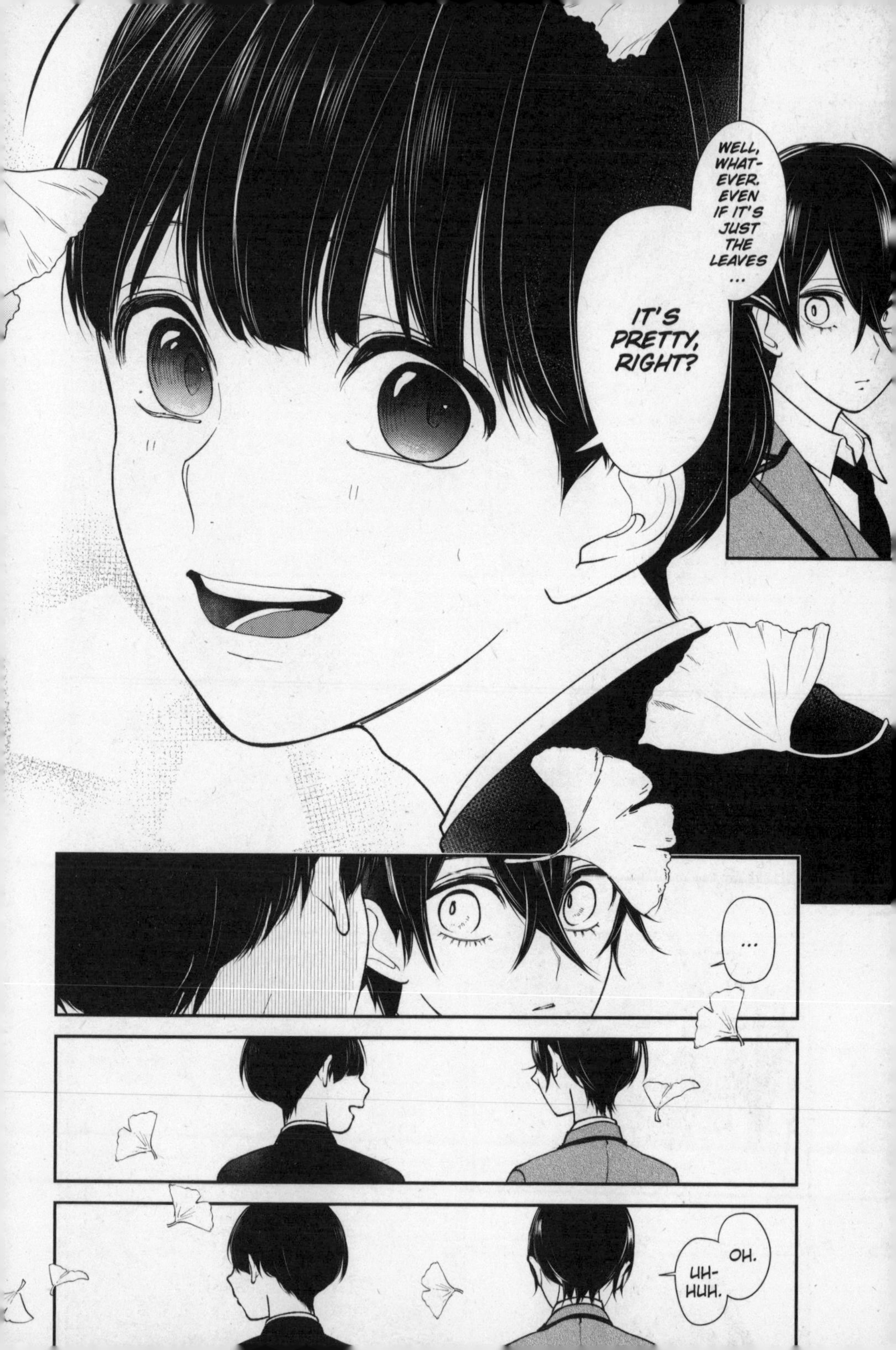
WELL, WHATEVER. EVEN IF IT'S JUST THE LEAVES...
IT'S PRETTY, RIGHT?
...
OH. UH-HUH.

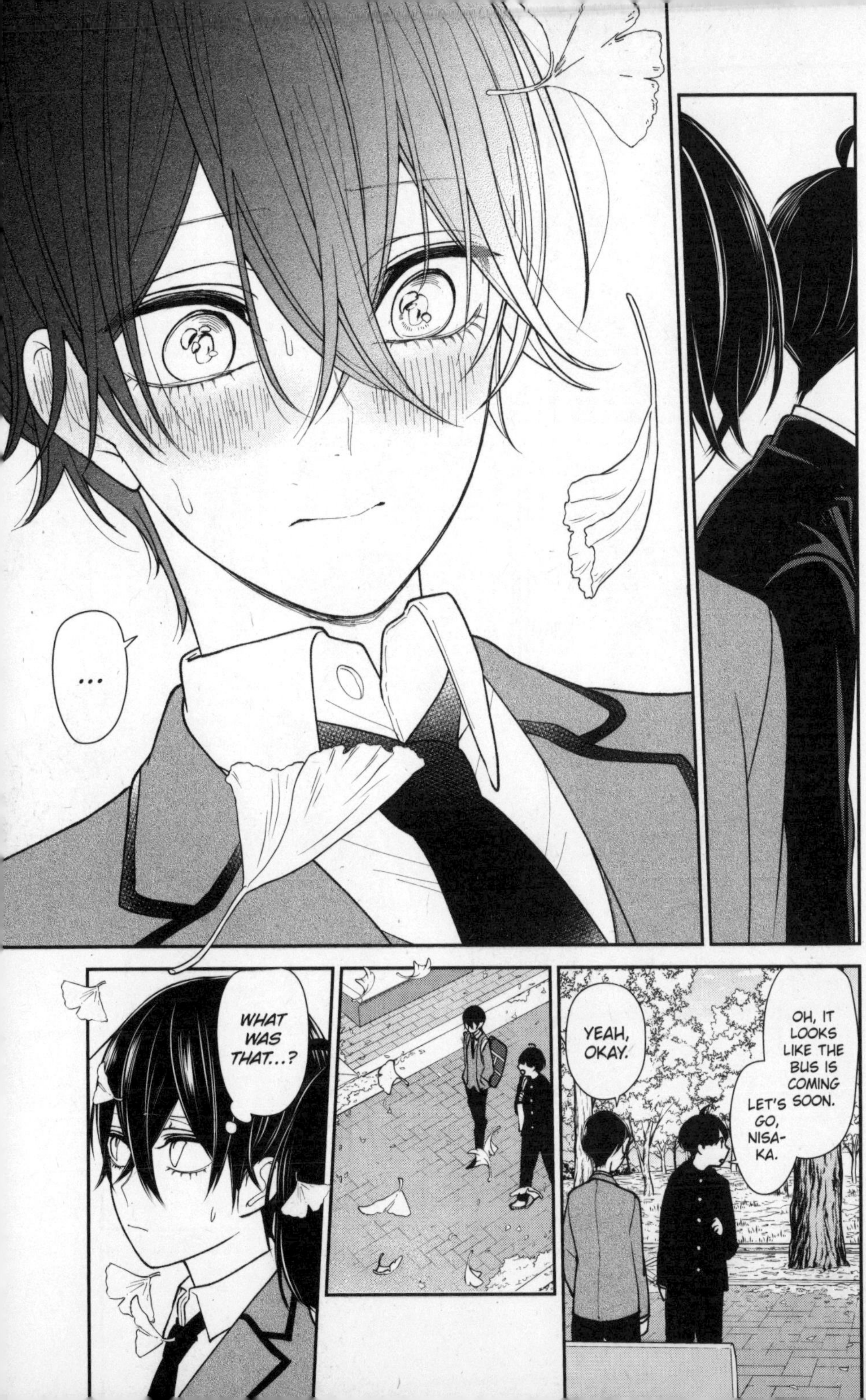
...
OH, IT LOOKS LIKE THE BUS IS COMING SOON.
LET'S GO, NISA-KA.
YEAH, OKAY.
WHAT WAS THAT...?

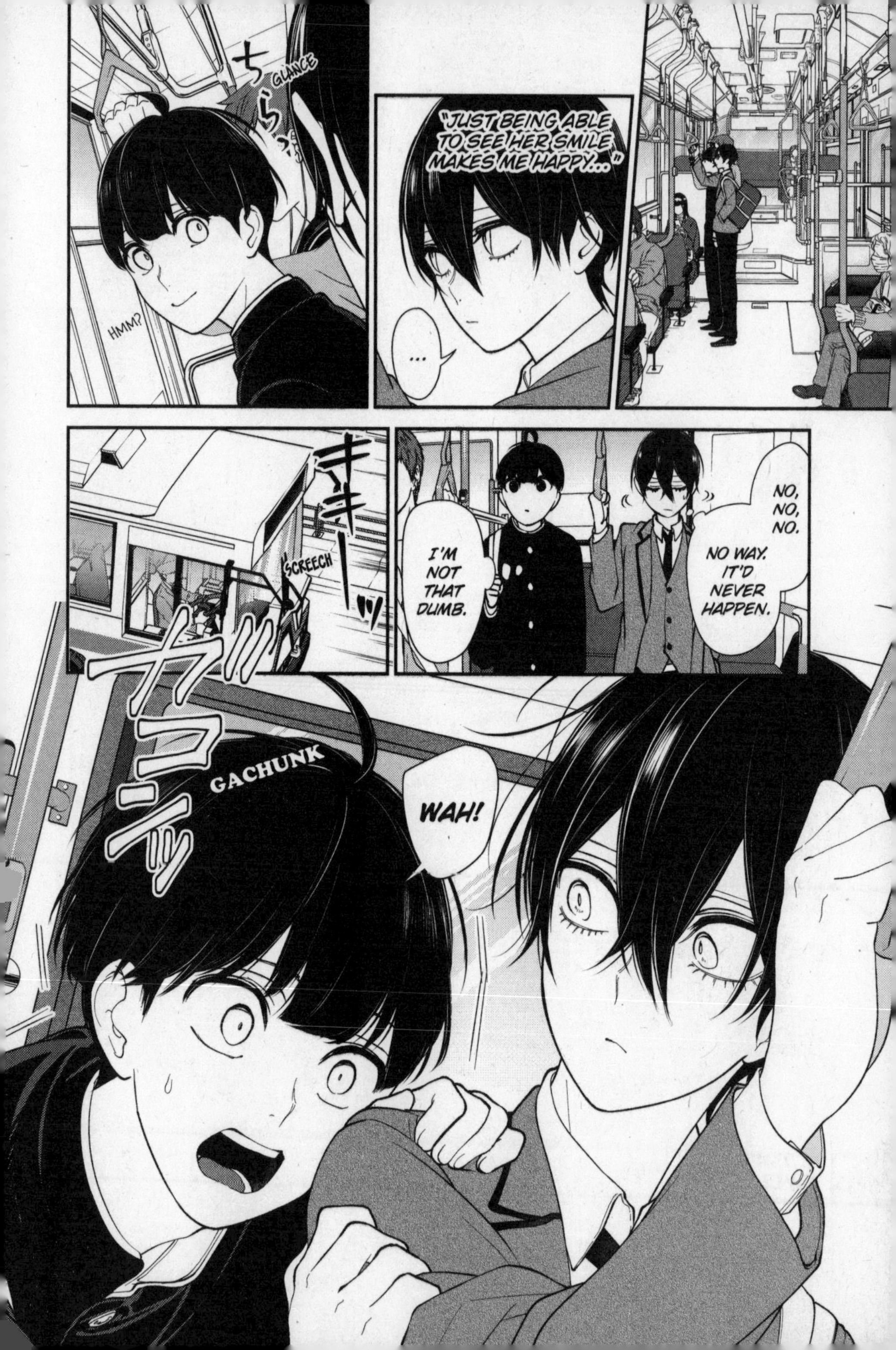
"JUST BEING ABLE TO SEE HER SMILE MAKES ME HAPPY..."
...
ちら
GLANCE
HMM?
NO, NO, NO.
NO WAY. IT'D NEVER HAPPEN.
I'M NOT THAT DUMB.
キキーッ
SCREECH
ガコンッ
GACHUNK
WAH!

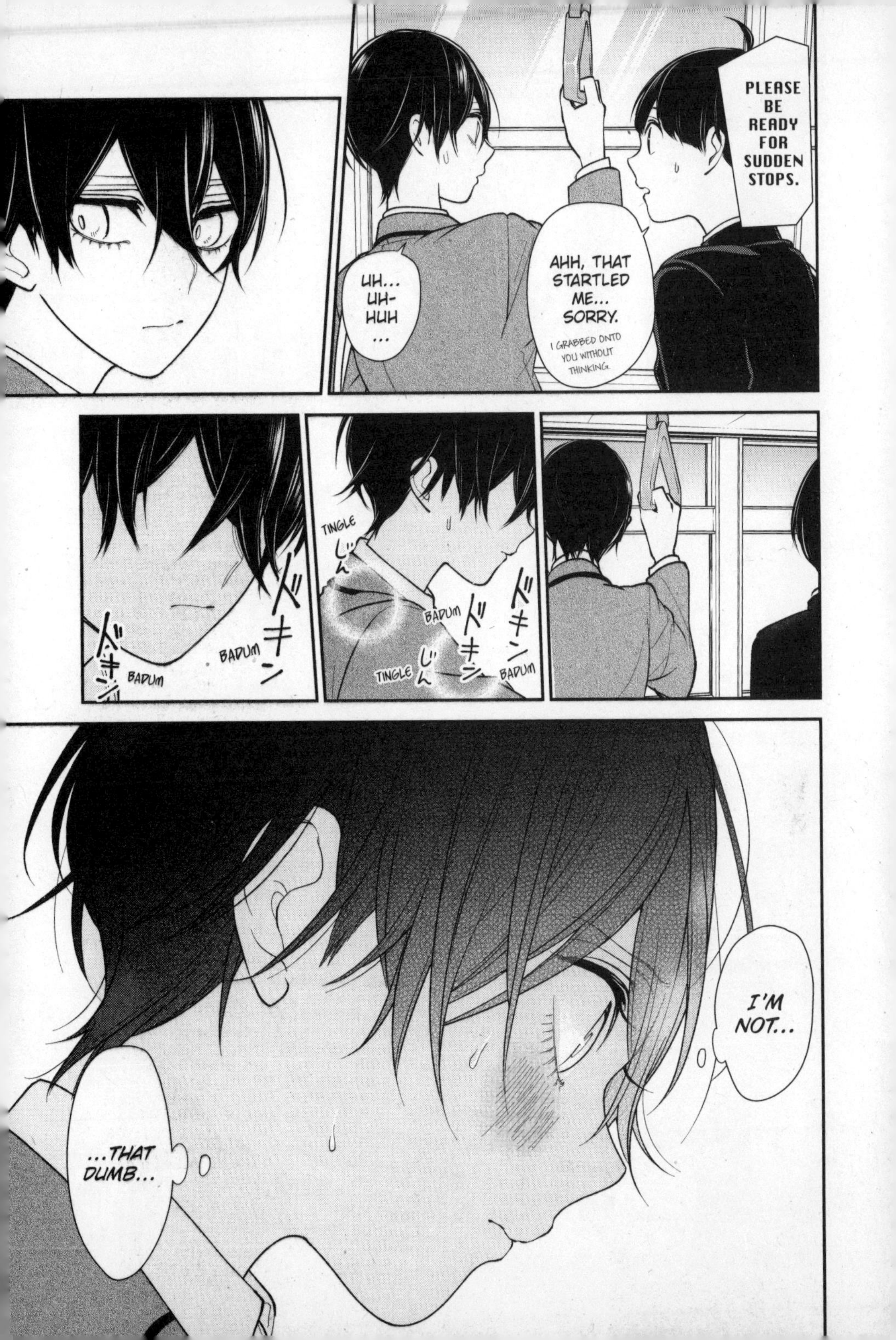
PLEASE BE READY FOR SUDDEN STOPS.
AHH, THAT STARTLED ME... SORRY.
I GRABBED ONTO YOU WITHOUT THINKING.
UH... UH-HUH...
ドキン
BADUM
ドキン
BADUM
じん
TINGLE
じん
TINGLE
ドキン
BADUM
ドキン
BADUM
I'M NOT...
...THAT DUMB...

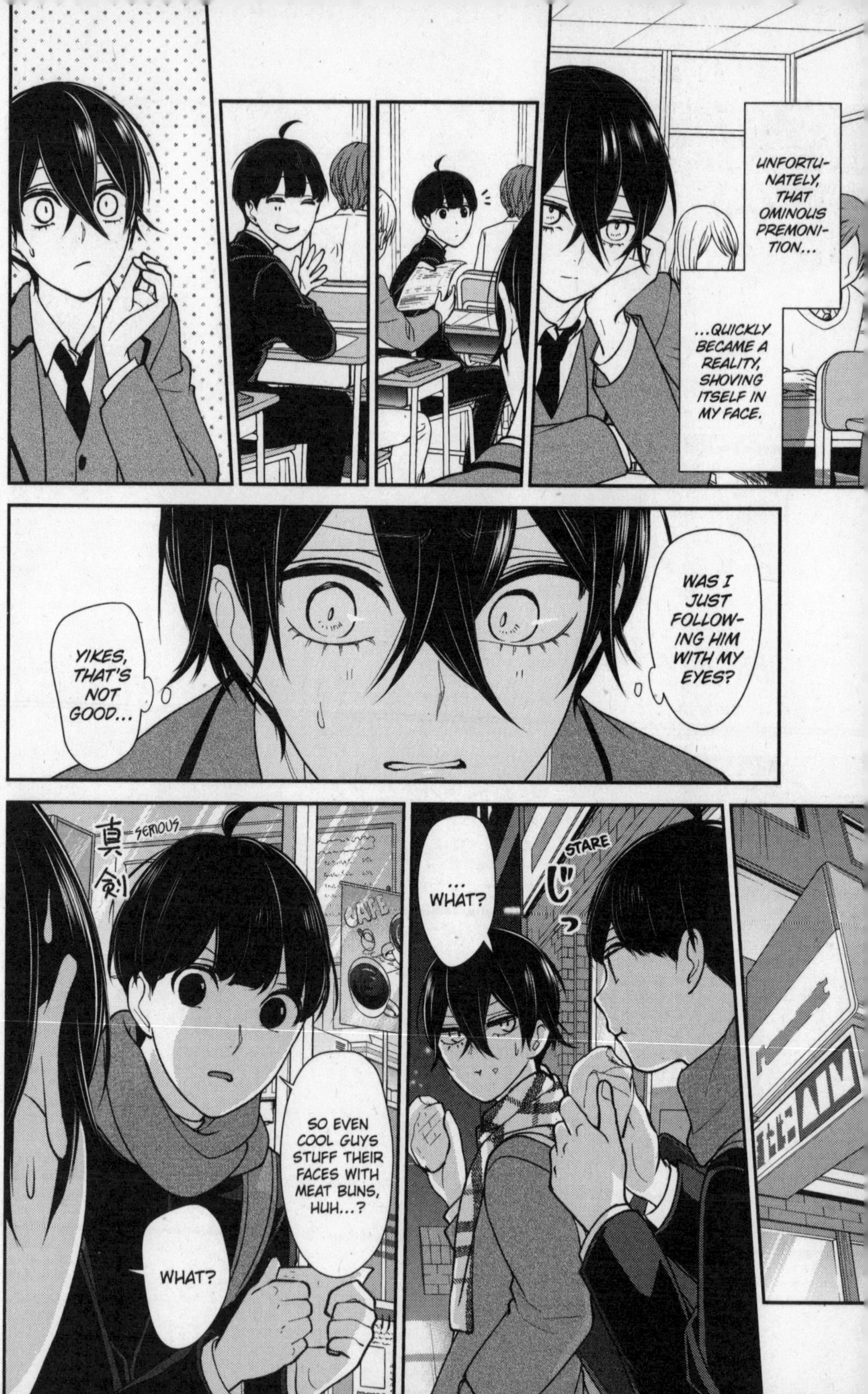
UNFORTU-
NATELY,
THAT
OMINOUS
PREMONI-
TION...
...QUICKLY
BECAME A
REALITY,
SHOVING
ITSELF IN
MY FACE.
WAS I JUST FOLLOW-ING HIM WITH MY EYES?
YIKES, THAT'S NOT GOOD...
STARE
じっ
...WHAT?
真剣 SERIOUS
CAFE
SO EVEN COOL GUYS STUFF THEIR FACES WITH MEAT BUNS, HUH...?
WHAT?

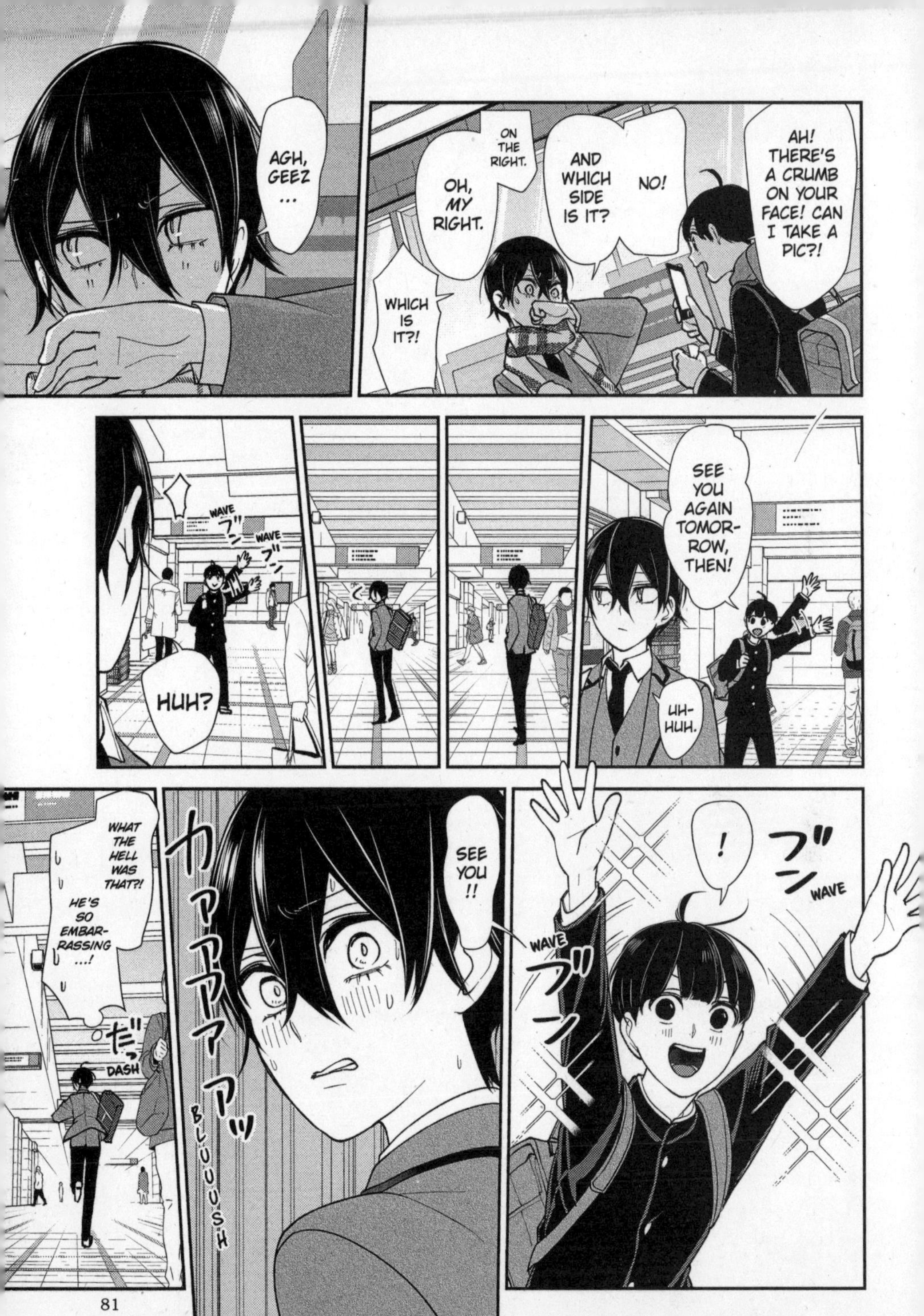
AH! THERE'S A CRUMB ON YOUR FACE! CAN I TAKE A PIC?!
NO!
AND WHICH SIDE IS IT?
ON THE RIGHT.
OH, MY RIGHT.
WHICH IS IT?!
AGH, GEEZ ...
SEE YOU AGAIN TOMORROW, THEN!
UH-HUH.
ブン WAVE
ブン WAVE
HUH?
!
ブン WAVE
ブン WAVE
SEE YOU!!
カァァァァァッ BLUUUUSH
WHAT THE HELL WAS THAT?!
HE'S SO EMBARRASSING...!
だっ DASH

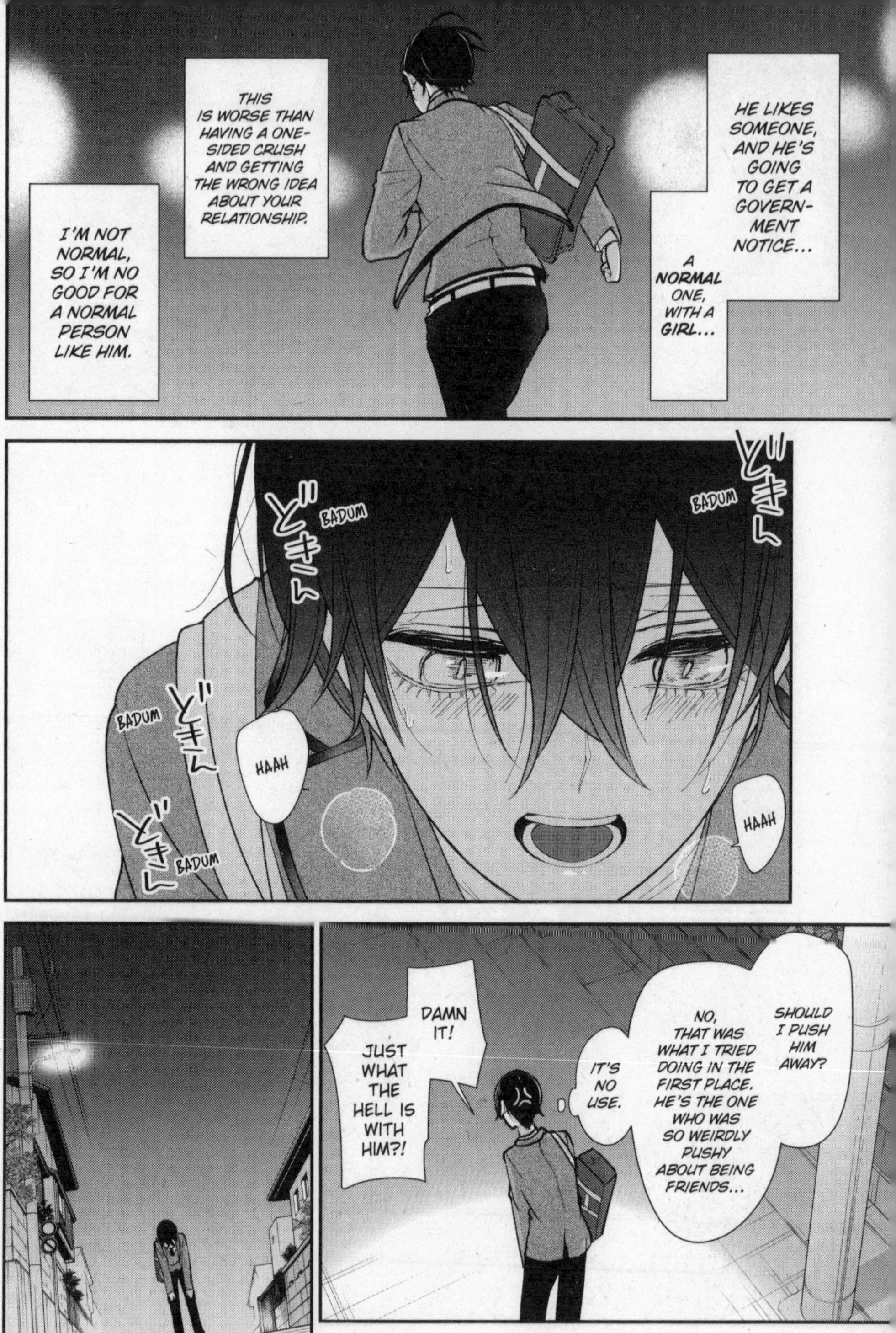
HE LIKES SOMEONE, AND HE'S GOING TO GET A GOVERNMENT NOTICE...
A NORMAL ONE, WITH A GIRL...
THIS IS WORSE THAN HAVING A ONE-SIDED CRUSH AND GETTING THE WRONG IDEA ABOUT YOUR RELATIONSHIP.
I'M NOT NORMAL, SO I'M NO GOOD FOR A NORMAL PERSON LIKE HIM.
どきん
BADUM
HAAH
どきん
BADUM
HAAH
どきん
BADUM
どきん
BADUM
SHOULD I PUSH HIM AWAY?
NO, THAT WAS WHAT I TRIED DOING IN THE FIRST PLACE. HE'S THE ONE WHO WAS SO WEIRDLY PUSHY ABOUT BEING FRIENDS...
IT'S NO USE.
DAMN IT!
JUST WHAT THE HELL IS WITH HIM?!

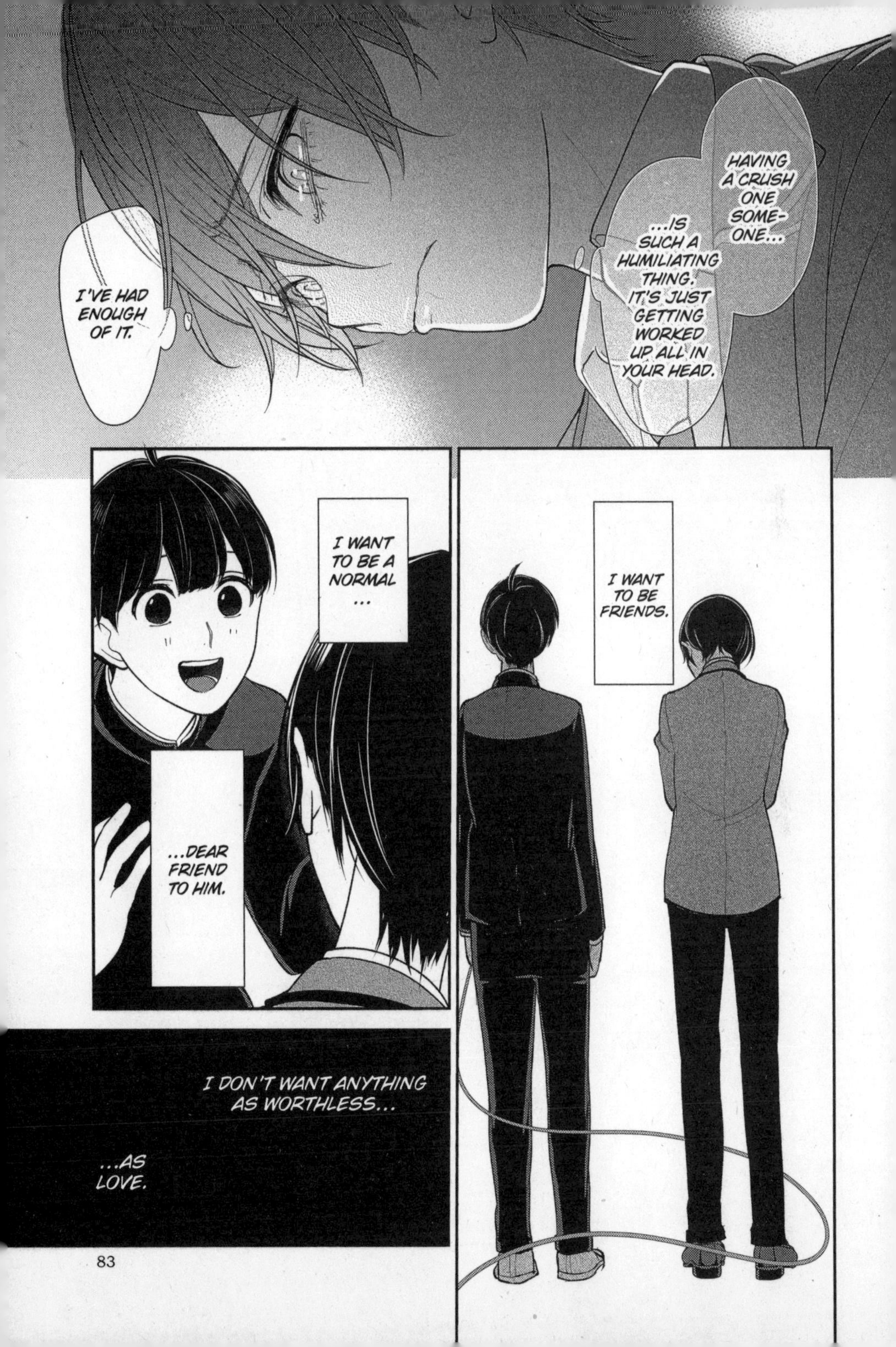
HAVING A CRUSH ONE SOME-ONE...
...IS SUCH A HUMILIATING THING. IT'S JUST GETTING WORKED UP ALL IN YOUR HEAD.
I'VE HAD ENOUGH OF IT.
I WANT TO BE FRIENDS.
I WANT TO BE A NORMAL ...
...DEAR FRIEND TO HIM.
I DON'T WANT ANYTHING AS WORTHLESS...
...AS LOVE.

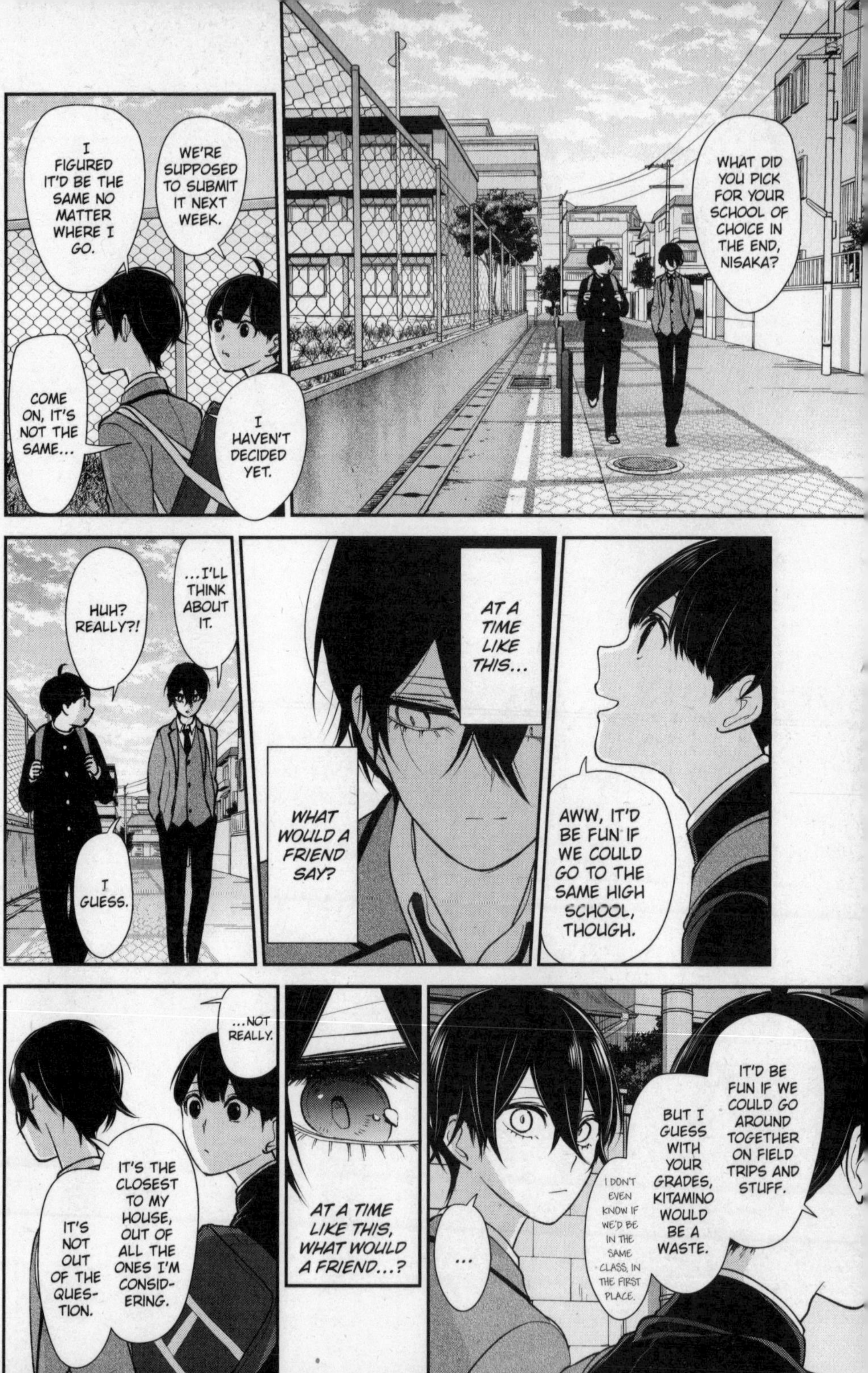
WHAT DID YOU PICK FOR YOUR SCHOOL OF CHOICE IN THE END, NISAKA?
I HAVEN'T DECIDED YET.
WE'RE SUPPOSED TO SUBMIT IT NEXT WEEK.
I FIGURED IT'D BE THE SAME NO MATTER WHERE I GO.
COME ON, IT'S NOT THE SAME...
AWW, IT'D BE FUN IF WE COULD GO TO THE SAME HIGH SCHOOL, THOUGH.
AT A TIME LIKE THIS...
WHAT WOULD A FRIEND SAY?
...I'LL THINK ABOUT IT.
HUH? REALLY?!
I GUESS.
IT'D BE FUN IF WE COULD GO AROUND TOGETHER ON FIELD TRIPS AND STUFF.
BUT I GUESS WITH YOUR GRADES, KITAMINO WOULD BE A WASTE.
I DON'T EVEN KNOW IF WE'D BE IN THE SAME CLASS, IN THE FIRST PLACE.
...
AT A TIME LIKE THIS, WHAT WOULD A FRIEND...?
...NOT REALLY.
IT'S THE CLOSEST TO MY HOUSE, OUT OF ALL THE ONES I'M CONSIDER-ING.
IT'S NOT OUT OF THE QUES-TION.

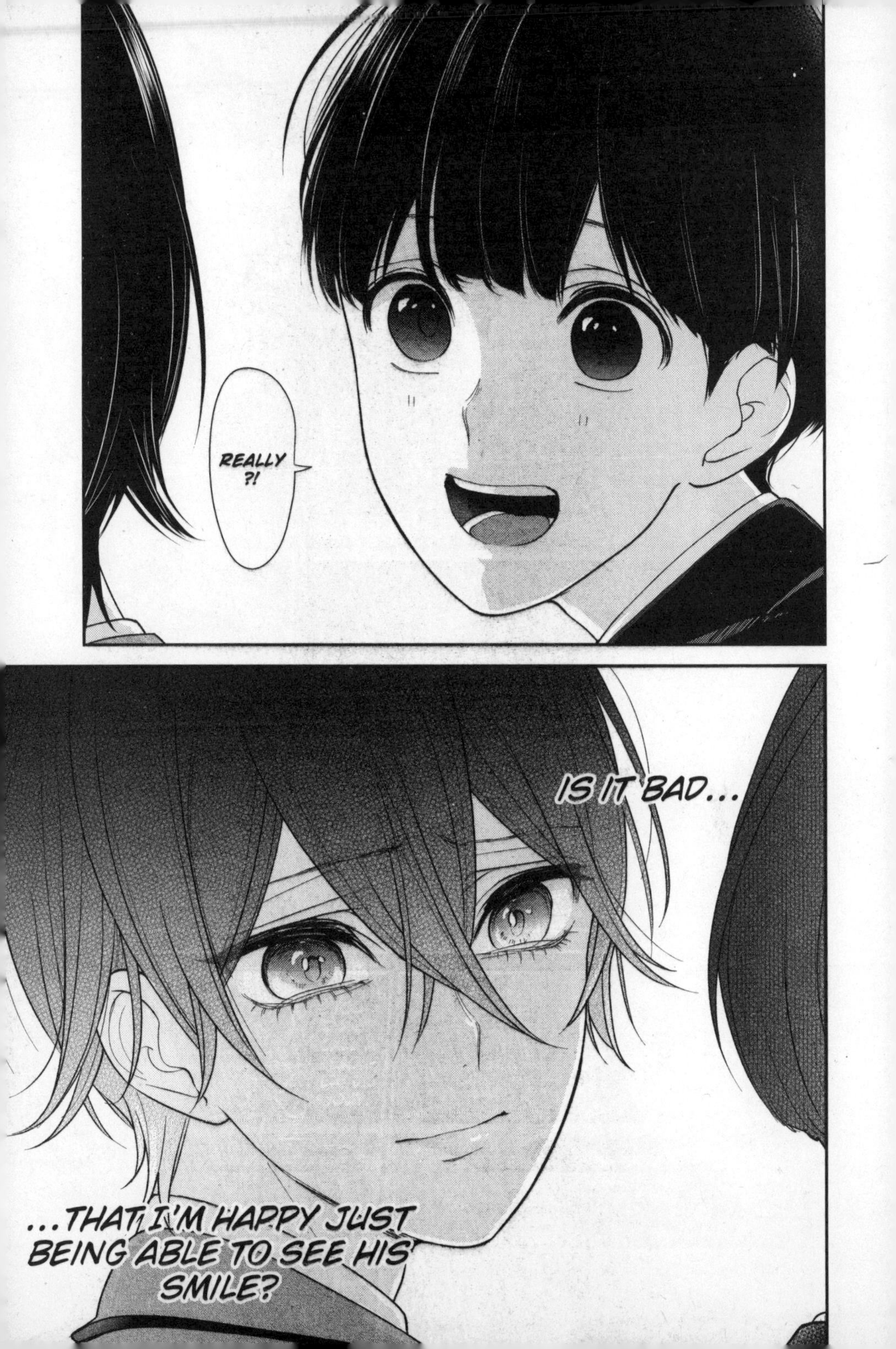
REALLY ?!
IS IT BAD...
...THAT I'M HAPPY JUST BEING ABLE TO SEE HIS SMILE?

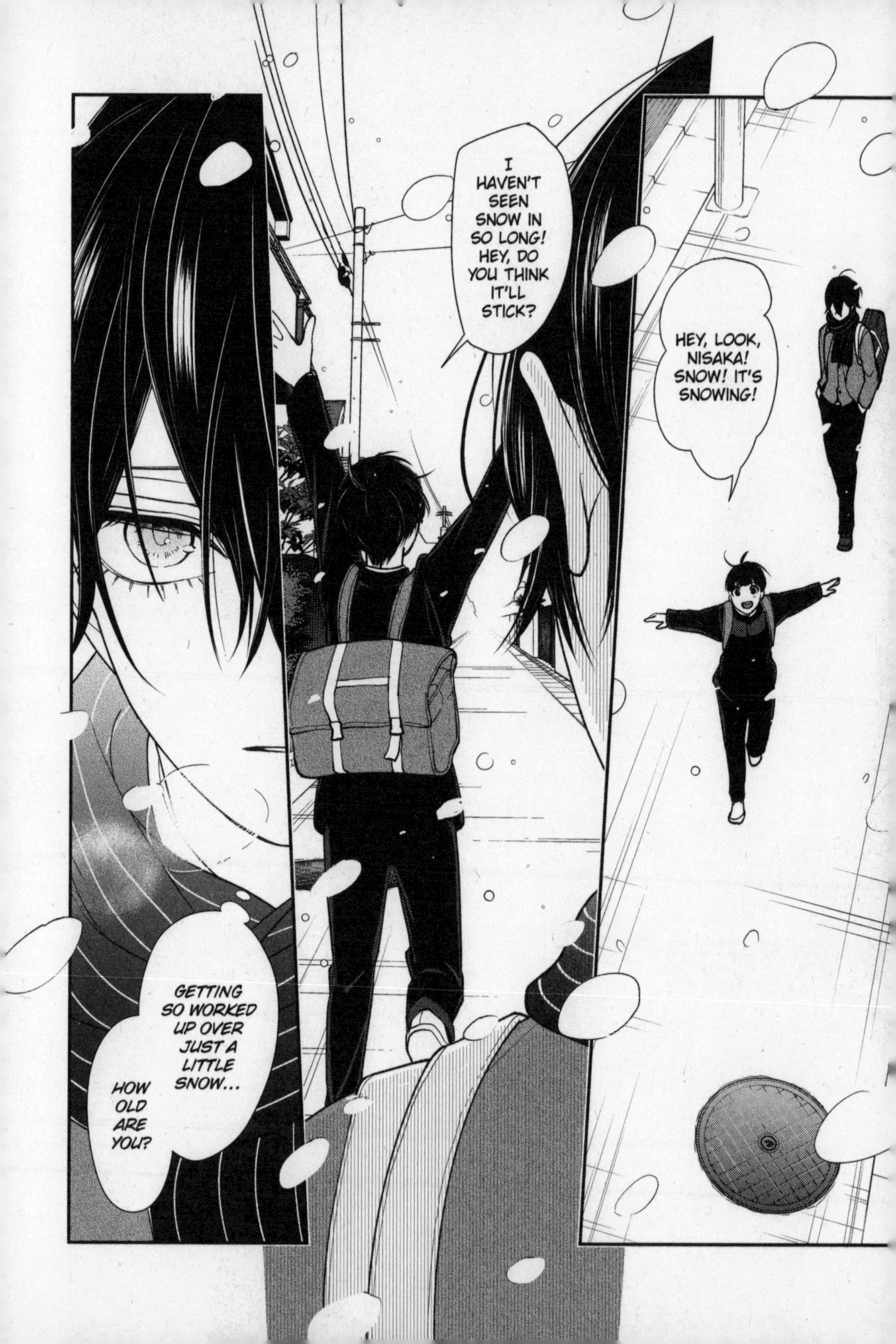
HEY, LOOK, NISAKA! SNOW! IT'S SNOWING!
I HAVEN'T SEEN SNOW IN SO LONG! HEY, DO YOU THINK IT'LL STICK?
GETTING SO WORKED UP OVER JUST A LITTLE SNOW...
HOW OLD ARE YOU?

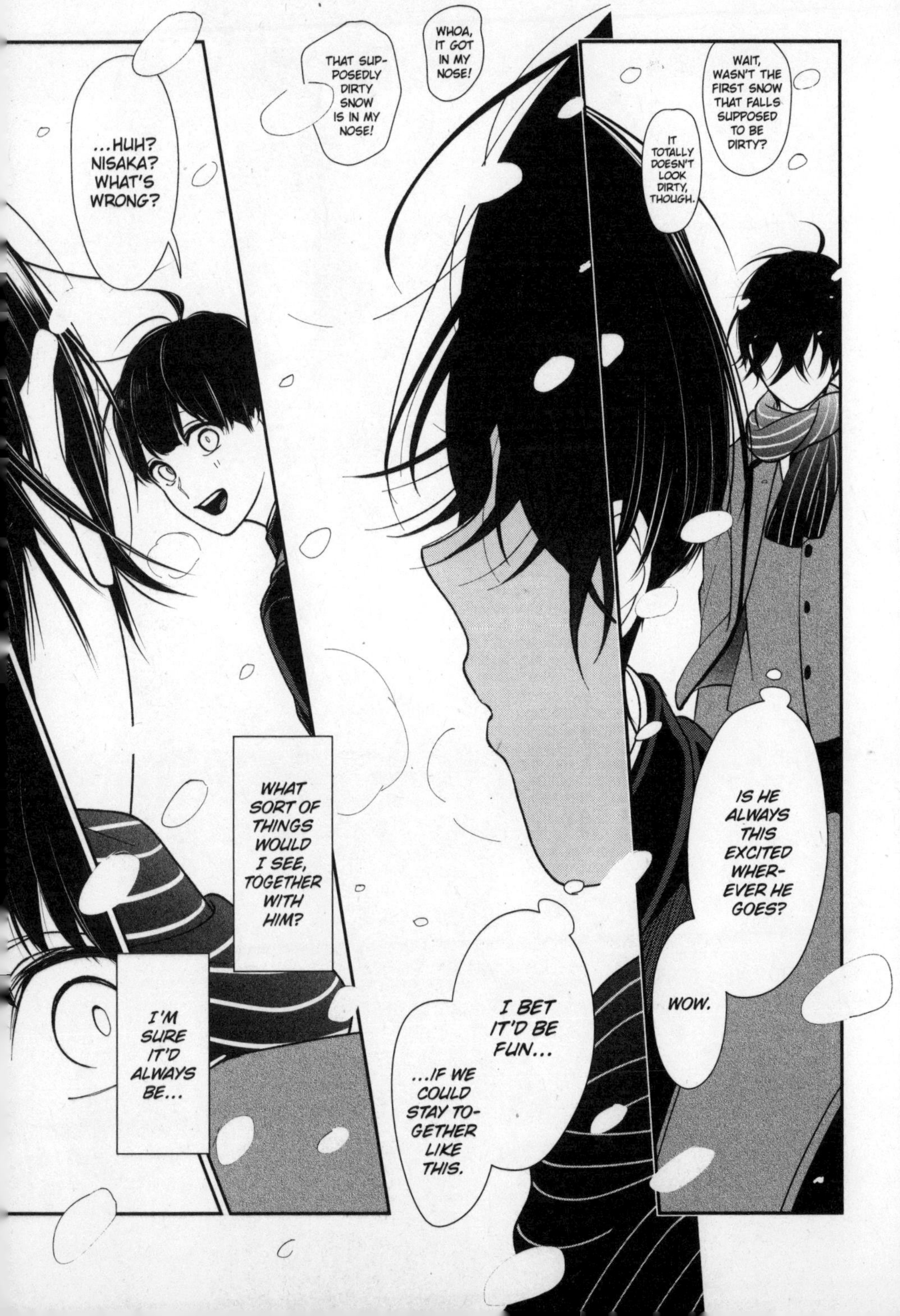
WAIT, WASN'T THE FIRST SNOW THAT FALLS SUPPOSED TO BE DIRTY?
IT TOTALLY DOESN'T LOOK DIRTY, THOUGH.
WHOA, IT GOT IN MY NOSE!
THAT SUPPOSEDLY DIRTY SNOW IS IN MY NOSE!
IS HE ALWAYS THIS EXCITED WHEREVER HE GOES?
WOW.
I BET IT'D BE FUN...
...IF WE COULD STAY TOGETHER LIKE THIS.
...HUH? NISAKA? WHAT'S WRONG?
WHAT SORT OF THINGS WOULD I SEE, TOGETHER WITH HIM?
I'M SURE IT'D ALWAYS BE...

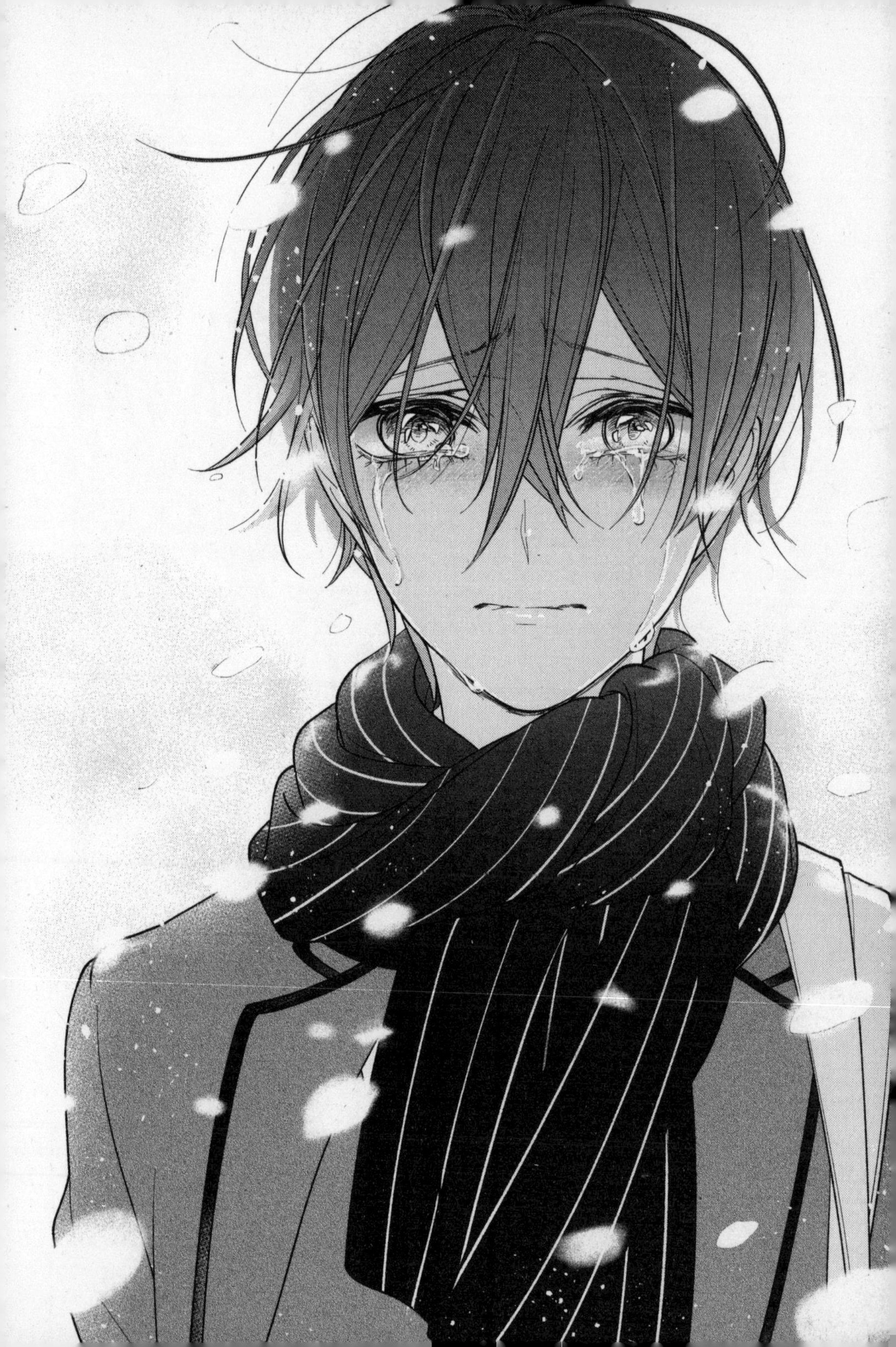

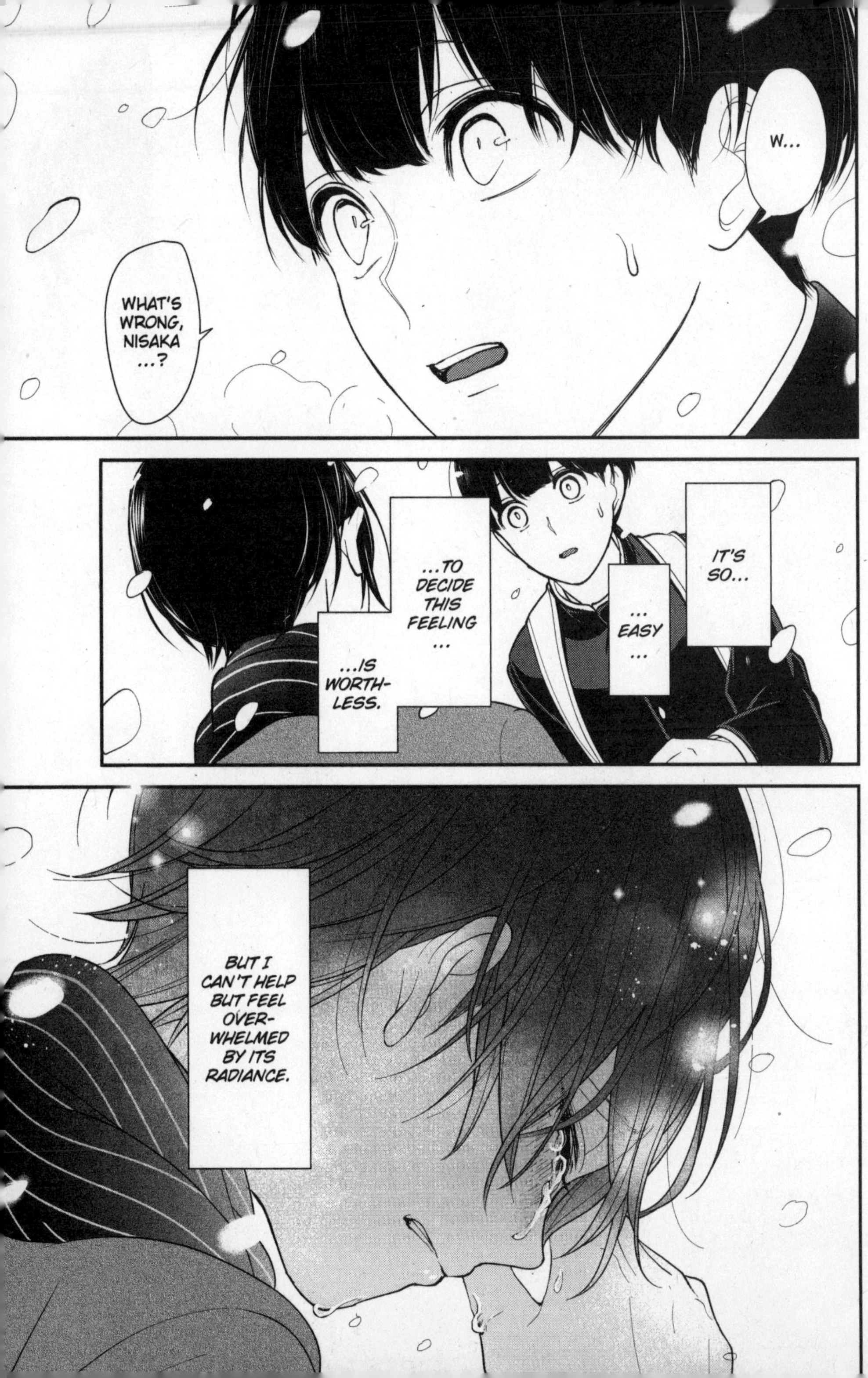
W...
WHAT'S WRONG, NISAKA ...?
IT'S SO...
... EASY ...
...TO DECIDE THIS FEELING ...
...IS WORTHLESS.
BUT I CAN'T HELP BUT FEEL OVERWHELMED BY ITS RADIANCE.

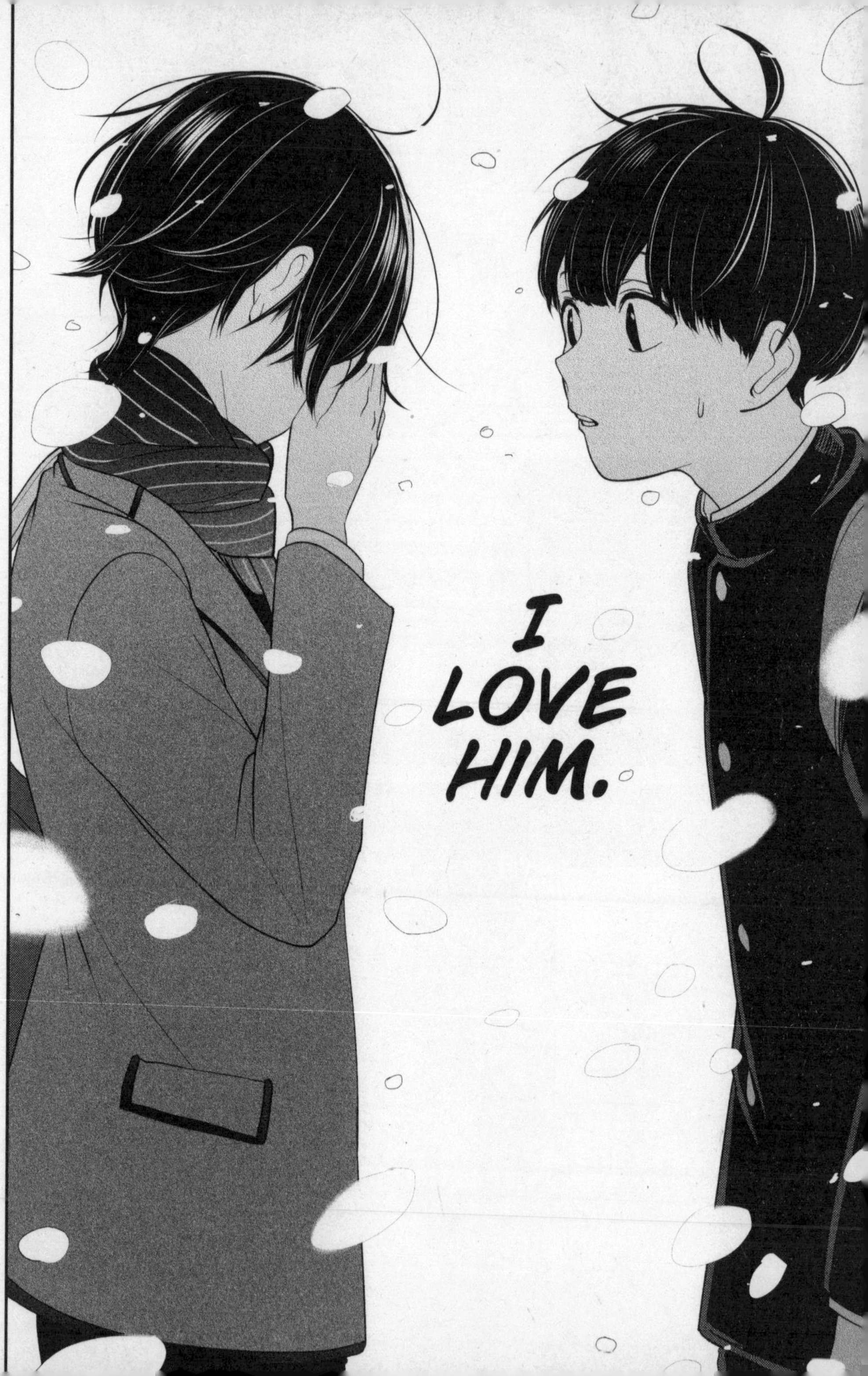
I LOVE HIM.

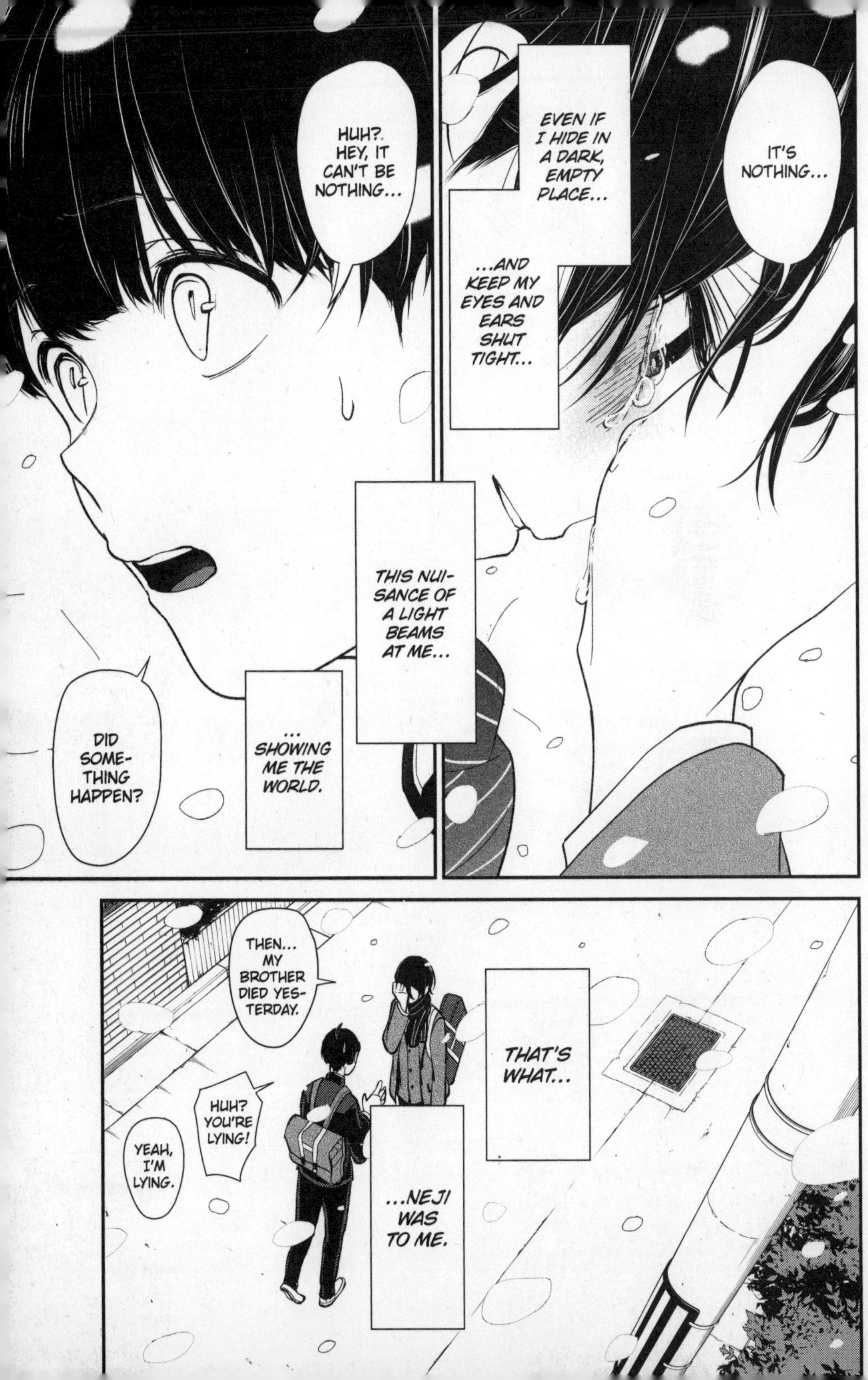
IT'S NOTHING...
EVEN IF I HIDE IN A DARK, EMPTY PLACE...
...AND KEEP MY EYES AND EARS SHUT TIGHT...
THIS NUI-SANCE OF A LIGHT BEAMS AT ME...
HUH? HEY, IT CAN'T BE NOTHING...
... SHOWING ME THE WORLD.
DID SOME-THING HAPPEN?
THAT'S WHAT...
...NEJI WAS TO ME.
THEN... MY BROTHER DIED YES-TERDAY.
HUH? YOU'RE LYING!
YEAH, I'M LYING.

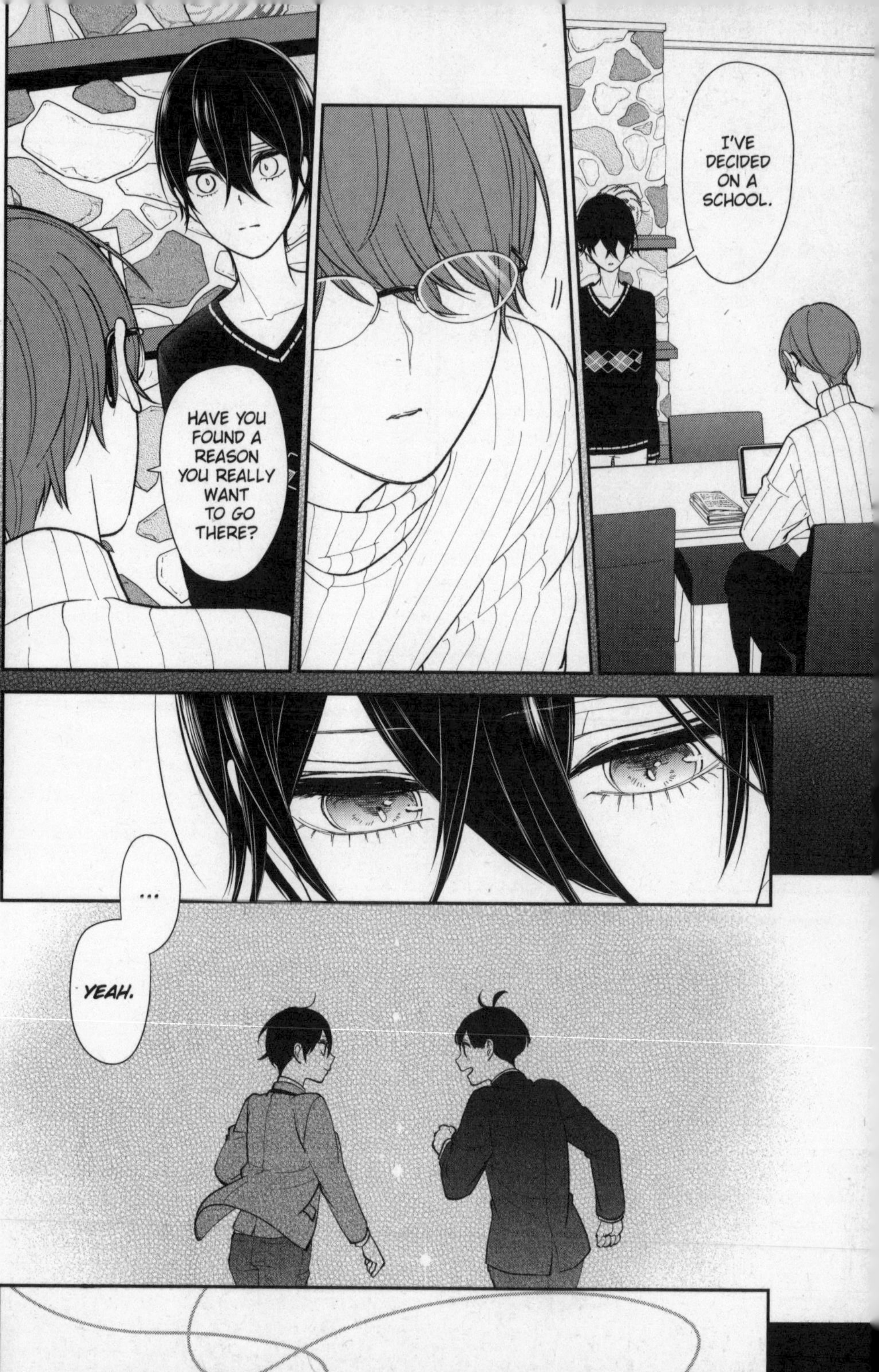

I'VE DECIDED ON A SCHOOL.
HAVE YOU FOUND A REASON YOU REALLY WANT TO GO THERE?
...
YEAH.

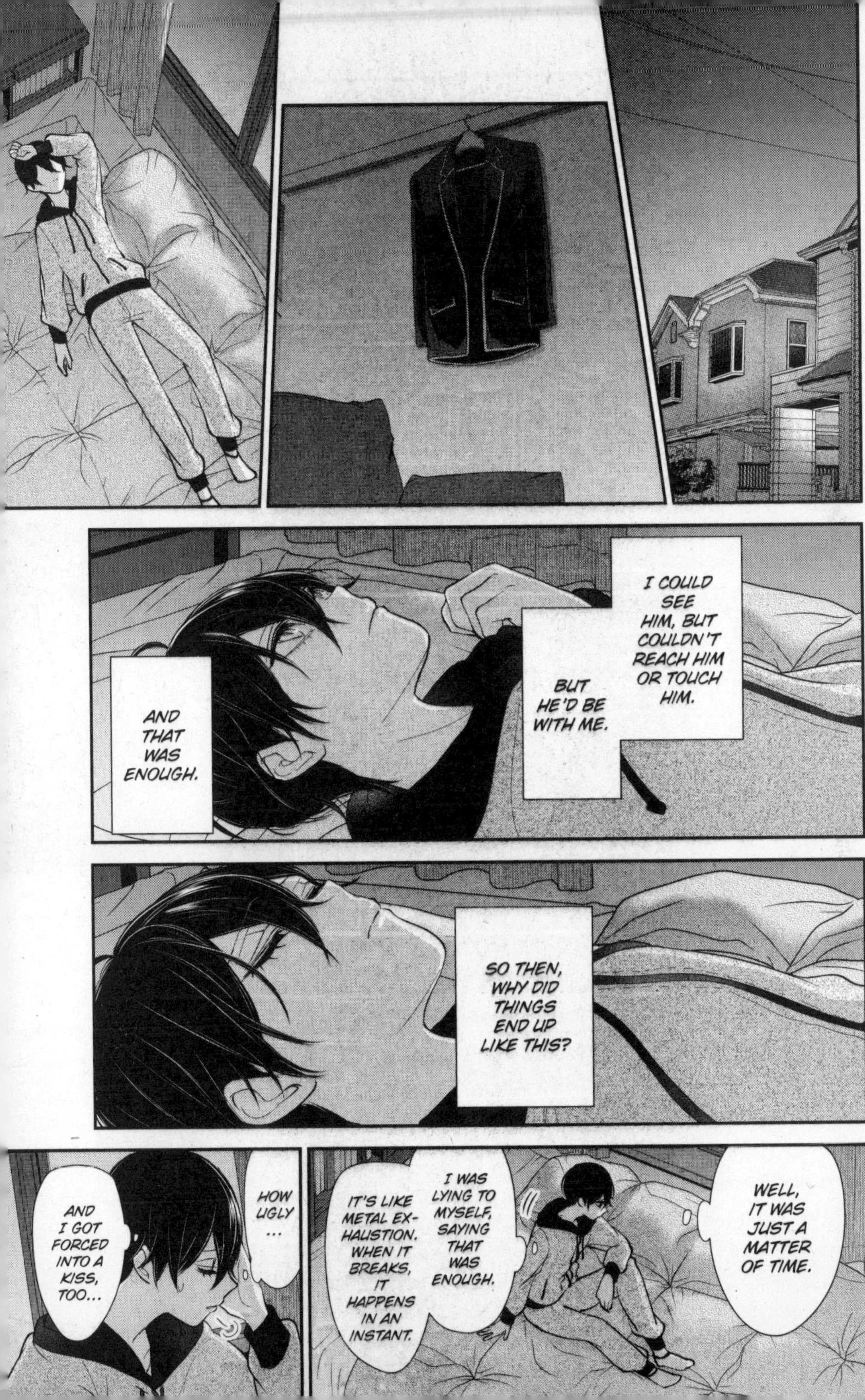
I COULD SEE HIM, BUT COULDN'T REACH HIM OR TOUCH HIM.
BUT HE'D BE WITH ME.
AND THAT WAS ENOUGH.
SO THEN, WHY DID THINGS END UP LIKE THIS?
WELL, IT WAS JUST A MATTER OF TIME.
I WAS LYING TO MYSELF, SAYING THAT WAS ENOUGH.
IT'S LIKE METAL EX-HAUSTION. WHEN IT BREAKS, IT HAPPENS IN AN INSTANT.
HOW UGLY...
AND I GOT FORCED INTO A KISS, TOO...

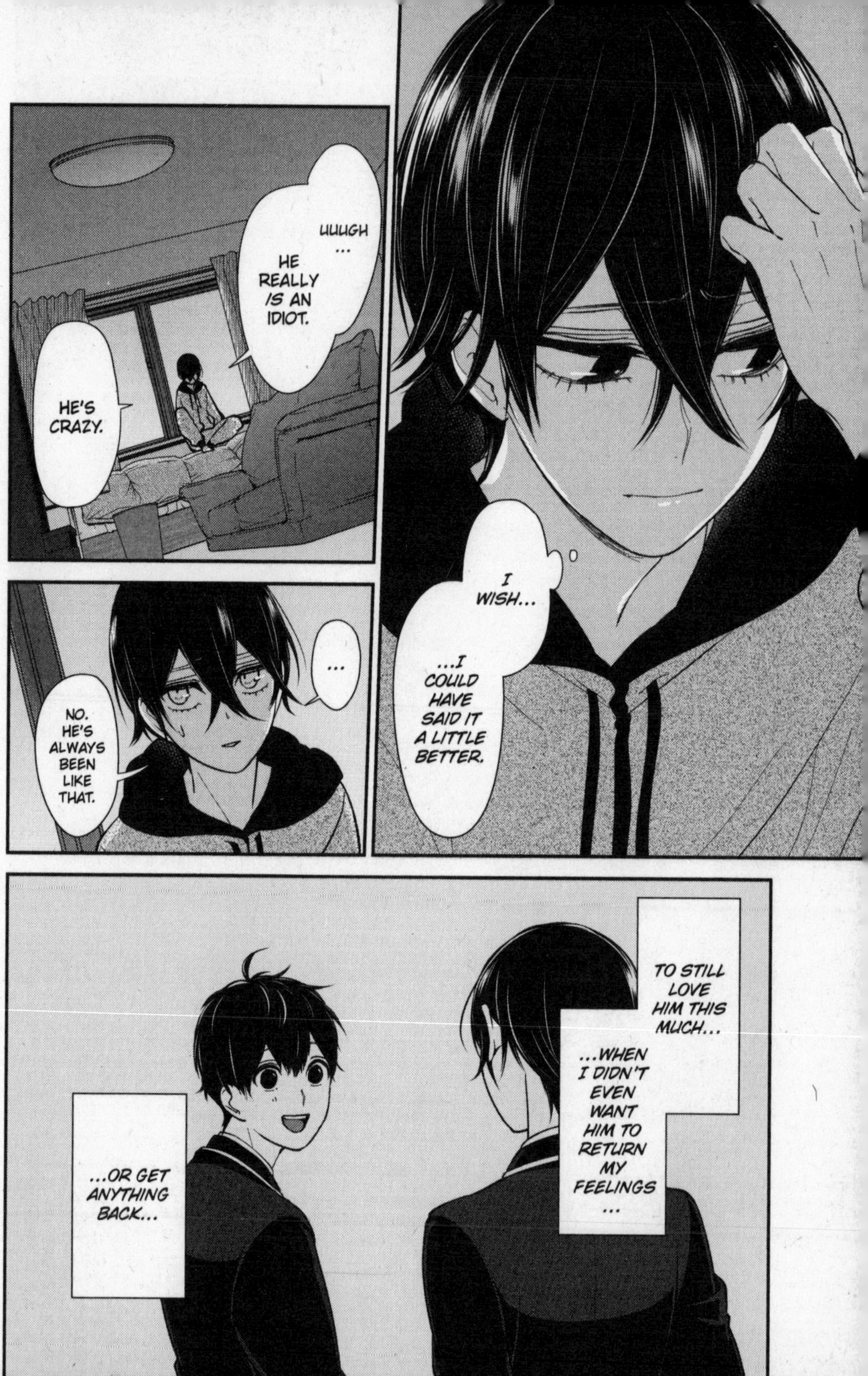
I WISH...
...I COULD HAVE SAID IT A LITTLE BETTER.
UUUGH...
HE REALLY IS AN IDIOT.
HE'S CRAZY.
...
NO. HE'S ALWAYS BEEN LIKE THAT.
TO STILL LOVE HIM THIS MUCH...
...WHEN I DIDN'T EVEN WANT HIM TO RETURN MY FEELINGS...
...OR GET ANYTHING BACK...

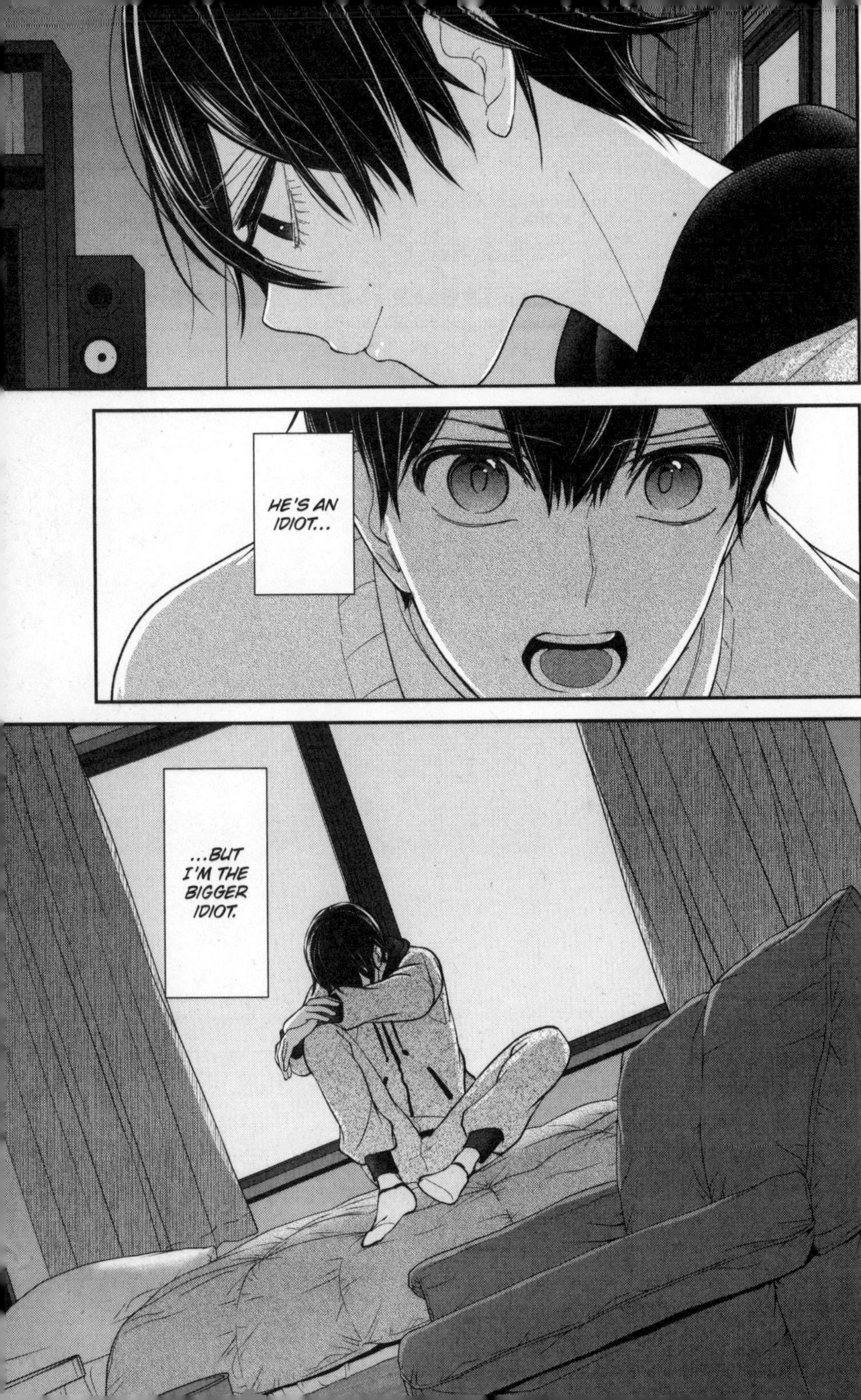
HE'S AN IDIOT...
...BUT I'M THE BIGGER IDIOT.

Love & Lies

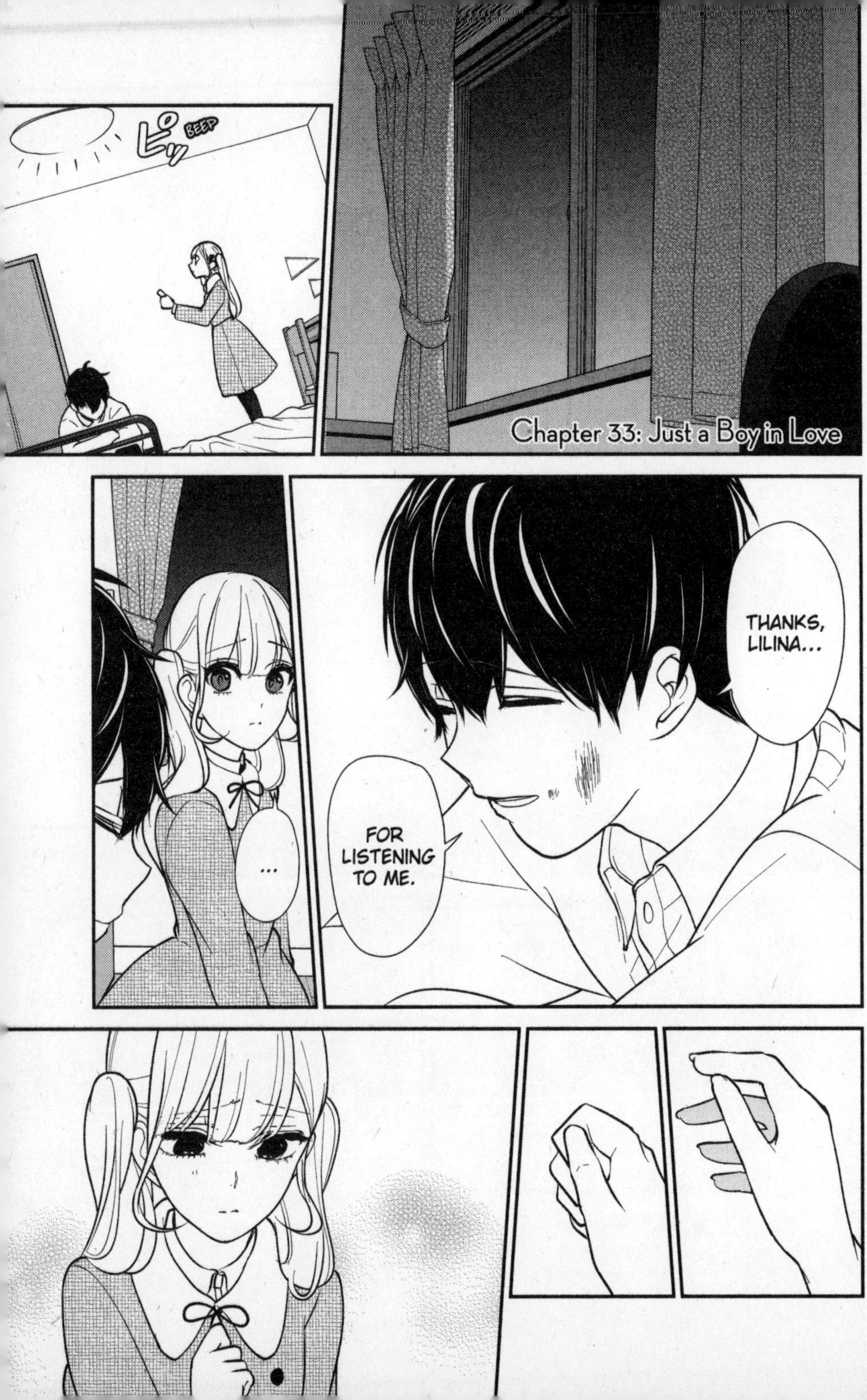
Chapter 33: Just a Boy in Love
ピッ BEEP
THANKS, LILINA...
FOR LISTENING TO ME.
...

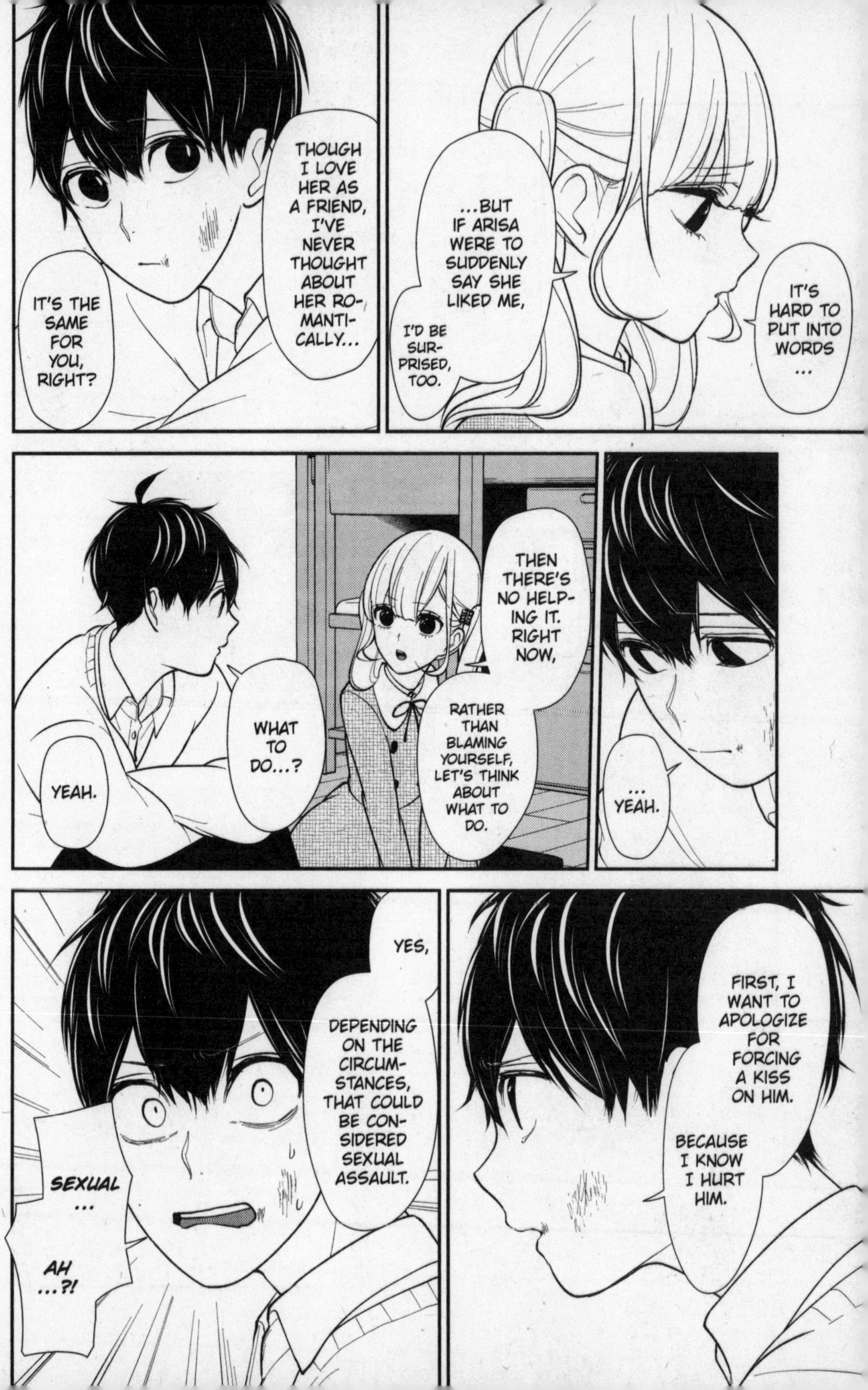
IT'S HARD TO PUT INTO WORDS ...
...BUT IF ARISA WERE TO SUDDENLY SAY SHE LIKED ME,
I'D BE SURPRISED, TOO.
THOUGH I LOVE HER AS A FRIEND, I'VE NEVER THOUGHT ABOUT HER ROMANTICALLY...
IT'S THE SAME FOR YOU, RIGHT?
... YEAH.
THEN THERE'S NO HELPING IT. RIGHT NOW,
RATHER THAN BLAMING YOURSELF, LET'S THINK ABOUT WHAT TO DO.
WHAT TO DO...?
YEAH.
FIRST, I WANT TO APOLOGIZE FOR FORCING A KISS ON HIM.
BECAUSE I KNOW I HURT HIM.
YES,
DEPENDING ON THE CIRCUMSTANCES, THAT COULD BE CONSIDERED SEXUAL ASSAULT.
SEXUAL ...
AH ...?!

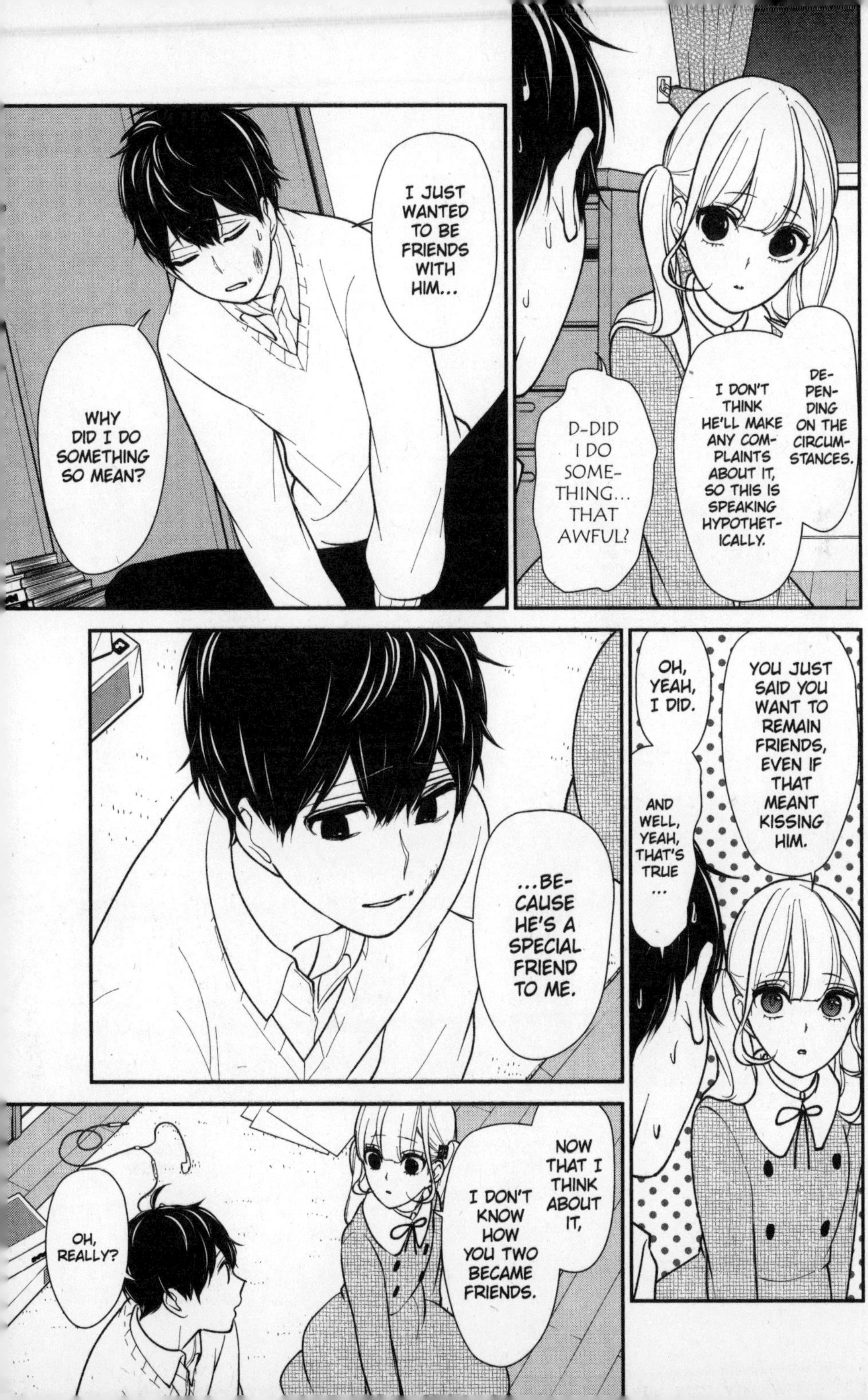
DE-PENDING ON THE CIRCUMSTANCES.
I DON'T THINK HE'LL MAKE ANY COMPLAINTS ABOUT IT, SO THIS IS SPEAKING HYPOTHETICALLY.
D-DID I DO SOMETHING... THAT AWFUL?
I JUST WANTED TO BE FRIENDS WITH HIM...
WHY DID I DO SOMETHING SO MEAN?
YOU JUST SAID YOU WANT TO REMAIN FRIENDS, EVEN IF THAT MEANT KISSING HIM.
OH, YEAH, I DID.
AND WELL, YEAH, THAT'S TRUE...
...BECAUSE HE'S A SPECIAL FRIEND TO ME.
NOW THAT I THINK ABOUT IT,
I DON'T KNOW HOW YOU TWO BECAME FRIENDS.
OH, REALLY?

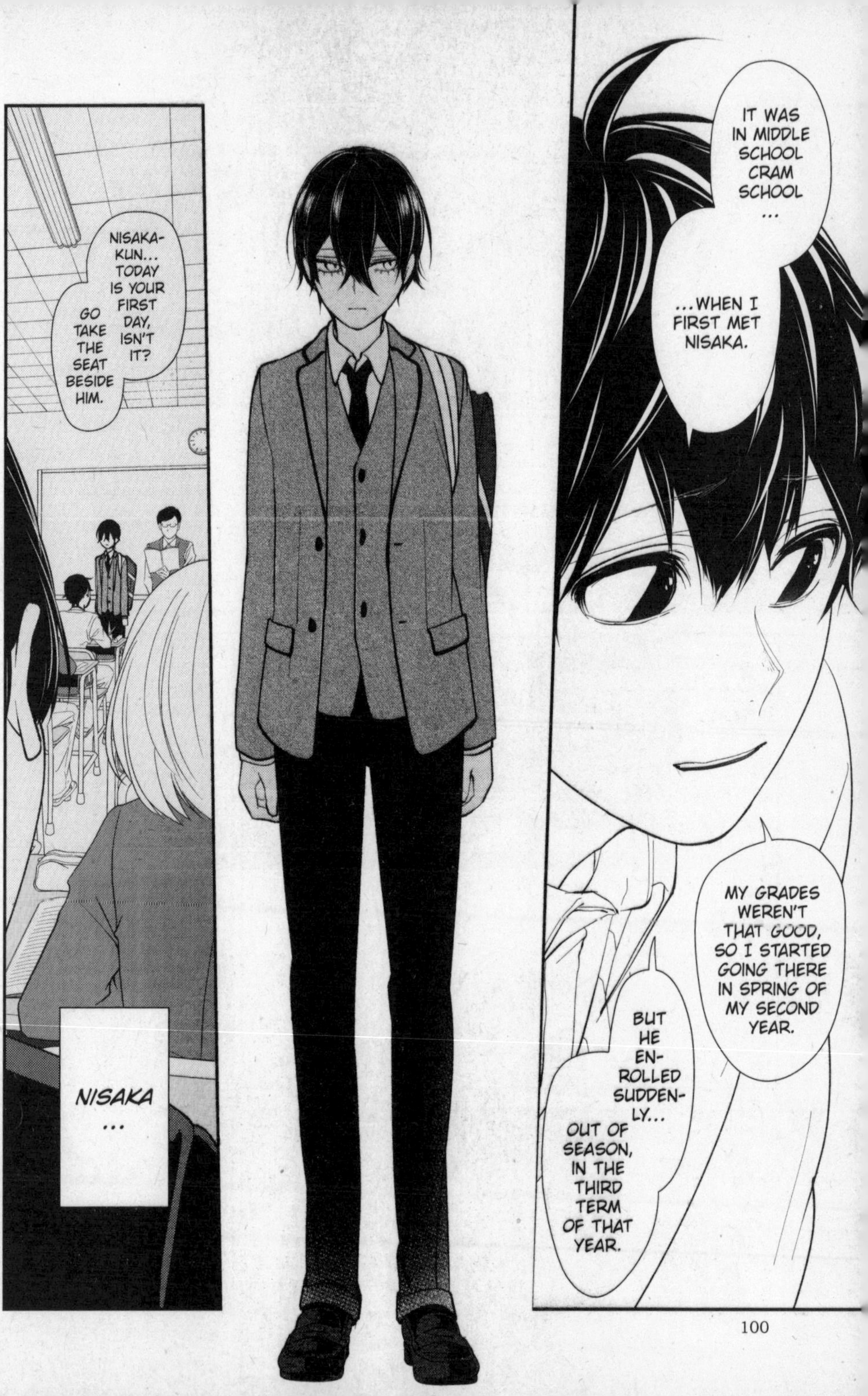
IT WAS IN MIDDLE SCHOOL CRAM SCHOOL ...
...WHEN I FIRST MET NISAKA.
MY GRADES WEREN'T THAT GOOD, SO I STARTED GOING THERE IN SPRING OF MY SECOND YEAR.
BUT HE EN-ROLLED SUDDEN-LY...
OUT OF SEASON, IN THE THIRD TERM OF THAT YEAR.
NISAKA-KUN... TODAY IS YOUR FIRST DAY, ISN'T IT?
GO TAKE THE SEAT BESIDE HIM.
NISAKA ...

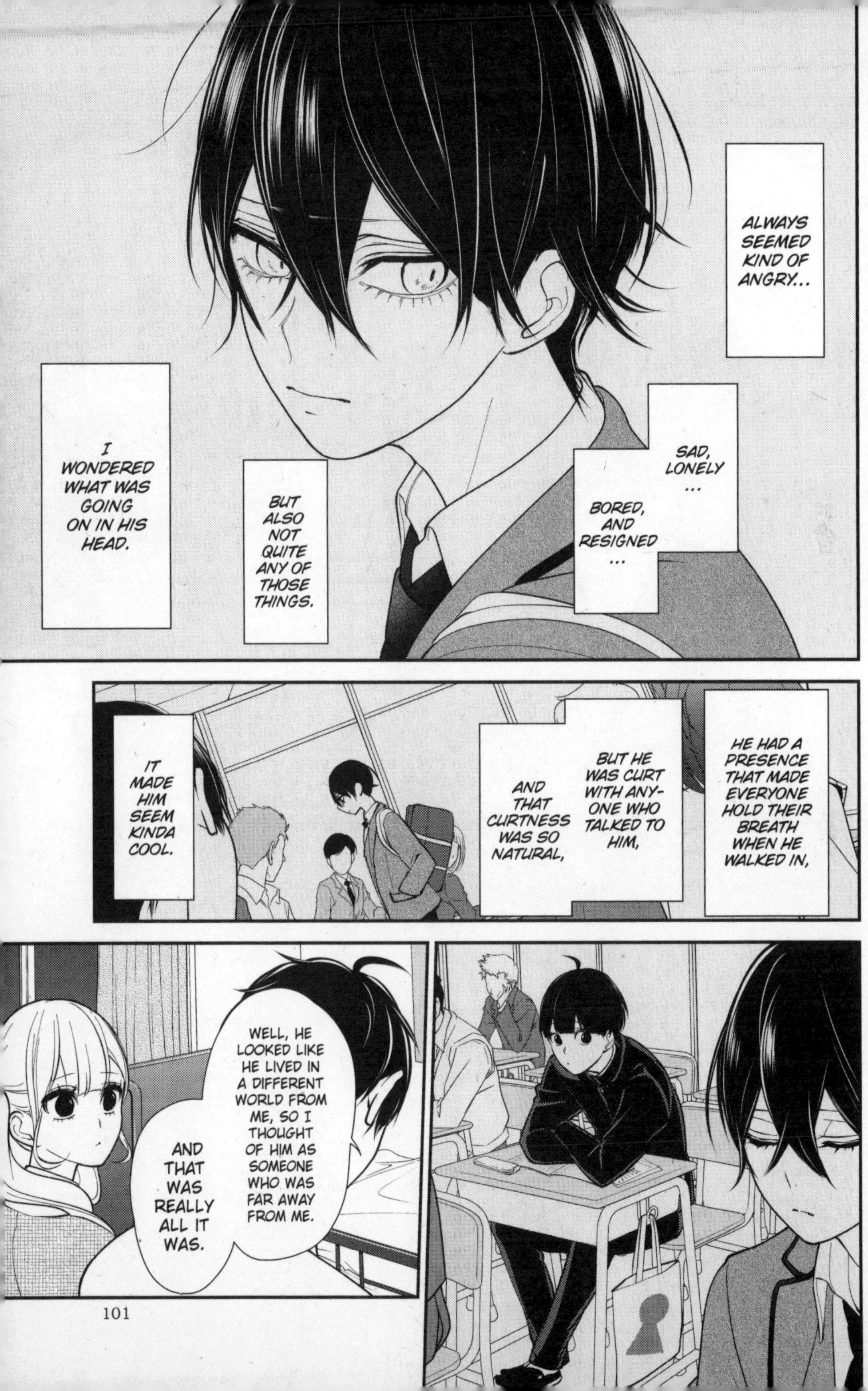
ALWAYS SEEMED KIND OF ANGRY...
SAD, LONELY ...
BORED, AND RESIGNED ...
BUT ALSO NOT QUITE ANY OF THOSE THINGS.
I WONDERED WHAT WAS GOING ON IN HIS HEAD.
HE HAD A PRESENCE THAT MADE EVERYONE HOLD THEIR BREATH WHEN HE WALKED IN,
BUT HE WAS CURT WITH ANY-ONE WHO TALKED TO HIM,
AND THAT CURTNESS WAS SO NATURAL,
IT MADE HIM SEEM KINDA COOL.
WELL, HE LOOKED LIKE HE LIVED IN A DIFFERENT WORLD FROM ME, SO I THOUGHT OF HIM AS SOMEONE WHO WAS FAR AWAY FROM ME.
AND THAT WAS REALLY ALL IT WAS.

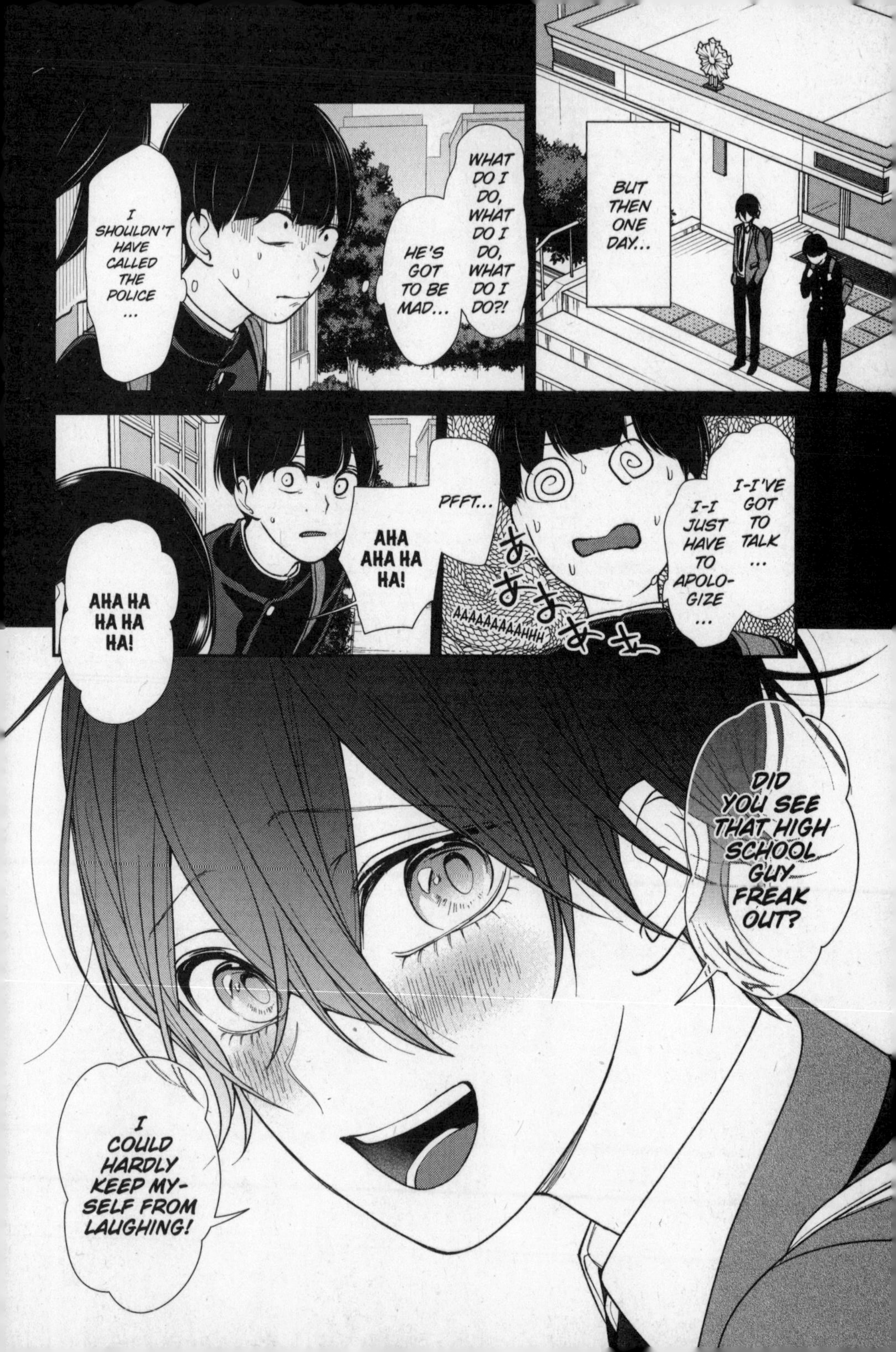
BUT THEN ONE DAY...
WHAT DO I DO, WHAT DO I DO, WHAT DO I DO?!
HE'S GOT TO BE MAD...
I SHOULDN'T HAVE CALLED THE POLICE...
I-I'VE GOT TO TALK...
I-I JUST HAVE TO APOLOGIZE...
AAAAAAAAAAHHH
PFFT...
AHA AHA HA HA!
AHA HA HA HA HA!
DID YOU SEE THAT HIGH SCHOOL GUY FREAK OUT?
I COULD HARDLY KEEP MY-SELF FROM LAUGHING!

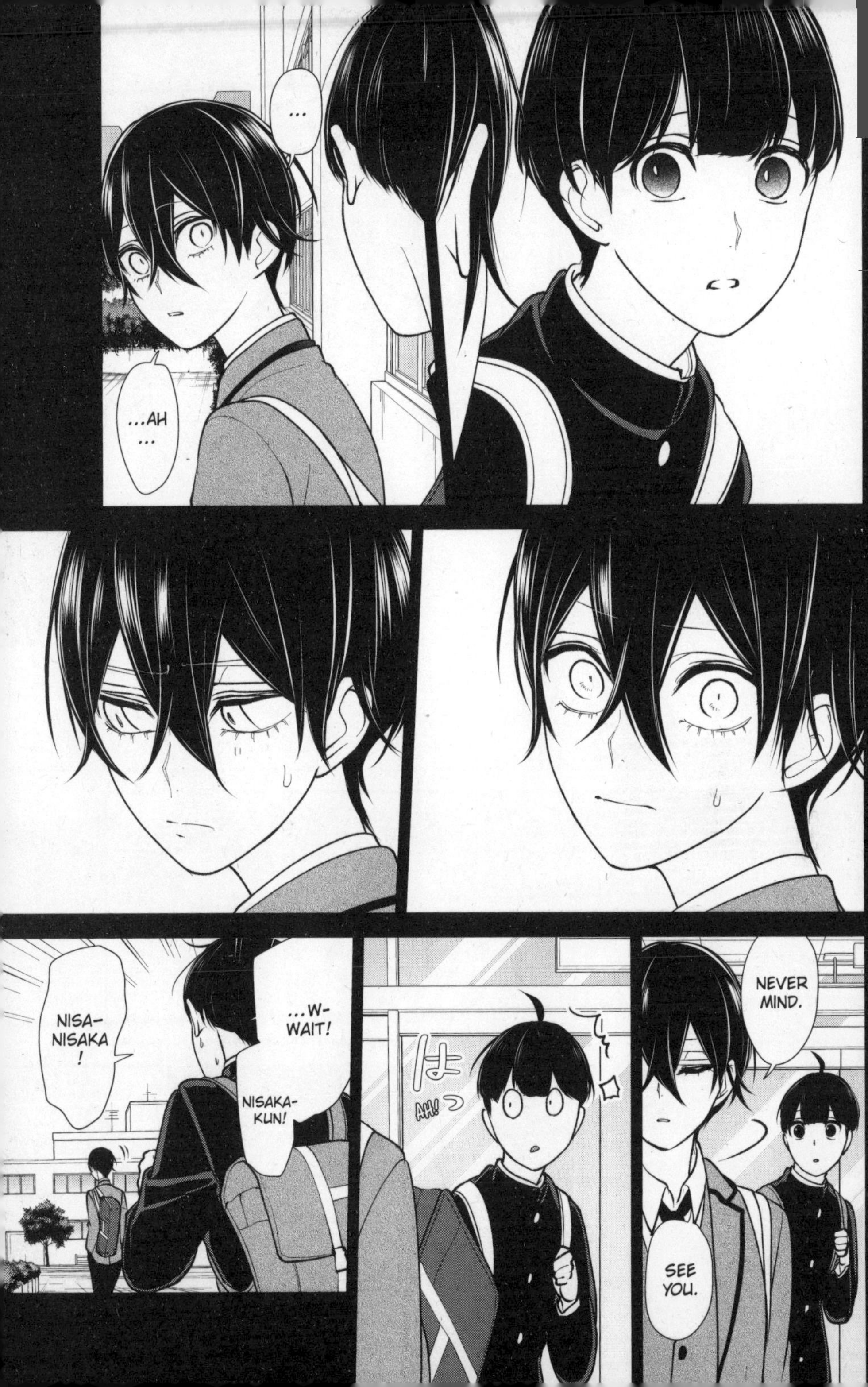
...
...AH ...
NEVER MIND.
SEE YOU.
はっ
AH!
...W- WAIT!
NISAKA-KUN!
NISA- NISAKA!

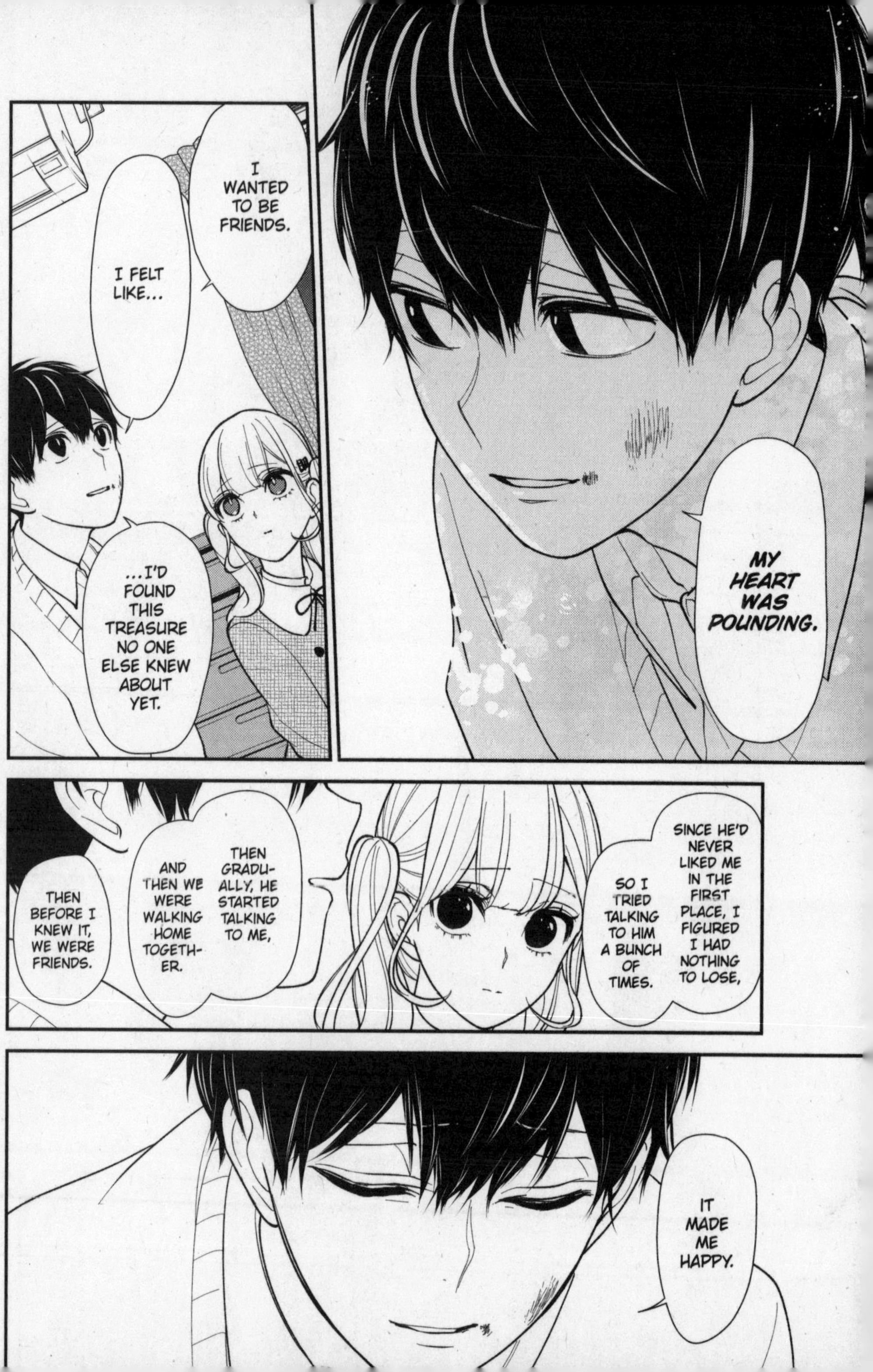
MY HEART WAS POUNDING.
I WANTED TO BE FRIENDS.
I FELT LIKE...
...I'D FOUND THIS TREASURE NO ONE ELSE KNEW ABOUT YET.
SINCE HE'D NEVER LIKED ME IN THE FIRST PLACE, I FIGURED I HAD NOTHING TO LOSE,
SO I TRIED TALKING TO HIM A BUNCH OF TIMES.
THEN GRADU-ALLY, HE STARTED TALKING TO ME,
AND THEN WE WERE WALKING HOME TOGETH-ER.
THEN BEFORE I KNEW IT, WE WERE FRIENDS.
IT MADE ME HAPPY.

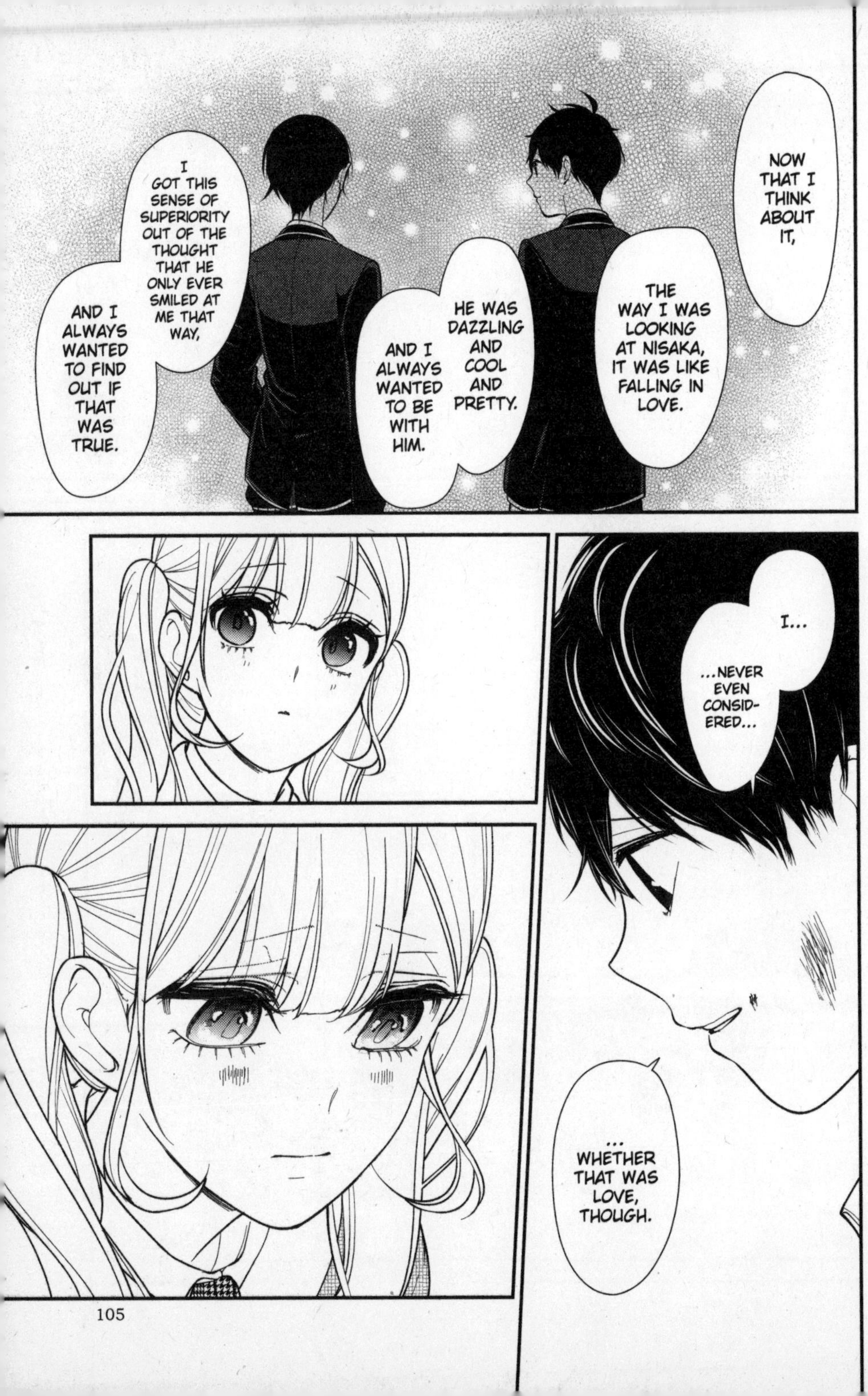
NOW THAT I THINK ABOUT IT,
THE WAY I WAS LOOKING AT NISAKA, IT WAS LIKE FALLING IN LOVE.
HE WAS DAZZLING AND COOL AND PRETTY.
AND I ALWAYS WANTED TO BE WITH HIM.
I GOT THIS SENSE OF SUPERIORITY OUT OF THE THOUGHT THAT HE ONLY EVER SMILED AT ME THAT WAY,
AND I ALWAYS WANTED TO FIND OUT IF THAT WAS TRUE.
I...
...NEVER EVEN CONSID-ERED...
...WHETHER THAT WAS LOVE, THOUGH.

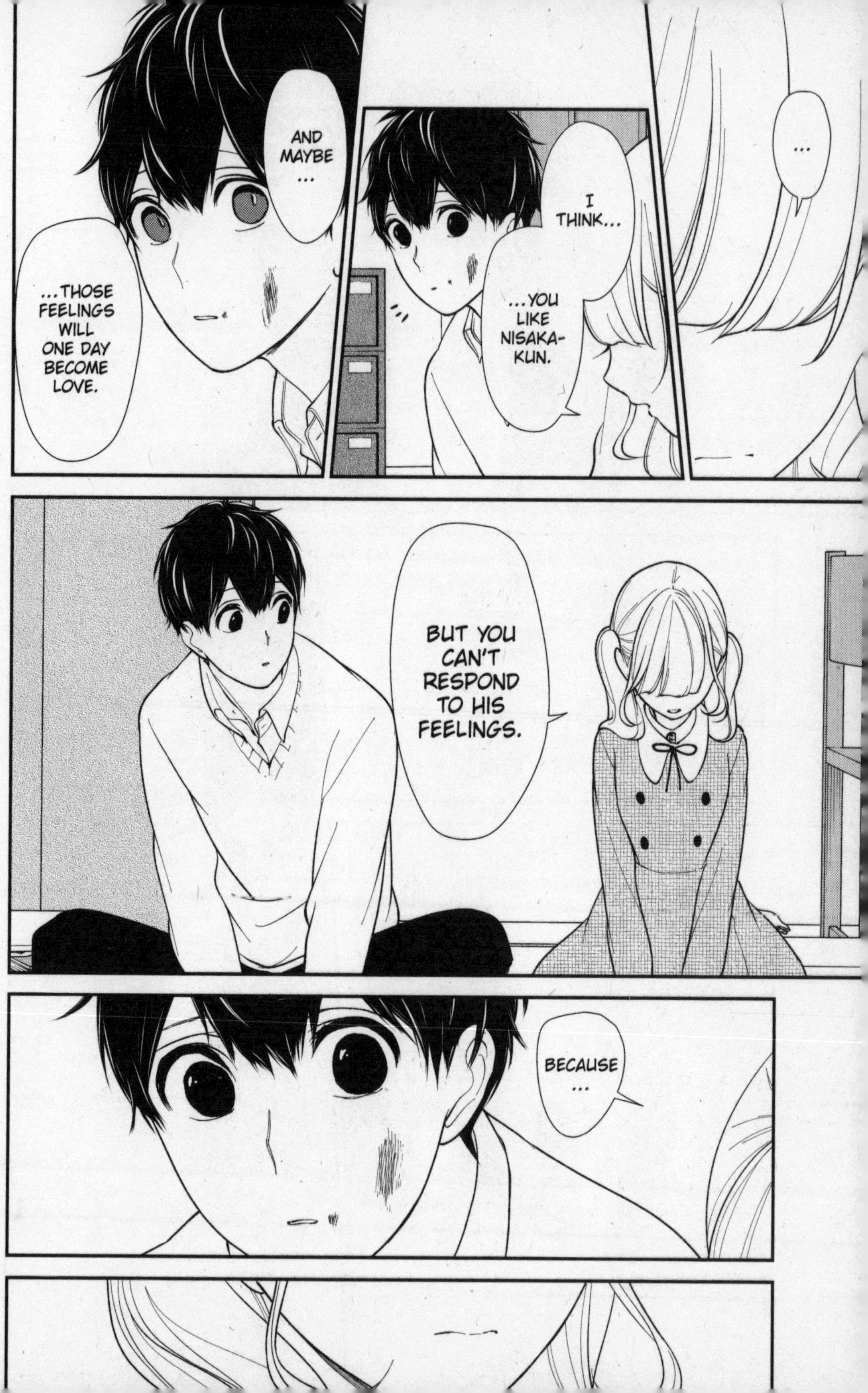
...
I THINK...
...YOU LIKE NISAKA-KUN.
AND MAYBE ...
...THOSE FEELINGS WILL ONE DAY BECOME LOVE.
BUT YOU CAN'T RESPOND TO HIS FEELINGS.
BECAUSE ...

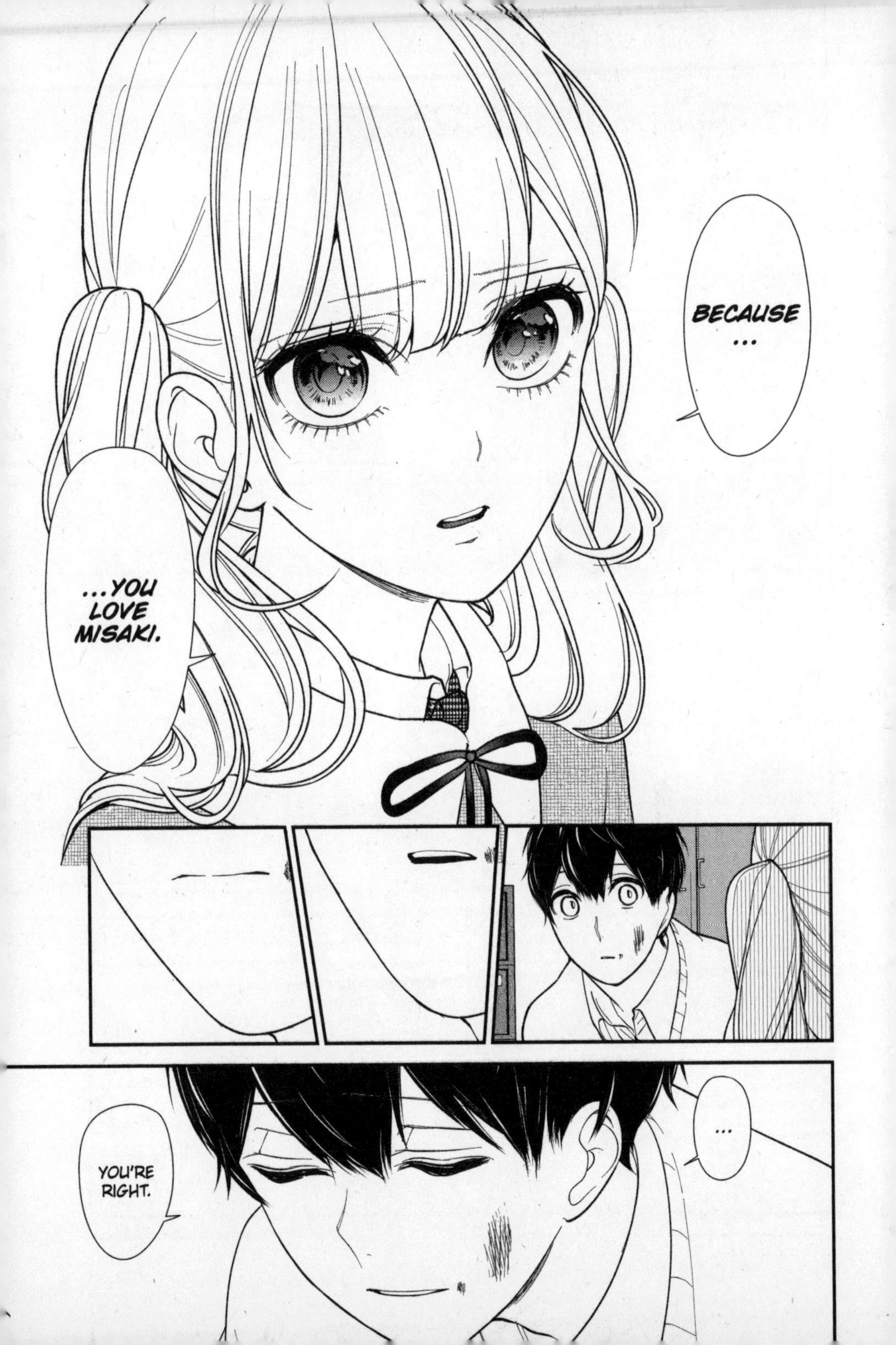
BECAUSE ...
...YOU LOVE MISAKI.
...
YOU'RE RIGHT.

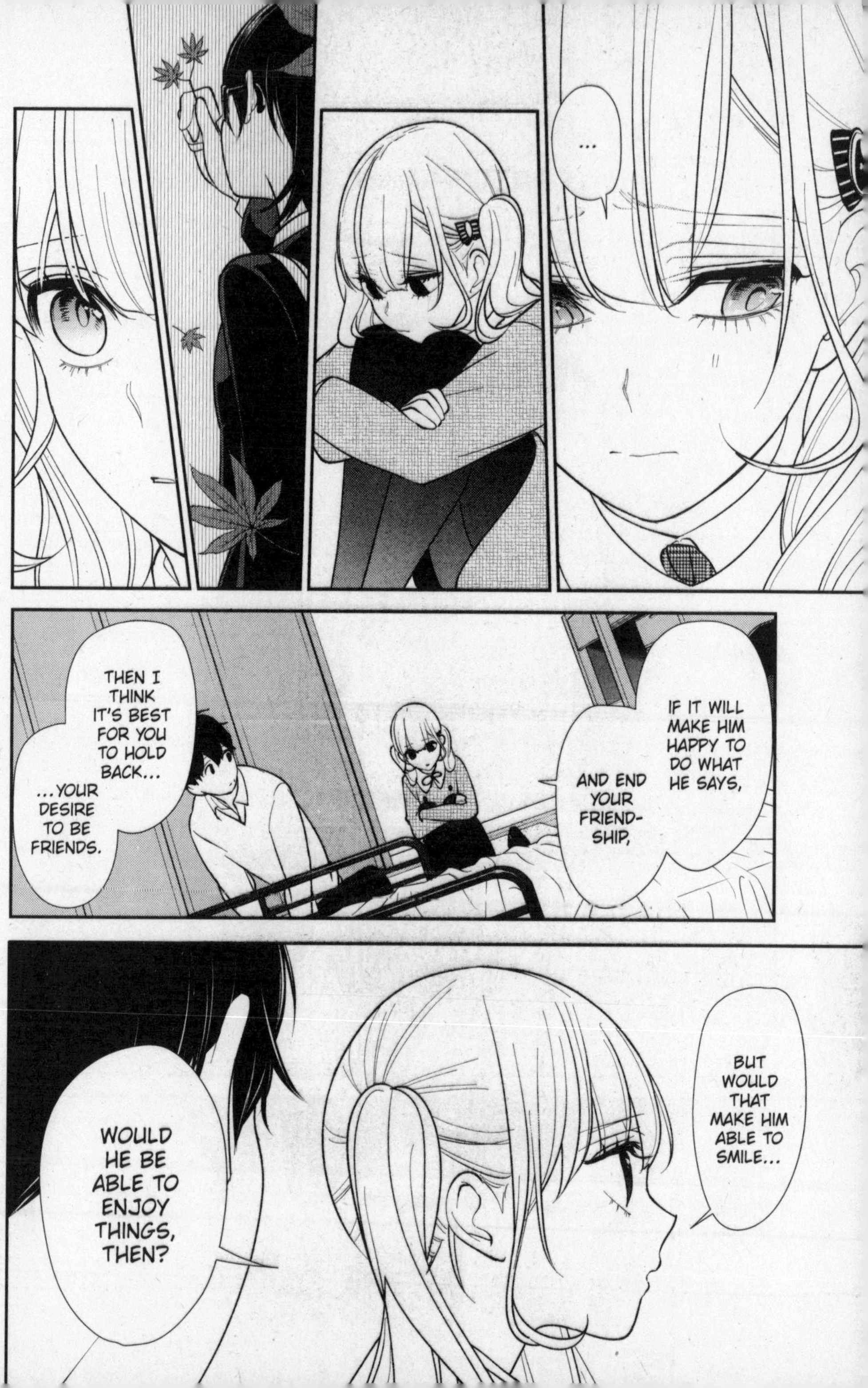
…
IF IT WILL MAKE HIM HAPPY TO DO WHAT HE SAYS,
AND END YOUR FRIENDSHIP,
THEN I THINK IT'S BEST FOR YOU TO HOLD BACK…
…YOUR DESIRE TO BE FRIENDS.
BUT WOULD THAT MAKE HIM ABLE TO SMILE…
WOULD HE BE ABLE TO ENJOY THINGS, THEN?

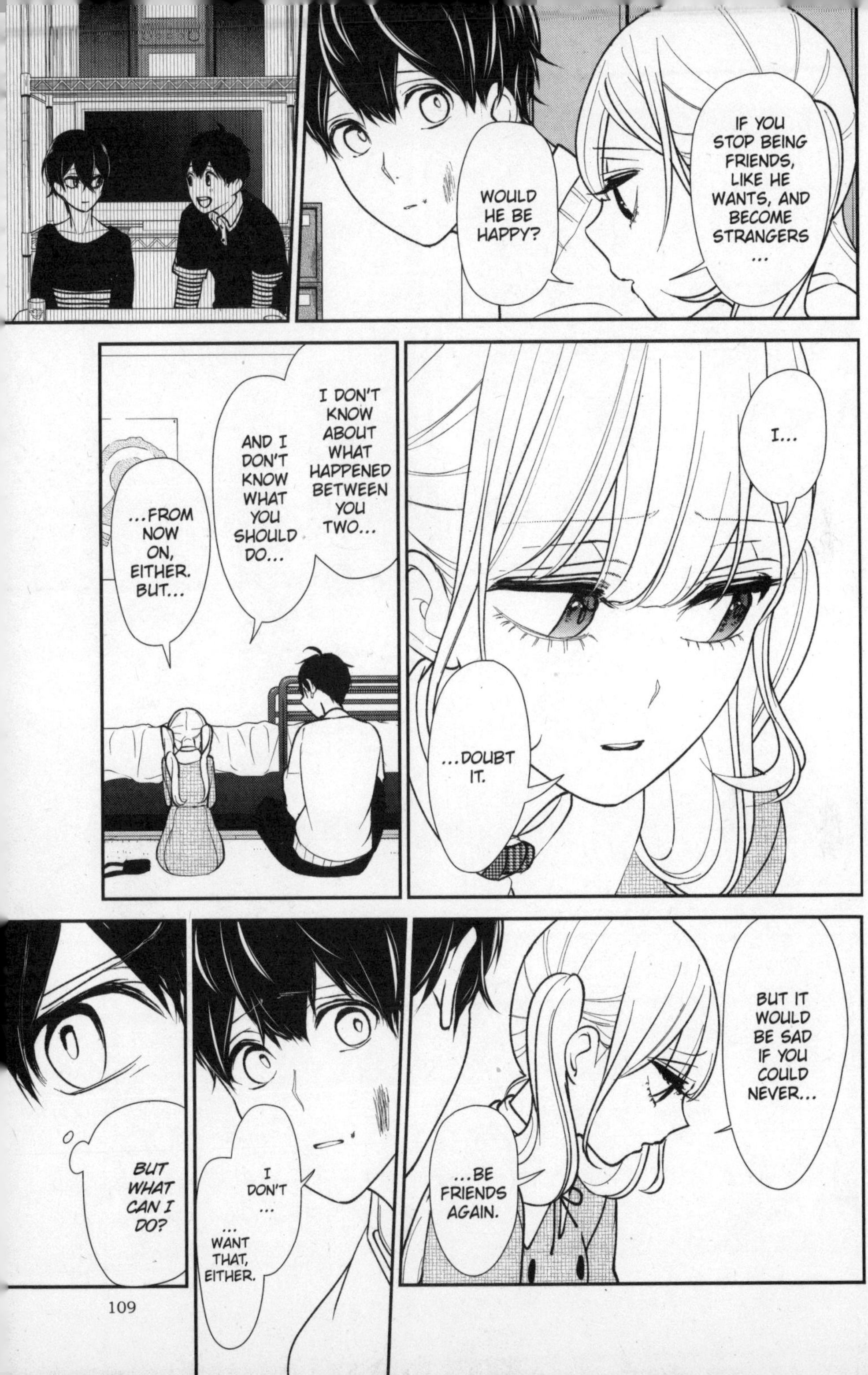
IF YOU STOP BEING FRIENDS, LIKE HE WANTS, AND BECOME STRANGERS...
WOULD HE BE HAPPY?
I...
...DOUBT IT.
I DON'T KNOW ABOUT WHAT HAPPENED BETWEEN YOU TWO...
AND I DON'T KNOW WHAT YOU SHOULD DO...
...FROM NOW ON, EITHER. BUT...
BUT IT WOULD BE SAD IF YOU COULD NEVER...
...BE FRIENDS AGAIN.
I DON'T ...
... WANT THAT, EITHER.
BUT WHAT CAN I DO?

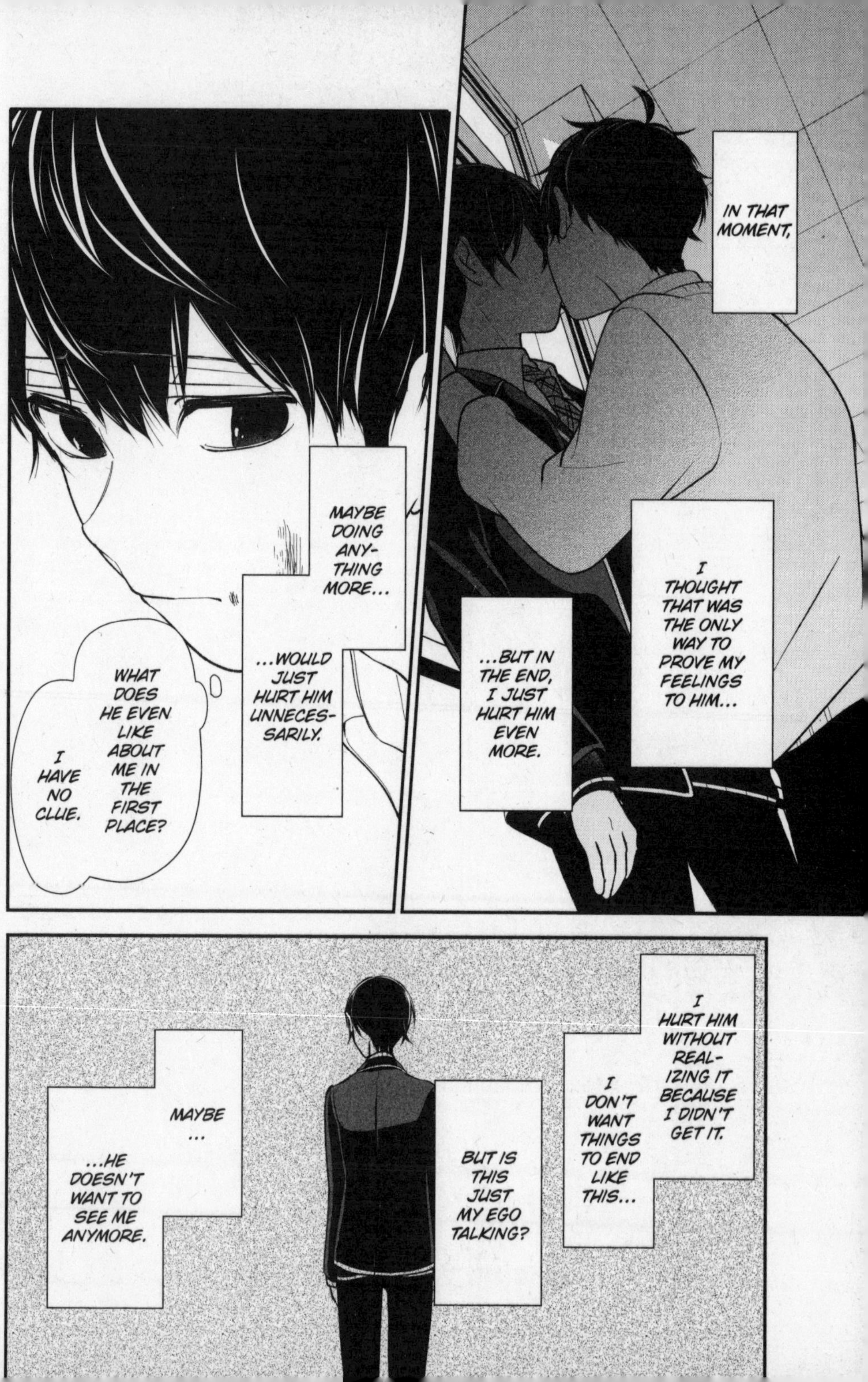
IN THAT MOMENT,
I THOUGHT THAT WAS THE ONLY WAY TO PROVE MY FEELINGS TO HIM...
...BUT IN THE END, I JUST HURT HIM EVEN MORE.
MAYBE DOING ANYTHING MORE...
...WOULD JUST HURT HIM UNNECESSARILY.
WHAT DOES HE EVEN LIKE ABOUT ME IN THE FIRST PLACE?
I HAVE NO CLUE.
I HURT HIM WITHOUT REALIZING IT BECAUSE I DIDN'T GET IT.
I DON'T WANT THINGS TO END LIKE THIS...
BUT IS THIS JUST MY EGO TALKING?
MAYBE...
...HE DOESN'T WANT TO SEE ME ANYMORE.

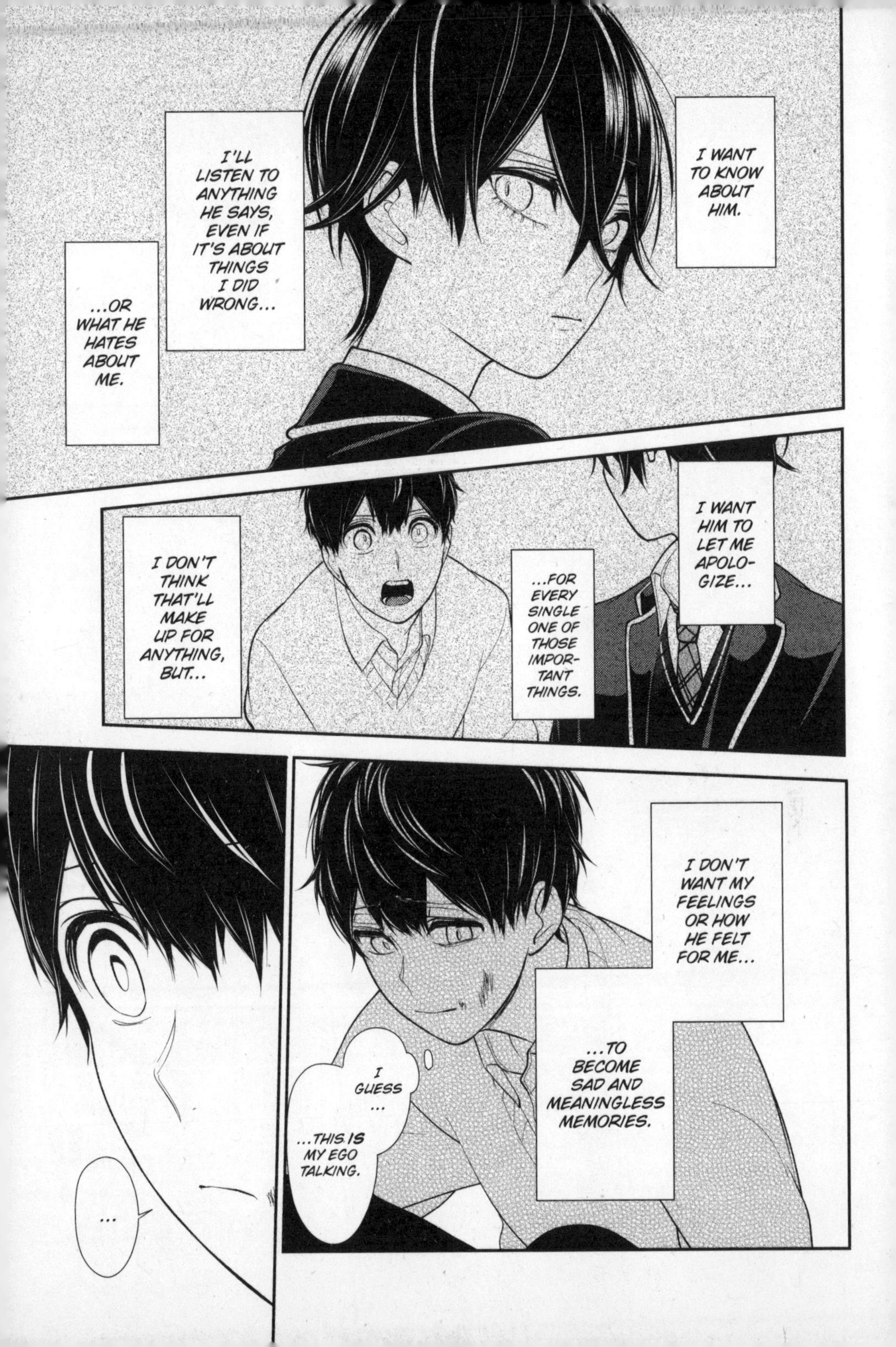
I WANT TO KNOW ABOUT HIM.
I'LL LISTEN TO ANYTHING HE SAYS, EVEN IF IT'S ABOUT THINGS I DID WRONG...
...OR WHAT HE HATES ABOUT ME.
I WANT HIM TO LET ME APOLOGIZE...
...FOR EVERY SINGLE ONE OF THOSE IMPORTANT THINGS.
I DON'T THINK THAT'LL MAKE UP FOR ANYTHING, BUT...
I DON'T WANT MY FEELINGS OR HOW HE FELT FOR ME...
...TO BECOME SAD AND MEANINGLESS MEMORIES.
I GUESS...
...THIS IS MY EGO TALKING.
...

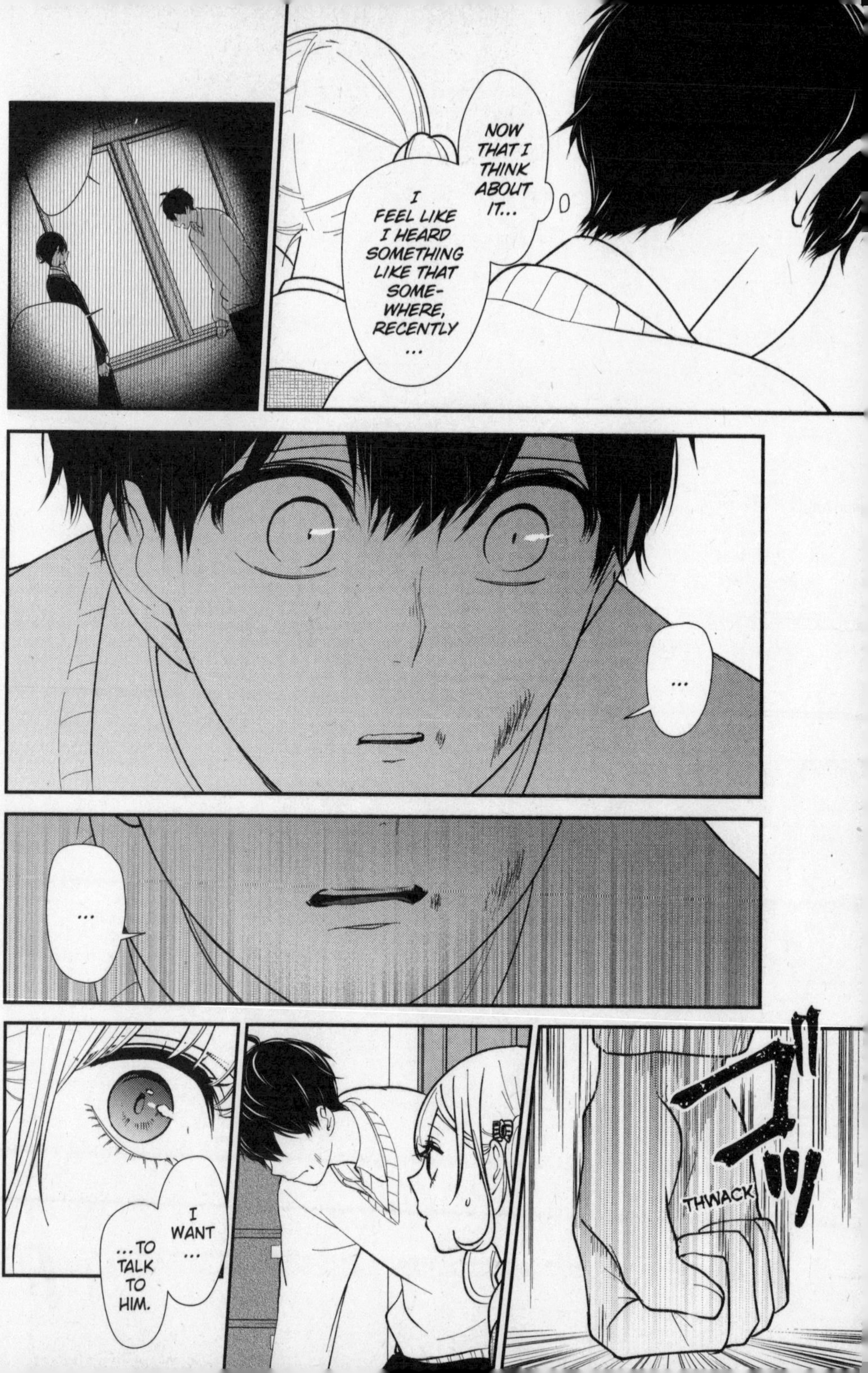
NOW THAT I THINK ABOUT IT...
I FEEL LIKE I HEARD SOMETHING LIKE THAT SOME-WHERE, RECENTLY...
...
...
ゴッ
THWACK
I WANT...
...TO TALK TO HIM.

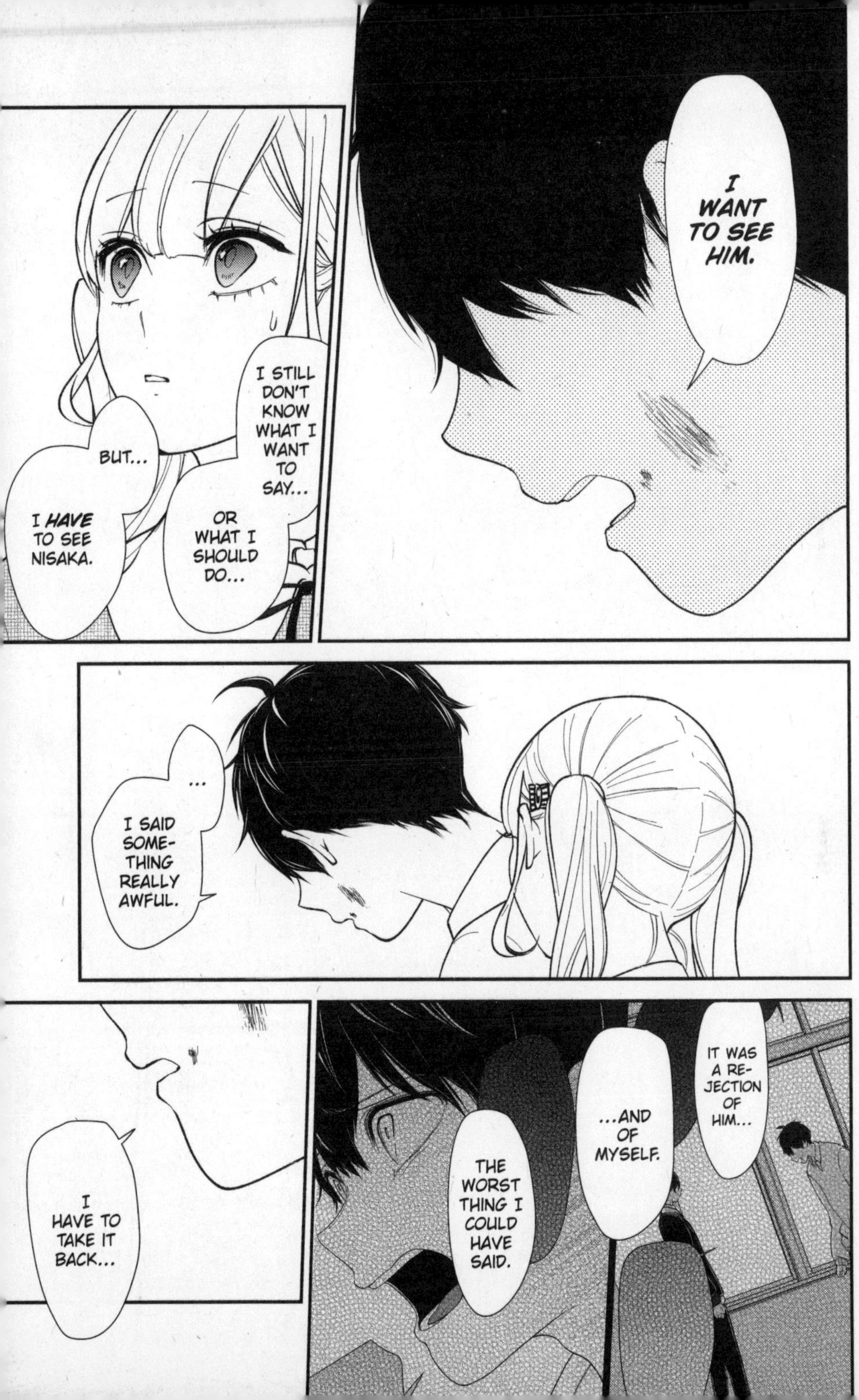
I WANT TO SEE HIM.
I STILL DON'T KNOW WHAT I WANT TO SAY...
OR WHAT I SHOULD DO...
BUT...
I *HAVE* TO SEE NISAKA.
...
I SAID SOME-THING REALLY AWFUL.
IT WAS A RE-JECTION OF HIM...
...AND OF MYSELF.
THE WORST THING I COULD HAVE SAID.
I HAVE TO TAKE IT BACK...

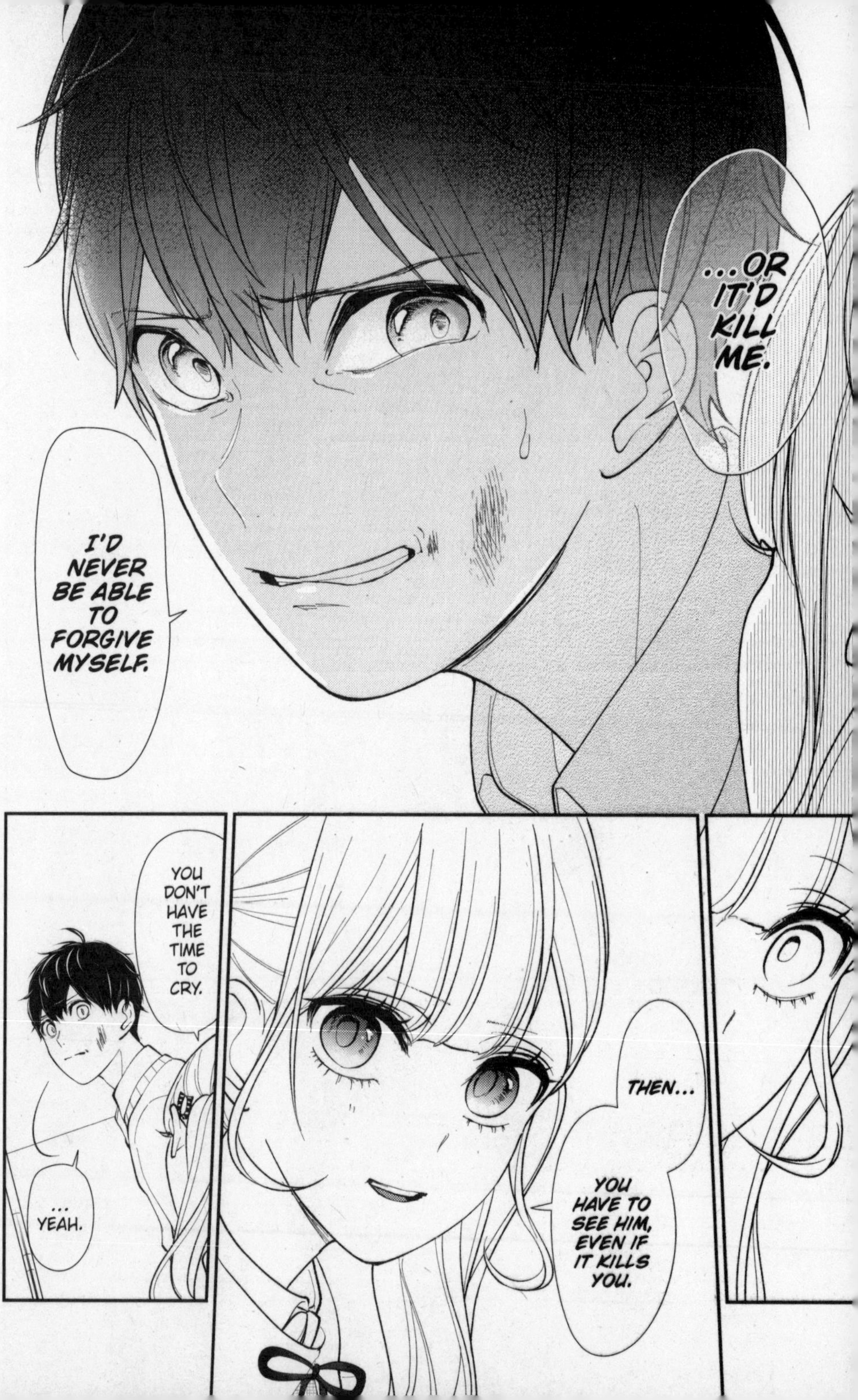
...OR IT'D KILL ME.
I'D NEVER BE ABLE TO FORGIVE MYSELF.
THEN...
YOU HAVE TO SEE HIM, EVEN IF IT KILLS YOU.
YOU DON'T HAVE THE TIME TO CRY.
...YEAH.

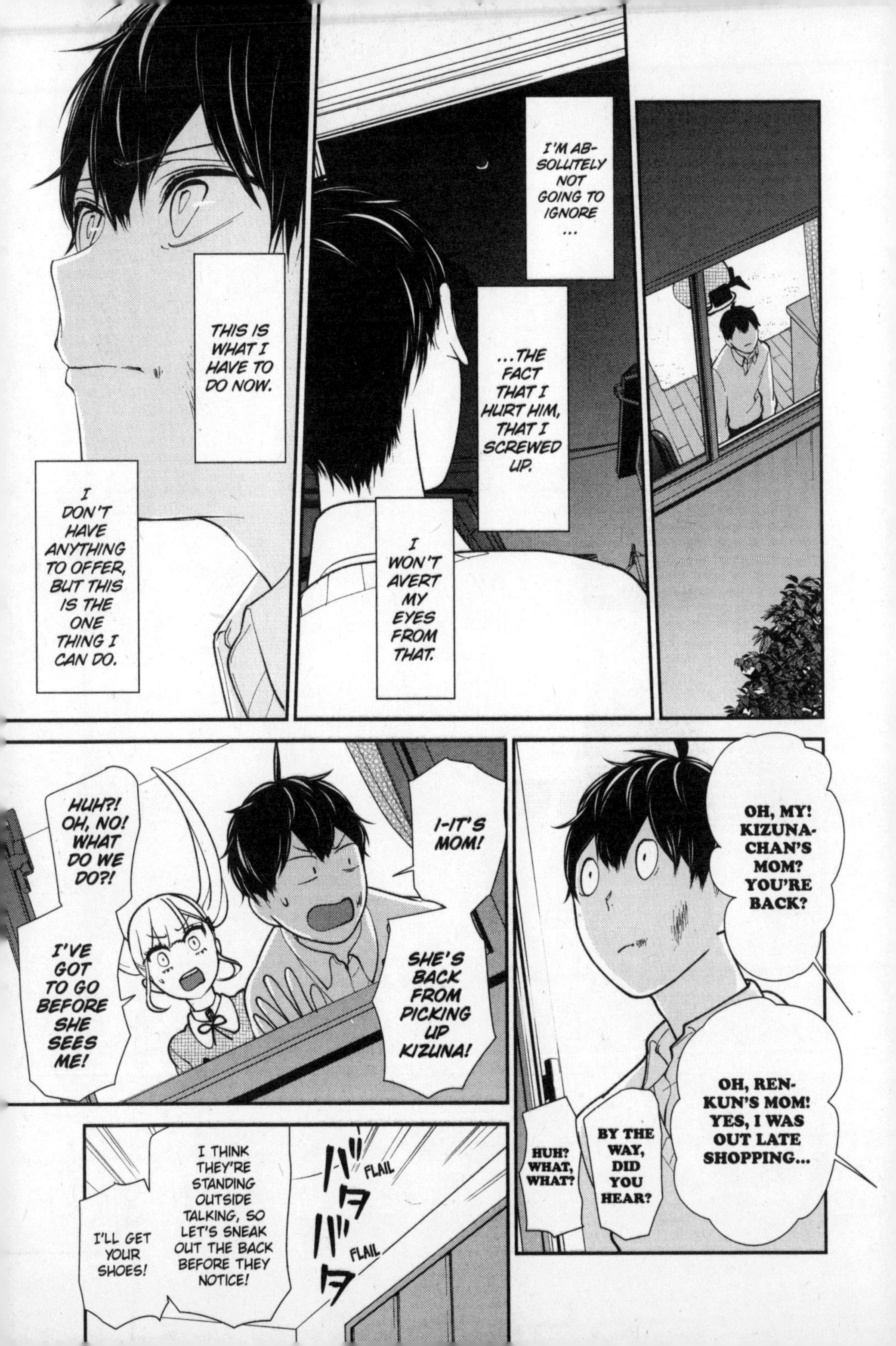
I'M AB-SOLUTELY NOT GOING TO IGNORE ...
...THE FACT THAT I HURT HIM, THAT I SCREWED UP.
I WON'T AVERT MY EYES FROM THAT.
THIS IS WHAT I HAVE TO DO NOW.
I DON'T HAVE ANYTHING TO OFFER, BUT THIS IS THE ONE THING I CAN DO.
OH, MY! KIZUNA-CHAN'S MOM? YOU'RE BACK?
OH, REN-KUN'S MOM! YES, I WAS OUT LATE SHOPPING...
BY THE WAY, DID YOU HEAR?
HUH? WHAT, WHAT?
I-IT'S MOM!
SHE'S BACK FROM PICKING UP KIZUNA!
HUH?! OH, NO! WHAT DO WE DO?!
I'VE GOT TO GO BEFORE SHE SEES ME!
バタ FLAIL
バタ FLAIL
I THINK THEY'RE STANDING OUTSIDE TALKING, SO LET'S SNEAK OUT THE BACK BEFORE THEY NOTICE!
I'LL GET YOUR SHOES!

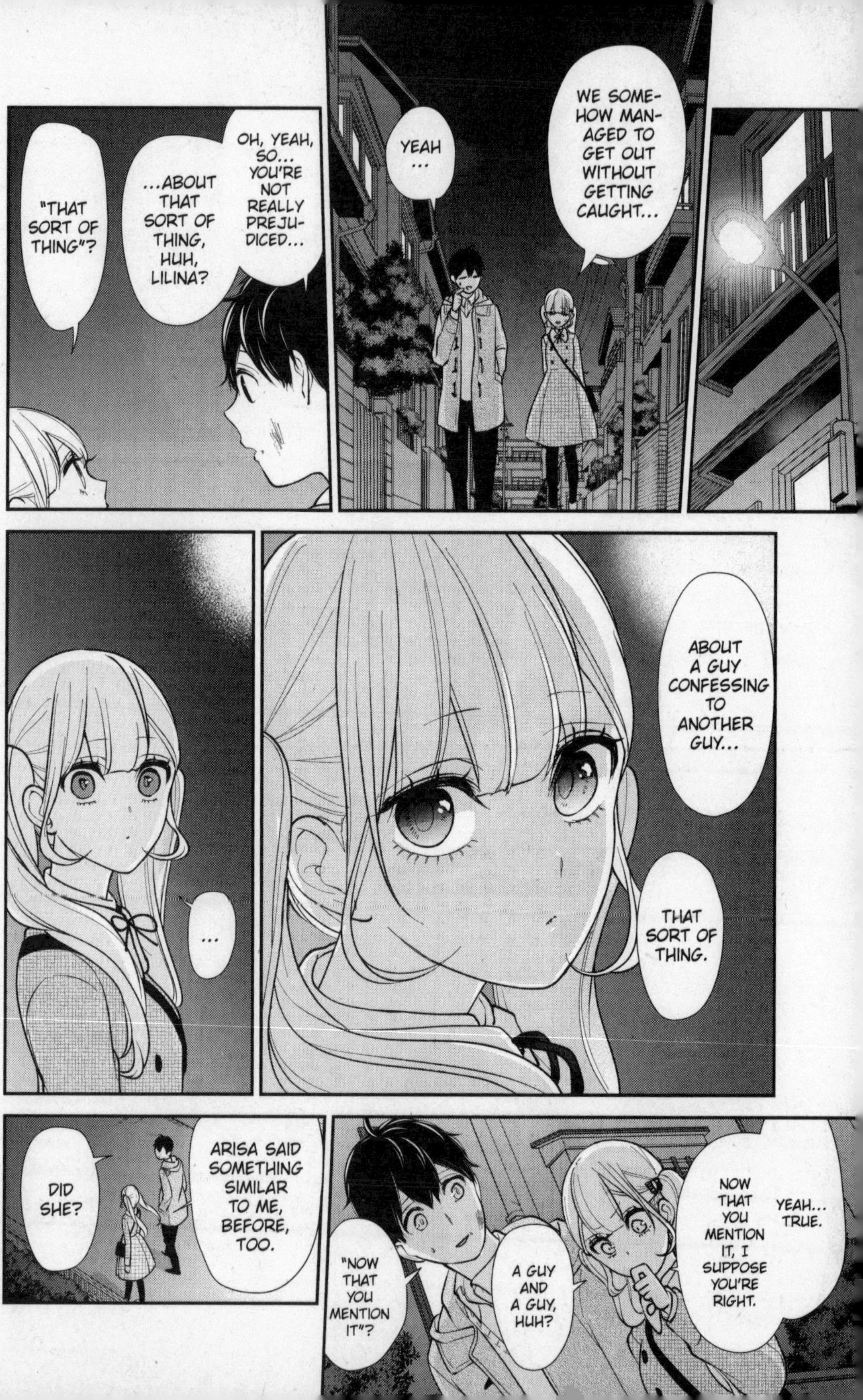
WE SOMEHOW MANAGED TO GET OUT WITHOUT GETTING CAUGHT...
YEAH...
OH, YEAH, SO... YOU'RE NOT REALLY PREJUDICED...
...ABOUT THAT SORT OF THING, HUH, LILINA?
"THAT SORT OF THING"?
ABOUT A GUY CONFESSING TO ANOTHER GUY...
THAT SORT OF THING.
...
YEAH... TRUE.
NOW THAT YOU MENTION IT, I SUPPOSE YOU'RE RIGHT.
A GUY AND A GUY, HUH?
"NOW THAT YOU MENTION IT"?
ARISA SAID SOMETHING SIMILAR TO ME, BEFORE, TOO.
DID SHE?

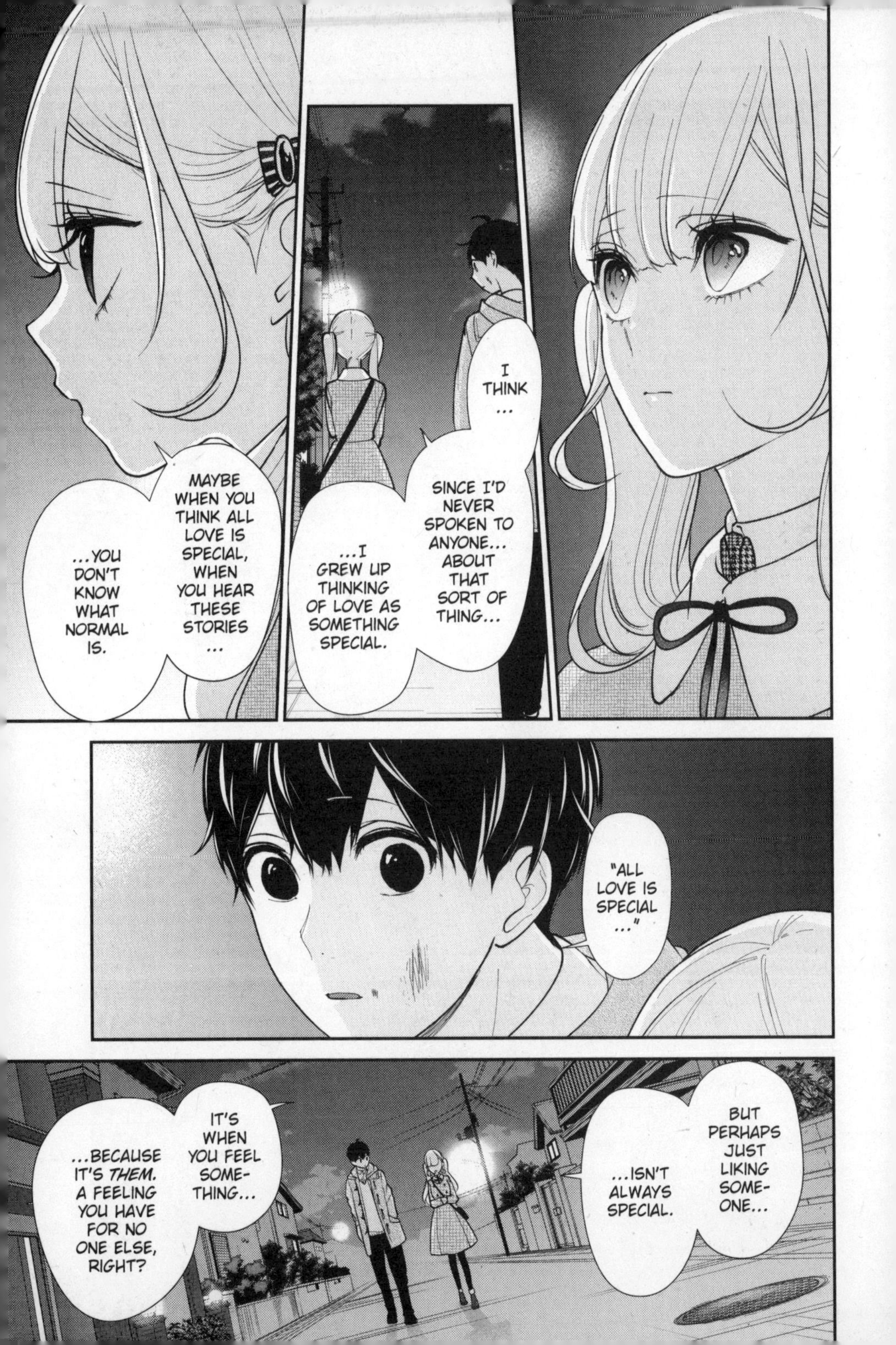
I THINK...
SINCE I'D NEVER SPOKEN TO ANYONE... ABOUT THAT SORT OF THING...
...I GREW UP THINKING OF LOVE AS SOMETHING SPECIAL.
MAYBE WHEN YOU THINK ALL LOVE IS SPECIAL, WHEN YOU HEAR THESE STORIES...
...YOU DON'T KNOW WHAT NORMAL IS.
"ALL LOVE IS SPECIAL..."
BUT PERHAPS JUST LIKING SOME-ONE...
...ISN'T ALWAYS SPECIAL.
IT'S WHEN YOU FEEL SOME-THING...
...BECAUSE IT'S *THEM*. A FEELING YOU HAVE FOR NO ONE ELSE, RIGHT?

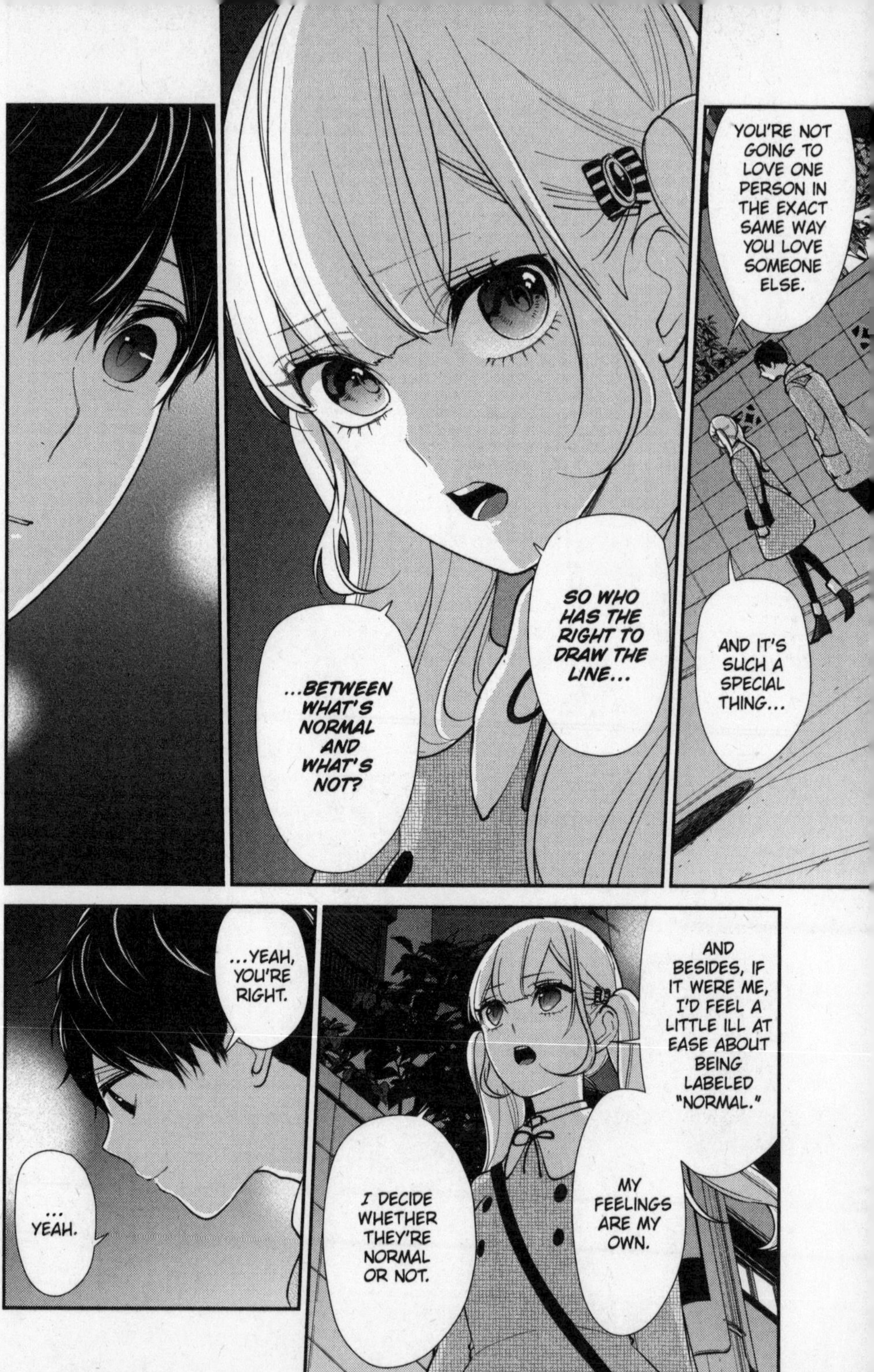
YOU'RE NOT GOING TO LOVE ONE PERSON IN THE EXACT SAME WAY YOU LOVE SOMEONE ELSE.
AND IT'S SUCH A SPECIAL THING...
SO WHO HAS THE RIGHT TO DRAW THE LINE...
...BETWEEN WHAT'S NORMAL AND WHAT'S NOT?
AND BESIDES, IF IT WERE ME, I'D FEEL A LITTLE ILL AT EASE ABOUT BEING LABELED "NORMAL."
MY FEELINGS ARE MY OWN.
I DECIDE WHETHER THEY'RE NORMAL OR NOT.
...YEAH, YOU'RE RIGHT.
... YEAH.

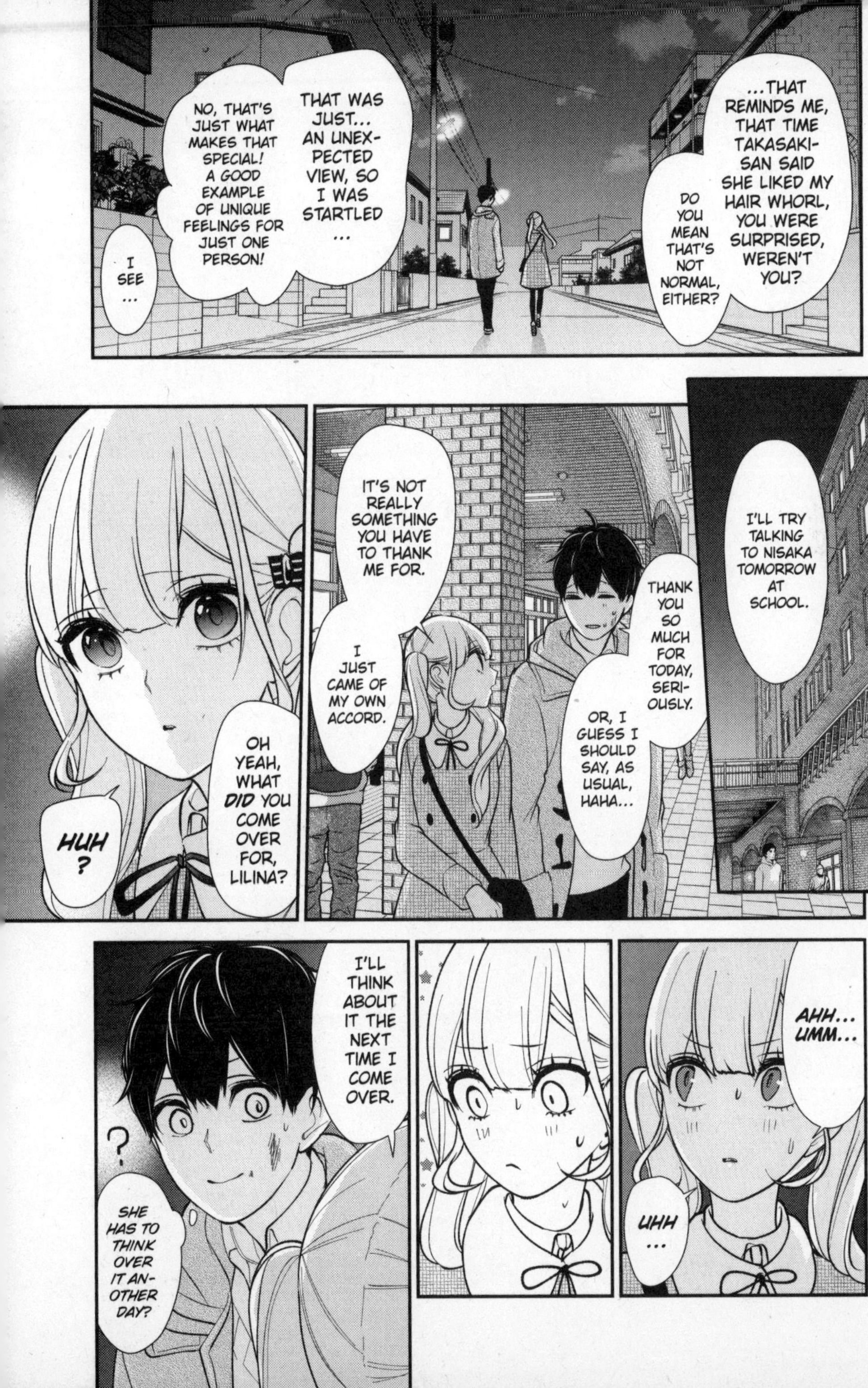
...THAT REMINDS ME, THAT TIME TAKASAKI-SAN SAID SHE LIKED MY HAIR WHORL, YOU WERE SURPRISED, WEREN'T YOU?
DO YOU MEAN THAT'S NOT NORMAL, EITHER?
THAT WAS JUST... AN UNEX-PECTED VIEW, SO I WAS STARTLED...
NO, THAT'S JUST WHAT MAKES THAT SPECIAL! A GOOD EXAMPLE OF UNIQUE FEELINGS FOR JUST ONE PERSON!
I SEE...
I'LL TRY TALKING TO NISAKA TOMORROW AT SCHOOL.
THANK YOU SO MUCH FOR TODAY, SERI-OUSLY.
OR, I GUESS I SHOULD SAY, AS USUAL, HAHA...
IT'S NOT REALLY SOMETHING YOU HAVE TO THANK ME FOR.
I JUST CAME OF MY OWN ACCORD.
OH YEAH, WHAT DID YOU COME OVER FOR, LILINA?
HUH?
AHH... UMM...
UHH...
I'LL THINK ABOUT IT THE NEXT TIME I COME OVER.
?
SHE HAS TO THINK OVER IT AN-OTHER DAY?

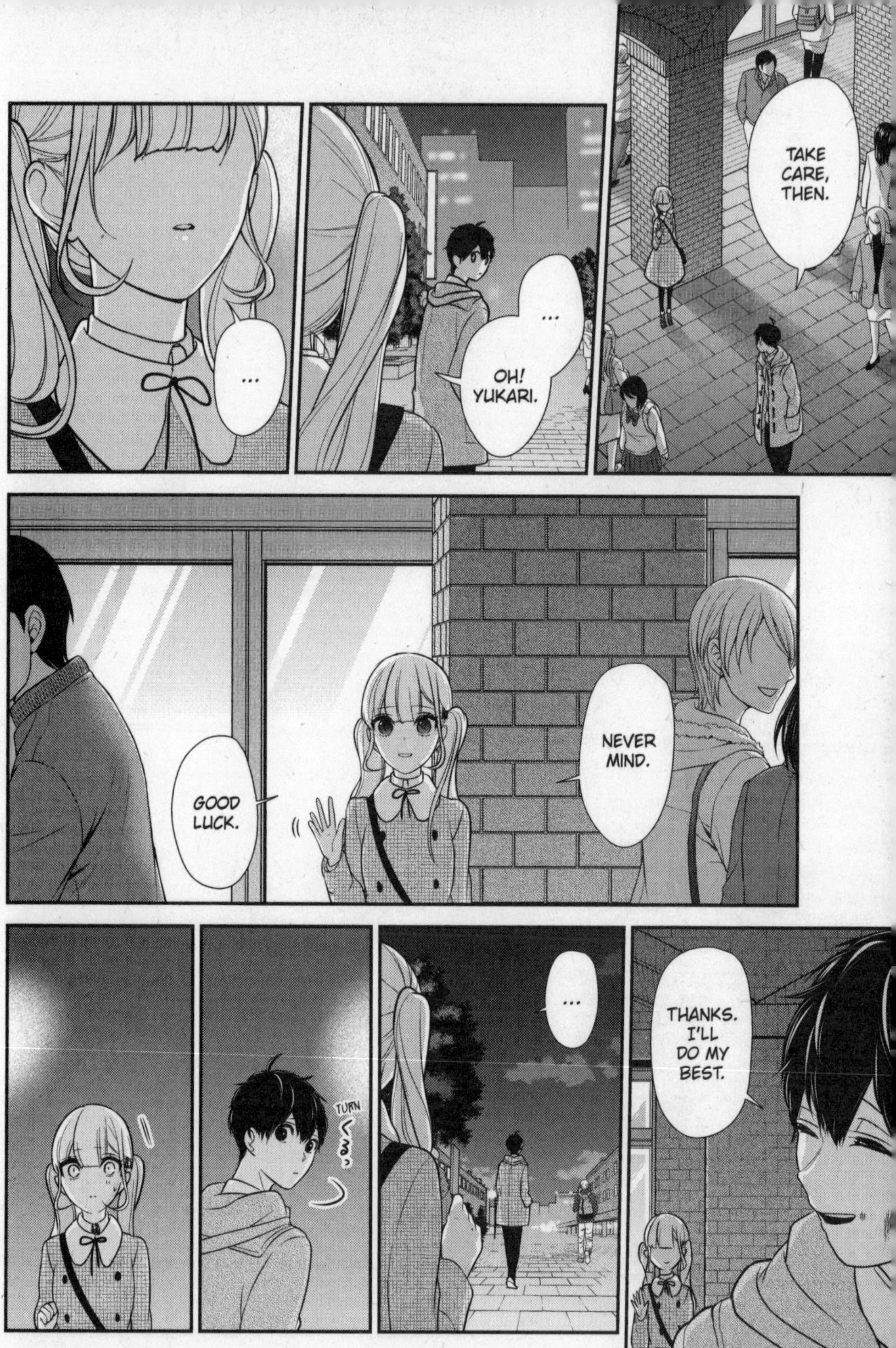
TAKE CARE, THEN.
...
OH! YUKARI.
...
NEVER MIND.
GOOD LUCK.
THANKS. I'LL DO MY BEST.
...
TURN

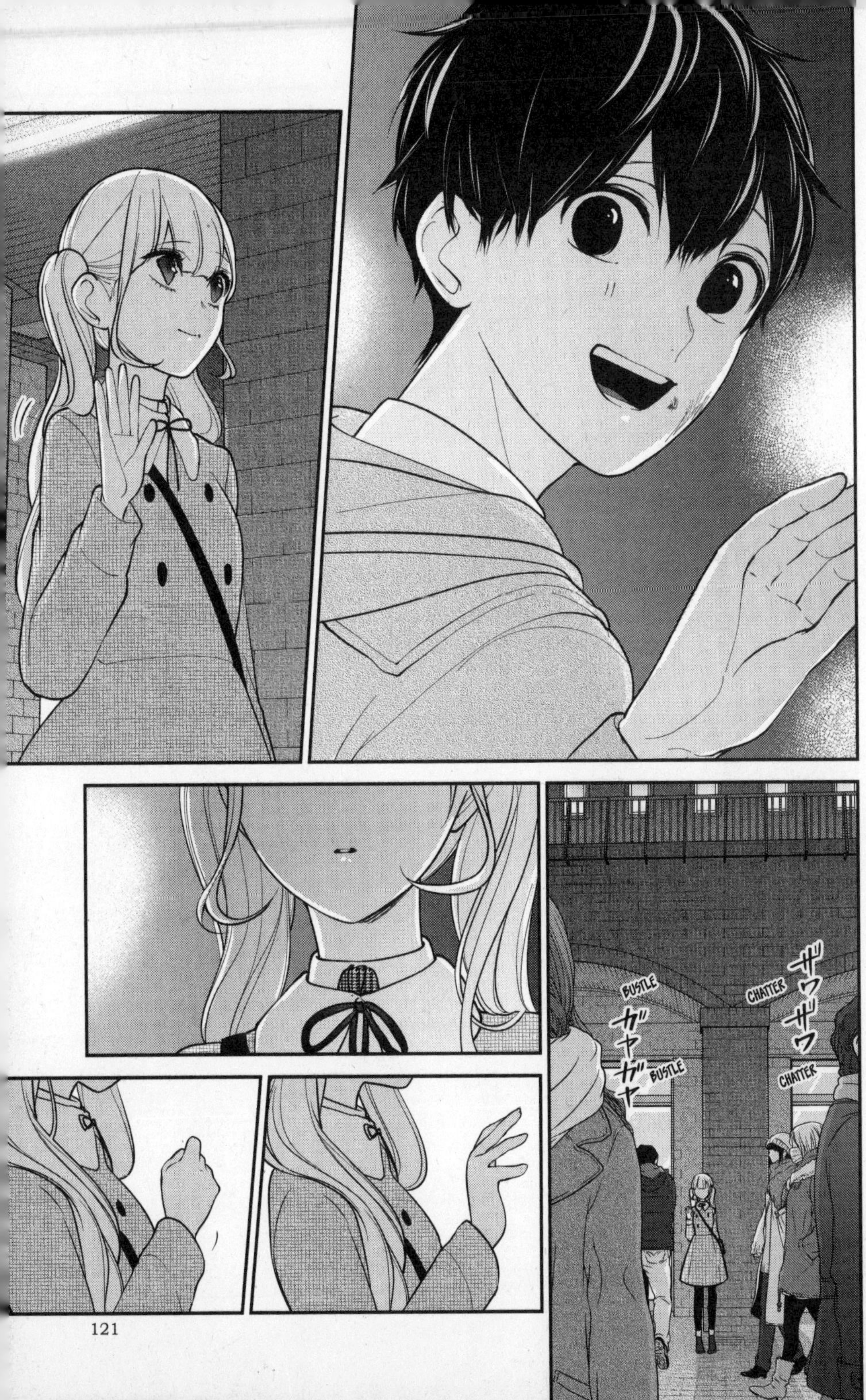
CHATTER
ザワザワ
CHATTER
BUSTLE
ガヤガヤ
BUSTLE

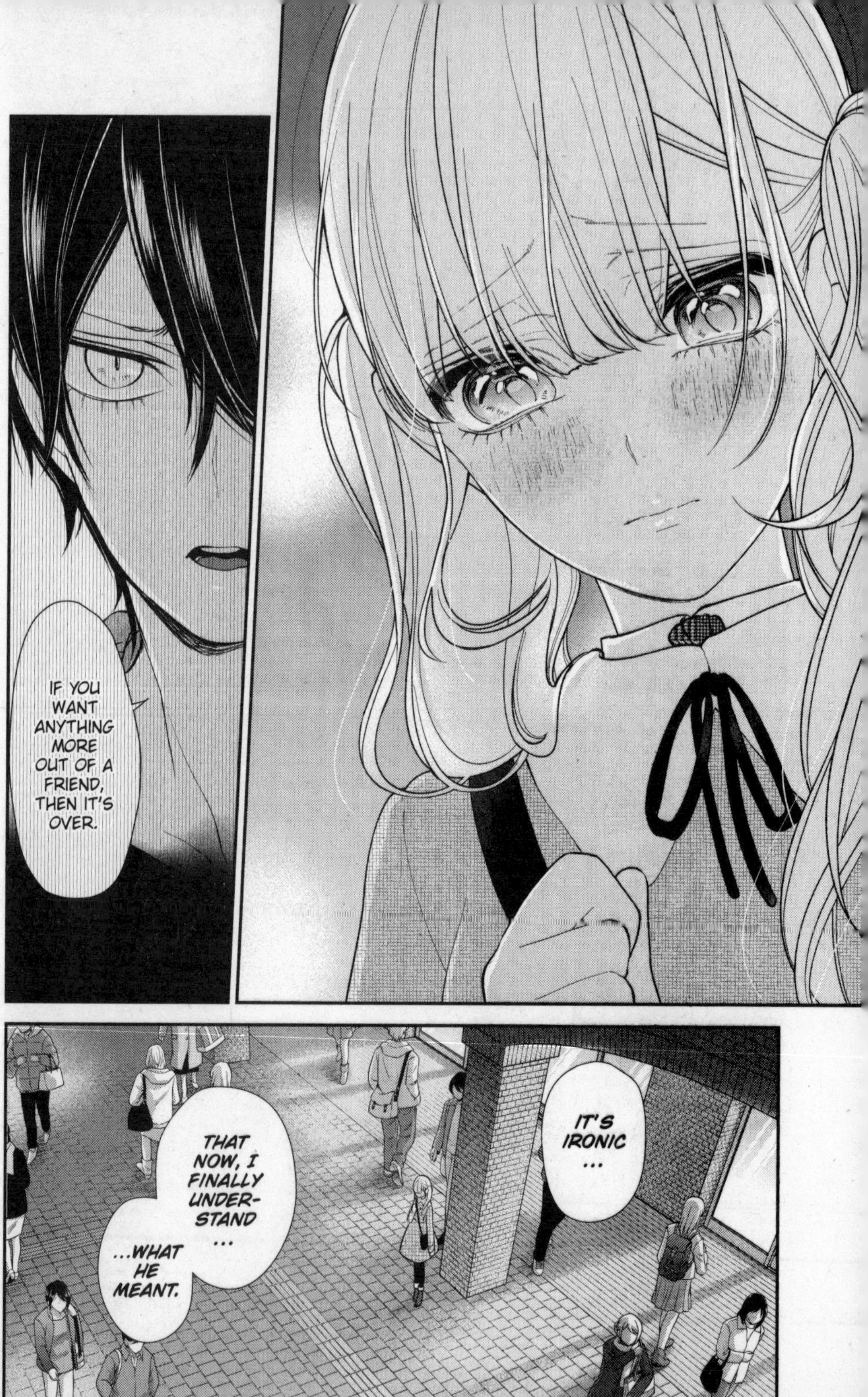
IF YOU WANT ANYTHING MORE OUT OF A FRIEND, THEN IT'S OVER.
IT'S IRONIC...
THAT NOW, I FINALLY UNDER-STAND...
...WHAT HE MEANT.

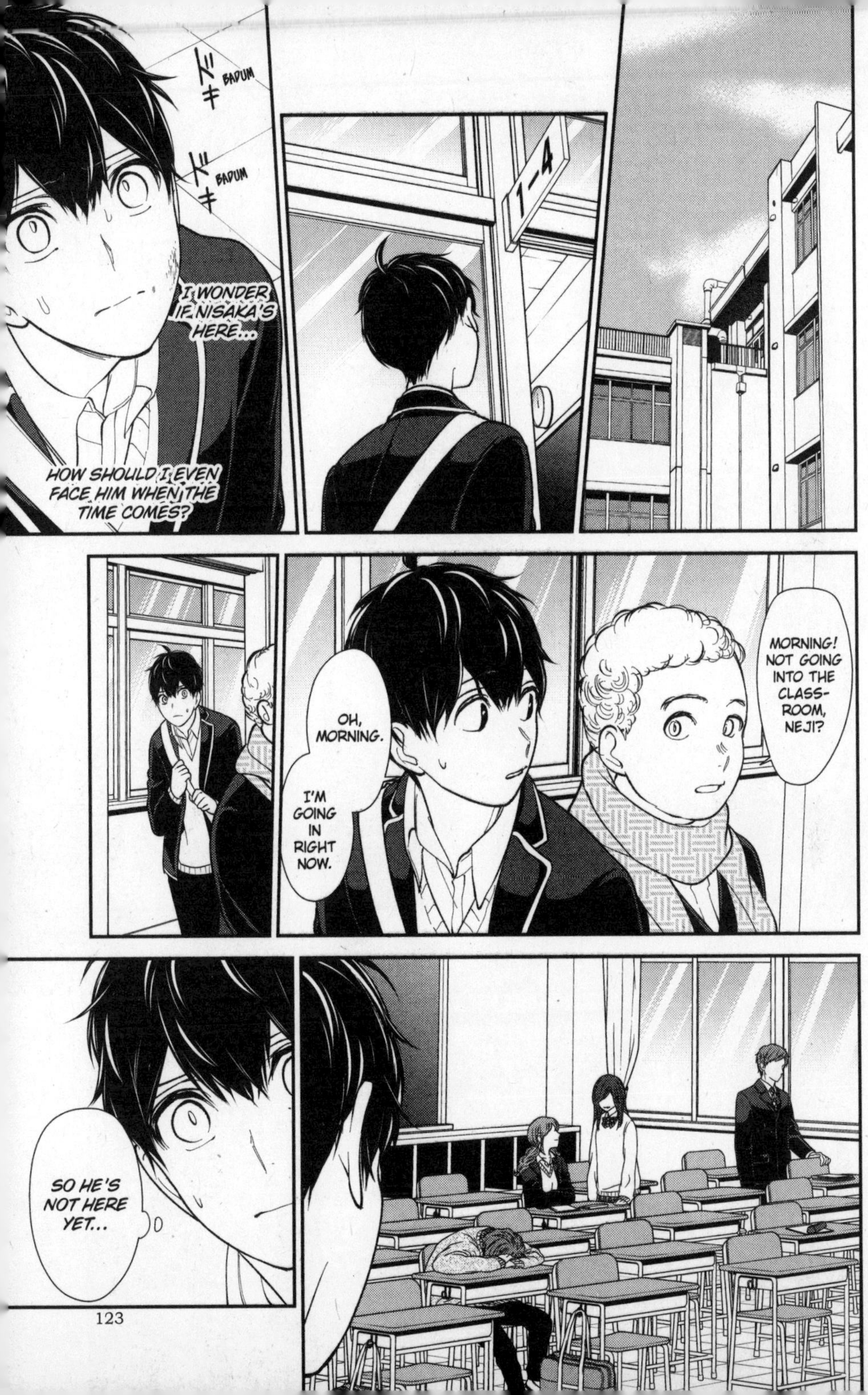
1-4
ドキ
BADUM
ドキ
BADUM
I WONDER IF NISAKA'S HERE...
HOW SHOULD I EVEN FACE HIM WHEN THE TIME COMES?
MORNING! NOT GOING INTO THE CLASSROOM, NEJI?
OH, MORNING.
I'M GOING IN RIGHT NOW.
SO HE'S NOT HERE YET...

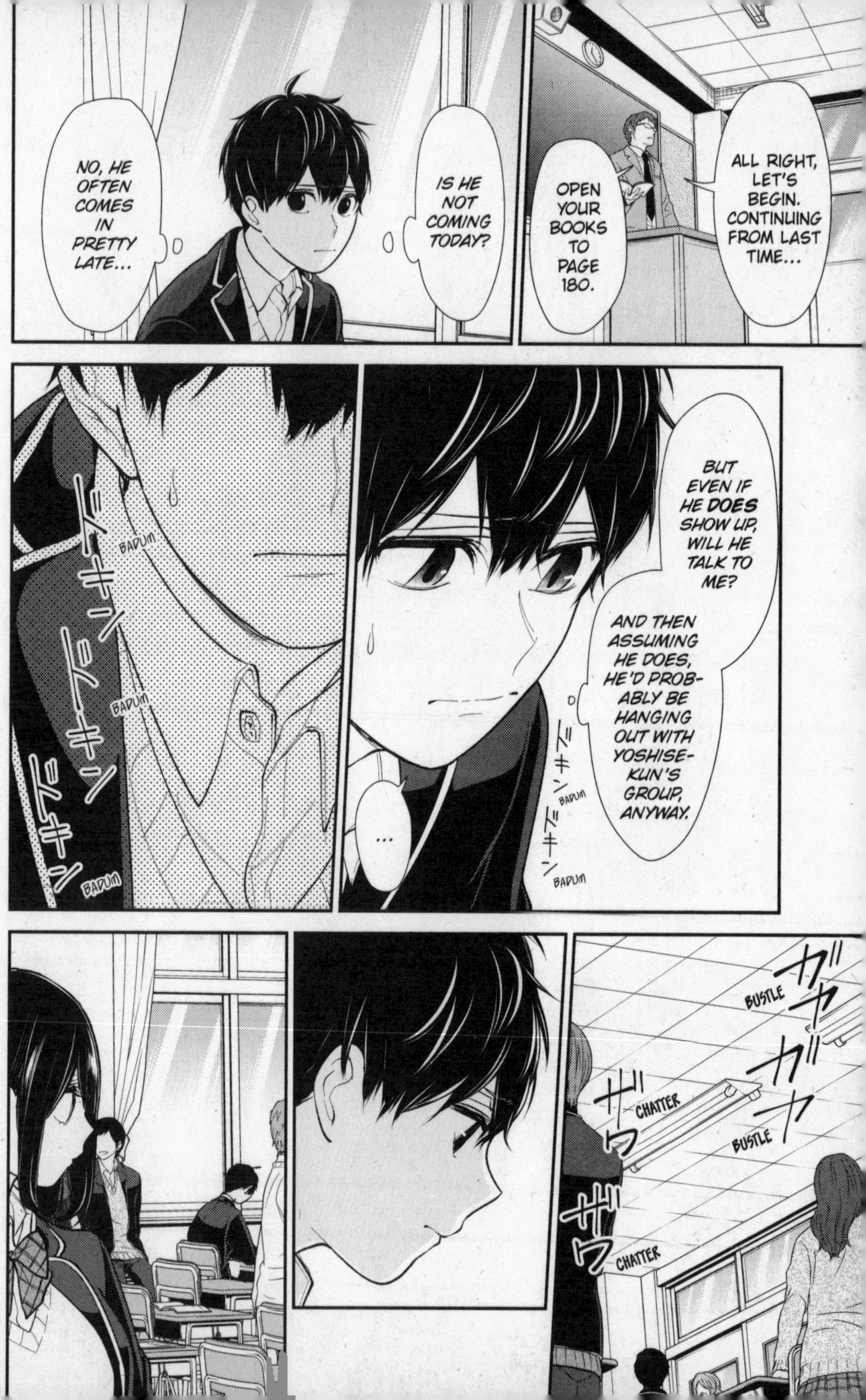
ALL RIGHT, LET'S BEGIN. CONTINUING FROM LAST TIME...
OPEN YOUR BOOKS TO PAGE 180.
IS HE NOT COMING TODAY?
NO, HE OFTEN COMES IN PRETTY LATE...
BUT EVEN IF HE DOES SHOW UP, WILL HE TALK TO ME?
AND THEN ASSUMING HE DOES, HE'D PROBABLY BE HANGING OUT WITH YOSHISE-KUN'S GROUP, ANYWAY.
...
ドキン BADUM
ドキン BADUM
ドキン BADUM
ドキン BADUM
ドキン BADUM
ガヤ BUSTLE
ガヤ BUSTLE
ザワ CHATTER
ザワ CHATTER

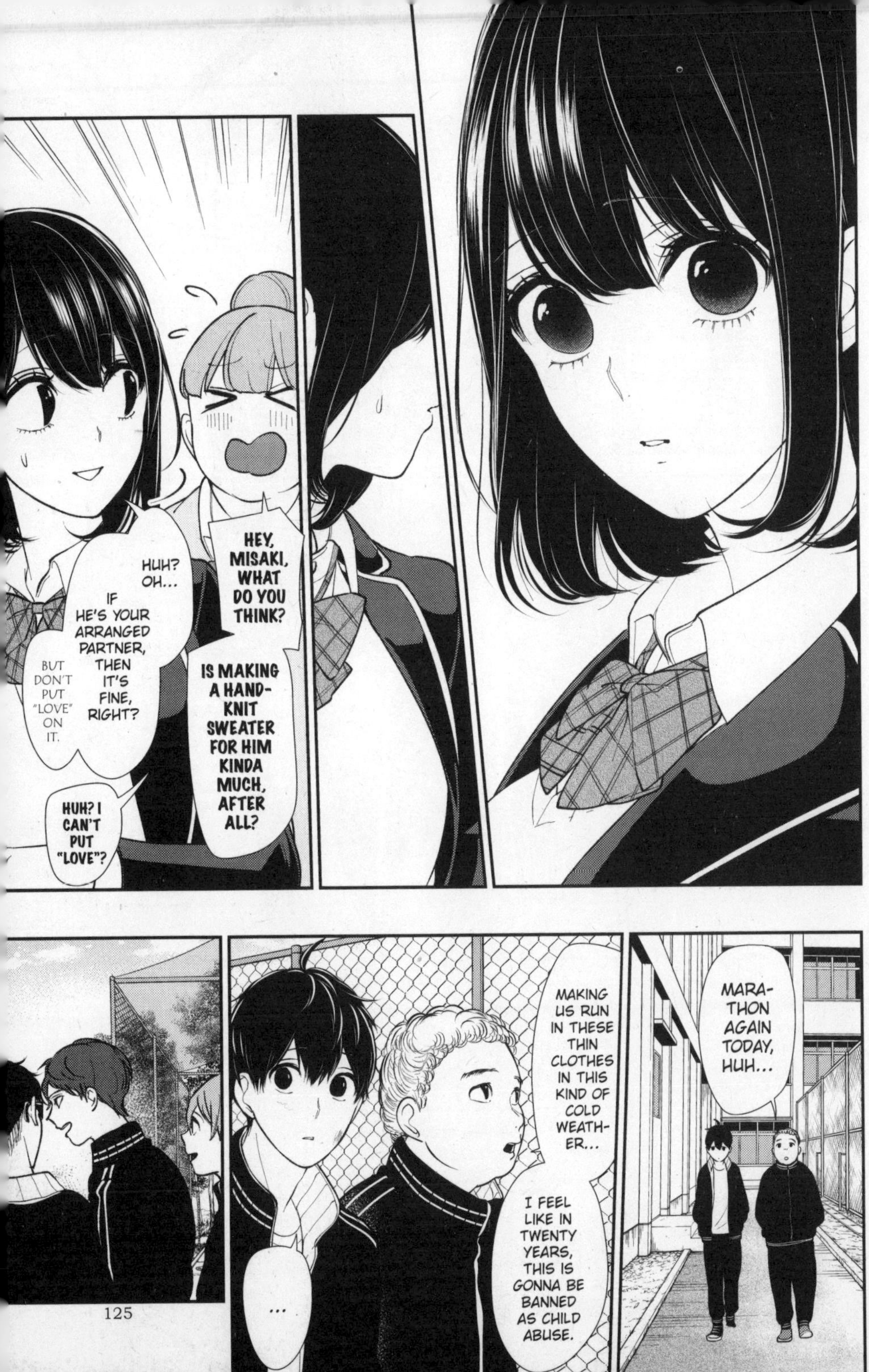
HEY, MISAKI, WHAT DO YOU THINK?
IS MAKING A HAND-KNIT SWEATER FOR HIM KINDA MUCH, AFTER ALL?
HUH? OH... IF HE'S YOUR ARRANGED PARTNER, THEN IT'S FINE, RIGHT?
BUT DON'T PUT "LOVE" ON IT.
HUH? I CAN'T PUT "LOVE"?
MARATHON AGAIN TODAY, HUH...
MAKING US RUN IN THESE THIN CLOTHES IN THIS KIND OF COLD WEATHER...
I FEEL LIKE IN TWENTY YEARS, THIS IS GONNA BE BANNED AS CHILD ABUSE.
...

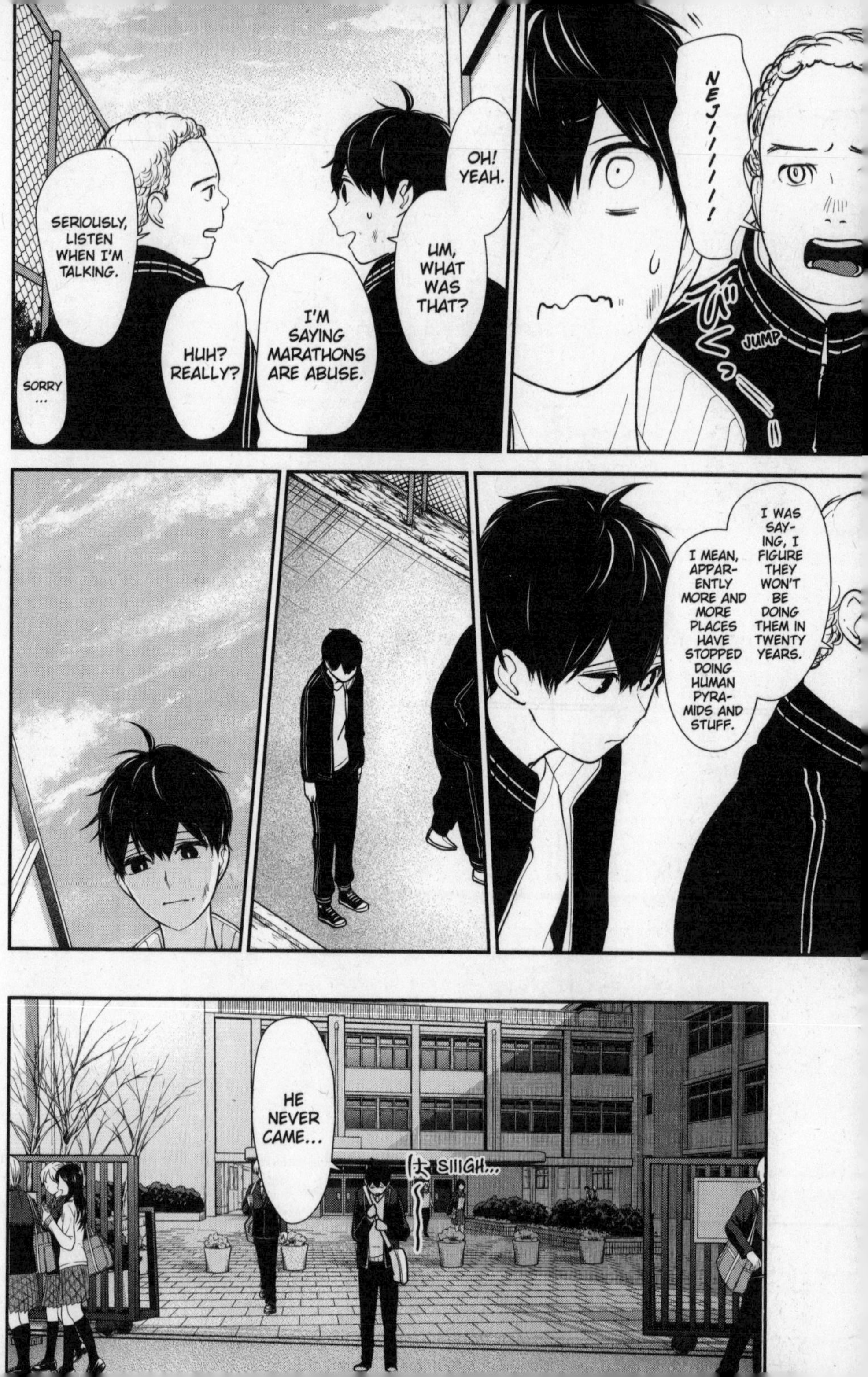
NEJI!!!!!!!
JUMP
OH! YEAH.
UM, WHAT WAS THAT?
I'M SAYING MARATHONS ARE ABUSE.
HUH? REALLY?
SERIOUSLY, LISTEN WHEN I'M TALKING.
SORRY...
I WAS SAYING, I FIGURE THEY WON'T BE DOING THEM IN TWENTY YEARS.
I MEAN, APPARENTLY MORE AND MORE PLACES HAVE STOPPED DOING HUMAN PYRAMIDS AND STUFF.
HE NEVER CAME...
SIIIGH...

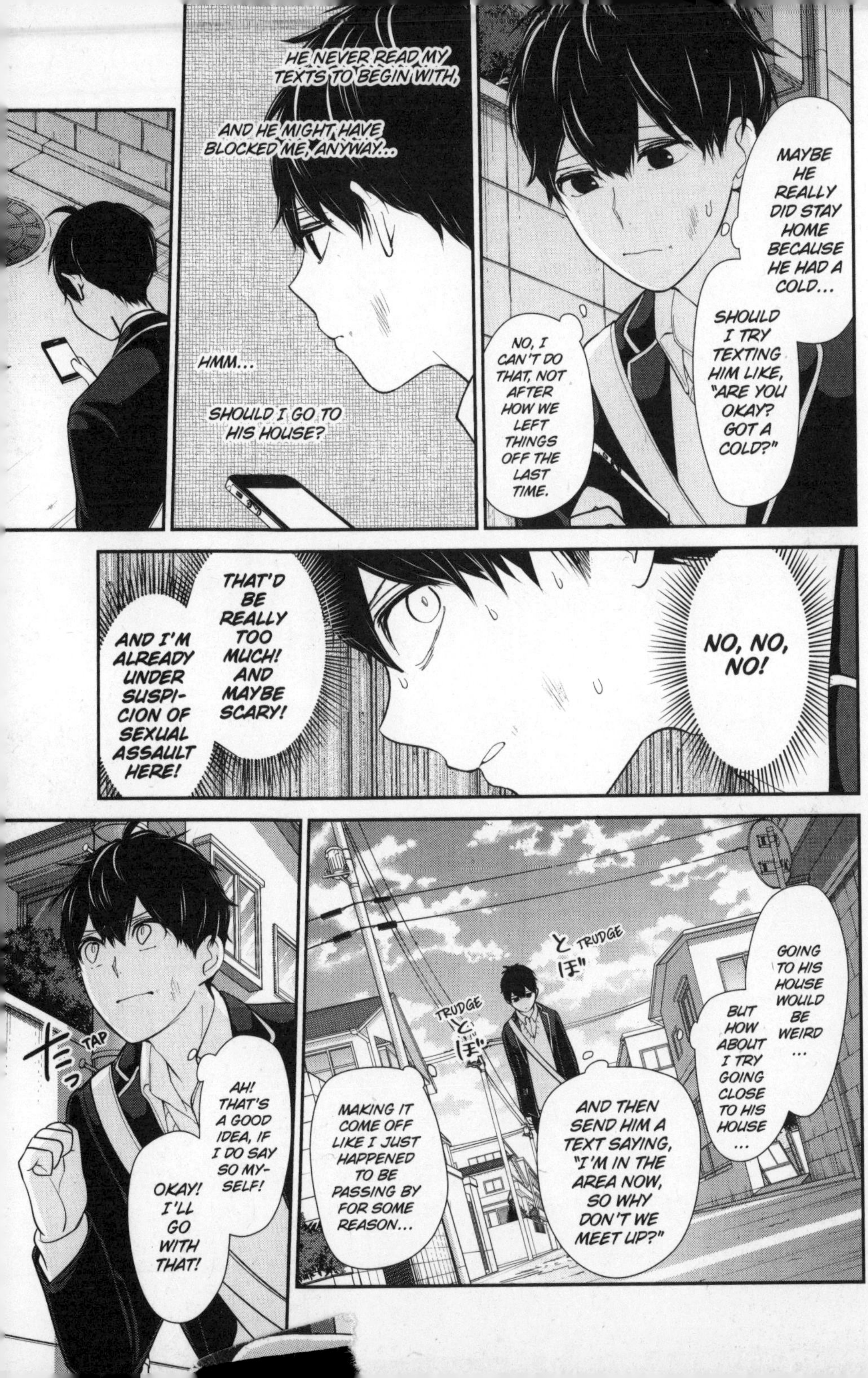
MAYBE HE REALLY DID STAY HOME BECAUSE HE HAD A COLD...
SHOULD I TRY TEXTING HIM LIKE, "ARE YOU OKAY? GOT A COLD?"
NO, I CAN'T DO THAT, NOT AFTER HOW WE LEFT THINGS OFF THE LAST TIME.
HE NEVER READ MY TEXTS TO BEGIN WITH,
AND HE MIGHT HAVE BLOCKED ME, ANYWAY...
HMM...
SHOULD I GO TO HIS HOUSE?
NO, NO, NO!
THAT'D BE REALLY TOO MUCH! AND MAYBE SCARY!
AND I'M ALREADY UNDER SUSPI-CION OF SEXUAL ASSAULT HERE!
GOING TO HIS HOUSE WOULD BE WEIRD...
BUT HOW ABOUT I TRY GOING CLOSE TO HIS HOUSE...
とぼ TRUDGE
TRUDGE とぼ
AND THEN SEND HIM A TEXT SAYING, "I'M IN THE AREA NOW, SO WHY DON'T WE MEET UP?"
MAKING IT COME OFF LIKE I JUST HAPPENED TO BE PASSING BY FOR SOME REASON...
AH! THAT'S A GOOD IDEA, IF I DO SAY SO MY-SELF!
TAP
OKAY! I'LL GO WITH THAT!

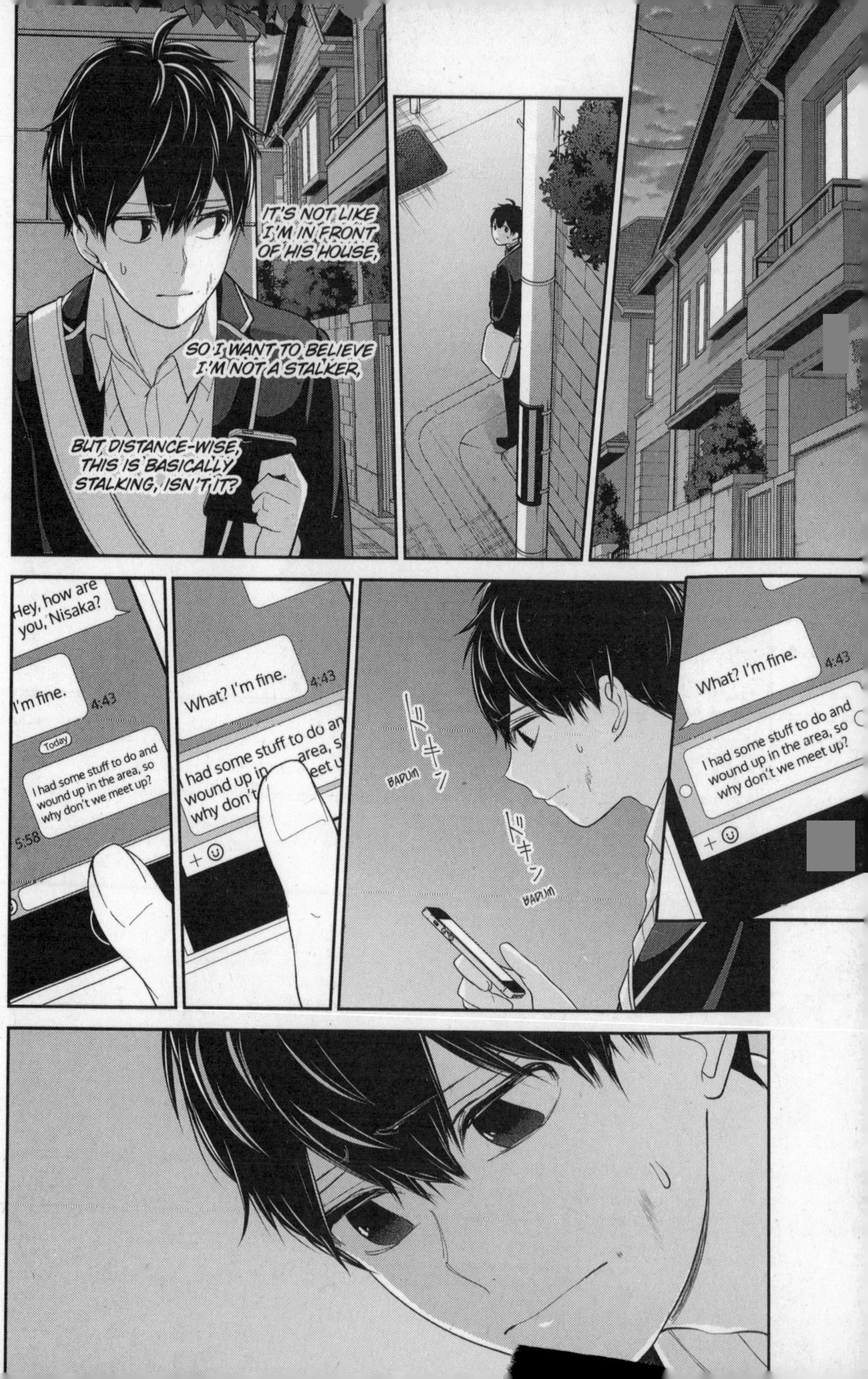
IT'S NOT LIKE I'M IN FRONT OF HIS HOUSE,
SO I WANT TO BELIEVE I'M NOT A STALKER,
BUT DISTANCE-WISE, THIS IS BASICALLY STALKING, ISN'T IT?
What? I'm fine.
4:43
I had some stuff to do and wound up in the area, so why don't we meet up?
ドキン
BADUM
ドキン
BADUM
What? I'm fine.
4:43
I had some stuff to do an
wound up in
area, s
why don't
eet u
Hey, how are you, Nisaka?
I'm fine.
4:43
Today
I had some stuff to do and wound up in the area, so why don't we meet up?
5:58

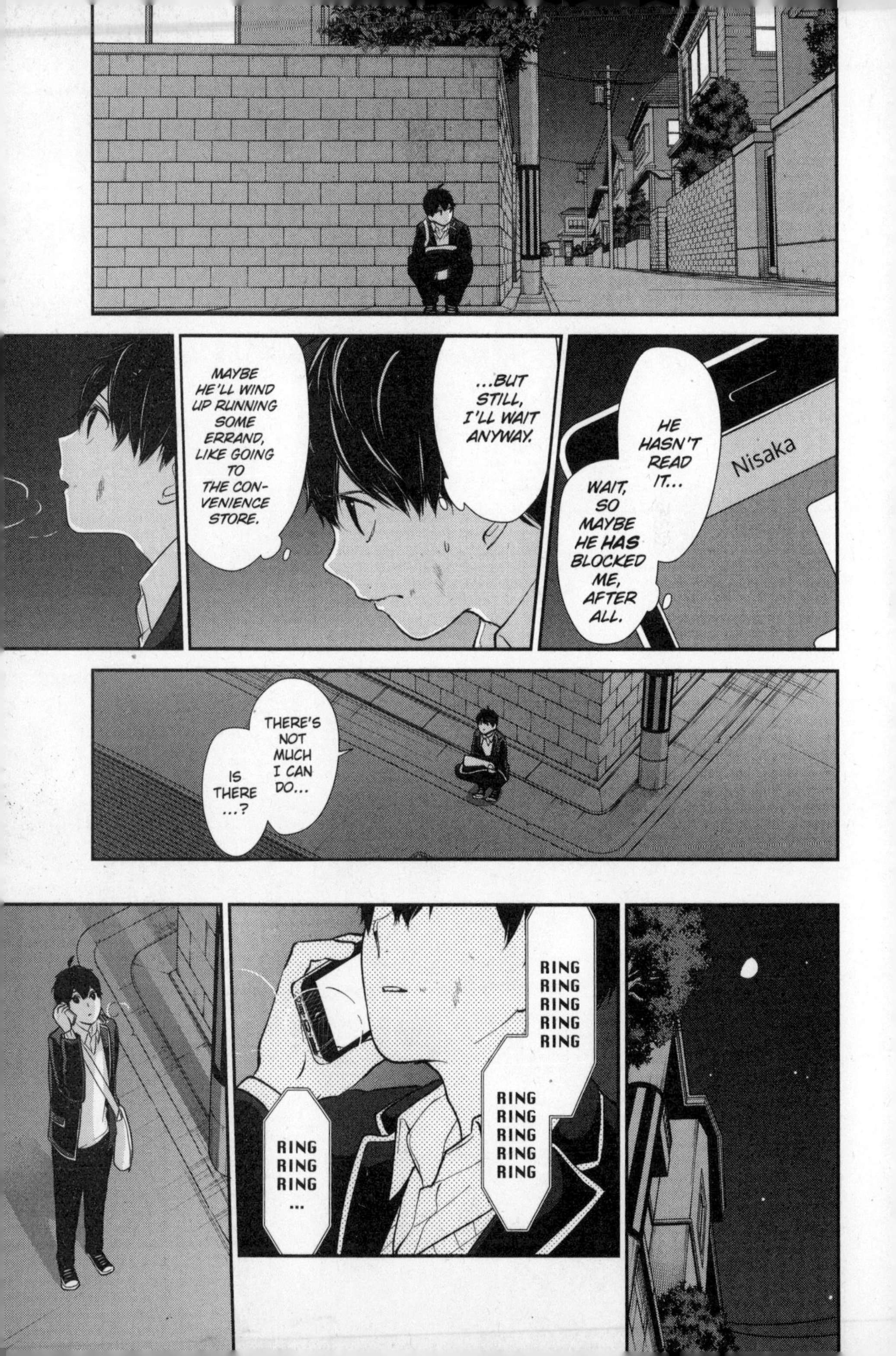
HE HASN'T READ IT...
Nisaka
WAIT, SO MAYBE HE HAS BLOCKED ME, AFTER ALL.
MAYBE HE'LL WIND UP RUNNING SOME ERRAND, LIKE GOING TO THE CON-VENIENCE STORE.
...BUT STILL, I'LL WAIT ANYWAY.
THERE'S NOT MUCH I CAN DO...
IS THERE ...?
RING RING RING RING RING
RING RING RING RING RING
RING RING RING ...

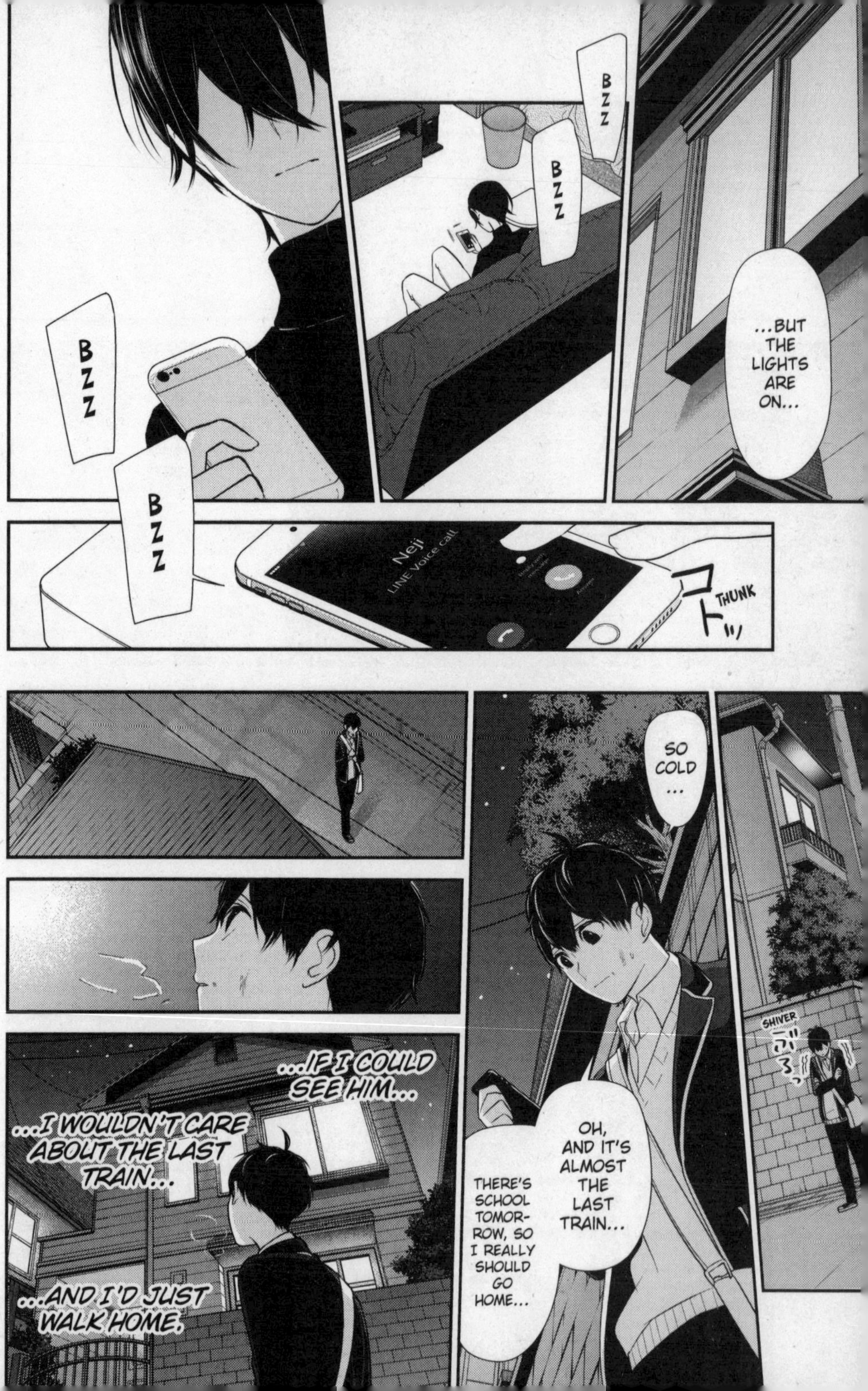
...BUT THE LIGHTS ARE ON...
BZZ
BZZ
BZZ
BZZ
Neji
LINE Voice call
THUNK
SHIVER
SO COLD...
OH, AND IT'S ALMOST THE LAST TRAIN...
THERE'S SCHOOL TOMOR-ROW, SO I REALLY SHOULD GO HOME...
...IF I COULD SEE HIM...
...I WOULDN'T CARE ABOUT THE LAST TRAIN...
...AND I'D JUST WALK HOME.

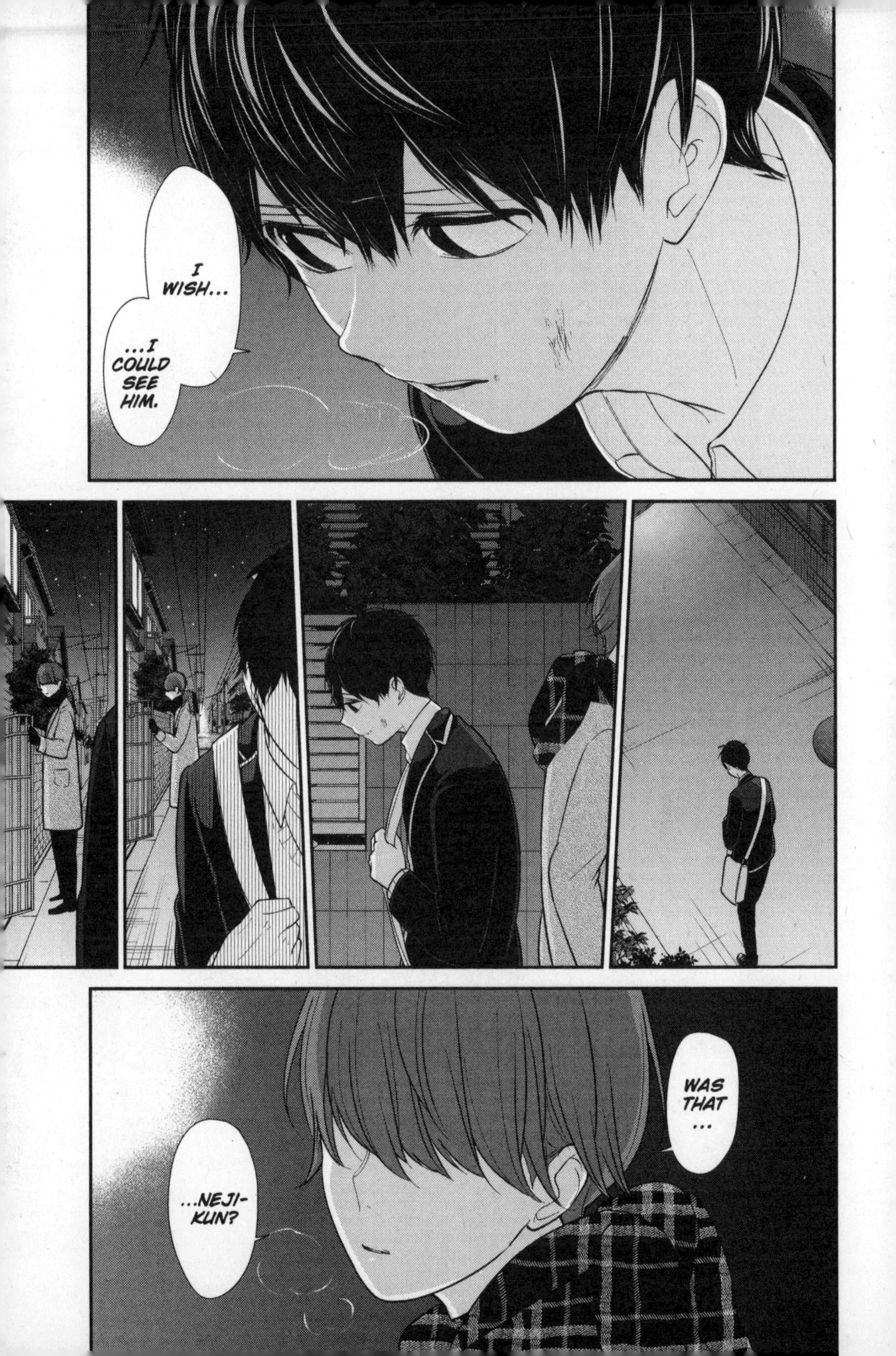
I WISH...
...I COULD SEE HIM.
WAS THAT...
...NEJI-KUN?

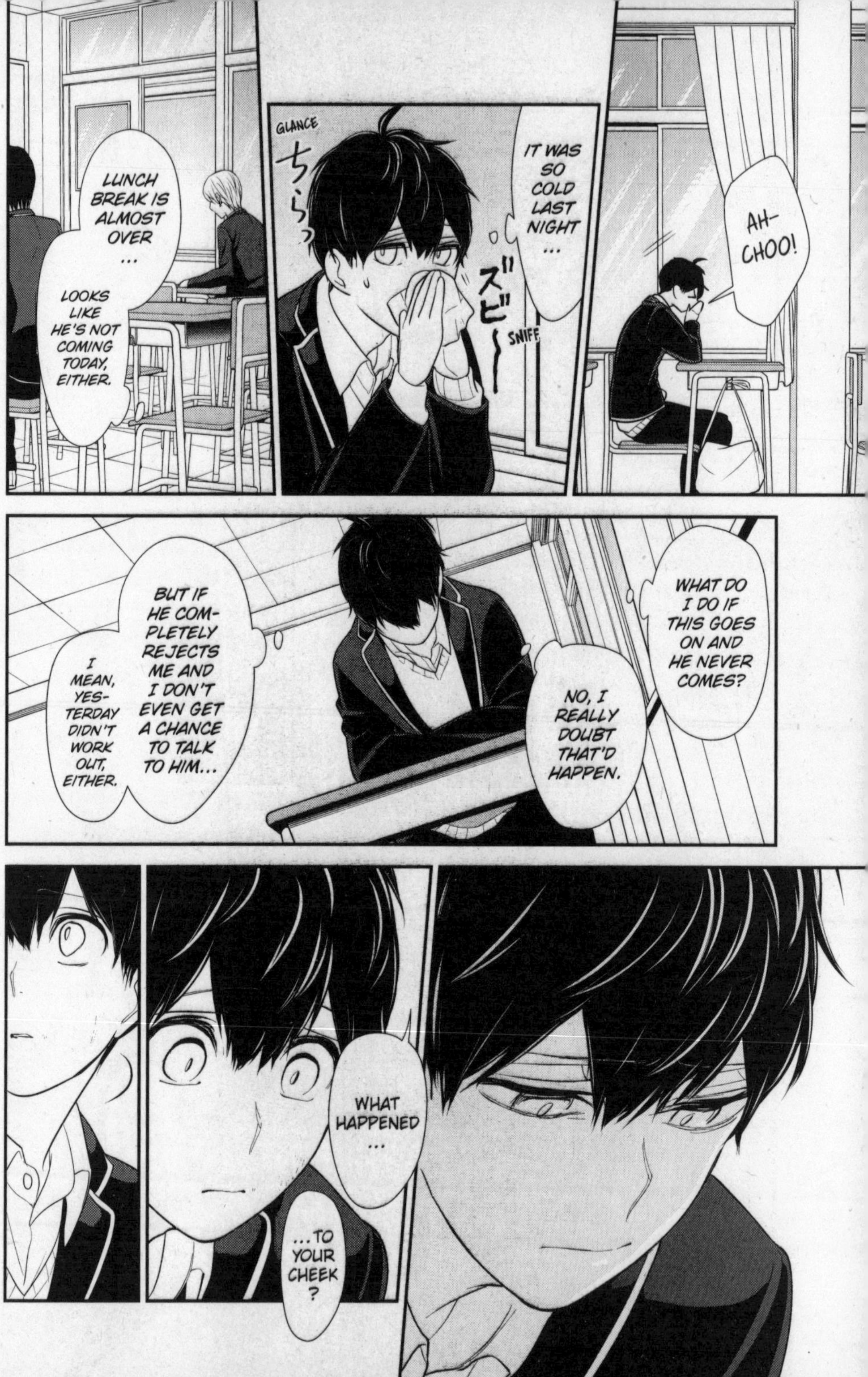
AH-CHOO!
IT WAS SO COLD LAST NIGHT...
GLANCE
ちらっ
ズビ~
SNIFF
LUNCH BREAK IS ALMOST OVER...
LOOKS LIKE HE'S NOT COMING TODAY, EITHER.
WHAT DO I DO IF THIS GOES ON AND HE NEVER COMES?
NO, I REALLY DOUBT THAT'D HAPPEN.
BUT IF HE COM-PLETELY REJECTS ME AND I DON'T EVEN GET A CHANCE TO TALK TO HIM...
I MEAN, YES-TERDAY DIDN'T WORK OUT, EITHER.
WHAT HAPPENED...
...TO YOUR CHEEK?

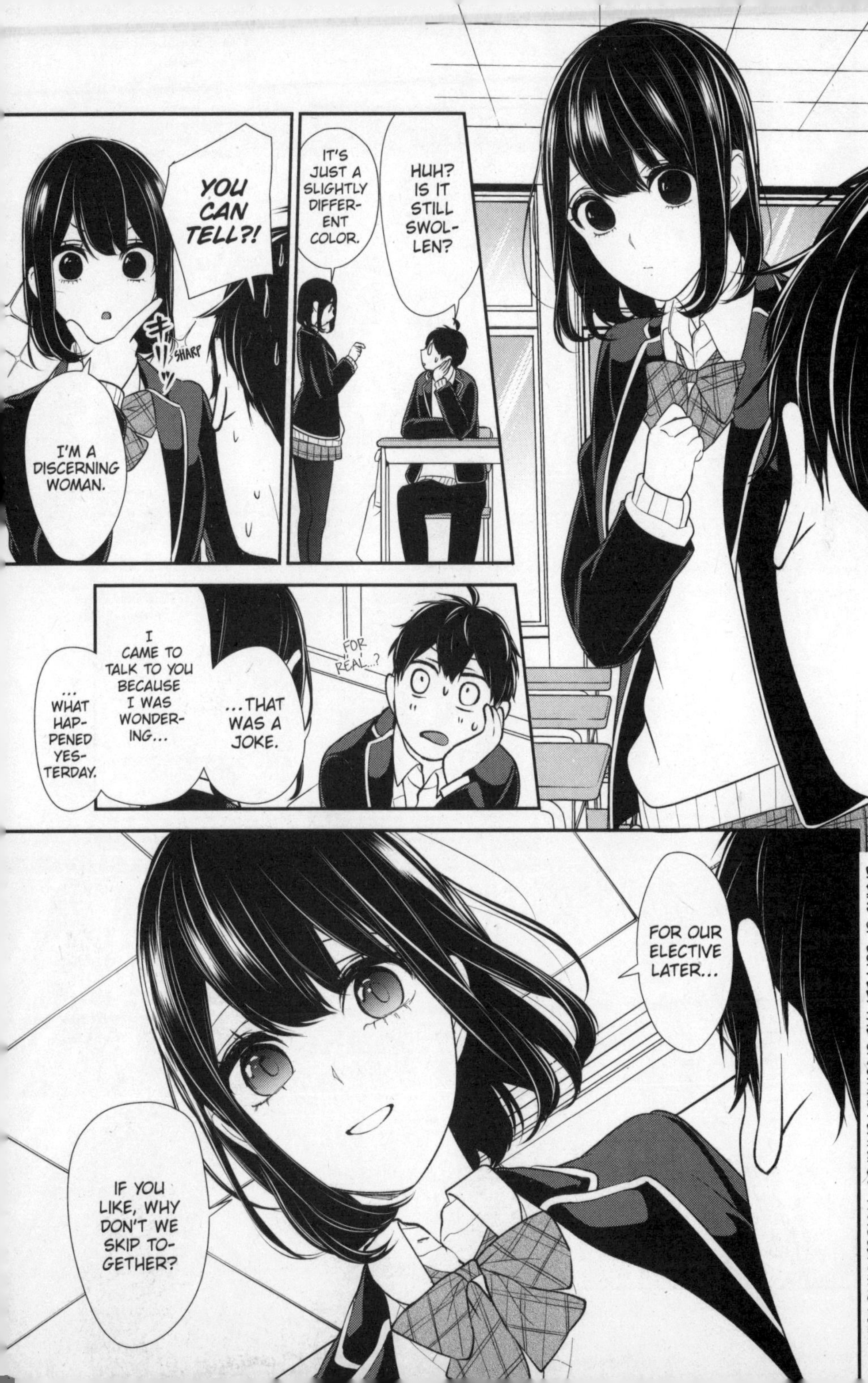
HUH? IS IT STILL SWOLLEN?
IT'S JUST A SLIGHTLY DIFFERENT COLOR.
YOU CAN TELL?!
SHARP
I'M A DISCERNING WOMAN.
FOR REAL...?
...THAT WAS A JOKE.
I CAME TO TALK TO YOU BECAUSE I WAS WONDERING...
...WHAT HAPPENED YESTERDAY.
FOR OUR ELECTIVE LATER...
IF YOU LIKE, WHY DON'T WE SKIP TOGETHER?

*MISAKI IS REFERENCING AN OLD, LONG-RUNNING AD CAMPAIGN FOR A BRAND OF COFFEE. THE ORIGINAL FEATURED "A DISCERNING MAN."

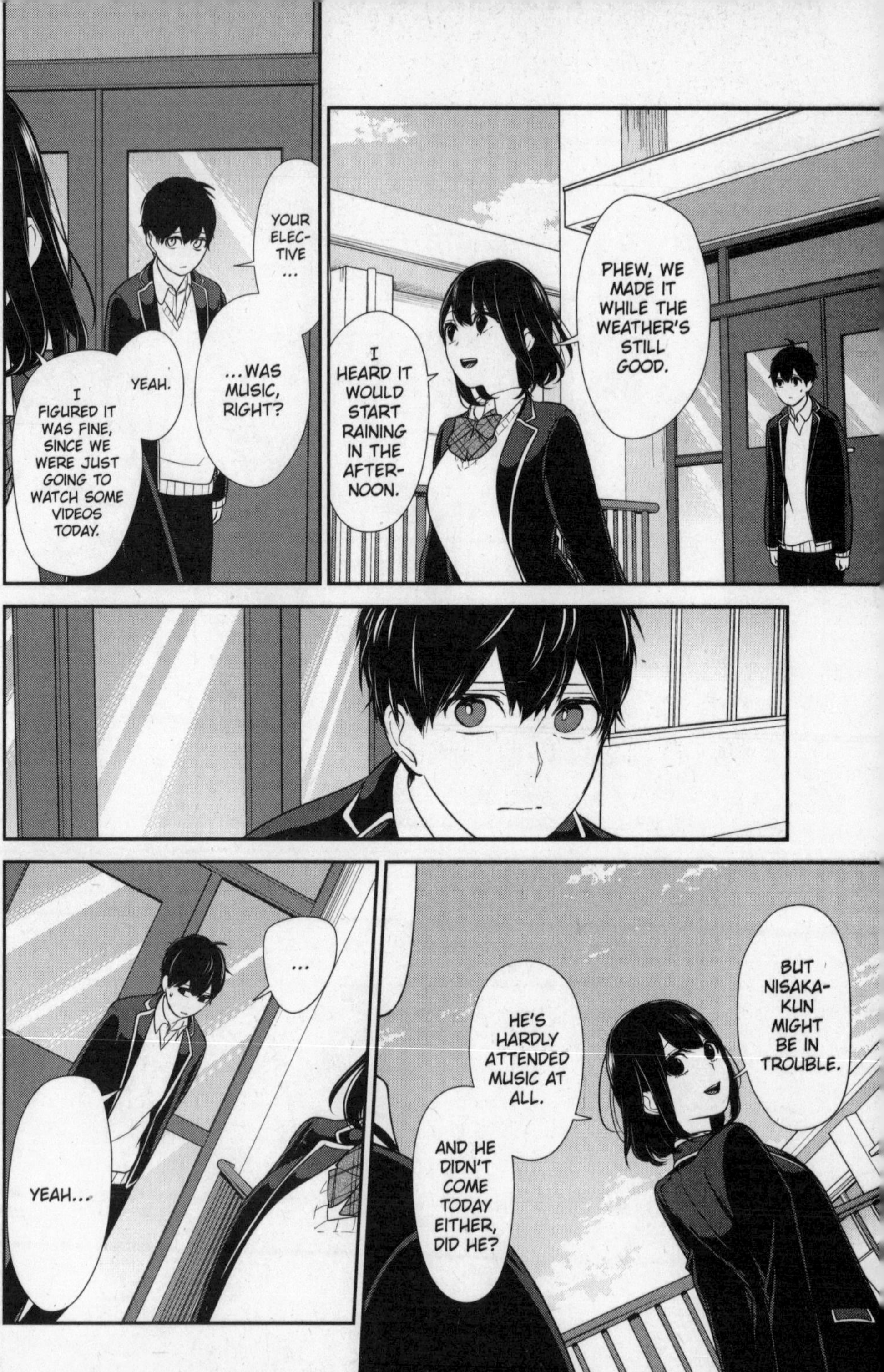
PHEW, WE MADE IT WHILE THE WEATHER'S STILL GOOD.
I HEARD IT WOULD START RAINING IN THE AFTER-NOON.
YOUR ELEC-TIVE ...
...WAS MUSIC, RIGHT?
YEAH.
I FIGURED IT WAS FINE, SINCE WE WERE JUST GOING TO WATCH SOME VIDEOS TODAY.
BUT NISAKA-KUN MIGHT BE IN TROUBLE.
HE'S HARDLY ATTENDED MUSIC AT ALL.
AND HE DIDN'T COME TODAY EITHER, DID HE?
...
YEAH...

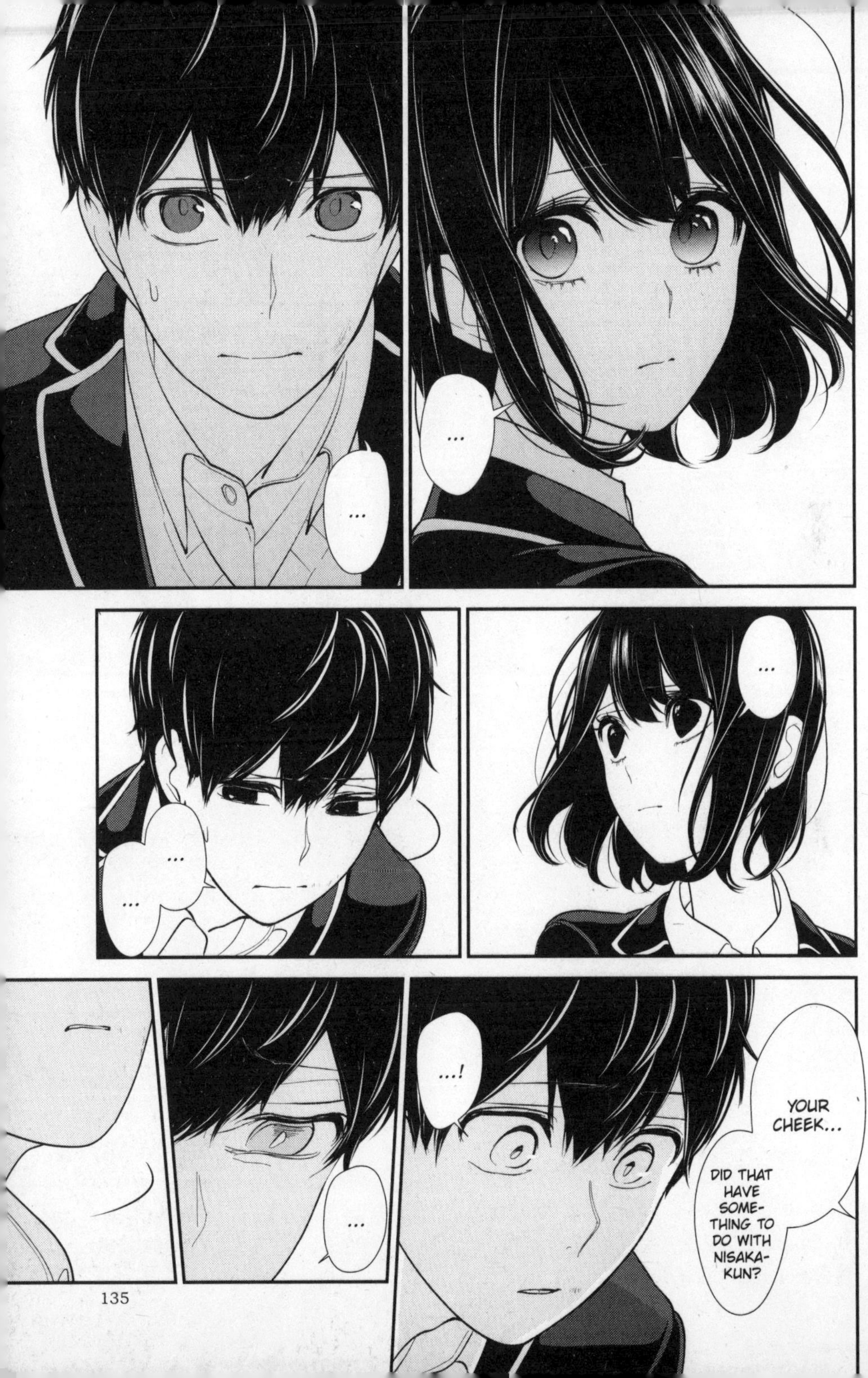
...
...
...
...
...
YOUR CHEEK...
DID THAT HAVE SOME-THING TO DO WITH NISAKA-KUN?
...!
...

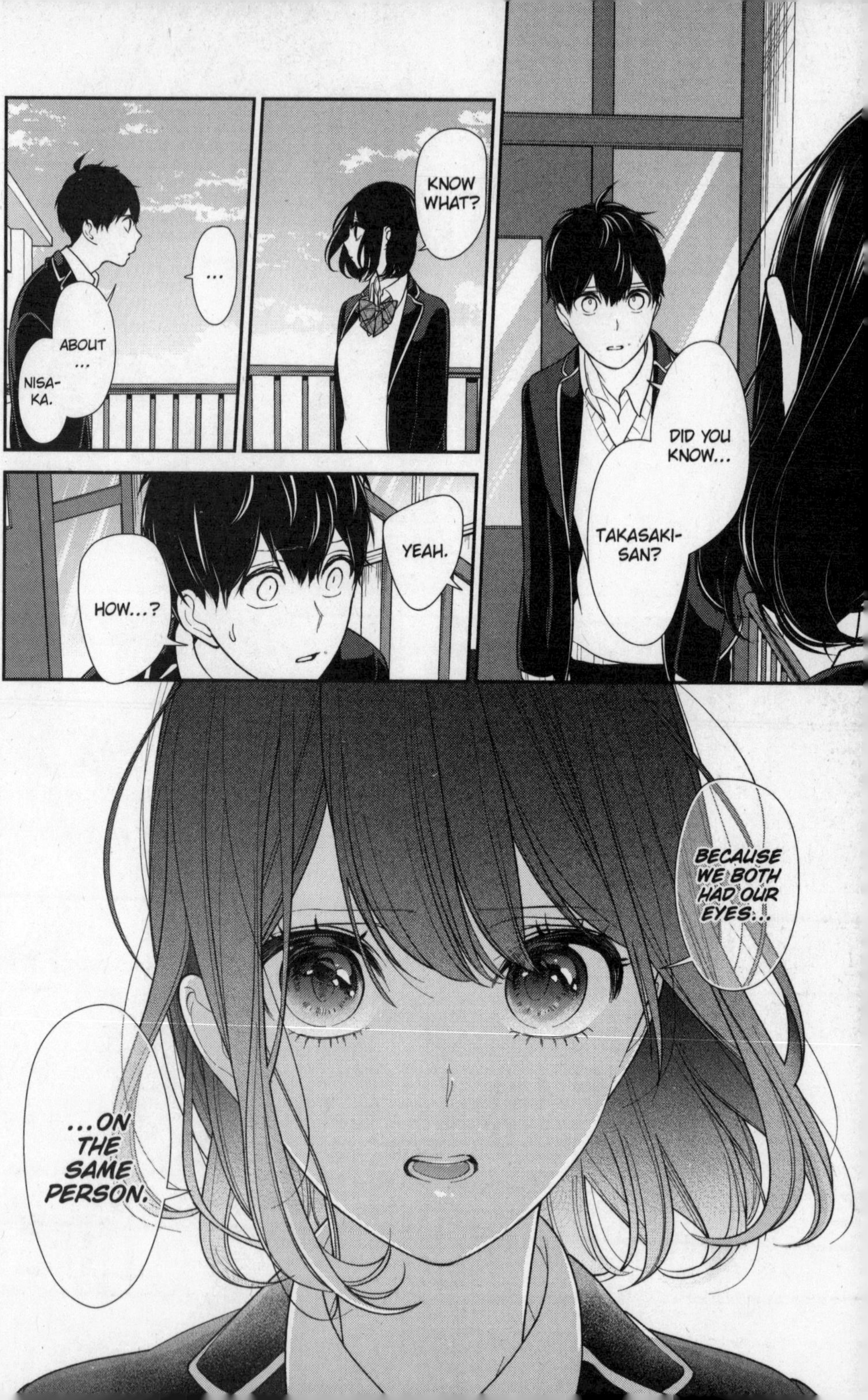
DID YOU KNOW...
TAKASAKI-SAN?
KNOW WHAT?
...
ABOUT ... NISA-KA.
YEAH.
HOW...?
BECAUSE WE BOTH HAD OUR EYES...
...ON THE SAME PERSON.

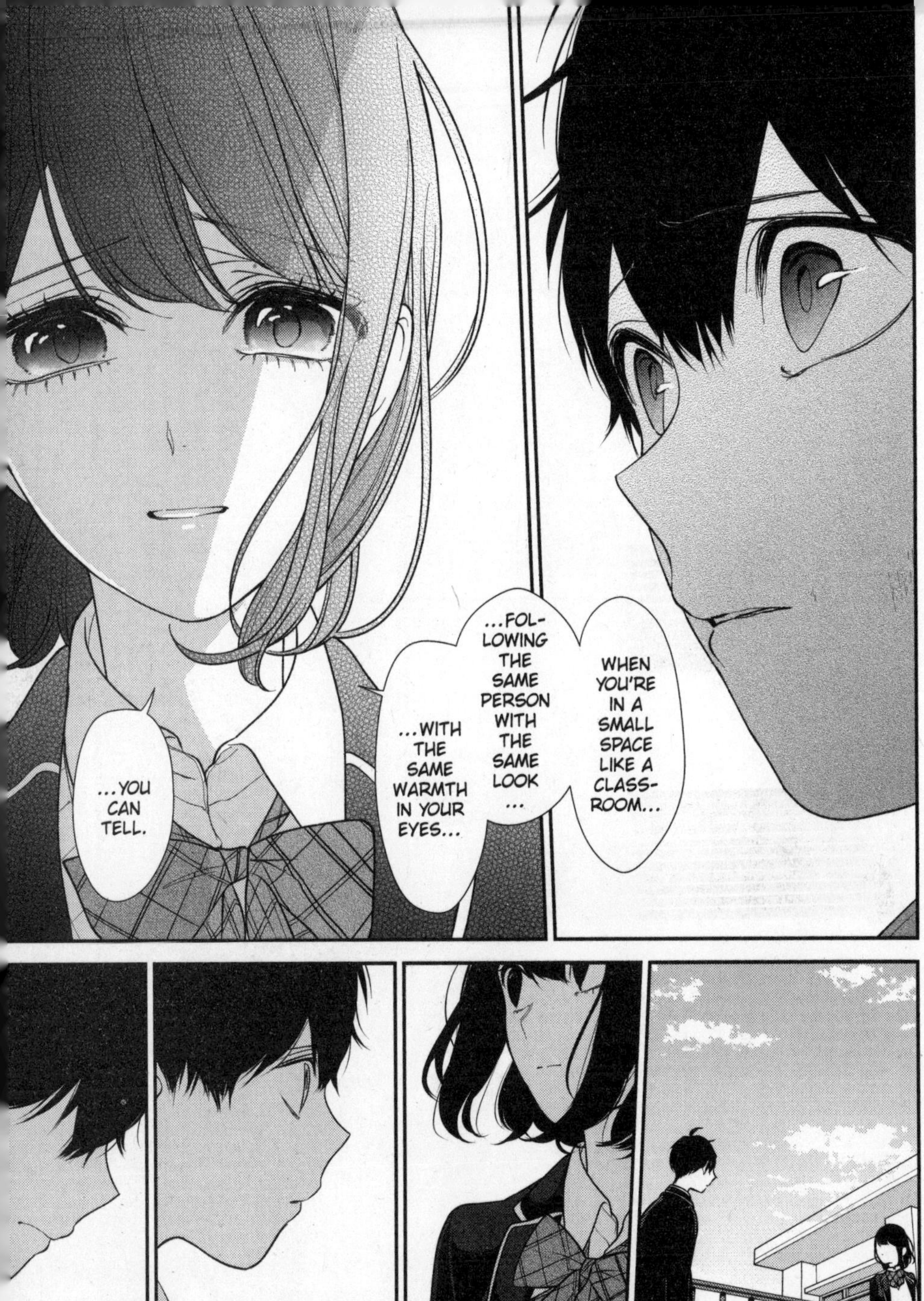
WHEN YOU'RE IN A SMALL SPACE LIKE A CLASS-ROOM...
...FOL-LOWING THE SAME PERSON WITH THE SAME LOOK ...
...WITH THE SAME WARMTH IN YOUR EYES...
...YOU CAN TELL.

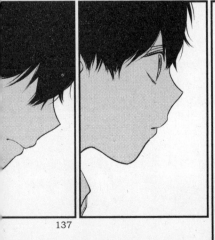

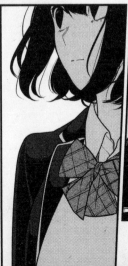

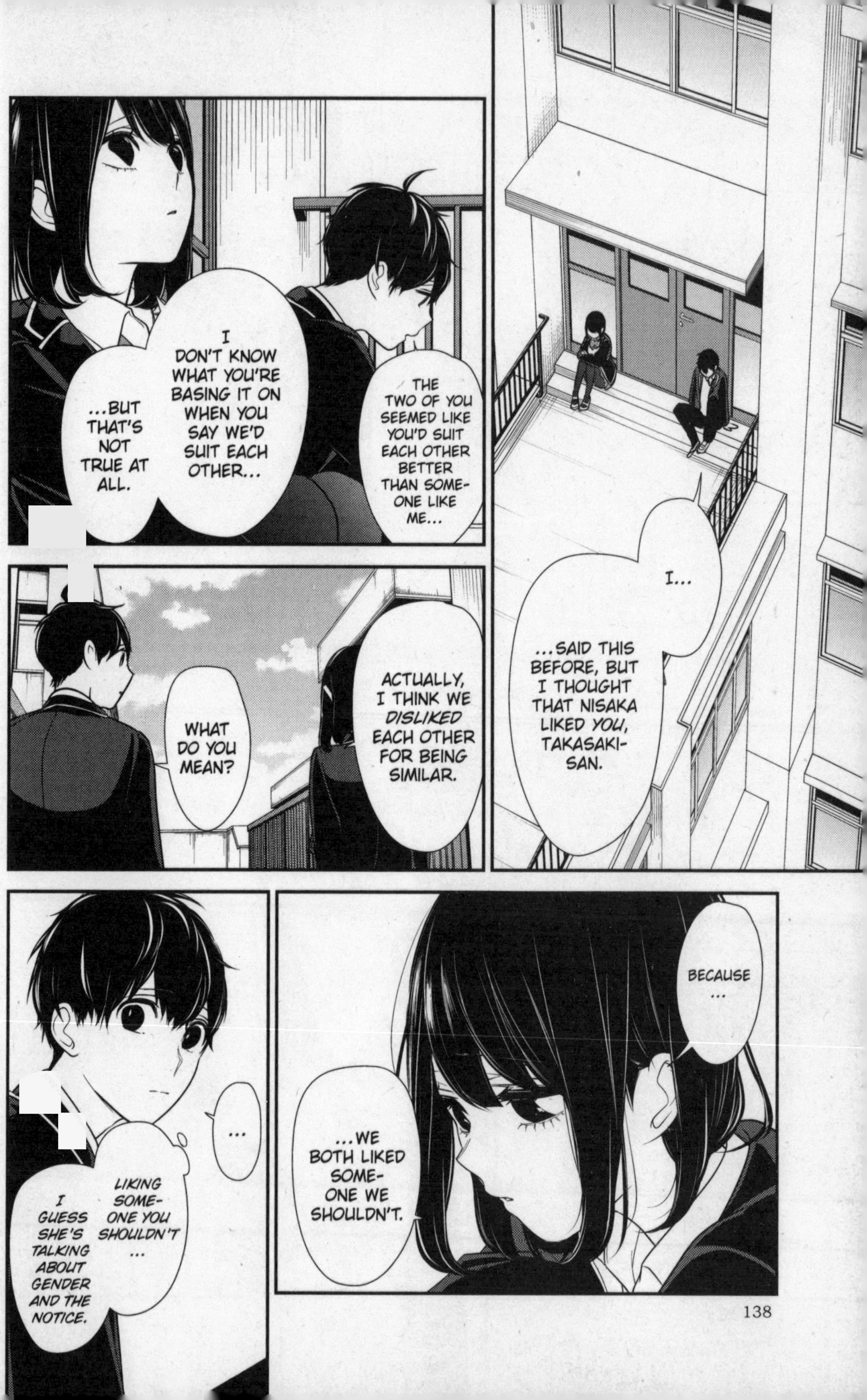
I...
...SAID THIS BEFORE, BUT I THOUGHT THAT NISAKA LIKED *YOU*, TAKASAKI-SAN.
THE TWO OF YOU SEEMED LIKE YOU'D SUIT EACH OTHER BETTER THAN SOME-ONE LIKE ME...
I DON'T KNOW WHAT YOU'RE BASING IT ON WHEN YOU SAY WE'D SUIT EACH OTHER...
...BUT THAT'S NOT TRUE AT ALL.
ACTUALLY, I THINK WE *DISLIKED* EACH OTHER FOR BEING SIMILAR.
WHAT DO YOU MEAN?
BECAUSE...
...WE BOTH LIKED SOME-ONE WE SHOULDN'T.
...
LIKING SOME-ONE YOU SHOULDN'T...
I GUESS SHE'S TALKING ABOUT GENDER AND THE NOTICE.

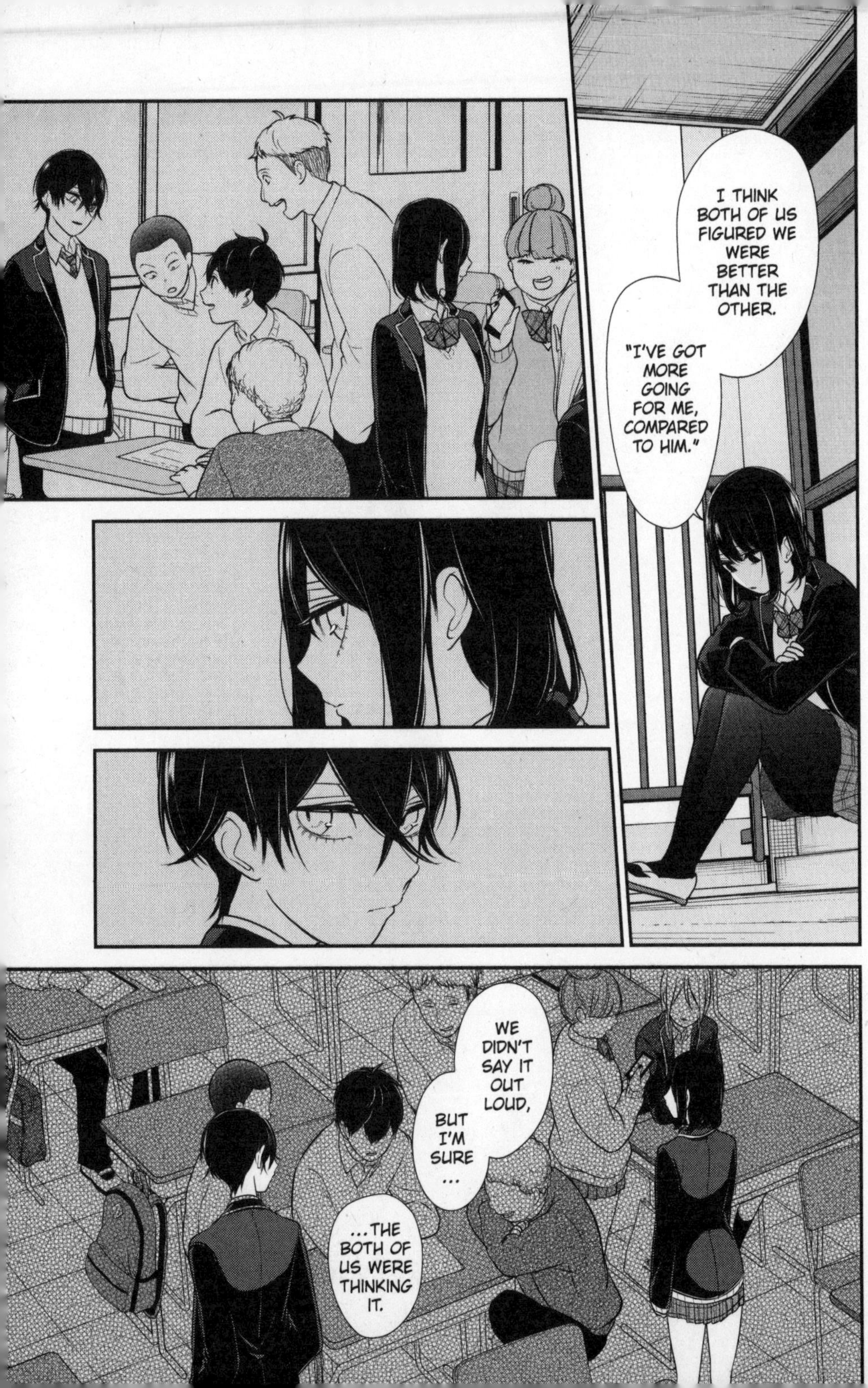
I THINK BOTH OF US FIGURED WE WERE BETTER THAN THE OTHER.
"I'VE GOT MORE GOING FOR ME, COMPARED TO HIM."
WE DIDN'T SAY IT OUT LOUD,
BUT I'M SURE ...
...THE BOTH OF US WERE THINKING IT.

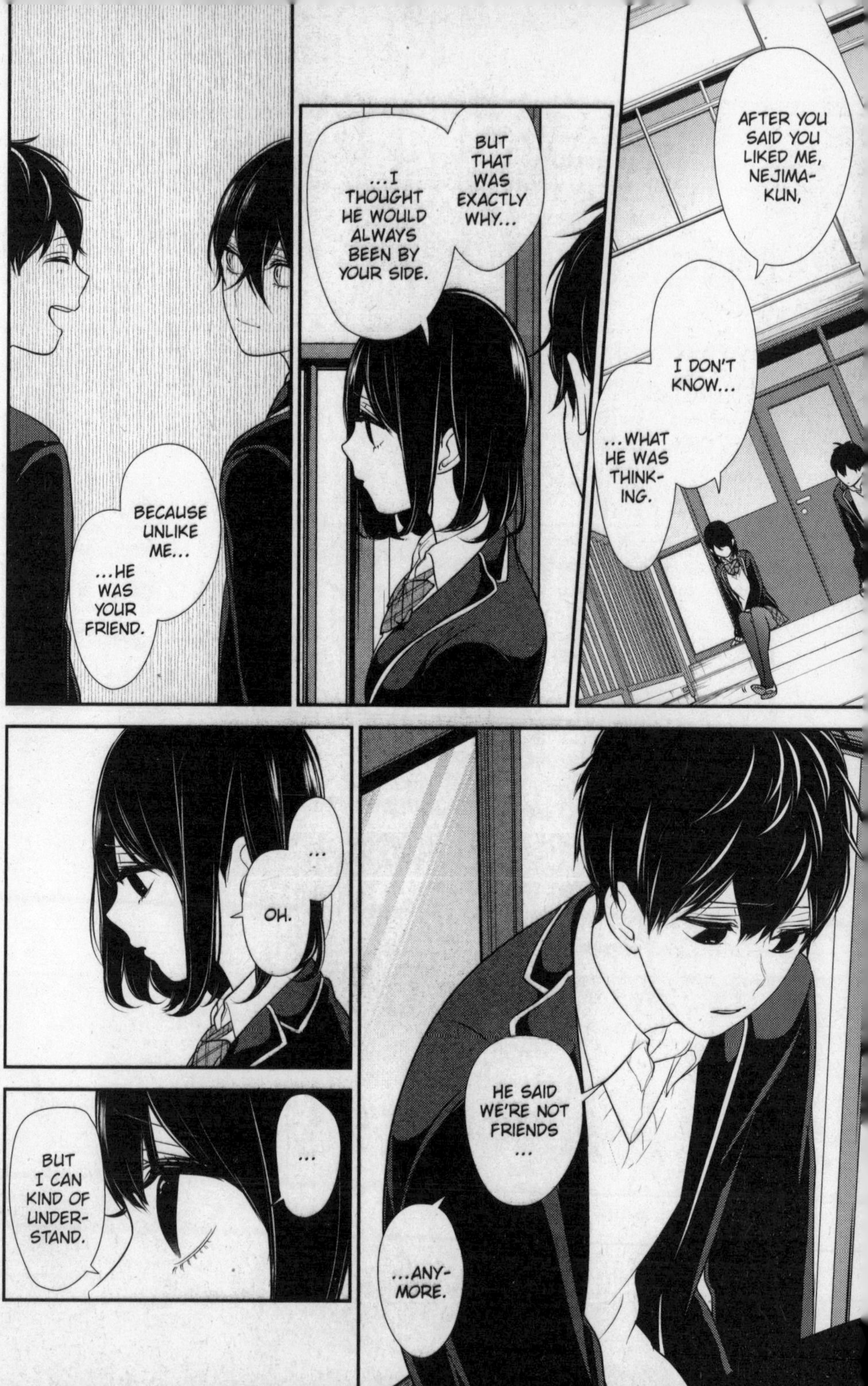
AFTER YOU SAID YOU LIKED ME, NEJIMA-KUN,
I DON'T KNOW...
...WHAT HE WAS THINKING.
BUT THAT WAS EXACTLY WHY...
...I THOUGHT HE WOULD ALWAYS BEEN BY YOUR SIDE.
BECAUSE UNLIKE ME...
...HE WAS YOUR FRIEND.
HE SAID WE'RE NOT FRIENDS ...
...ANY-MORE.
...
OH.
...
BUT I CAN KIND OF UNDER-STAND.

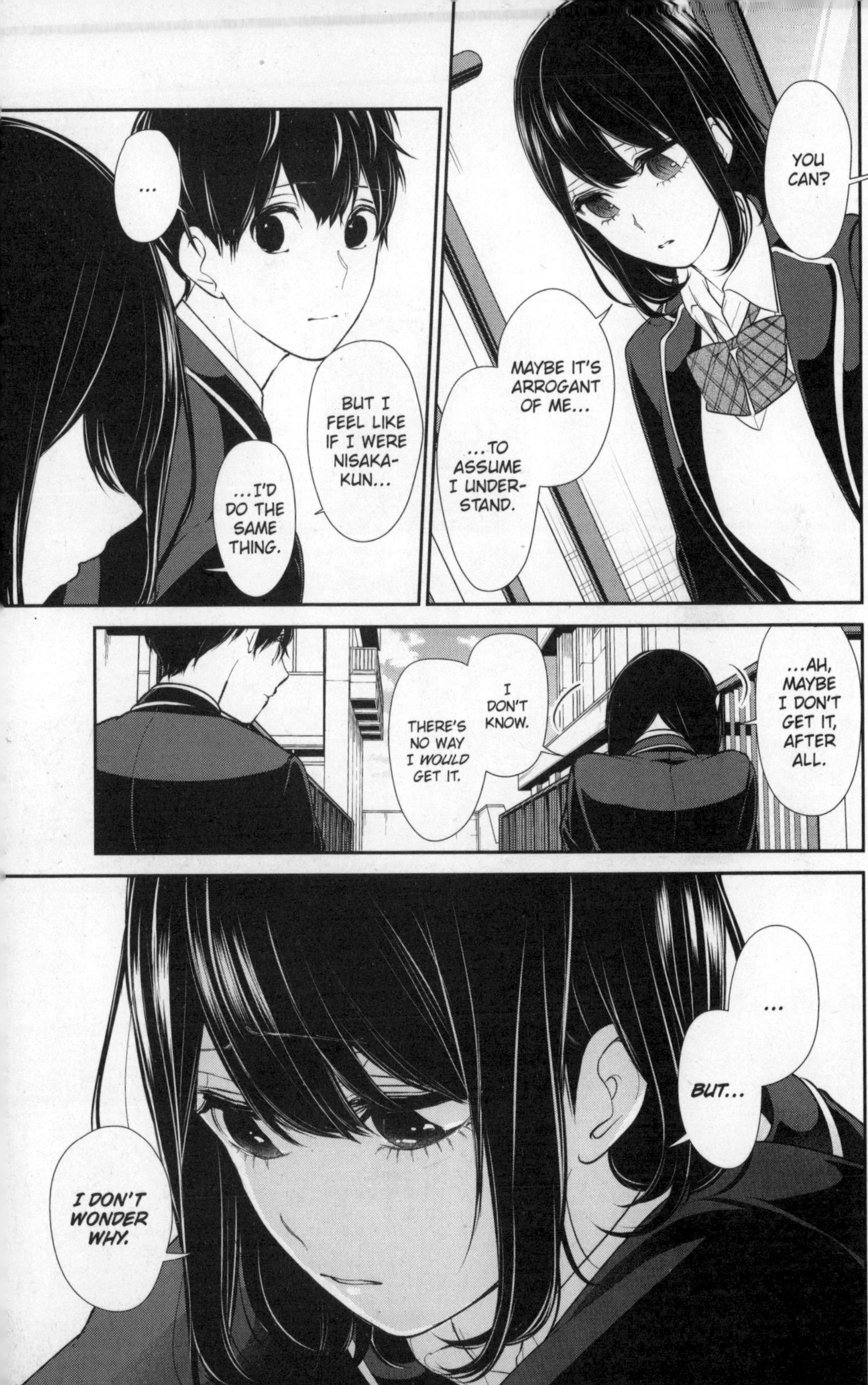
YOU CAN?
MAYBE IT'S ARROGANT OF ME...
...TO ASSUME I UNDERSTAND.
...
BUT I FEEL LIKE IF I WERE NISAKA-KUN...
...I'D DO THE SAME THING.
...AH, MAYBE I DON'T GET IT, AFTER ALL.
I DON'T KNOW.
THERE'S NO WAY I *WOULD* GET IT.
...
BUT...
I DON'T WONDER WHY.

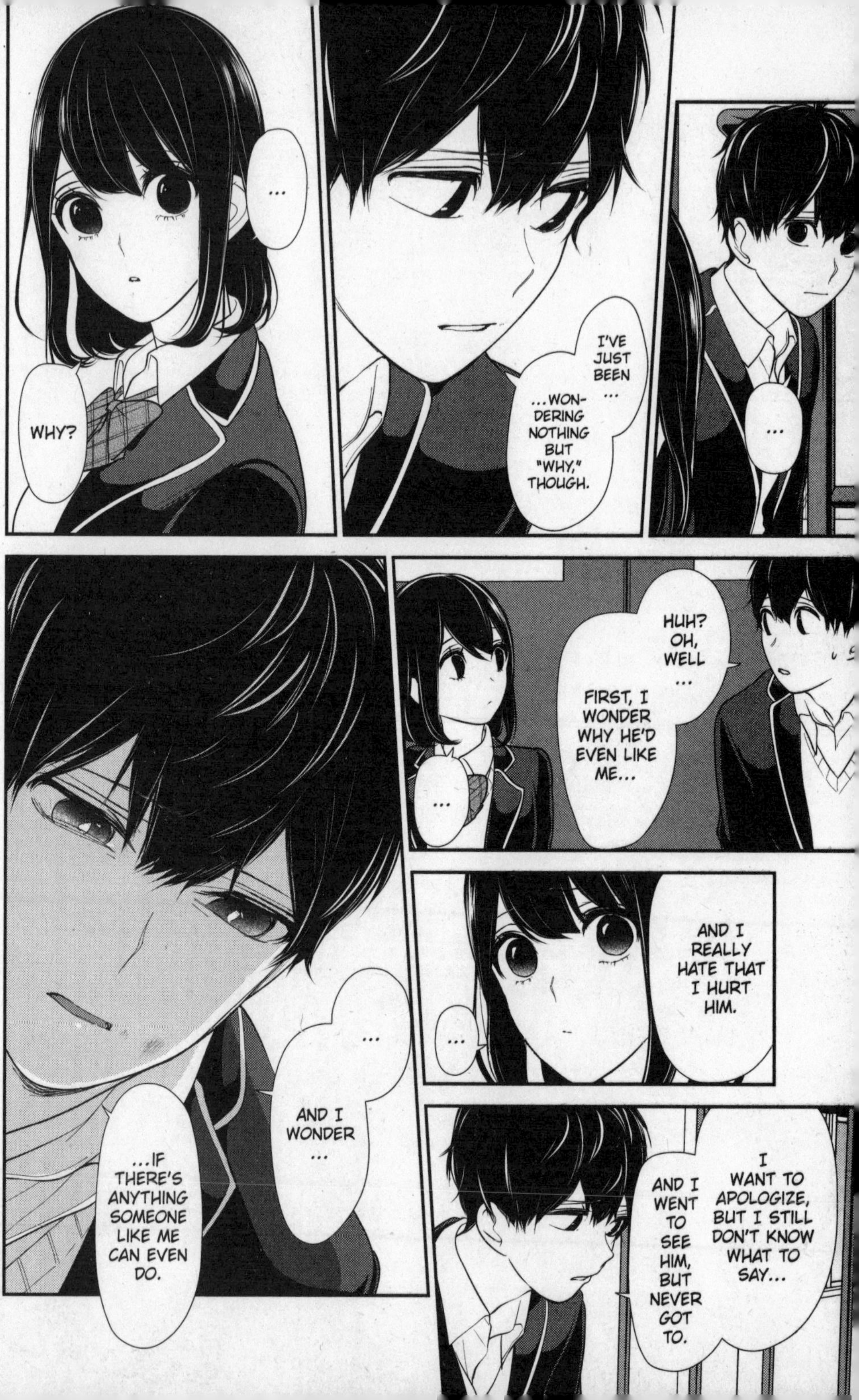
...
I'VE JUST BEEN...
...WONDERING NOTHING BUT "WHY," THOUGH.
...
WHY?
HUH? OH, WELL...
FIRST, I WONDER WHY HE'D EVEN LIKE ME...
...
AND I REALLY HATE THAT I HURT HIM.
...
I WANT TO APOLOGIZE, BUT I STILL DON'T KNOW WHAT TO SAY...
AND I WENT TO SEE HIM, BUT NEVER GOT TO.
...
AND I WONDER...
...IF THERE'S ANYTHING SOMEONE LIKE ME CAN EVEN DO.

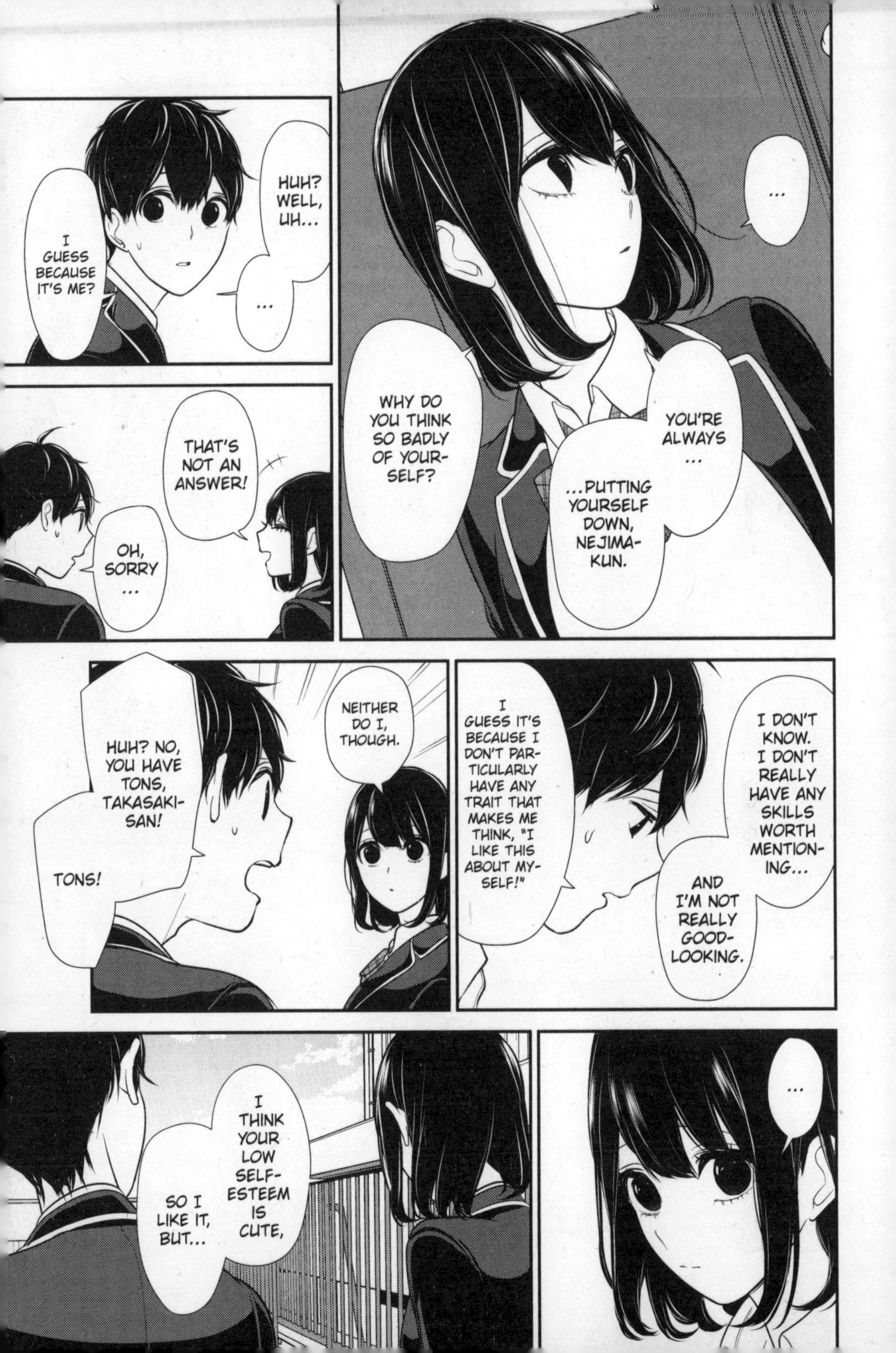
...
YOU'RE ALWAYS ...
...PUTTING YOURSELF DOWN, NEJIMA-KUN.
WHY DO YOU THINK SO BADLY OF YOURSELF?
HUH? WELL, UH...
...
I GUESS BECAUSE IT'S ME?
THAT'S NOT AN ANSWER!
OH, SORRY ...
I DON'T KNOW. I DON'T REALLY HAVE ANY SKILLS WORTH MENTIONING...
AND I'M NOT REALLY GOOD-LOOKING.
I GUESS IT'S BECAUSE I DON'T PARTICULARLY HAVE ANY TRAIT THAT MAKES ME THINK, "I LIKE THIS ABOUT MYSELF!"
NEITHER DO I, THOUGH.
HUH? NO, YOU HAVE TONS, TAKASAKI-SAN!
TONS!
...
I THINK YOUR LOW SELF-ESTEEM IS CUTE,
SO I LIKE IT, BUT...

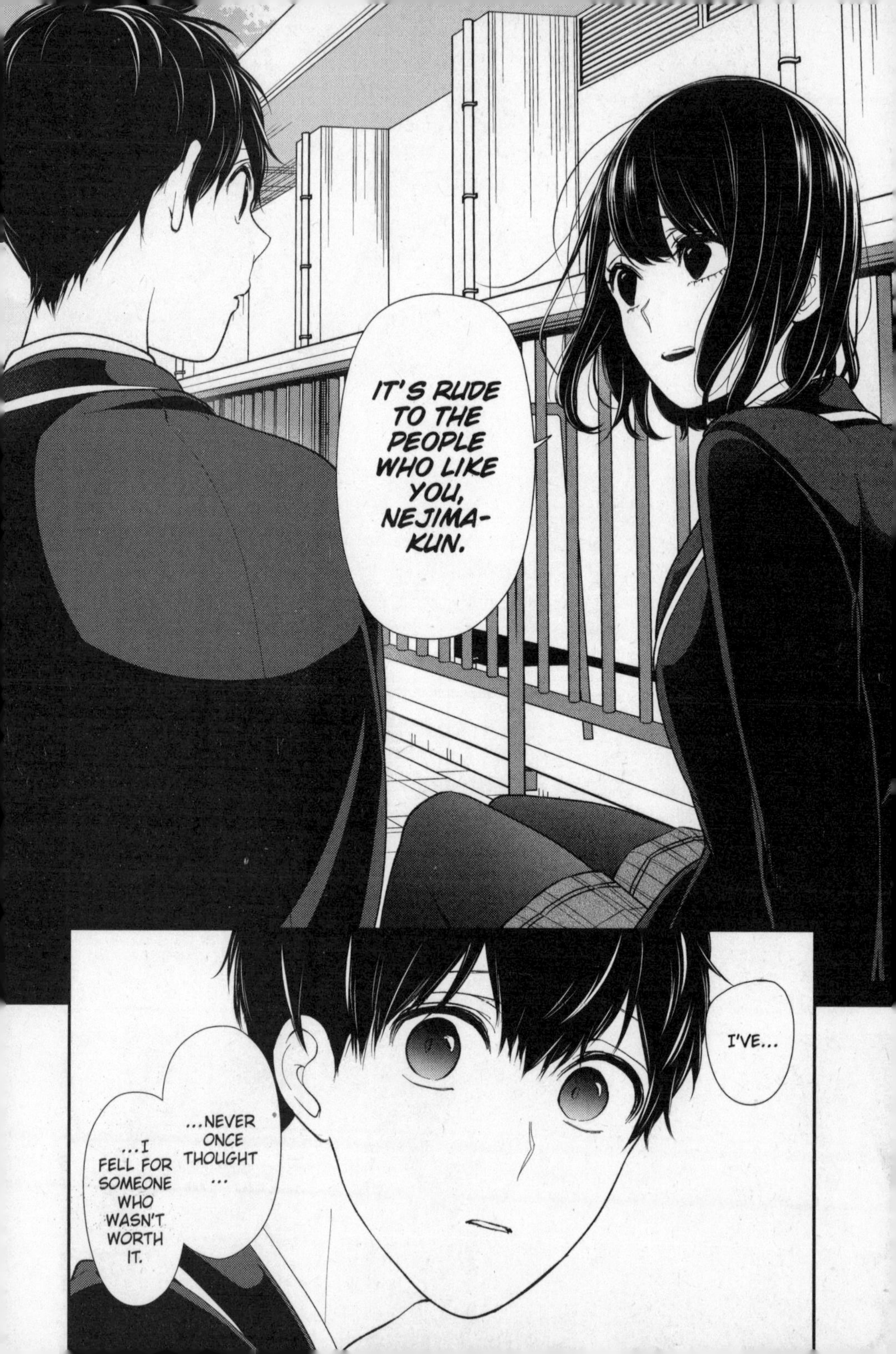
IT'S RUDE TO THE PEOPLE WHO LIKE YOU, NEJIMA-KUN.
I'VE...
...NEVER ONCE THOUGHT ...
...I FELL FOR SOMEONE WHO WASN'T WORTH IT.

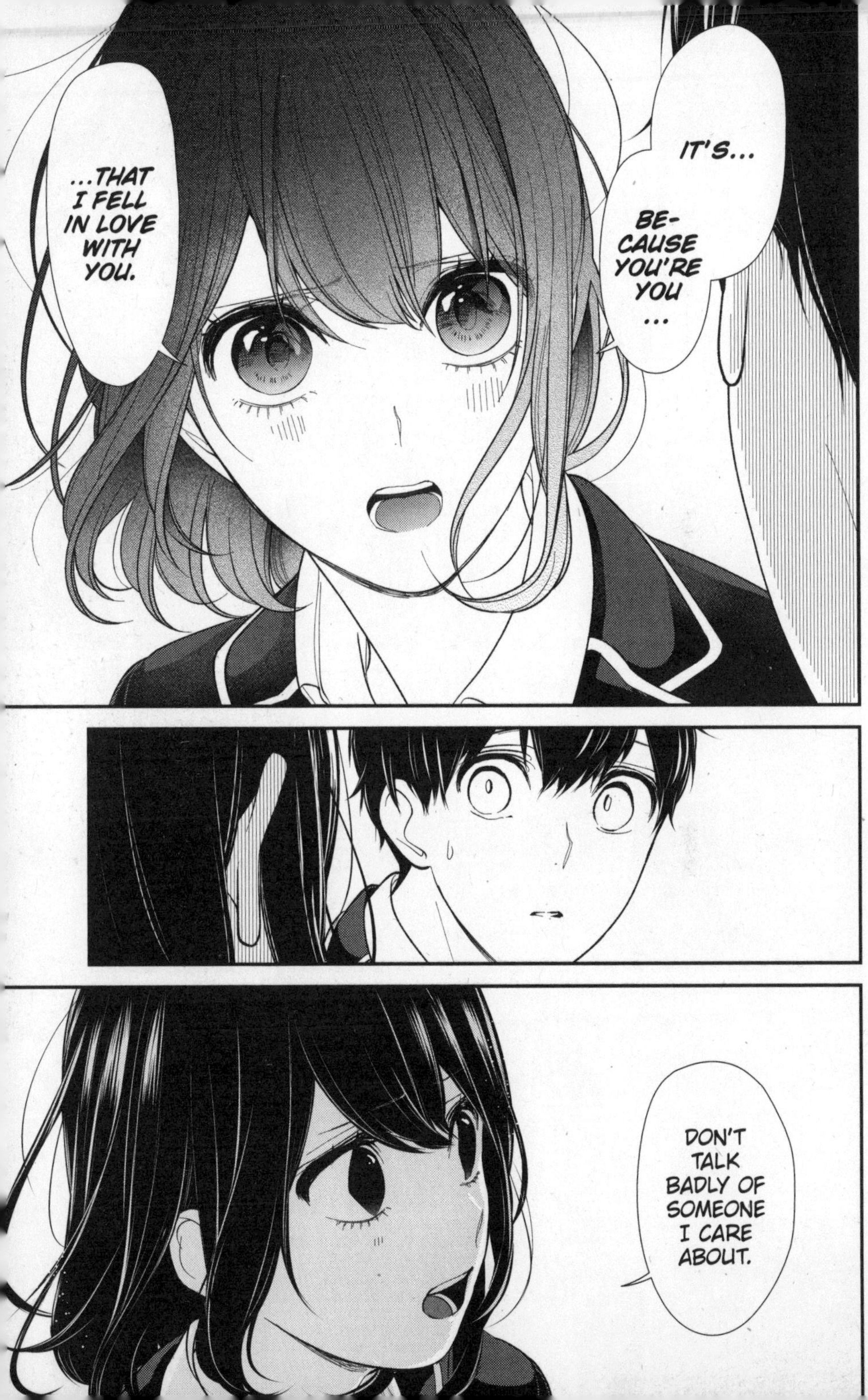
IT'S... BE-CAUSE YOU'RE YOU...
...THAT I FELL IN LOVE WITH YOU.
DON'T TALK BADLY OF SOMEONE I CARE ABOUT.

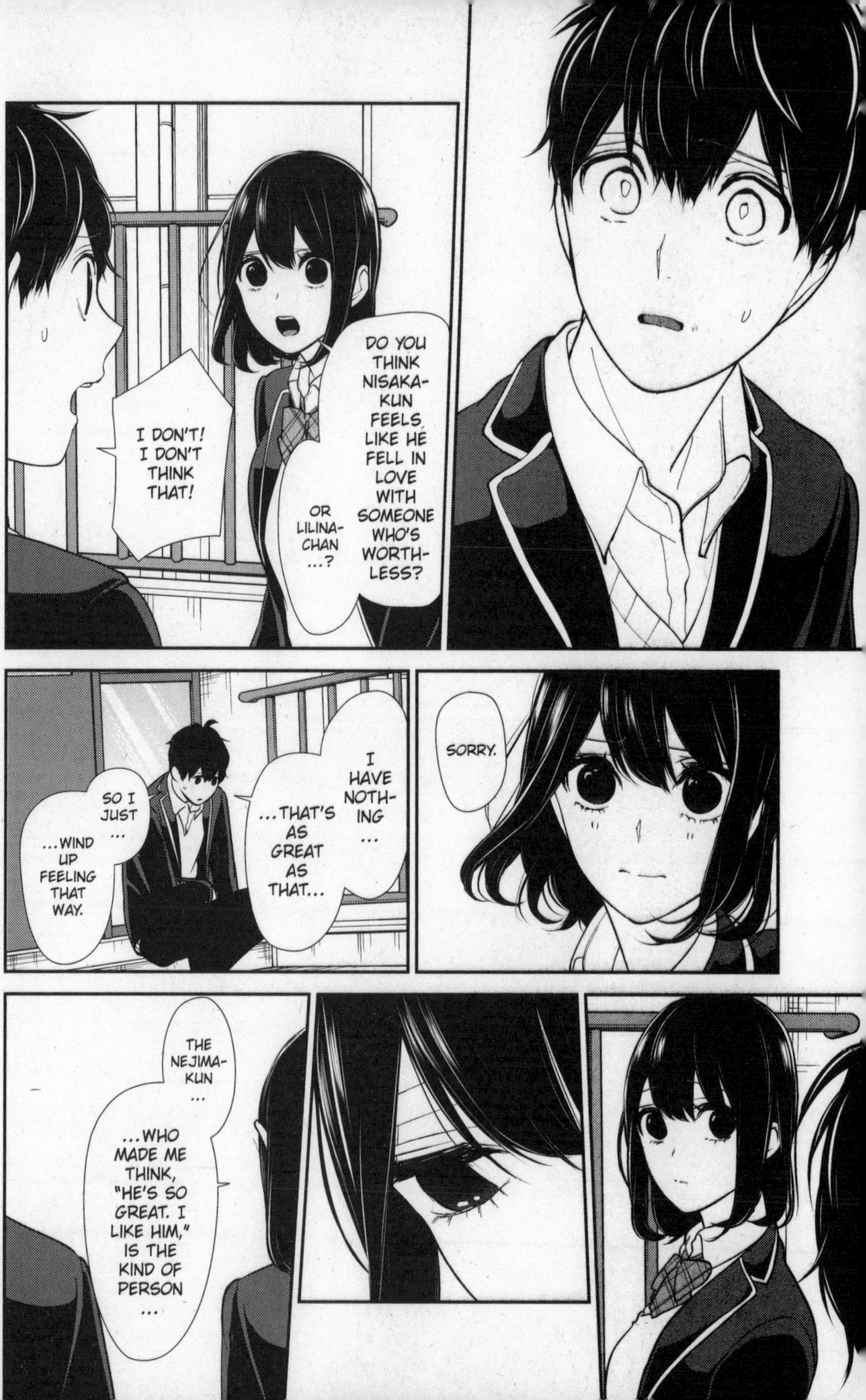
DO YOU THINK NISAKA-KUN FEELS LIKE HE FELL IN LOVE WITH SOMEONE WHO'S WORTHLESS?
OR LILINA-CHAN ...?
I DON'T! I DON'T THINK THAT!
SORRY.
I HAVE NOTHING-ING ...
...THAT'S AS GREAT AS THAT...
SO I JUST ...
...WIND UP FEELING THAT WAY.
THE NEJIMA-KUN ...
...WHO MADE ME THINK, "HE'S SO GREAT. I LIKE HIM," IS THE KIND OF PERSON ...

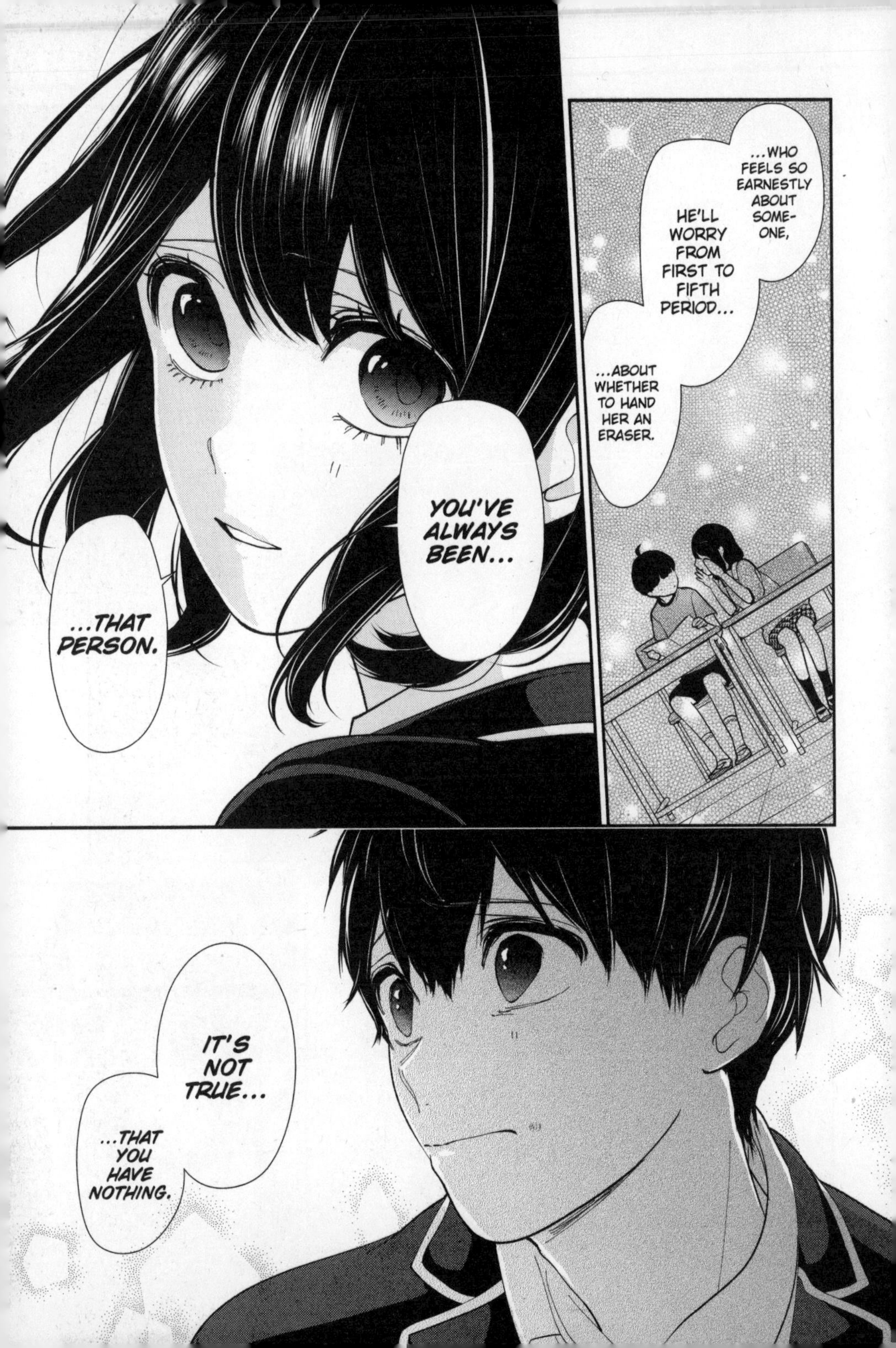
...WHO FEELS SO EARNESTLY ABOUT SOME-ONE,
HE'LL WORRY FROM FIRST TO FIFTH PERIOD...
...ABOUT WHETHER TO HAND HER AN ERASER.
YOU'VE ALWAYS BEEN...
...THAT PERSON.
IT'S NOT TRUE...
...THAT YOU HAVE NOTHING.

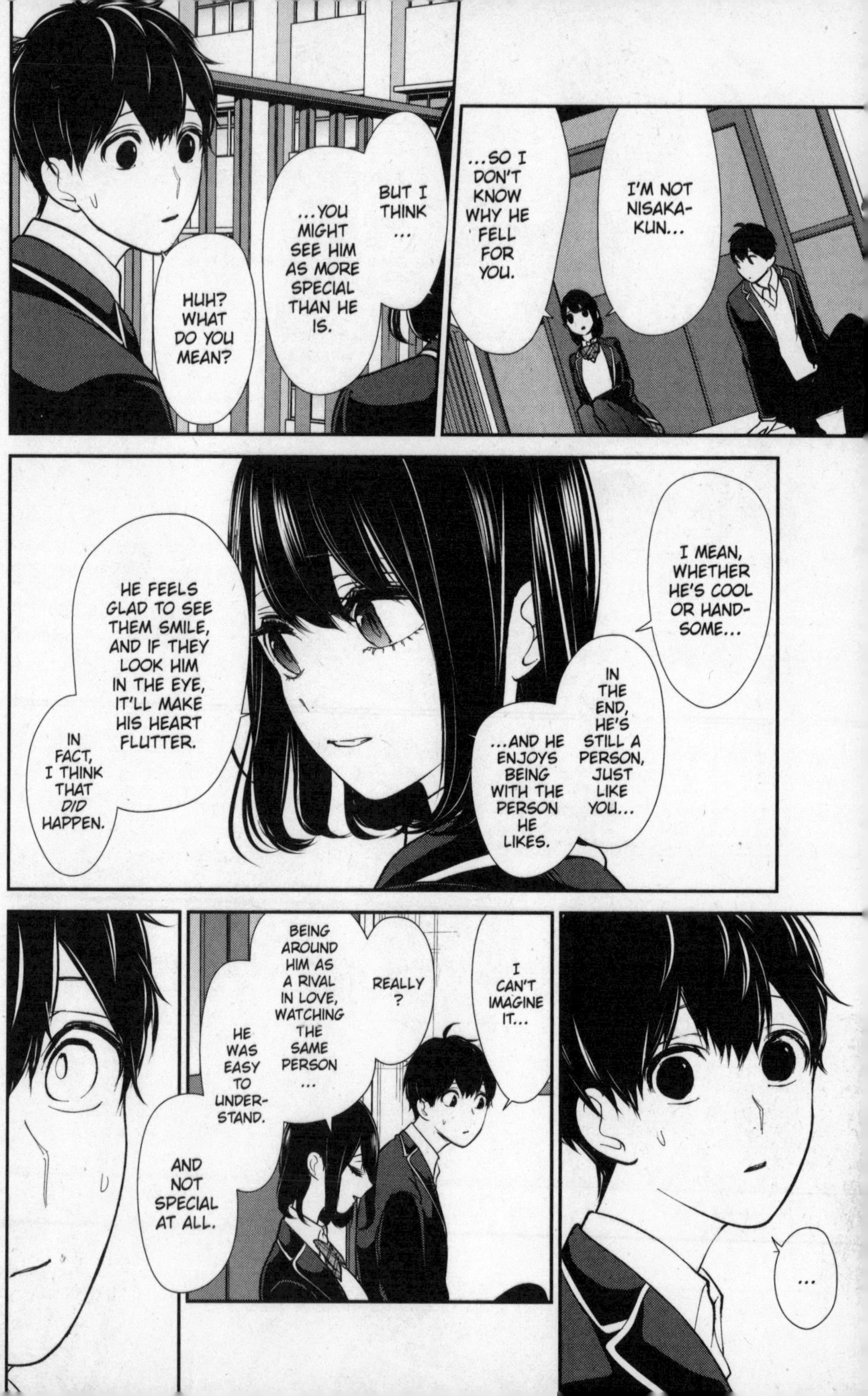
I'M NOT NISAKA-KUN...
...SO I DON'T KNOW WHY HE FELL FOR YOU.
BUT I THINK...
...YOU MIGHT SEE HIM AS MORE SPECIAL THAN HE IS.
HUH? WHAT DO YOU MEAN?
I MEAN, WHETHER HE'S COOL OR HAND-SOME...
IN THE END, HE'S STILL A PERSON, JUST LIKE YOU...
...AND HE ENJOYS BEING WITH THE PERSON HE LIKES.
HE FEELS GLAD TO SEE THEM SMILE, AND IF THEY LOOK HIM IN THE EYE, IT'LL MAKE HIS HEART FLUTTER.
IN FACT, I THINK THAT *DID* HAPPEN.
...
I CAN'T IMAGINE IT...
REALLY?
BEING AROUND HIM AS A RIVAL IN LOVE, WATCHING THE SAME PERSON...
HE WAS EASY TO UNDERSTAND.
AND NOT SPECIAL AT ALL.

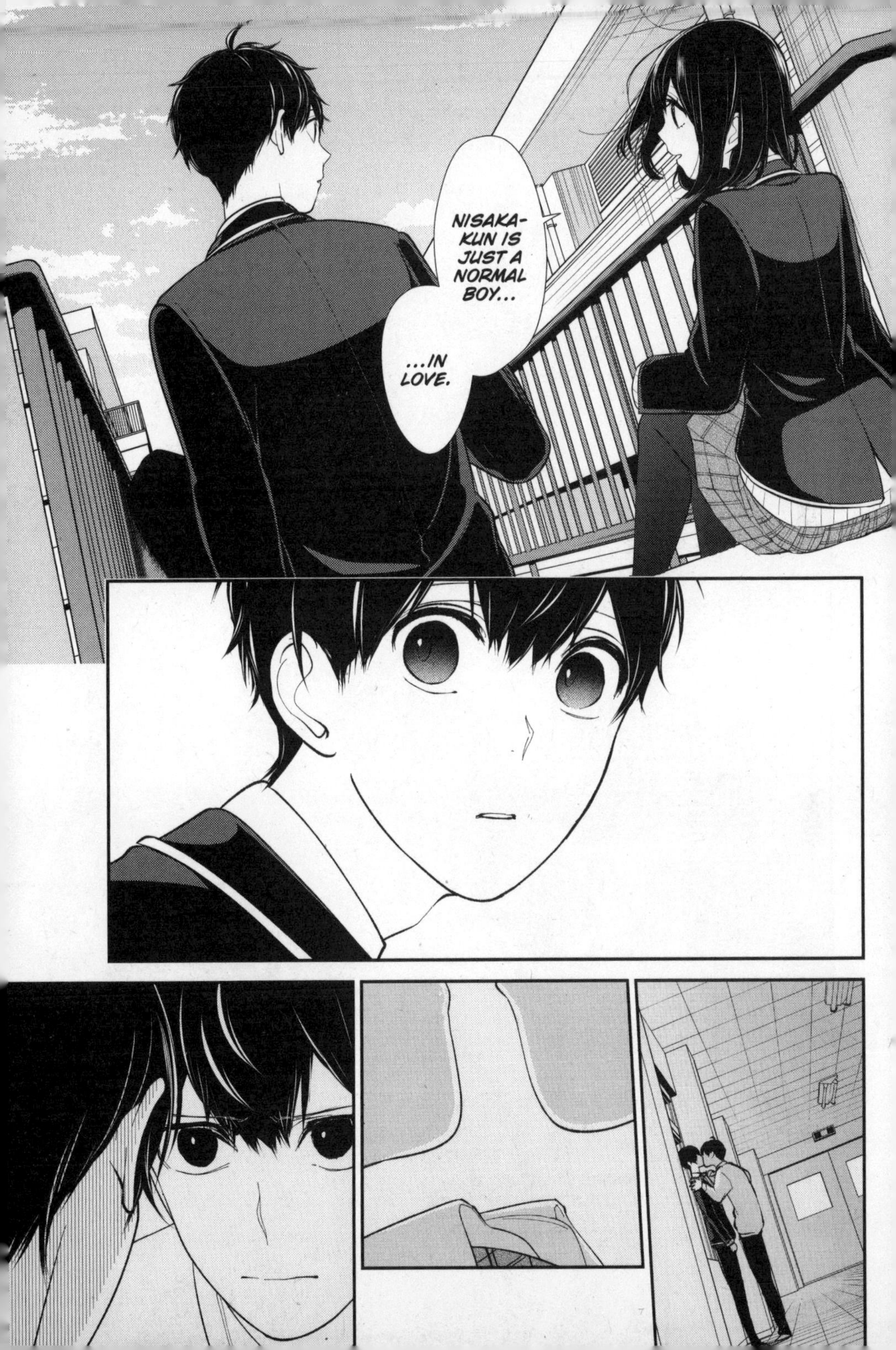
NISAKA-KUN IS JUST A NORMAL BOY...
...IN LOVE.

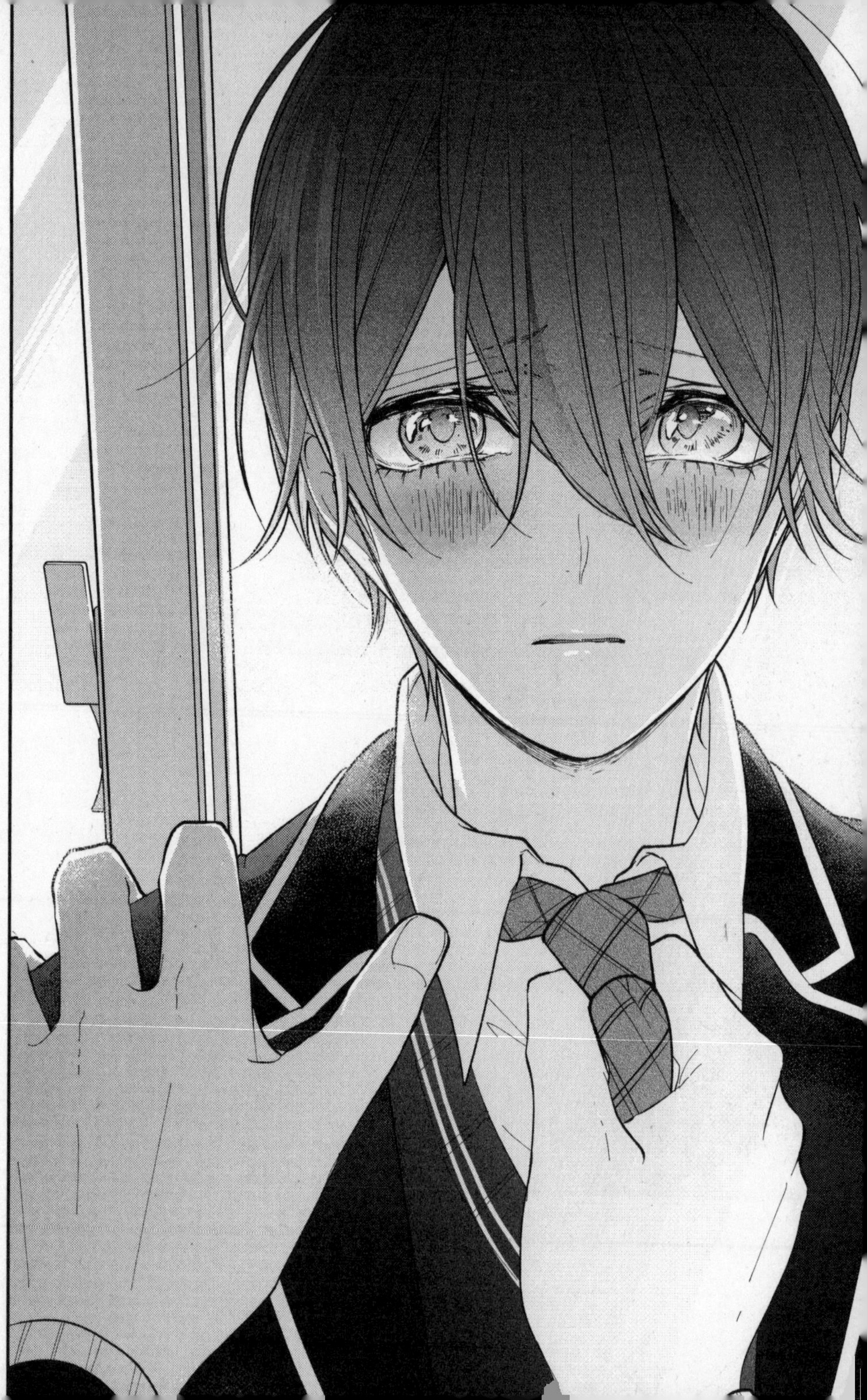

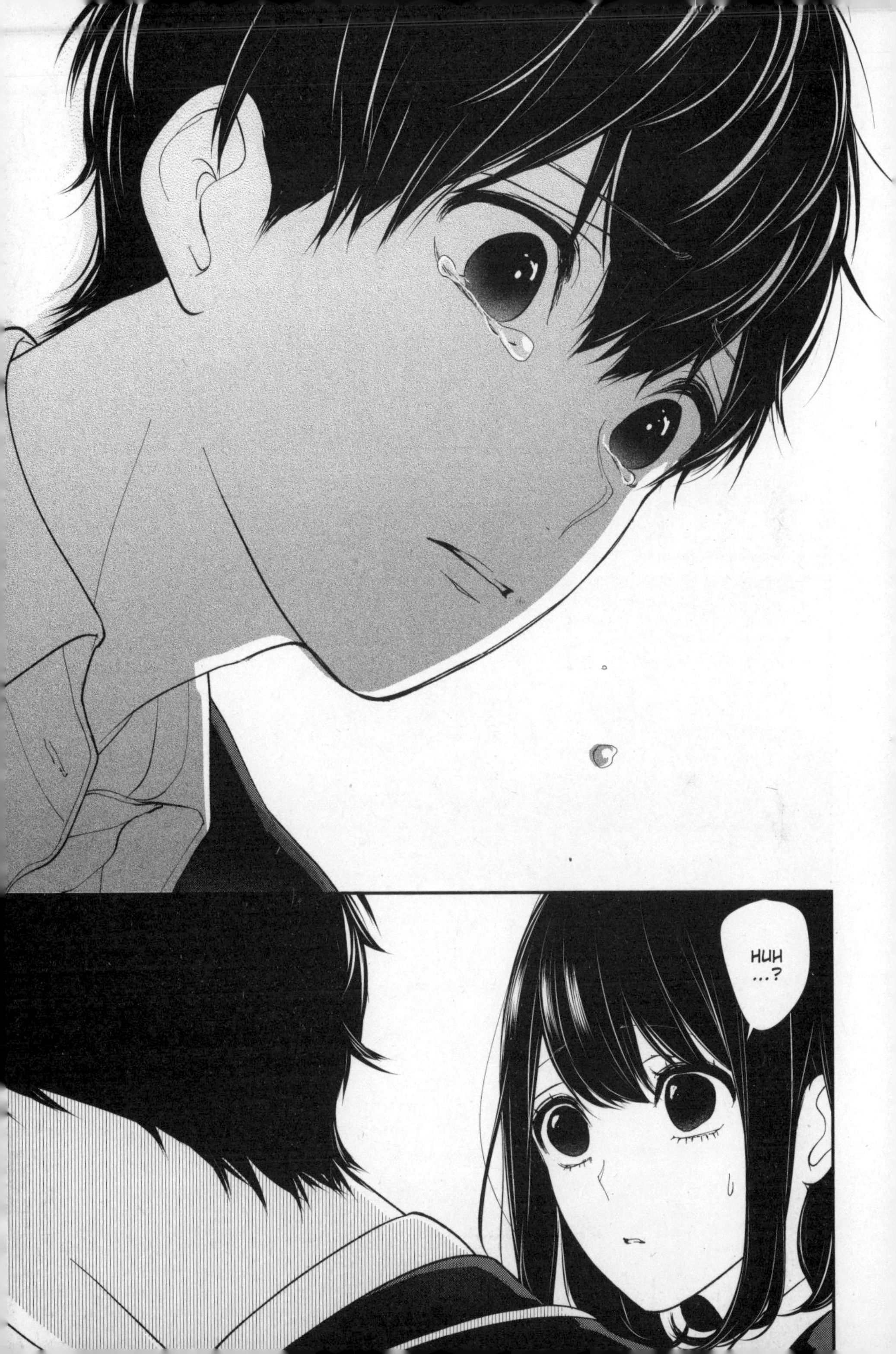
HUH …?

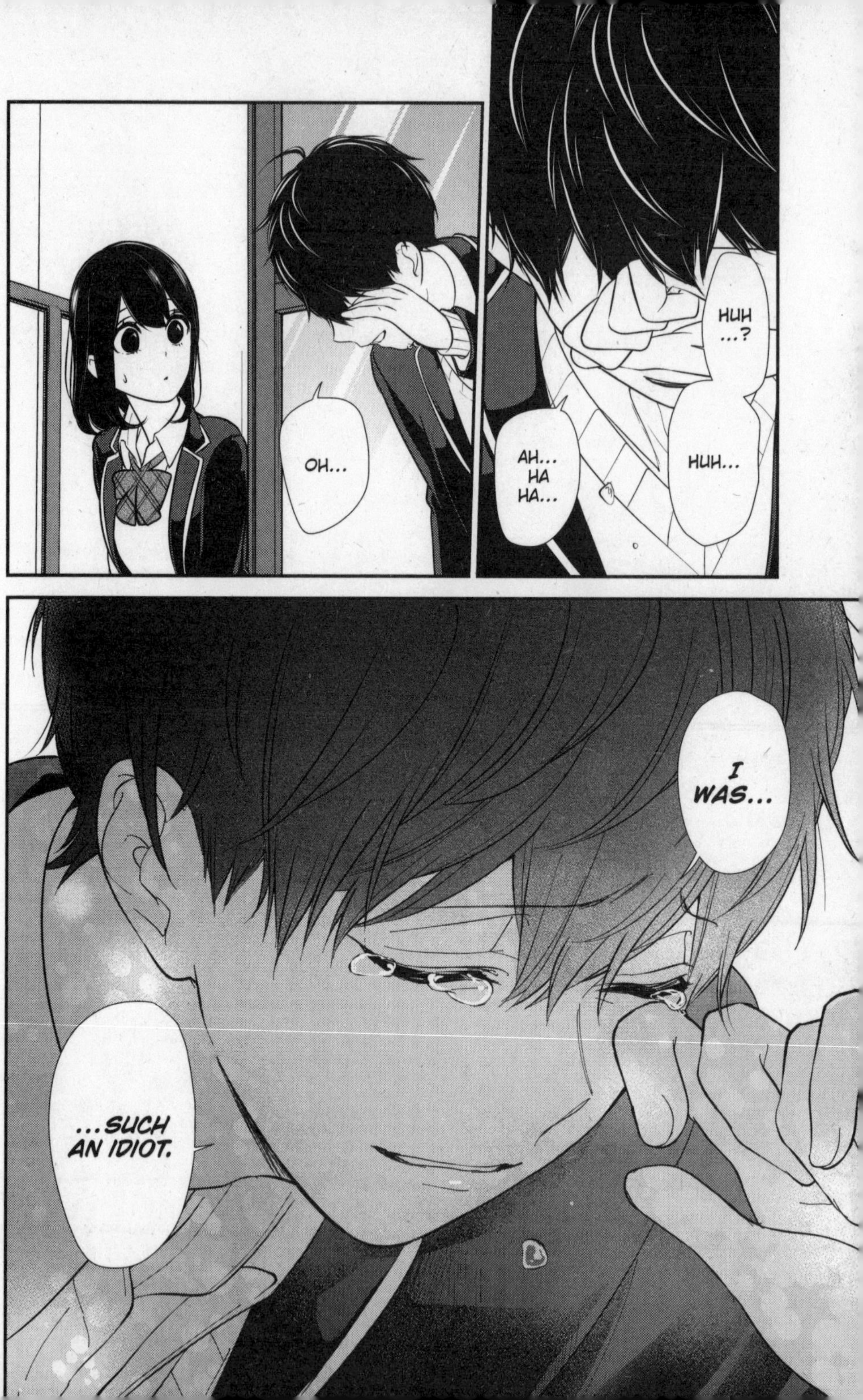
HUH ...?
HUH...
AH... HA HA...
OH...
I WAS...
...SUCH AN IDIOT.

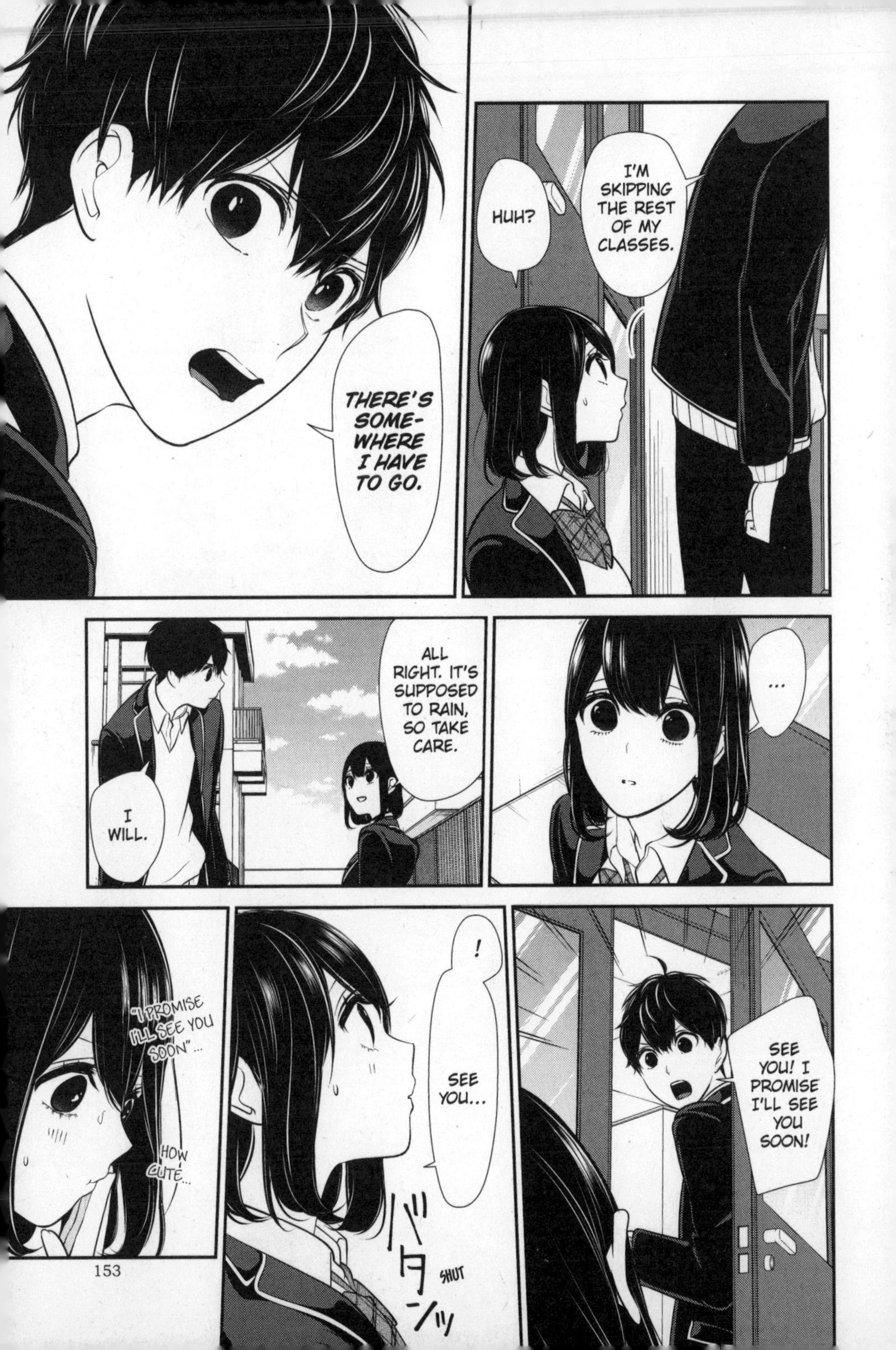
I'M SKIPPING THE REST OF MY CLASSES.
HUH?
THERE'S SOME-WHERE I HAVE TO GO.
...
ALL RIGHT. IT'S SUPPOSED TO RAIN, SO TAKE CARE.
I WILL.
SEE YOU! I PROMISE I'LL SEE YOU SOON!
!
SEE YOU...
SHUT
"I PROMISE I'LL SEE YOU SOON"...
HOW CUTE...

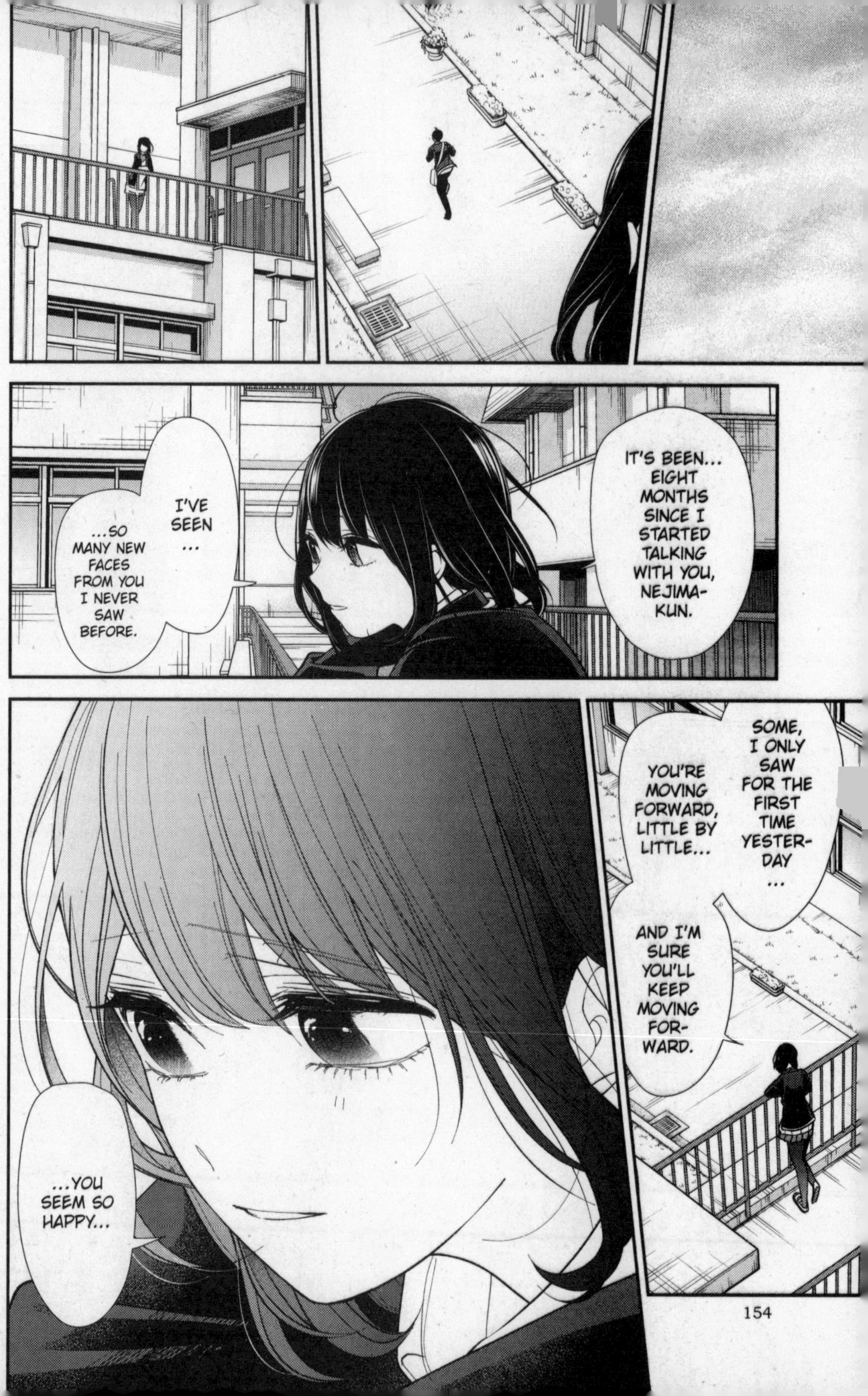
IT'S BEEN... EIGHT MONTHS SINCE I STARTED TALKING WITH YOU, NEJIMA-KUN.
I'VE SEEN...
...SO MANY NEW FACES FROM YOU I NEVER SAW BEFORE.
SOME, I ONLY SAW FOR THE FIRST TIME YESTER-DAY...
YOU'RE MOVING FORWARD, LITTLE BY LITTLE...
AND I'M SURE YOU'LL KEEP MOVING FOR-WARD.
...YOU SEEM SO HAPPY...

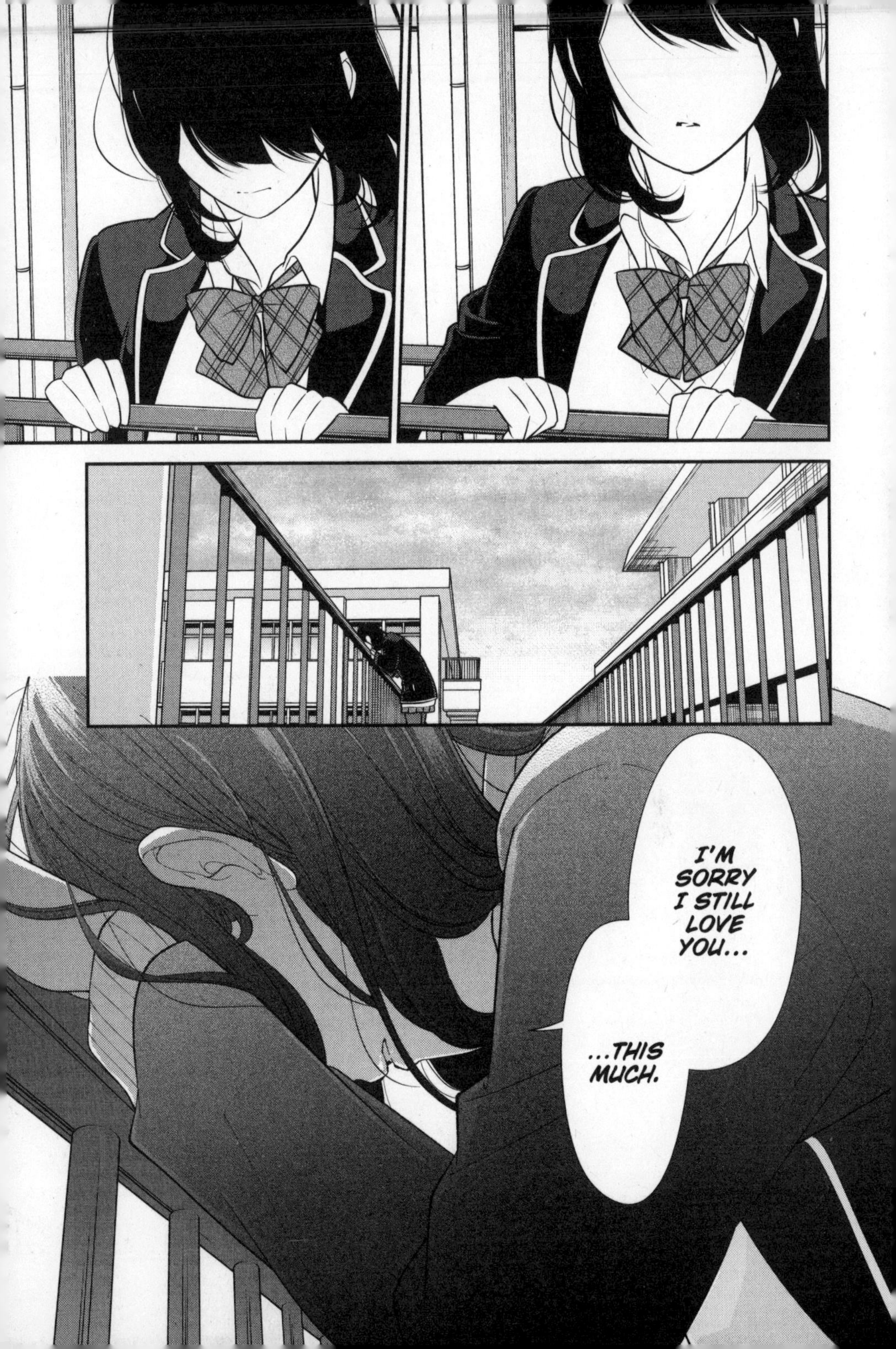
I'M SORRY I STILL LOVE YOU...
...THIS MUCH.

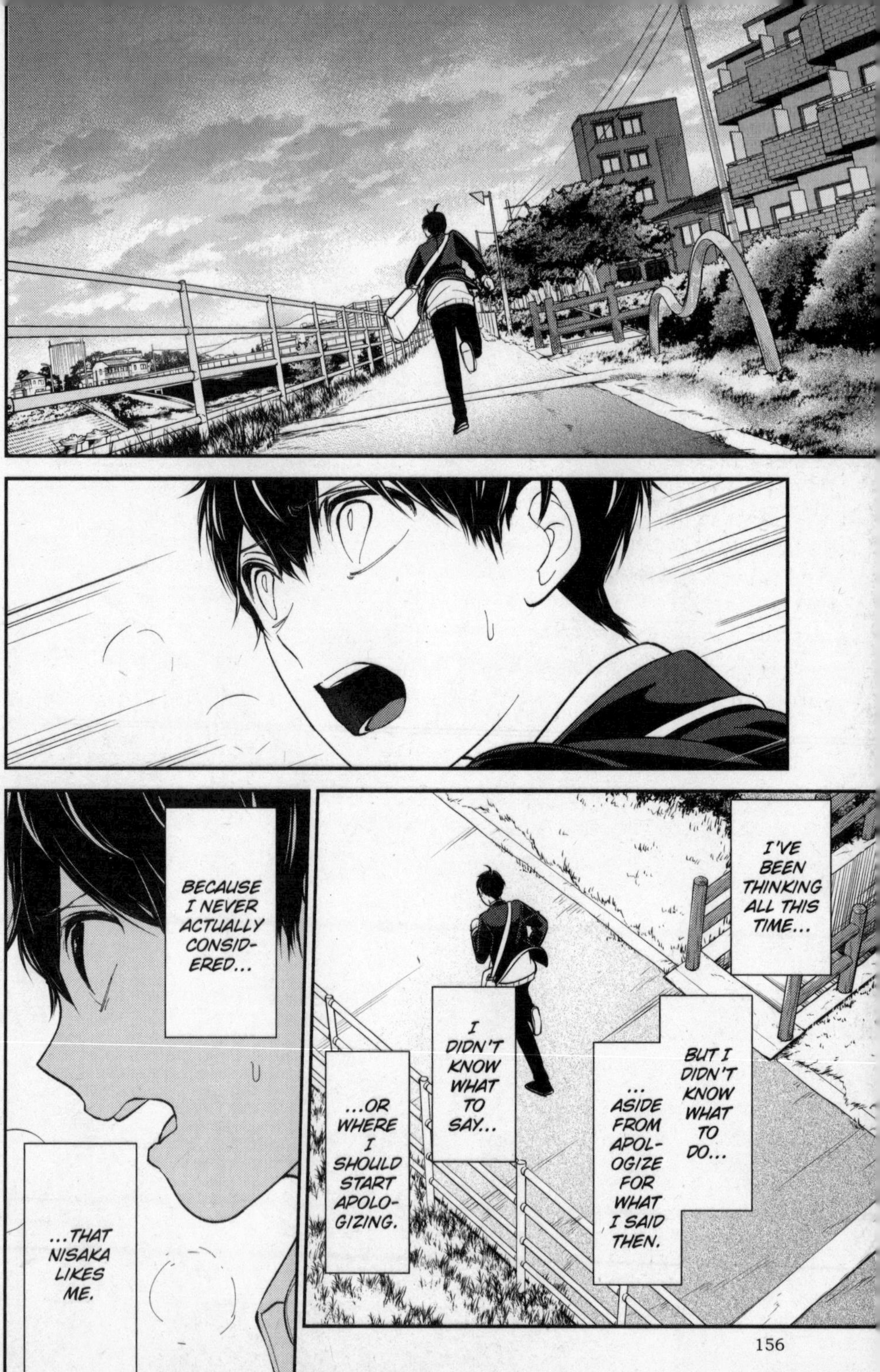
I'VE BEEN THINKING ALL THIS TIME...
BUT I DIDN'T KNOW WHAT TO DO...
... ASIDE FROM APOLOGIZE FOR WHAT I SAID THEN.
I DIDN'T KNOW WHAT TO SAY...
...OR WHERE I SHOULD START APOLOGIZING.
BECAUSE I NEVER ACTUALLY CONSIDERED...
...THAT NISAKA LIKES ME.

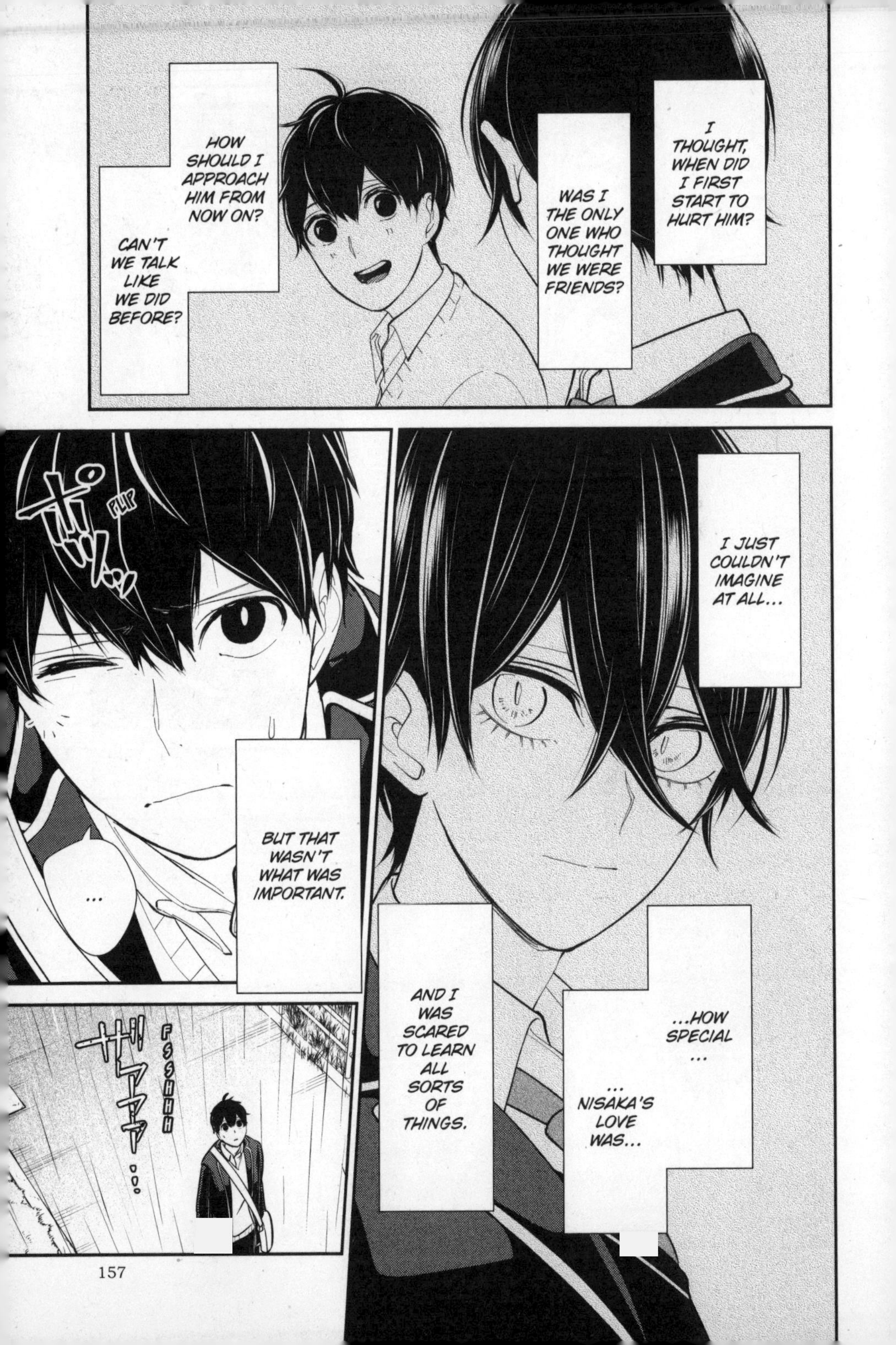
I THOUGHT, WHEN DID I FIRST START TO HURT HIM?
WAS I THE ONLY ONE WHO THOUGHT WE WERE FRIENDS?
HOW SHOULD I APPROACH HIM FROM NOW ON?
CAN'T WE TALK LIKE WE DID BEFORE?
I JUST COULDN'T IMAGINE AT ALL...
...HOW SPECIAL ...
... NISAKA'S LOVE WAS...
AND I WAS SCARED TO LEARN ALL SORTS OF THINGS.
FLIP
BUT THAT WASN'T WHAT WAS IMPORTANT.
...
FSSHHH

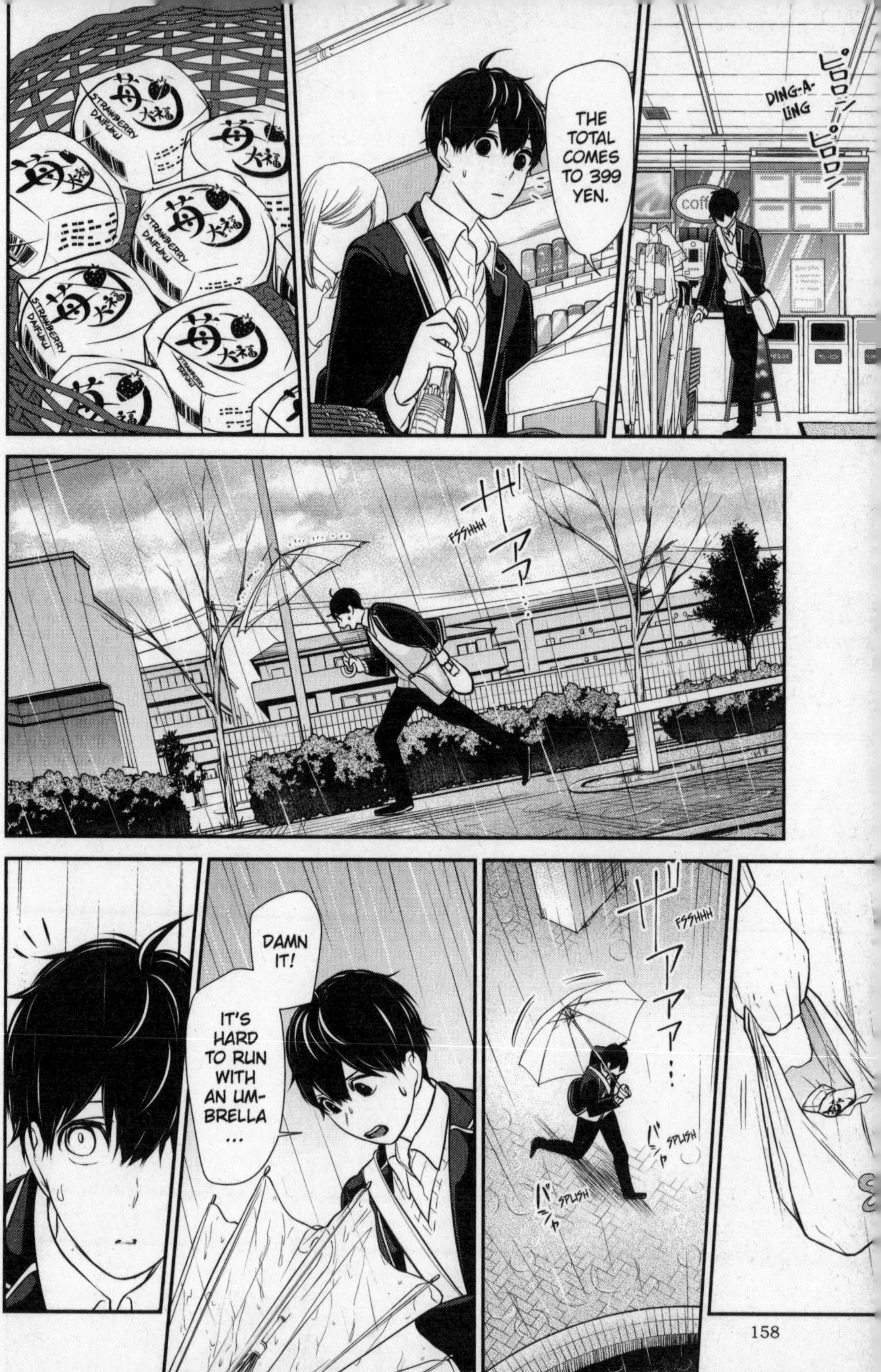
DING-A-LING
ピロロン
ピロロン
THE TOTAL COMES TO 399 YEN.
苺大福
STRAWBERRY DAIFUKU
ザアア…
FSSHHH
ザアアア…
FSSHHH
バシャ
SPLISH
バシャ
SPLISH
DAMN IT!
IT'S HARD TO RUN WITH AN UM-BRELLA …

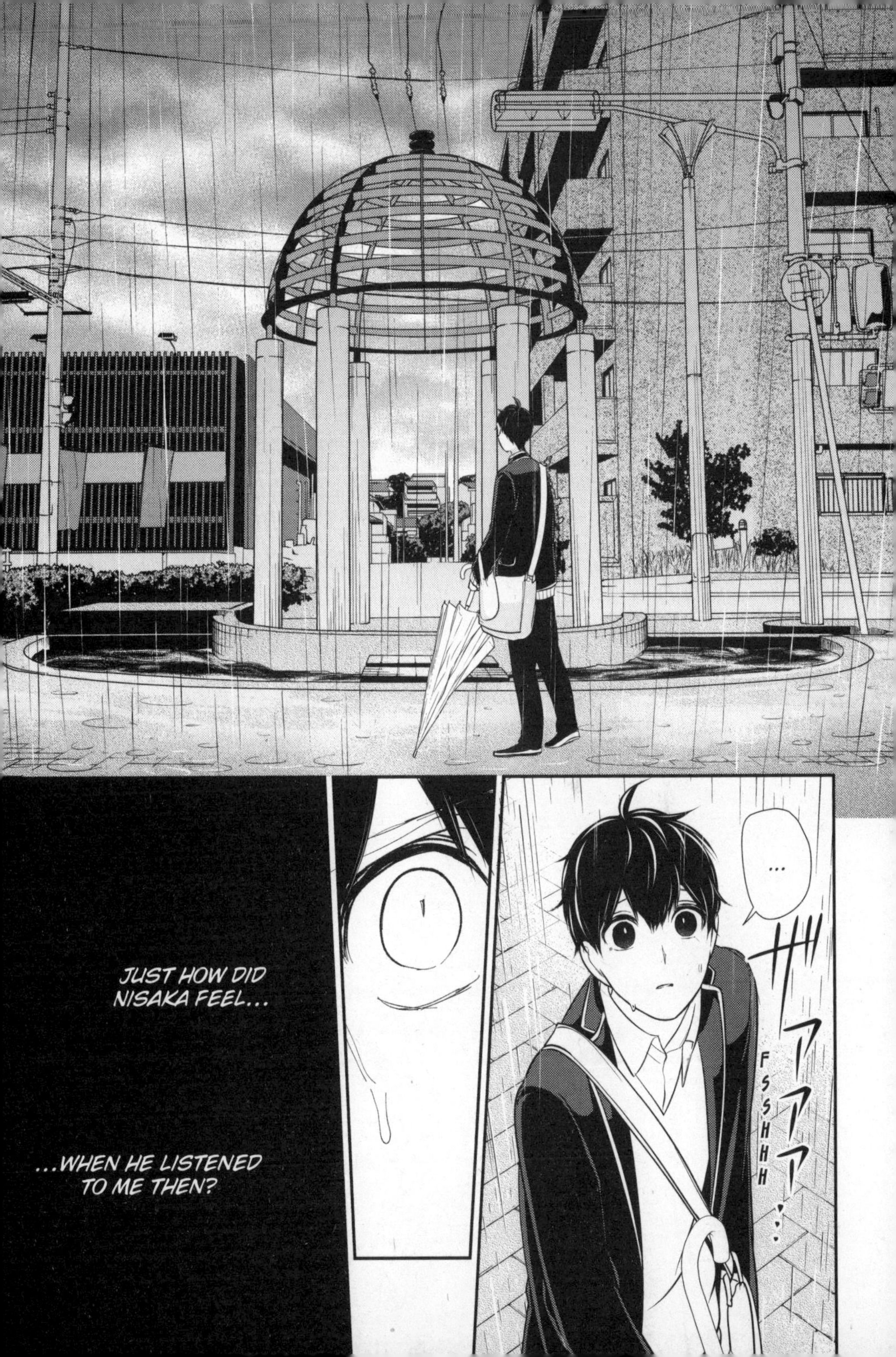
...
FSSHHH
JUST HOW DID NISAKA FEEL...
...WHEN HE LISTENED TO ME THEN?

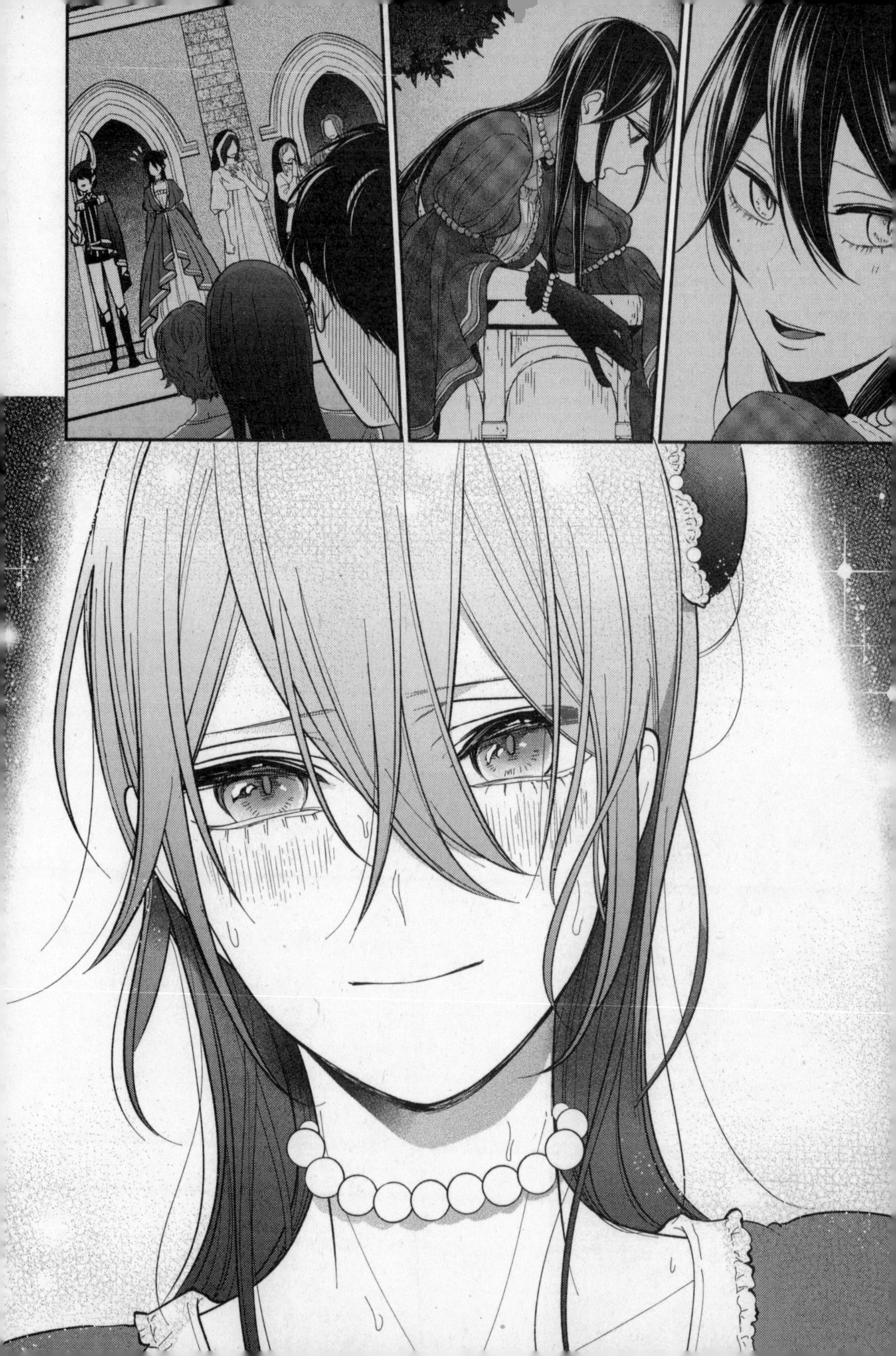

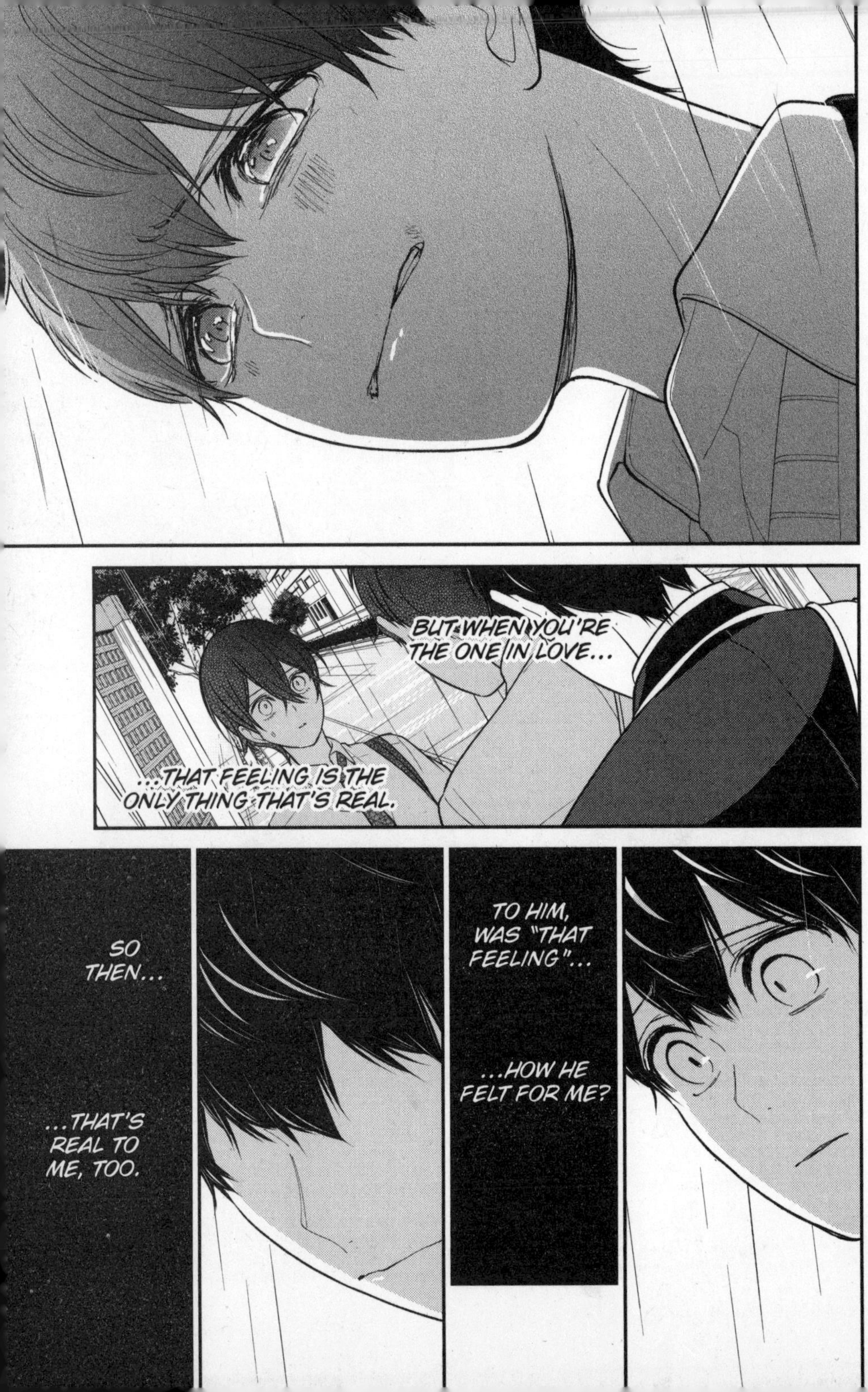
BUT WHEN YOU'RE THE ONE IN LOVE...
...THAT FEELING IS THE ONLY THING THAT'S REAL.
TO HIM, WAS "THAT FEELING"...
...HOW HE FELT FOR ME?
SO THEN...
...THAT'S REAL TO ME, TOO.

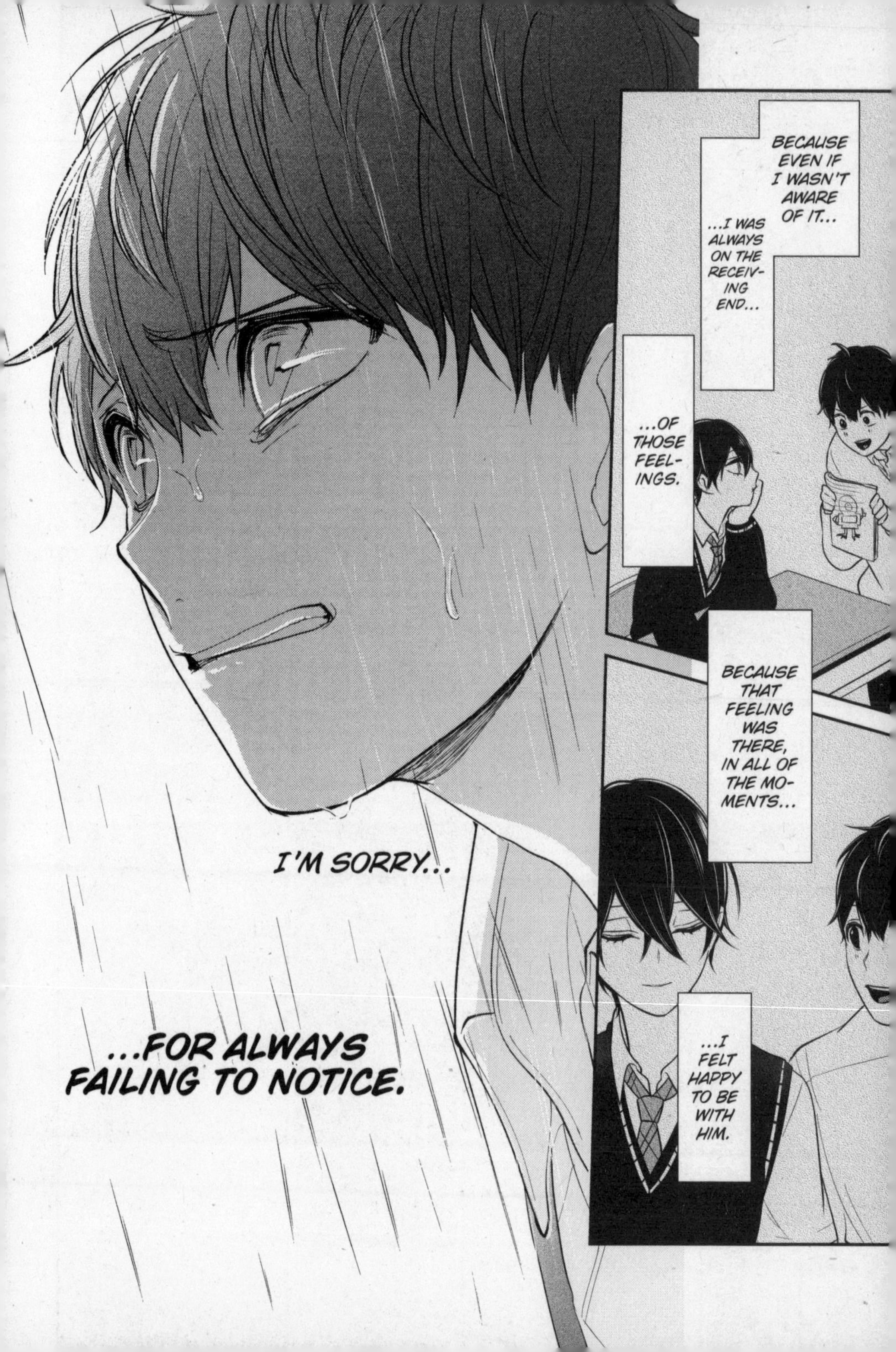
BECAUSE EVEN IF I WASN'T AWARE OF IT...
...I WAS ALWAYS ON THE RECEIV-ING END...
...OF THOSE FEEL-INGS.
BECAUSE THAT FEELING WAS THERE, IN ALL OF THE MO-MENTS...
...I FELT HAPPY TO BE WITH HIM.
I'M SORRY...
...FOR ALWAYS FAILING TO NOTICE.

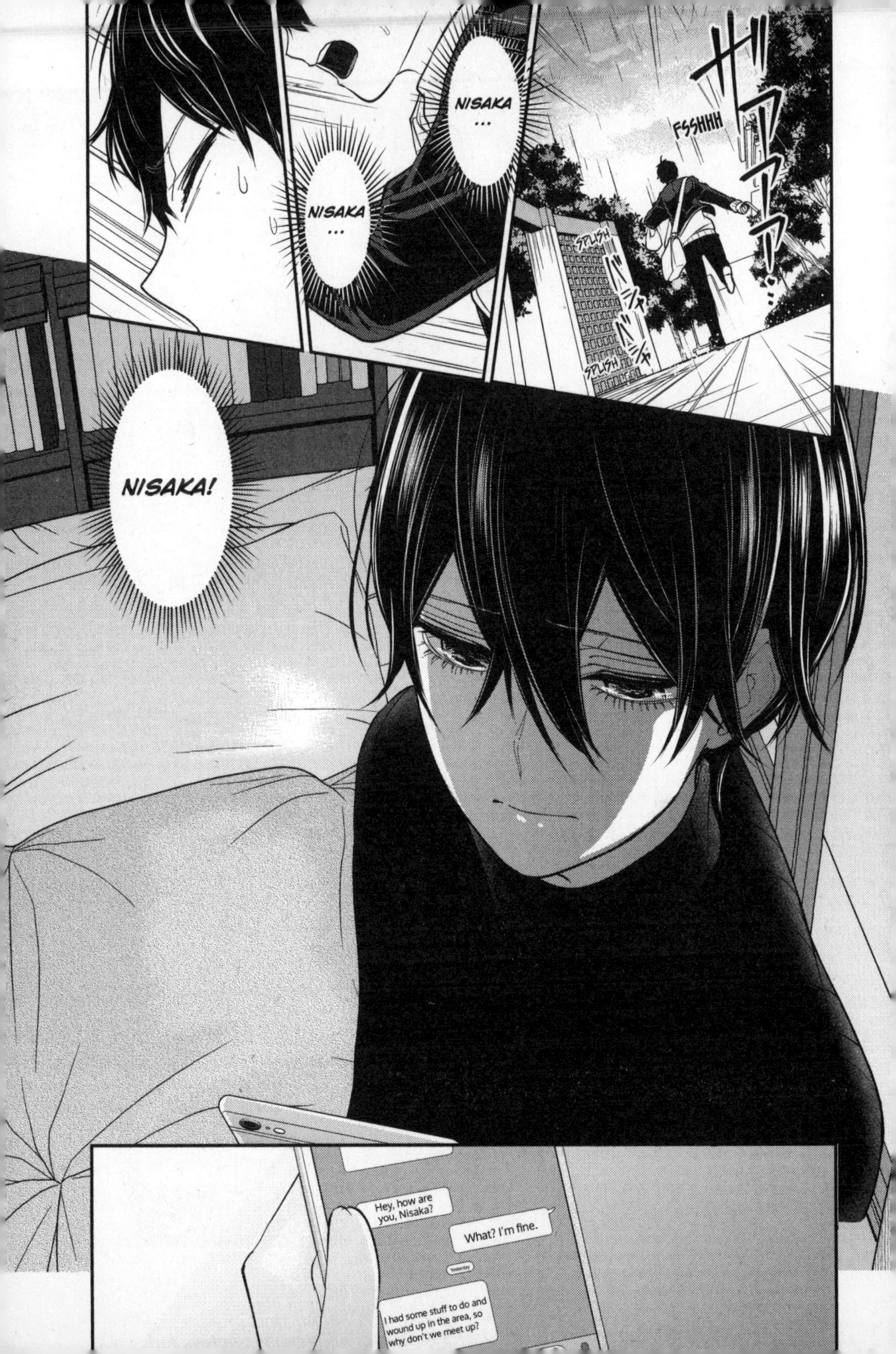

ザァァァァ…
FSSHHH
SPLISH
バシャ
バシャ
SPLISH
NISAKA …
NISAKA …
NISAKA!
Hey, how are you, Nisaka?
What? I'm fine.
Yesterday
I had some stuff to do and wound up in the area, so why don't we meet up?

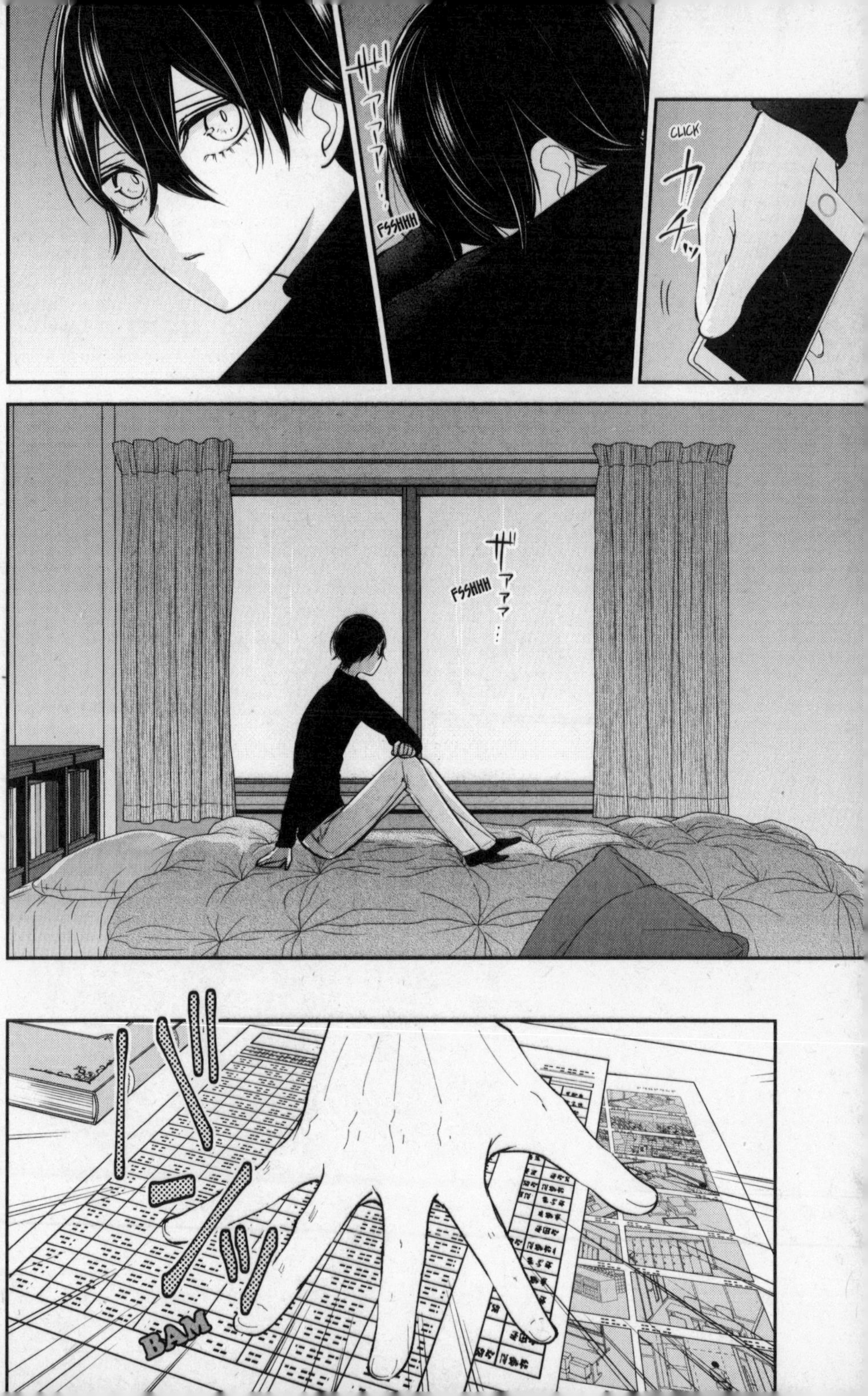

CLICK
カチッ
ザァァァ…!
FSSHHH
ザァァ…
FSSHHH
BAM

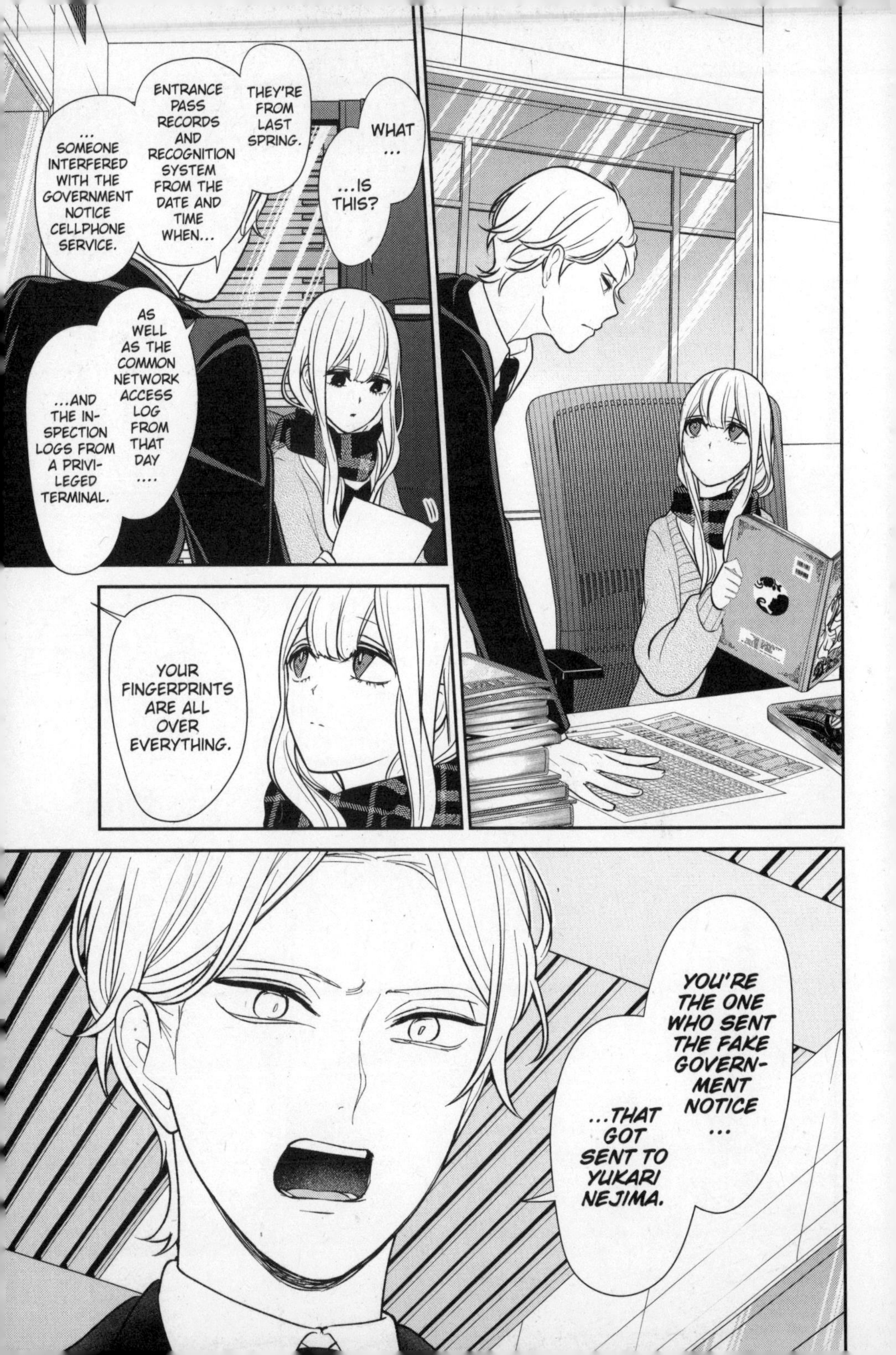
WHAT ...
...IS THIS?
THEY'RE FROM LAST SPRING.
ENTRANCE PASS RECORDS AND RECOGNITION SYSTEM FROM THE DATE AND TIME WHEN...
... SOMEONE INTERFERED WITH THE GOVERNMENT NOTICE CELLPHONE SERVICE.
AS WELL AS THE COMMON NETWORK ACCESS LOG FROM THAT DAY ....
...AND THE INSPECTION LOGS FROM A PRIVILEGED TERMINAL.
YOUR FINGERPRINTS ARE ALL OVER EVERYTHING.
YOU'RE THE ONE WHO SENT THE FAKE GOVERNMENT NOTICE ...
...THAT GOT SENT TO YUKARI NEJIMA.

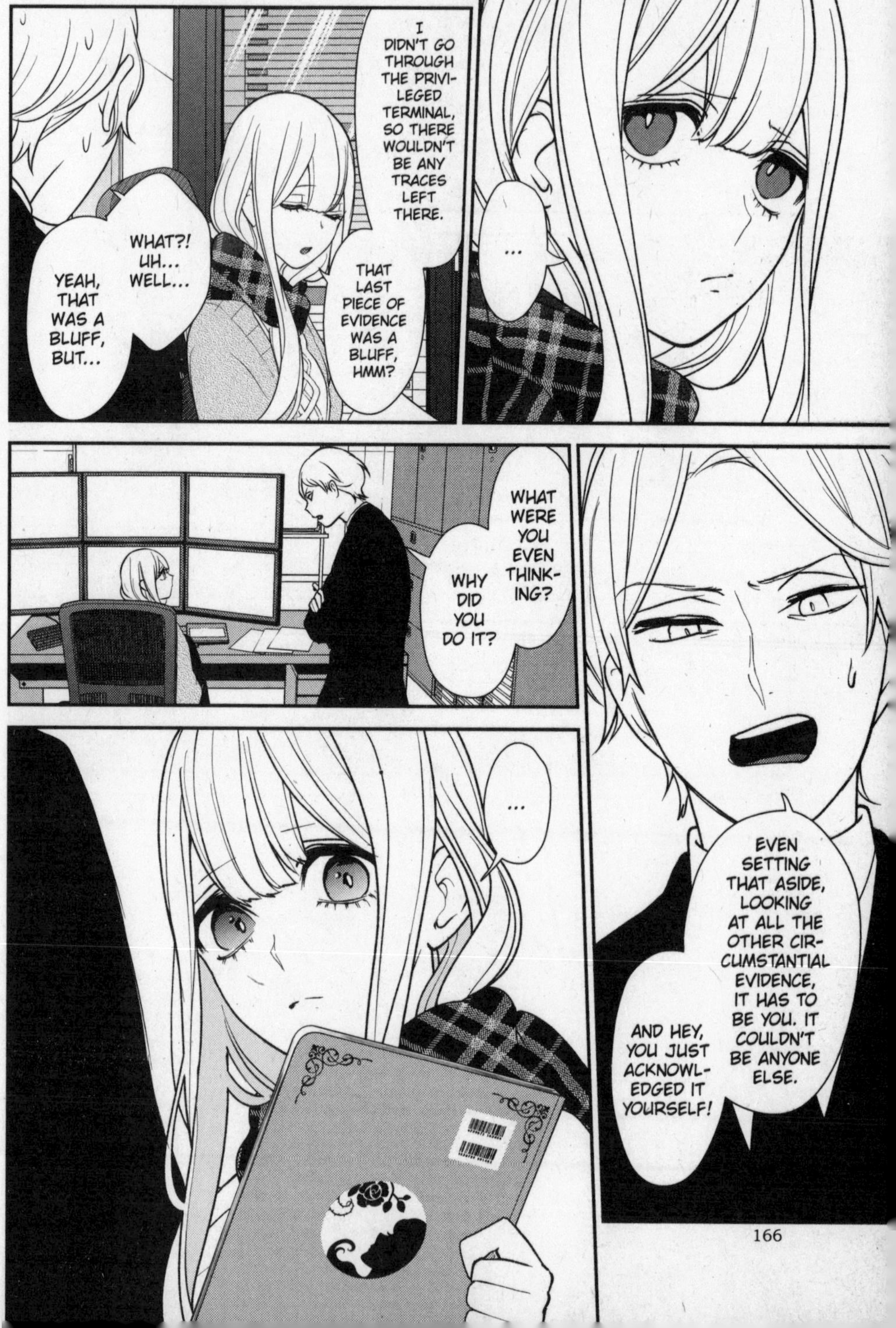
...
I DIDN'T GO THROUGH THE PRIVI-LEGED TERMINAL, SO THERE WOULDN'T BE ANY TRACES LEFT THERE.
THAT LAST PIECE OF EVIDENCE WAS A BLUFF, HMM?
WHAT?! UH... WELL...
YEAH, THAT WAS A BLUFF, BUT...
EVEN SETTING THAT ASIDE, LOOKING AT ALL THE OTHER CIR-CUMSTANTIAL EVIDENCE, IT HAS TO BE YOU. IT COULDN'T BE ANYONE ELSE.
AND HEY, YOU JUST ACKNOWL-EDGED IT YOURSELF!
WHAT WERE YOU EVEN THINK-ING?
WHY DID YOU DO IT?
...

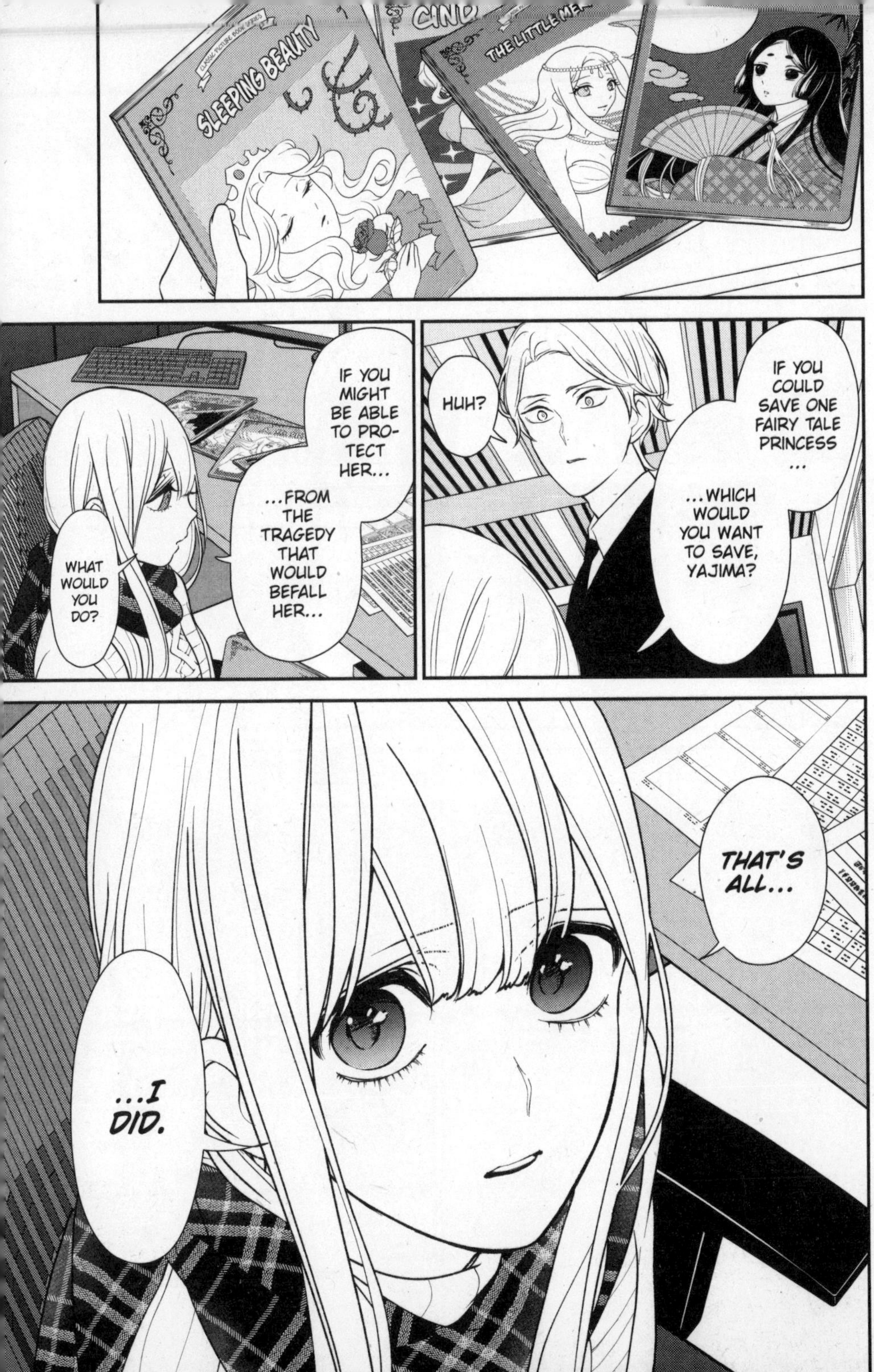
CLASSIC PICTURE BOOK SERIES
SLEEPING BEAUTY
THE LITTLE ME
IF YOU COULD SAVE ONE FAIRY TALE PRINCESS...
...WHICH WOULD YOU WANT TO SAVE, YAJIMA?
HUH?
IF YOU MIGHT BE ABLE TO PROTECT HER...
...FROM THE TRAGEDY THAT WOULD BEFALL HER...
WHAT WOULD YOU DO?
THAT'S ALL...
...I DID.

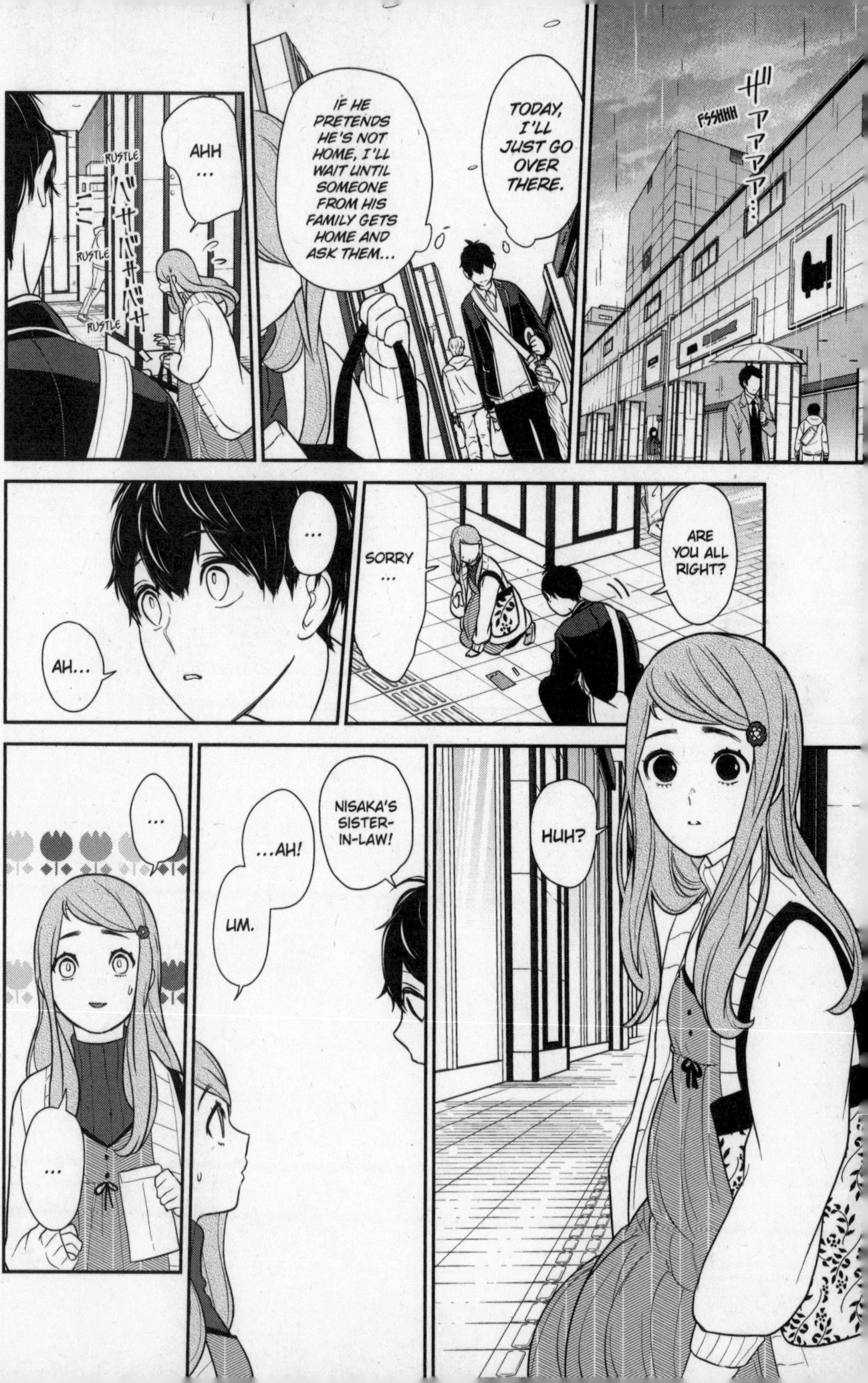

ザアアア…
FSSHHH
TODAY, I'LL JUST GO OVER THERE.
IF HE PRETENDS HE'S NOT HOME, I'LL WAIT UNTIL SOMEONE FROM HIS FAMILY GETS HOME AND ASK THEM...
AHH ...
RUSTLE
RUSTLE
RUSTLE
ARE YOU ALL RIGHT?
SORRY ...
...
AH...
HUH?
NISAKA'S SISTER-IN-LAW!
...AH!
UM.
...
...

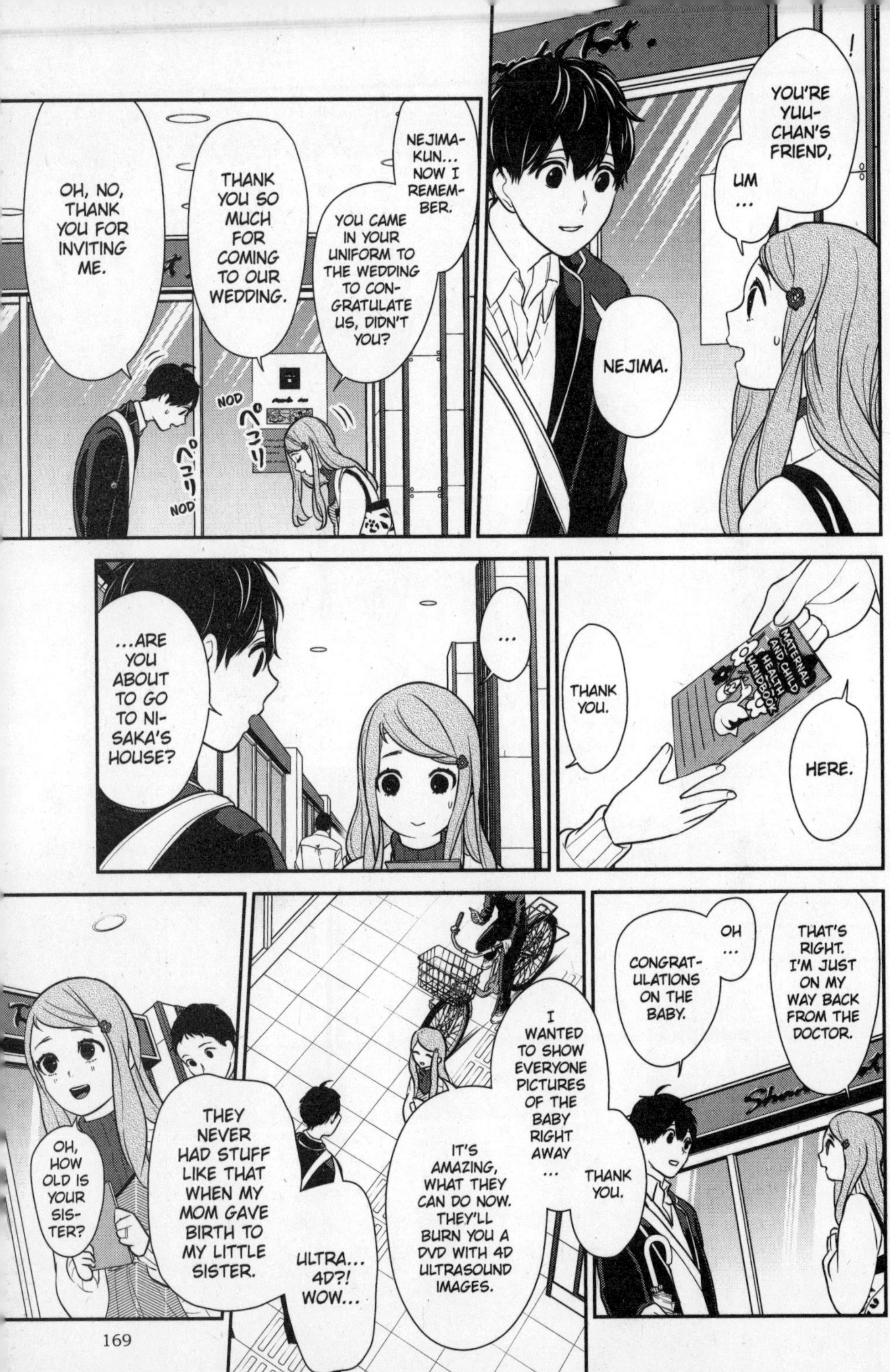
!
YOU'RE YUU-CHAN'S FRIEND,
UM ...
NEJIMA.
NEJIMA-KUN... NOW I REMEMBER.
YOU CAME IN YOUR UNIFORM TO THE WEDDING TO CONGRATULATE US, DIDN'T YOU?
THANK YOU SO MUCH FOR COMING TO OUR WEDDING.
OH, NO, THANK YOU FOR INVITING ME.
NOD ペコ
ペコリ NOD
HERE.
THANK YOU.
MATERIAL AND CHILD HEALTH HANDBOOK
...
...ARE YOU ABOUT TO GO TO NISAKA'S HOUSE?
THAT'S RIGHT. I'M JUST ON MY WAY BACK FROM THE DOCTOR.
OH ...
CONGRATULATIONS ON THE BABY.
THANK YOU.
I WANTED TO SHOW EVERYONE PICTURES OF THE BABY RIGHT AWAY ...
IT'S AMAZING, WHAT THEY CAN DO NOW. THEY'LL BURN YOU A DVD WITH 4D ULTRASOUND IMAGES.
ULTRA... 4D?! WOW...
THEY NEVER HAD STUFF LIKE THAT WHEN MY MOM GAVE BIRTH TO MY LITTLE SISTER.
OH, HOW OLD IS YOUR SISTER?

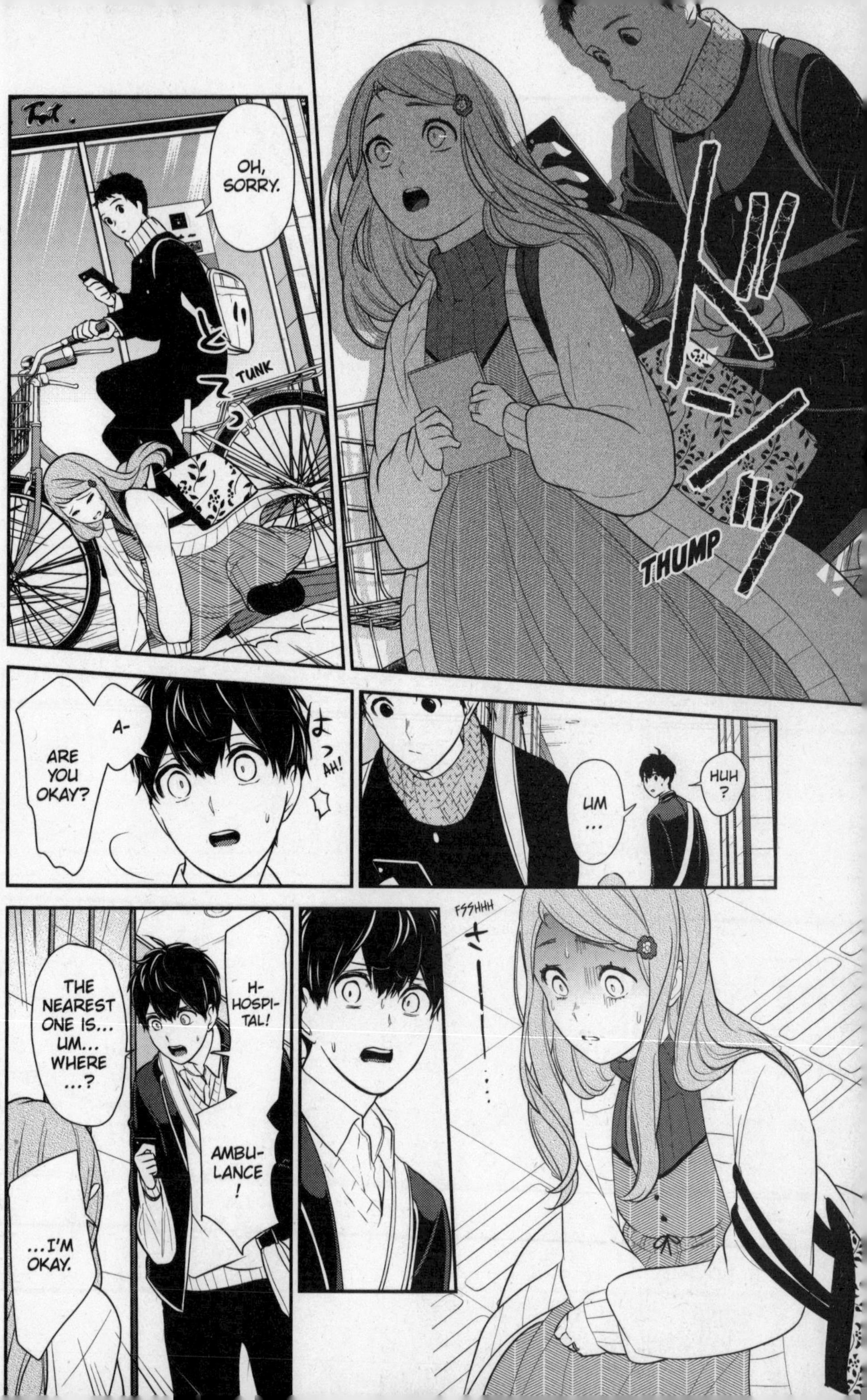
THUMP
OH, SORRY.
TUNK
HUH ?
UM ...
はっ AH!
A-
ARE YOU OKAY?
FSSHHH
さー…
H-HOSPITAL!
AMBULANCE!
THE NEAREST ONE IS... UM... WHERE ...?
...I'M OKAY.

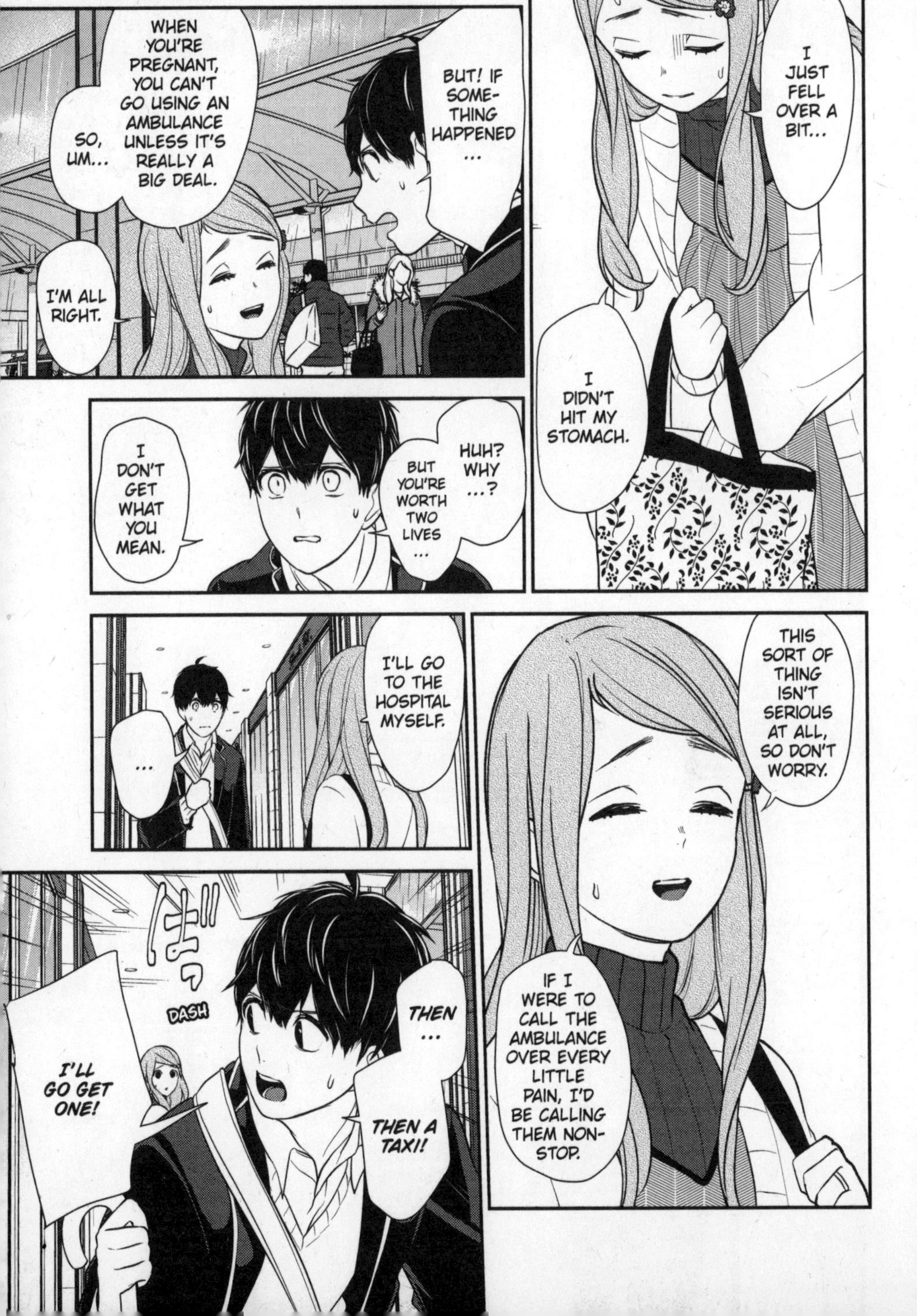
I JUST FELL OVER A BIT...
I DIDN'T HIT MY STOMACH.
BUT! IF SOMETHING HAPPENED...
WHEN YOU'RE PREGNANT, YOU CAN'T GO USING AN AMBULANCE UNLESS IT'S REALLY A BIG DEAL.
SO, UM...
I'M ALL RIGHT.
HUH? WHY...?
BUT YOU'RE WORTH TWO LIVES...
I DON'T GET WHAT YOU MEAN.
THIS SORT OF THING ISN'T SERIOUS AT ALL, SO DON'T WORRY.
IF I WERE TO CALL THE AMBULANCE OVER EVERY LITTLE PAIN, I'D BE CALLING THEM NON-STOP.
I'LL GO TO THE HOSPITAL MYSELF.
...
THEN...
THEN A TAXI!
はっ
DASH
I'LL GO GET ONE!

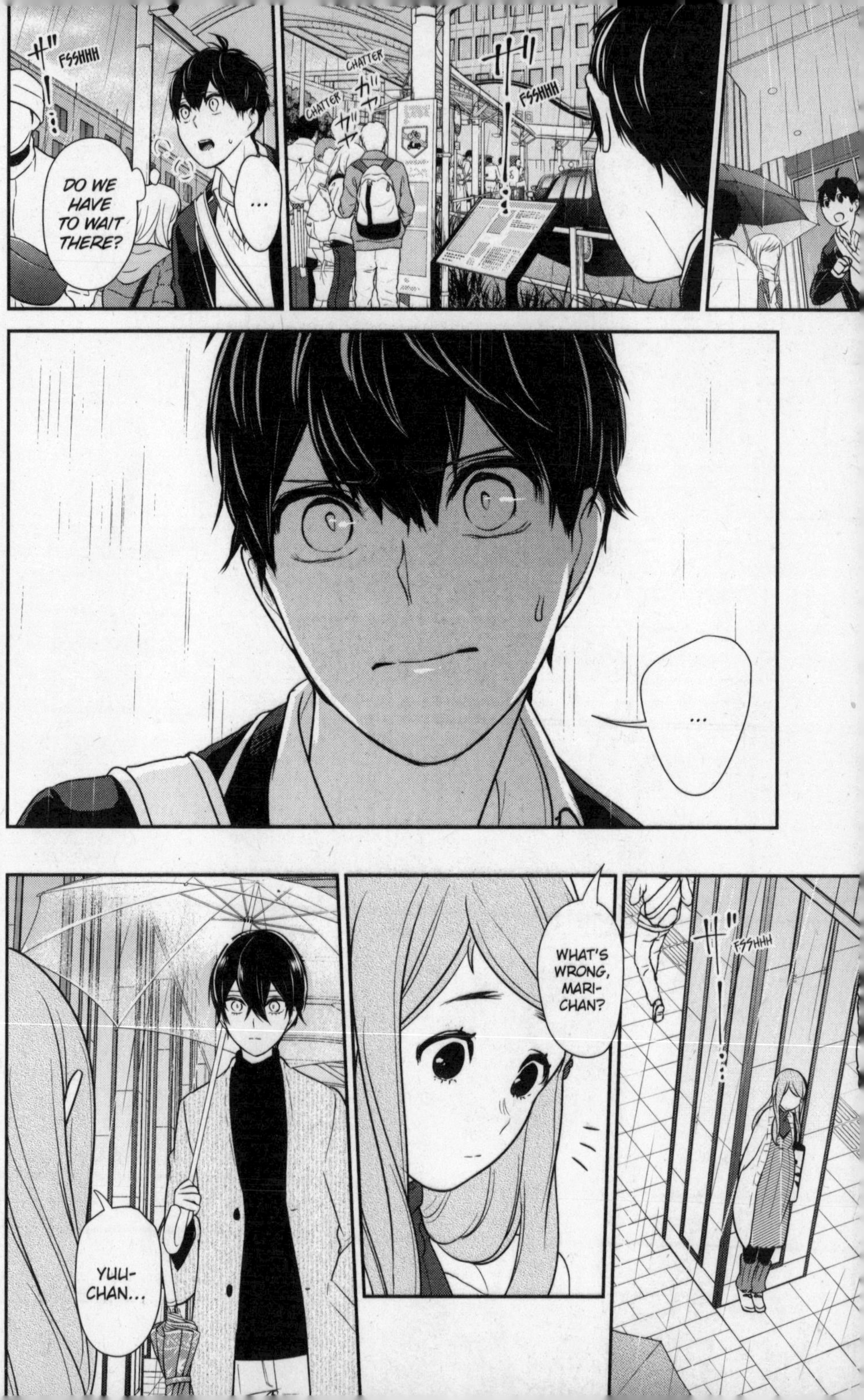
FSSHHH
CHATTER
CHATTER
FSSHHH
DO WE HAVE TO WAIT THERE?
...
...
FSSHHH
WHAT'S WRONG, MARI-CHAN?
YUU-CHAN...

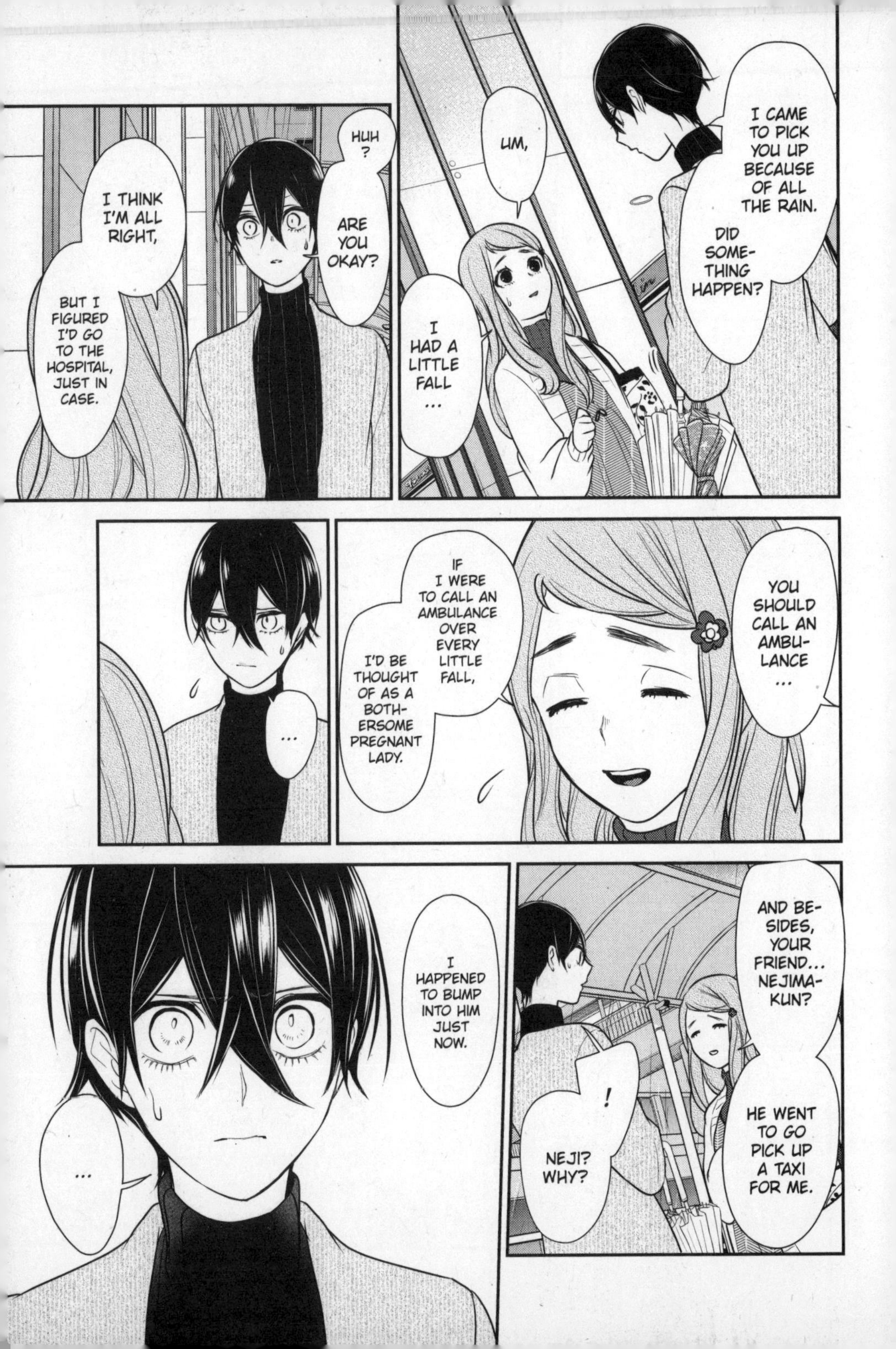
I CAME TO PICK YOU UP BECAUSE OF ALL THE RAIN.
DID SOME-THING HAPPEN?
UM,
I HAD A LITTLE FALL ...
HUH?
ARE YOU OKAY?
I THINK I'M ALL RIGHT,
BUT I FIGURED I'D GO TO THE HOSPITAL, JUST IN CASE.
YOU SHOULD CALL AN AMBU-LANCE ...
IF I WERE TO CALL AN AMBULANCE OVER EVERY LITTLE FALL,
I'D BE THOUGHT OF AS A BOTH-ERSOME PREGNANT LADY.
...
AND BE-SIDES, YOUR FRIEND... NEJIMA-KUN?
HE WENT TO GO PICK UP A TAXI FOR ME.
!
NEJI? WHY?
I HAPPENED TO BUMP INTO HIM JUST NOW.
...

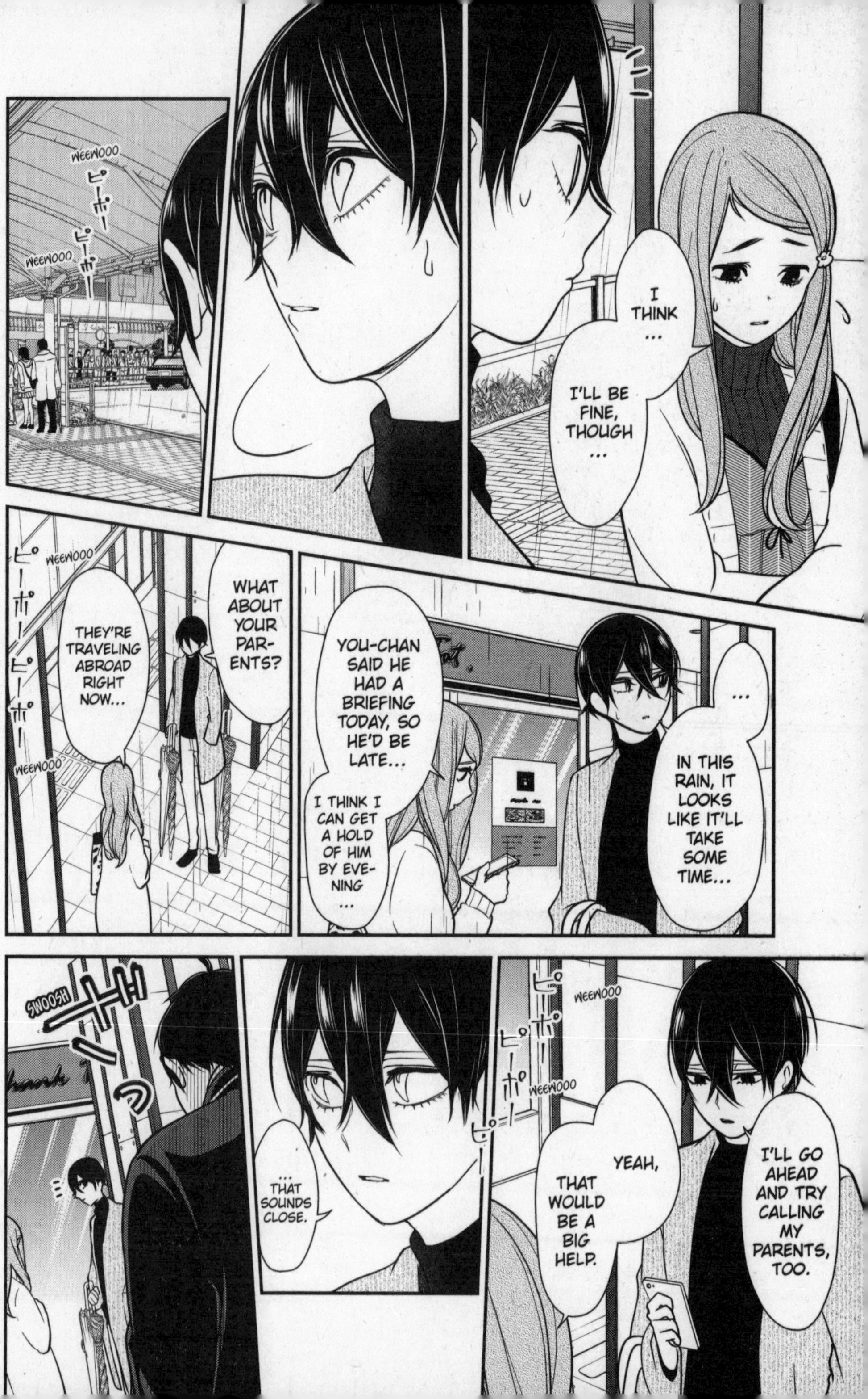
I THINK...
I'LL BE FINE, THOUGH...
WEEWOOO
WEEWOOO
...
IN THIS RAIN, IT LOOKS LIKE IT'LL TAKE SOME TIME...
YOU-CHAN SAID HE HAD A BRIEFING TODAY, SO HE'D BE LATE...
I THINK I CAN GET A HOLD OF HIM BY EVE-NING...
WHAT ABOUT YOUR PAR-ENTS?
THEY'RE TRAVELING ABROAD RIGHT NOW...
WEEWOOO
WEEWOOO
I'LL GO AHEAD AND TRY CALLING MY PARENTS, TOO.
YEAH,
THAT WOULD BE A BIG HELP.
WEEWOOO
WEEWOOO
...THAT SOUNDS CLOSE.
SWOOSH

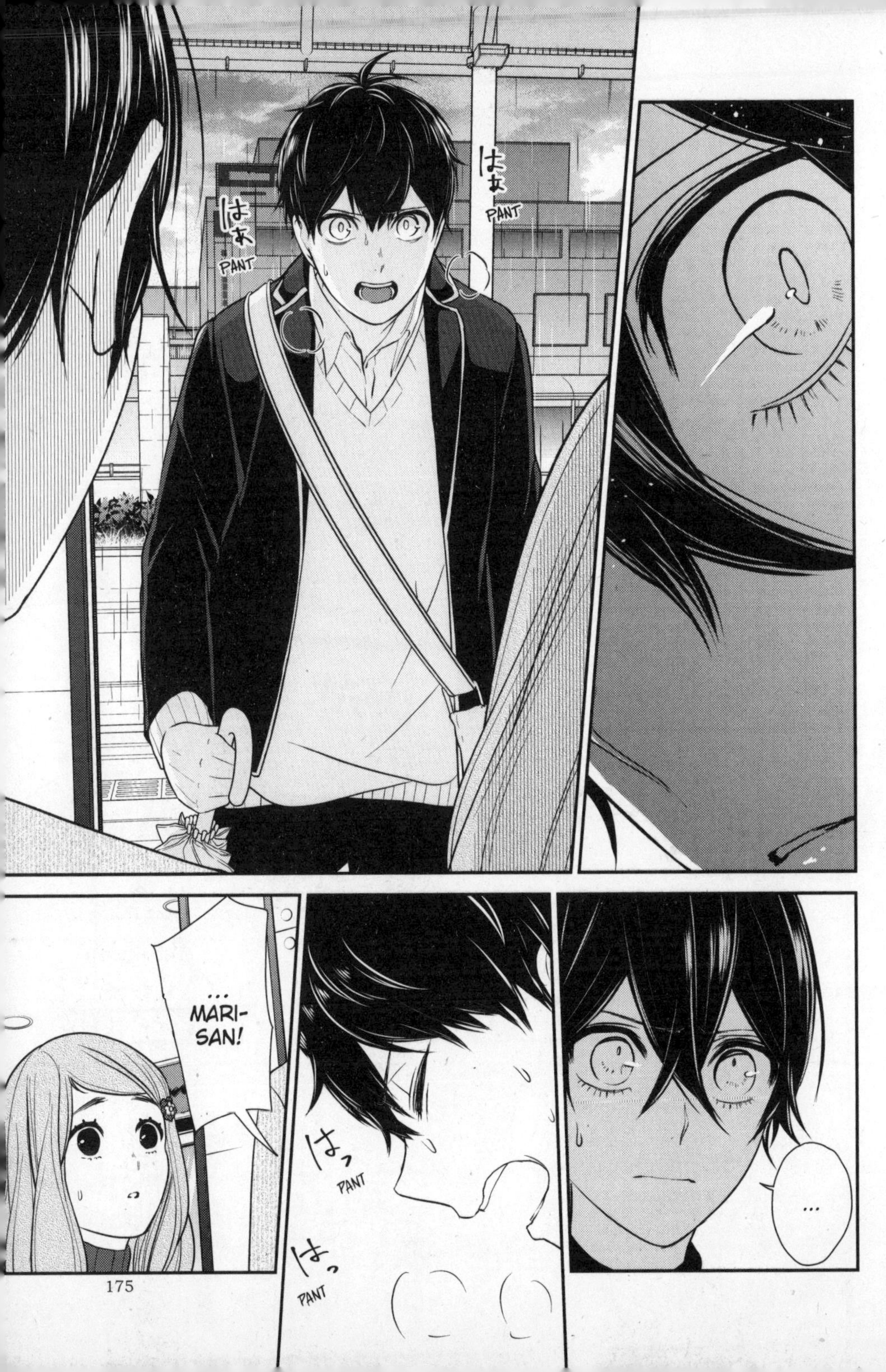
はぁ
PANT
はぁ
PANT
...
はっ
PANT
はっ
PANT
...
MARI-SAN!

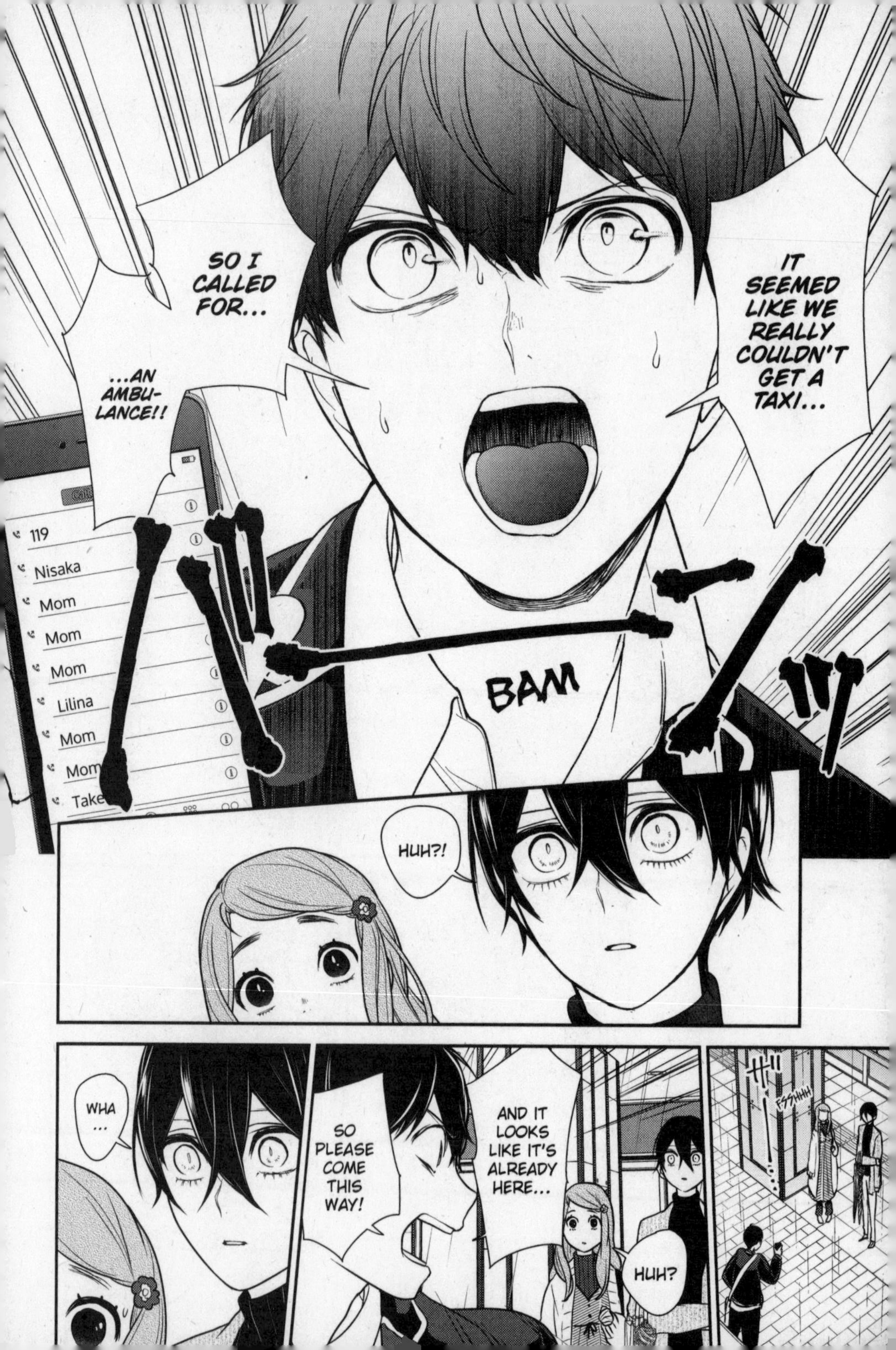
IT SEEMED LIKE WE REALLY COULDN'T GET A TAXI...
SO I CALLED FOR...
...AN AMBULANCE!!
119
Nisaka
Mom
Mom
Mom
Lilina
Mom
Mom
BAM
HUH?!
FSSHHH
AND IT LOOKS LIKE IT'S ALREADY HERE...
HUH?
SO PLEASE COME THIS WAY!
WHA ...

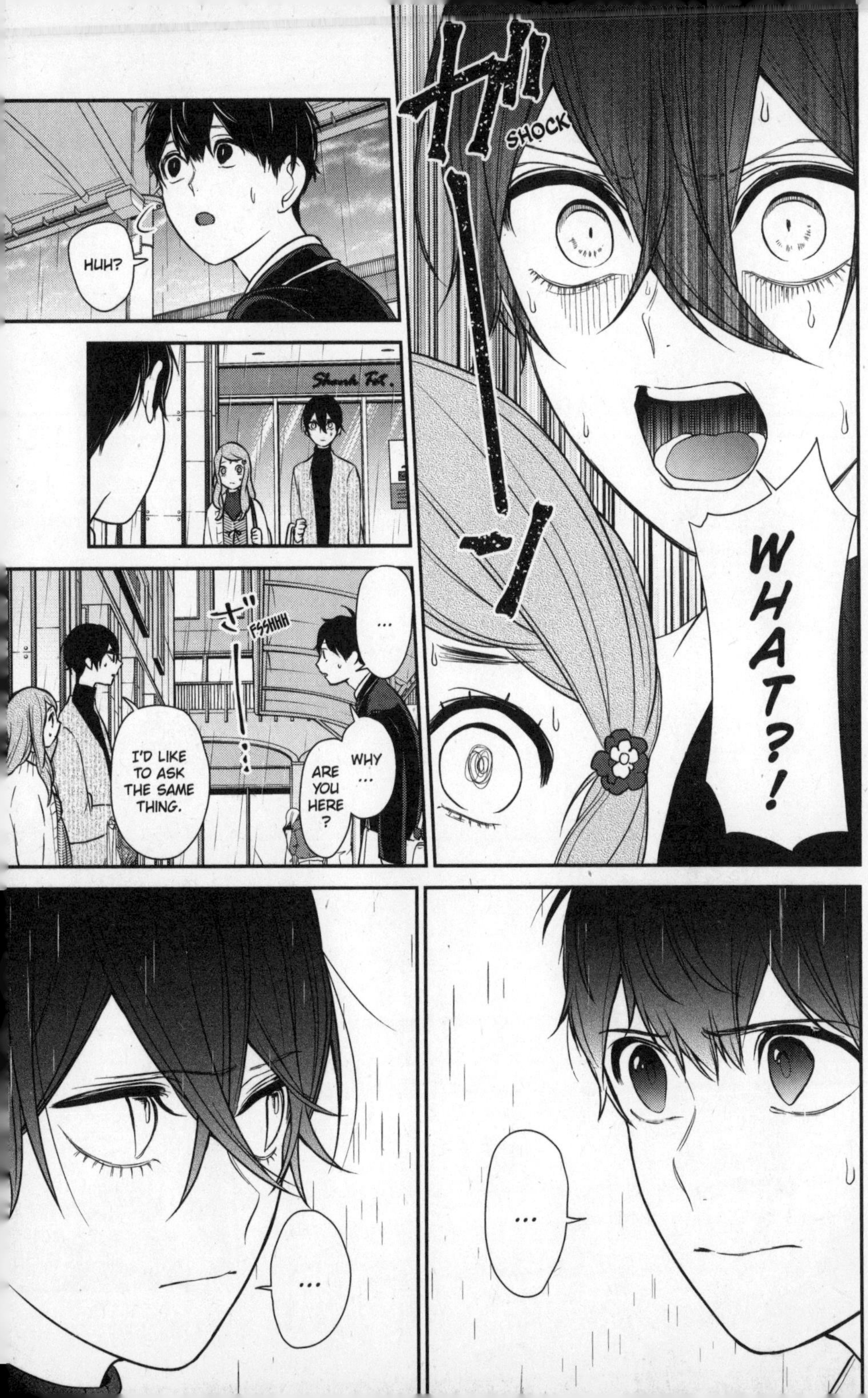

SHOCK
WHAT?!
HUH?
...
FSSHHH
WHY ... ARE YOU HERE?
I'D LIKE TO ASK THE SAME THING.
...
...

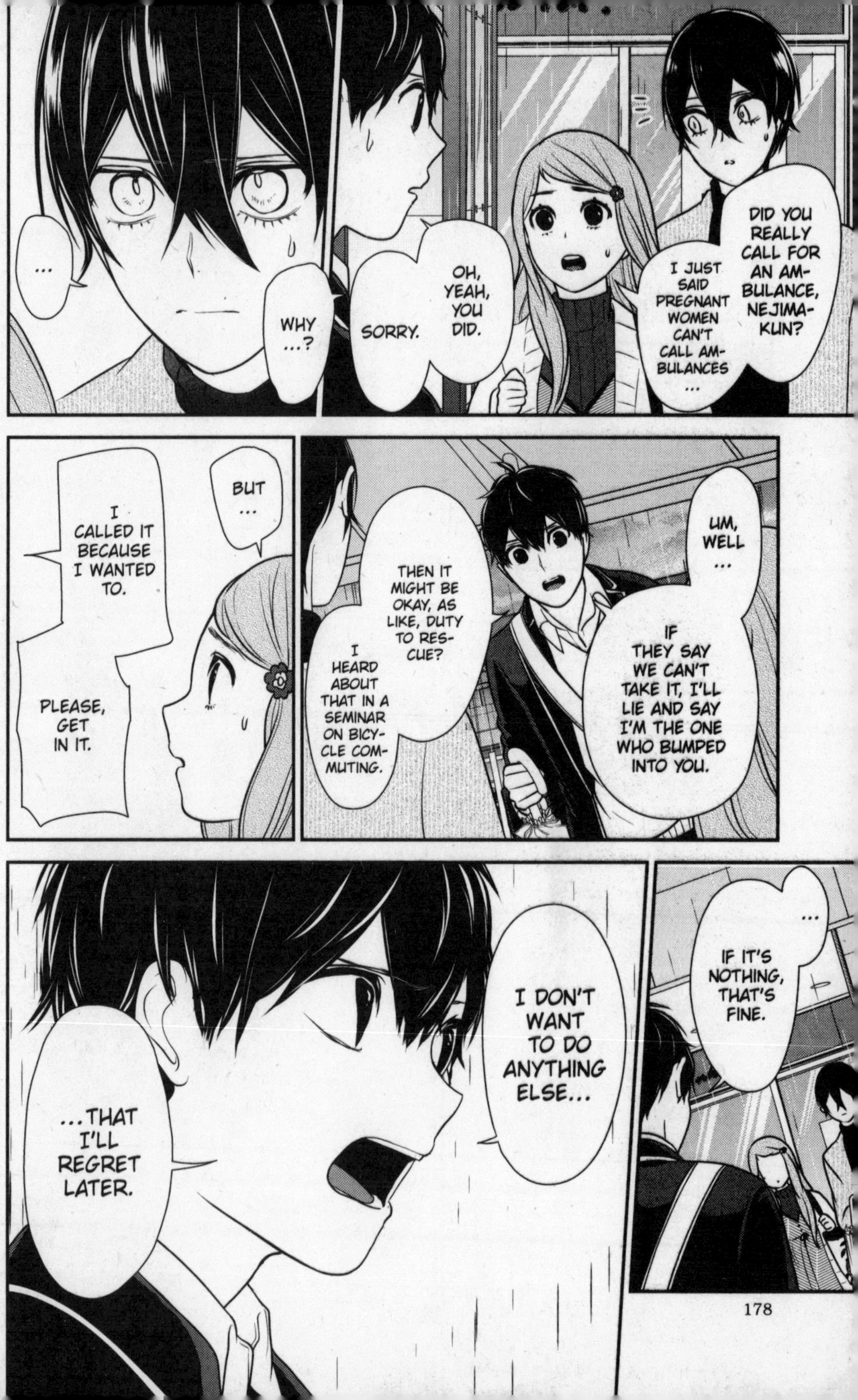
DID YOU REALLY CALL FOR AN AMBULANCE, NEJIMA-KUN?
I JUST SAID PREGNANT WOMEN CAN'T CALL AMBULANCES ...
OH, YEAH, YOU DID.
SORRY.
WHY ...?
...
UM, WELL ...
IF THEY SAY WE CAN'T TAKE IT, I'LL LIE AND SAY I'M THE ONE WHO BUMPED INTO YOU.
THEN IT MIGHT BE OKAY, AS LIKE, DUTY TO RESCUE?
I HEARD ABOUT THAT IN A SEMINAR ON BICYCLE COMMUTING.
BUT ...
I CALLED IT BECAUSE I WANTED TO.
PLEASE, GET IN IT.
...
IF IT'S NOTHING, THAT'S FINE.
I DON'T WANT TO DO ANYTHING ELSE...
...THAT I'LL REGRET LATER.

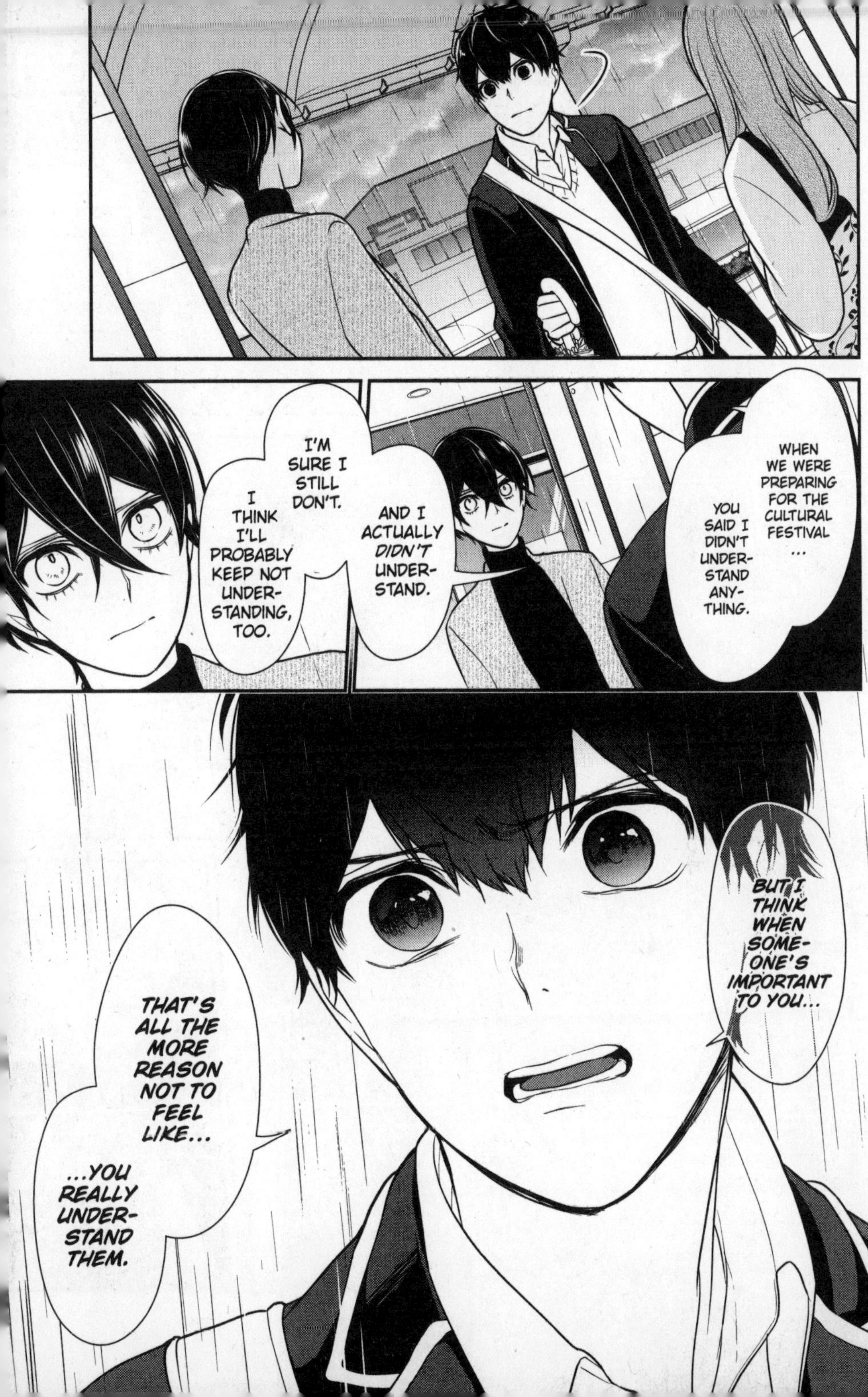
WHEN WE WERE PREPARING FOR THE CULTURAL FESTIVAL...
YOU SAID I DIDN'T UNDERSTAND ANYTHING.
AND I ACTUALLY *DIDN'T* UNDERSTAND.
I'M SURE I STILL DON'T.
I THINK I'LL PROBABLY KEEP NOT UNDERSTANDING, TOO.
BUT I THINK WHEN SOMEONE'S IMPORTANT TO YOU...
THAT'S ALL THE MORE REASON NOT TO FEEL LIKE...
...YOU REALLY UNDERSTAND THEM.

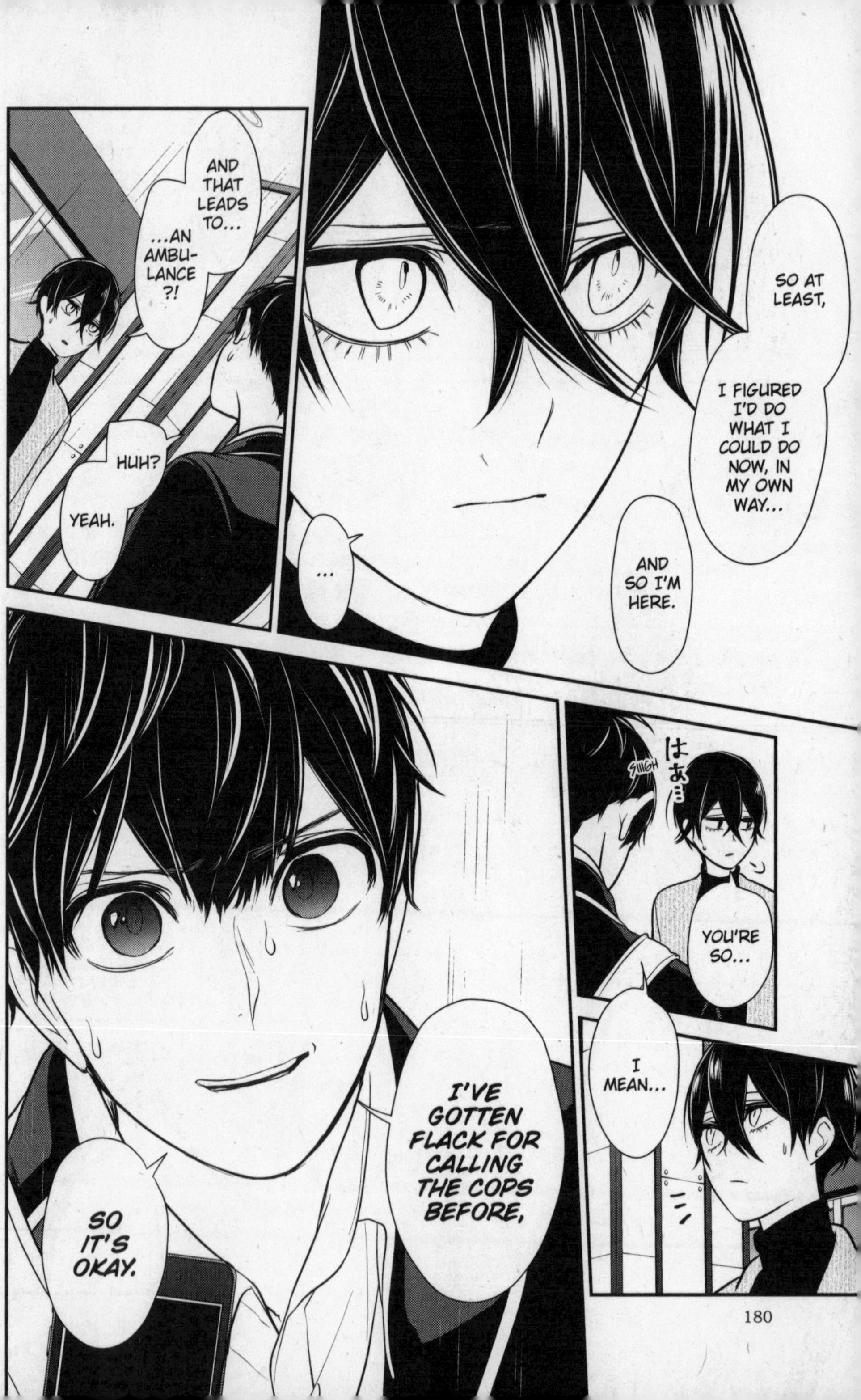
SO AT LEAST,
I FIGURED I'D DO WHAT I COULD DO NOW, IN MY OWN WAY...
AND SO I'M HERE.
...
AND THAT LEADS TO...
...AN AMBULANCE?!
HUH?
YEAH.
はぁ…
SIIGH
YOU'RE SO...
I MEAN...
I'VE GOTTEN FLACK FOR CALLING THE COPS BEFORE,
SO IT'S OKAY.

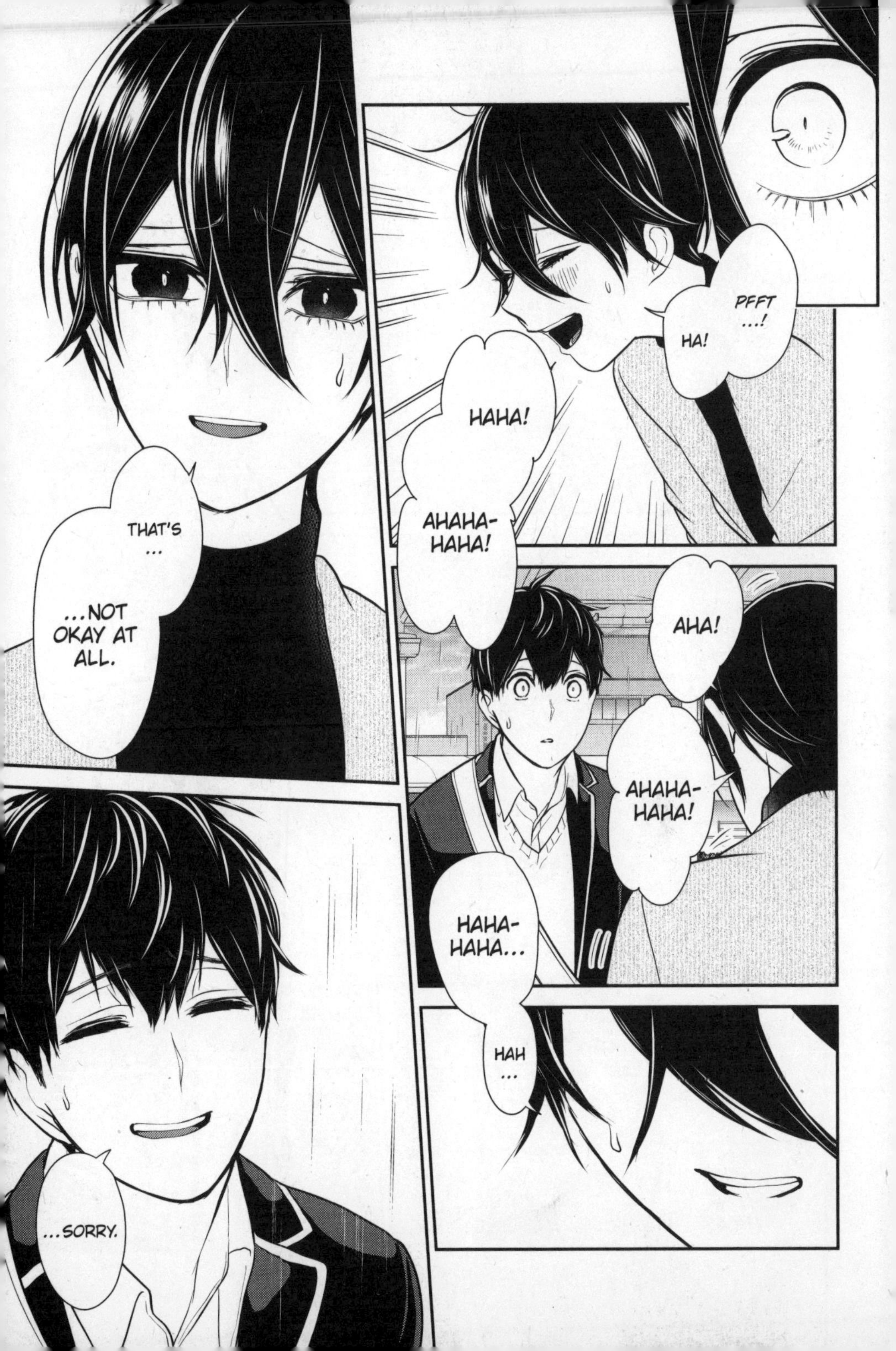
PFFT ...!
HA!
HAHA!
AHAHA-HAHA!
AHA!
AHAHA-HAHA!
HAHA-HAHA...
THAT'S ...
...NOT OKAY AT ALL.
HAH ...
...SORRY.

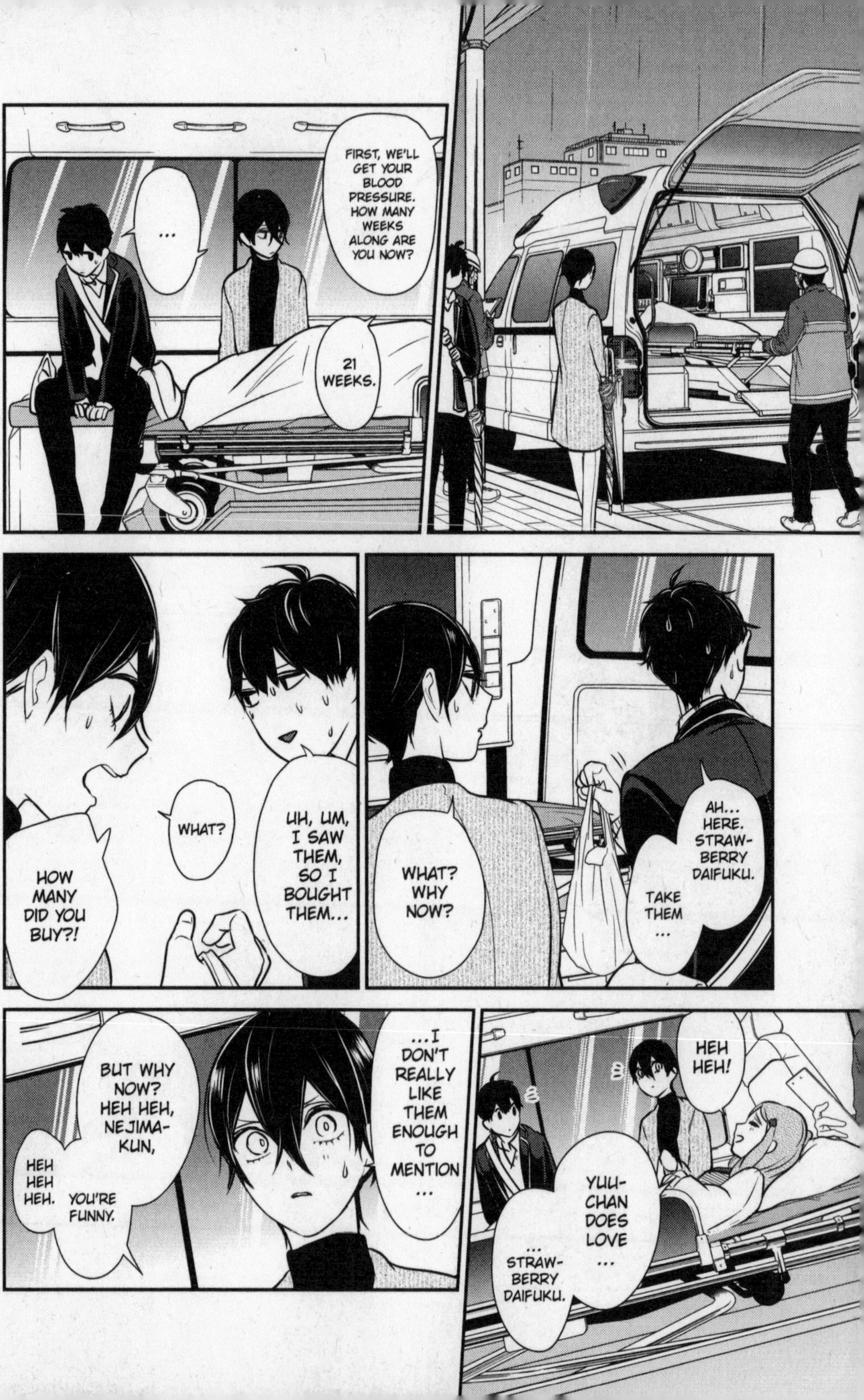
FIRST, WE'LL GET YOUR BLOOD PRESSURE. HOW MANY WEEKS ALONG ARE YOU NOW?
...
21 WEEKS.
AH... HERE. STRAW-BERRY DAIFUKU.
TAKE THEM ...
WHAT? WHY NOW?
UH, UM, I SAW THEM, SO I BOUGHT THEM...
WHAT?
HOW MANY DID YOU BUY?!
HEH HEH!
YUU-CHAN DOES LOVE ...
... STRAW-BERRY DAIFUKU.
...I DON'T REALLY LIKE THEM ENOUGH TO MENTION ...
BUT WHY NOW? HEH HEH, NEJIMA-KUN,
HEH HEH HEH.
YOU'RE FUNNY.

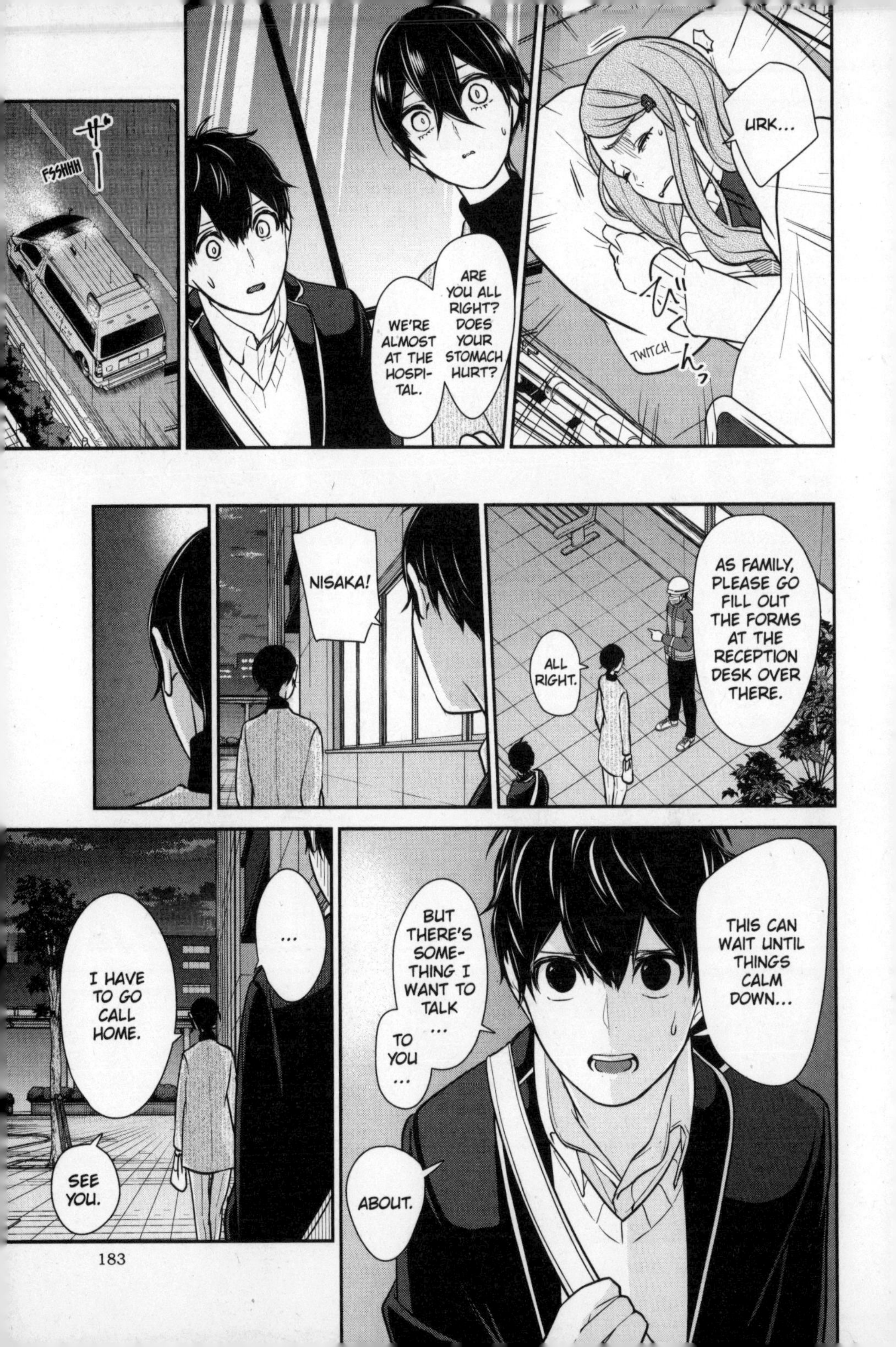
URK...
TWITCH
ARE YOU ALL RIGHT? DOES YOUR STOMACH HURT?
WE'RE ALMOST AT THE HOSPI-TAL.
FSSHHH
AS FAMILY, PLEASE GO FILL OUT THE FORMS AT THE RECEPTION DESK OVER THERE.
ALL RIGHT.
NISAKA!
THIS CAN WAIT UNTIL THINGS CALM DOWN...
BUT THERE'S SOME-THING I WANT TO TALK ...
TO YOU ...
ABOUT.
...
I HAVE TO GO CALL HOME.
SEE YOU.

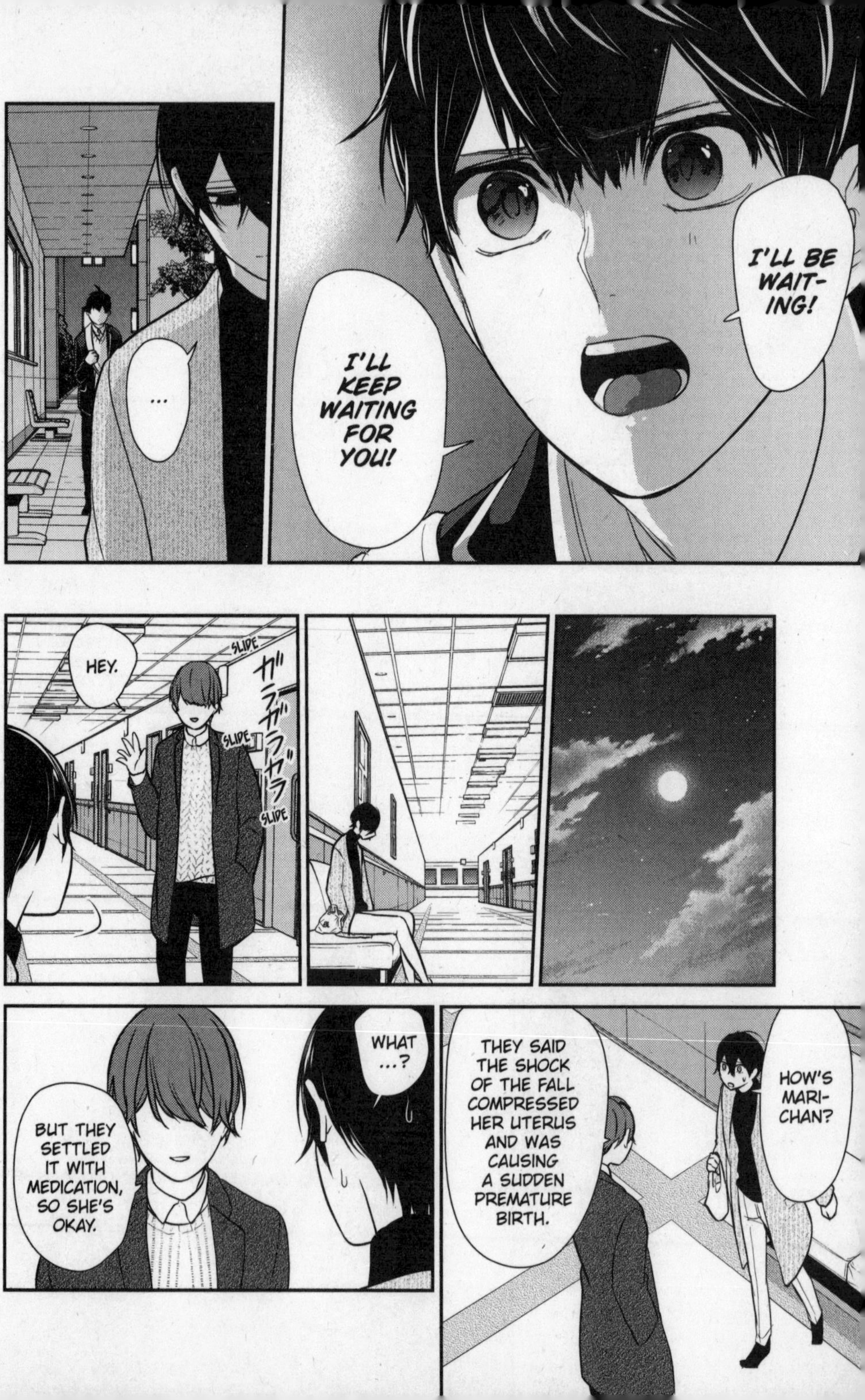
I'LL BE WAITING!
I'LL KEEP WAITING FOR YOU!
...
HEY.
SLIDE
ガラガラガラ
SLIDE
SLIDE
HOW'S MARI-CHAN?
THEY SAID THE SHOCK OF THE FALL COMPRESSED HER UTERUS AND WAS CAUSING A SUDDEN PREMATURE BIRTH.
WHAT ...?
BUT THEY SETTLED IT WITH MEDICATION, SO SHE'S OKAY.

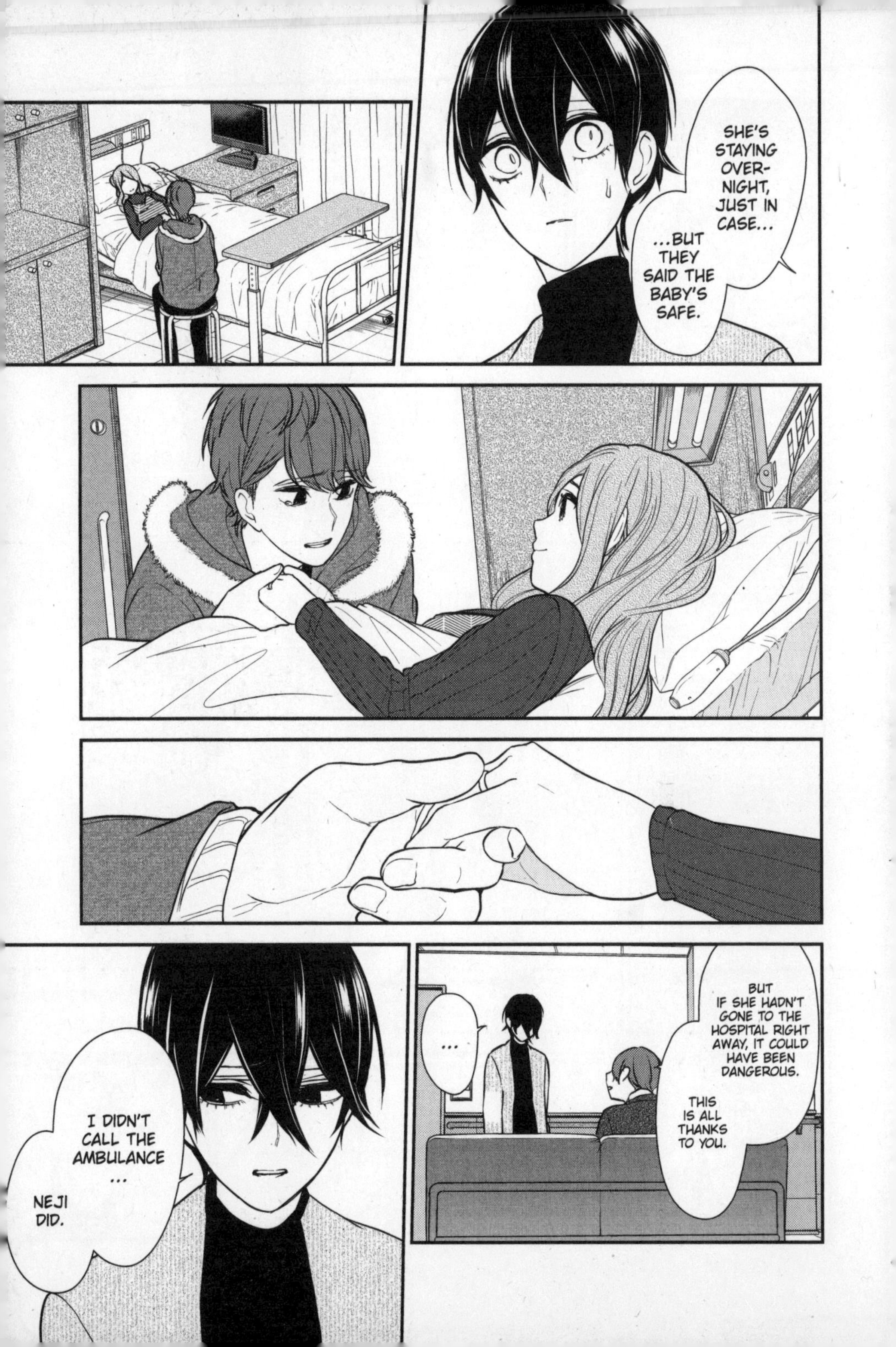
SHE'S STAYING OVER-NIGHT, JUST IN CASE...
...BUT THEY SAID THE BABY'S SAFE.
BUT IF SHE HADN'T GONE TO THE HOSPITAL RIGHT AWAY, IT COULD HAVE BEEN DANGEROUS.
THIS IS ALL THANKS TO YOU.
...
I DIDN'T CALL THE AMBULANCE ... NEJI DID.

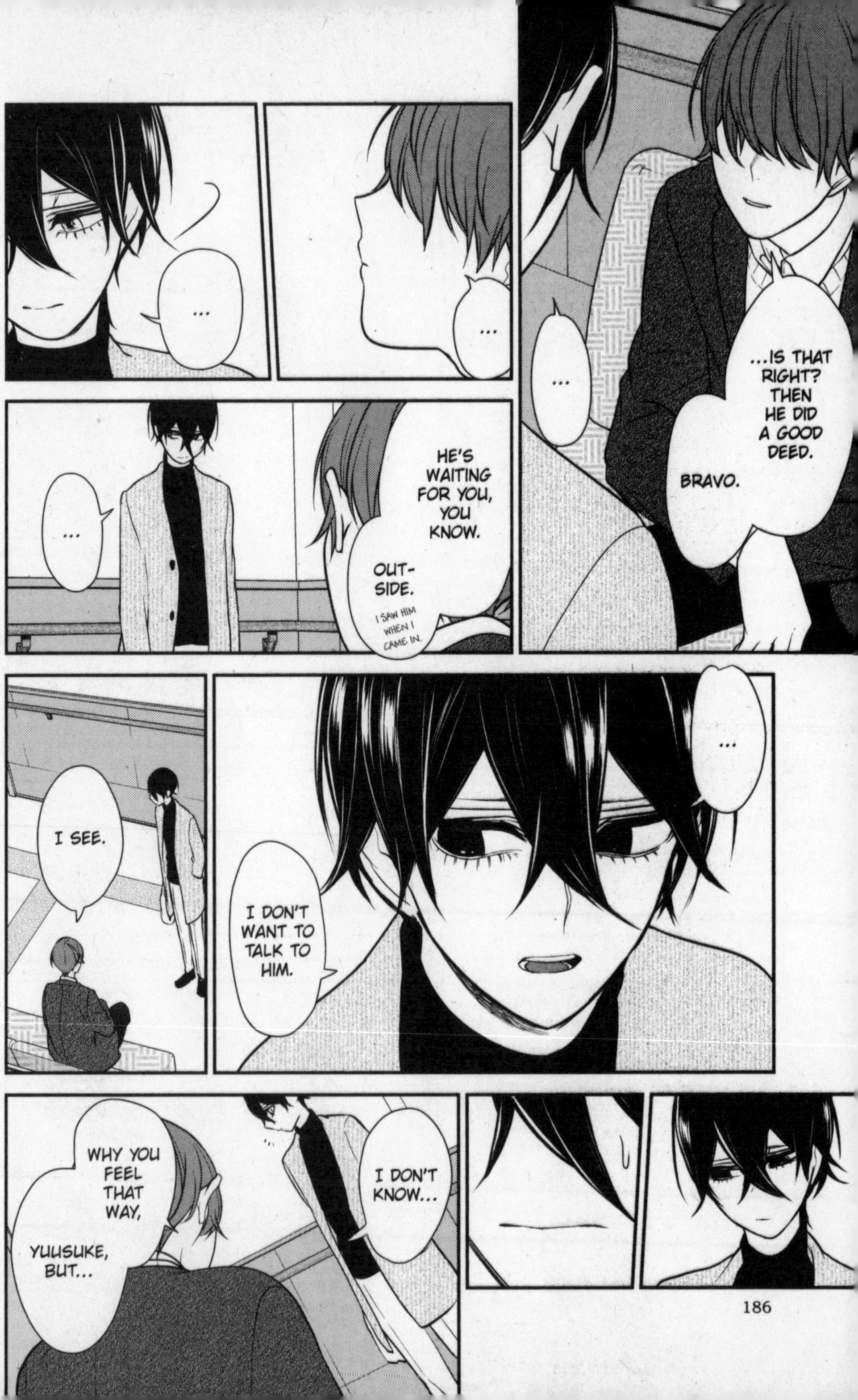
...IS THAT RIGHT? THEN HE DID A GOOD DEED.
BRAVO.
...
...
...
HE'S WAITING FOR YOU, YOU KNOW.
OUT-SIDE.
I SAW HIM WHEN I CAME IN.
...
...
I DON'T WANT TO TALK TO HIM.
I SEE.
I DON'T KNOW...
WHY YOU FEEL THAT WAY,
YUUSUKE, BUT...

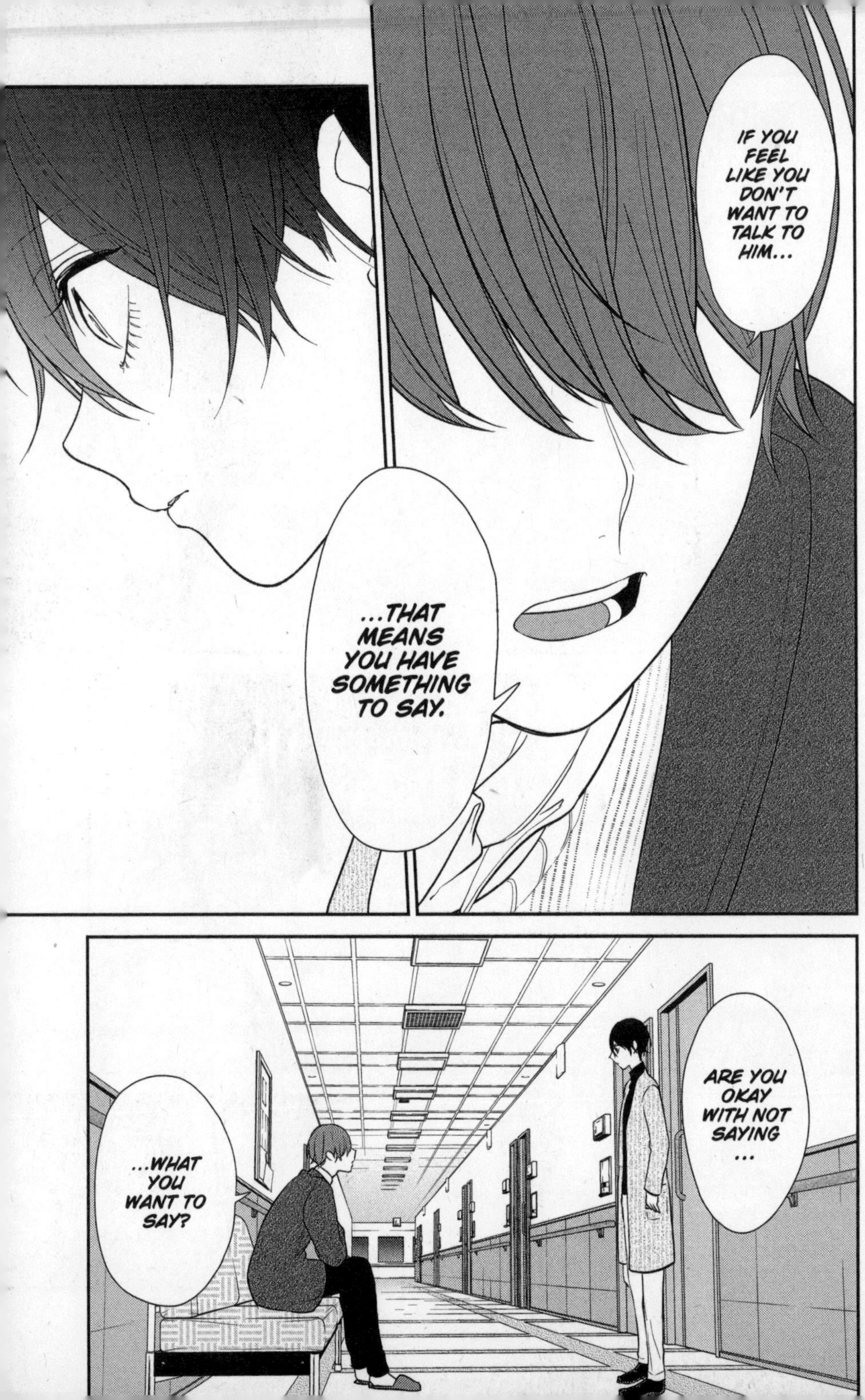

IF YOU FEEL LIKE YOU DON'T WANT TO TALK TO HIM...
...THAT MEANS YOU HAVE SOMETHING TO SAY.
ARE YOU OKAY WITH NOT SAYING ...
...WHAT YOU WANT TO SAY?

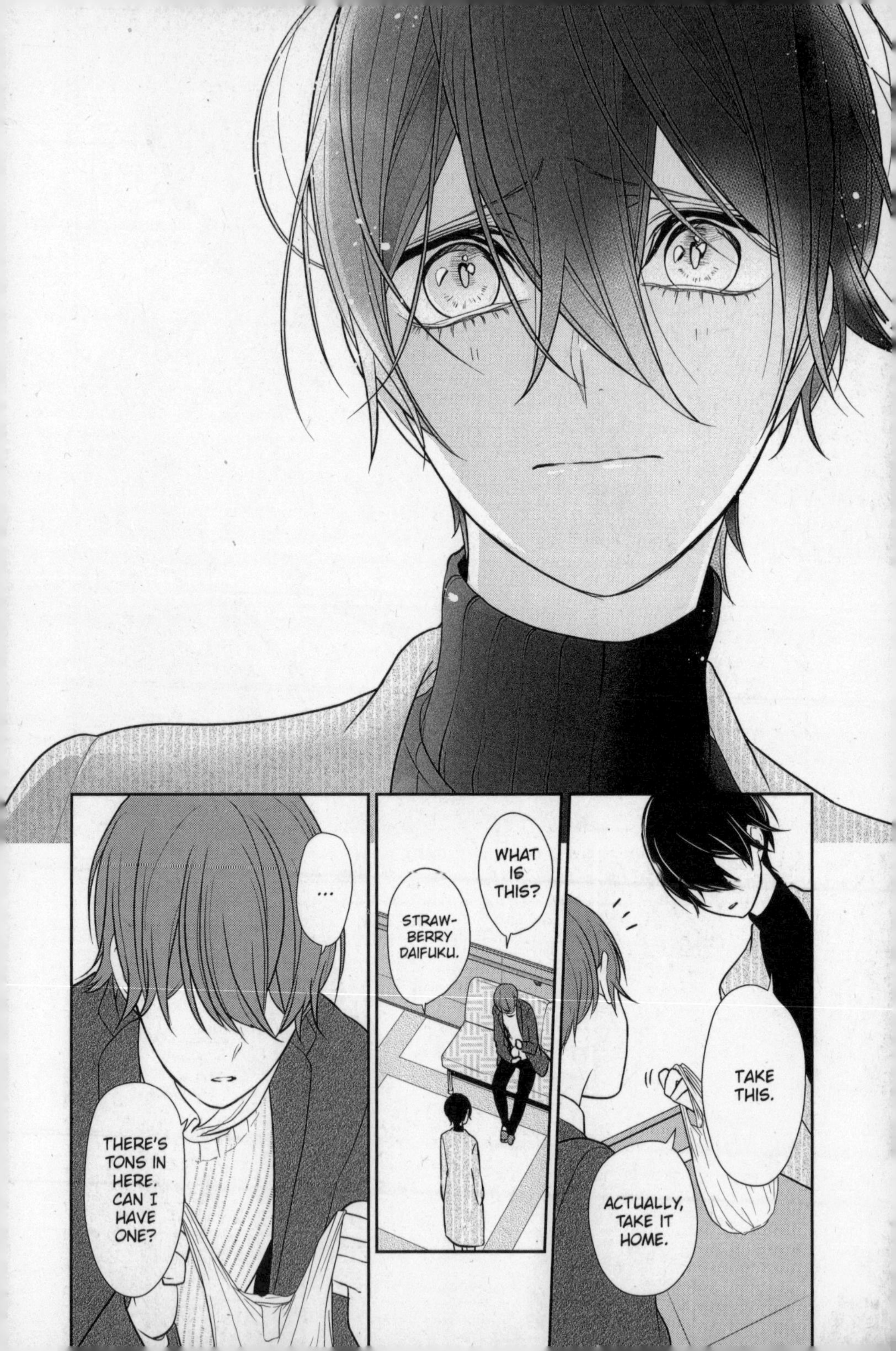
TAKE THIS.
ACTUALLY, TAKE IT HOME.
WHAT IS THIS?
STRAW-BERRY DAIFUKU.
...
THERE'S TONS IN HERE. CAN I HAVE ONE?

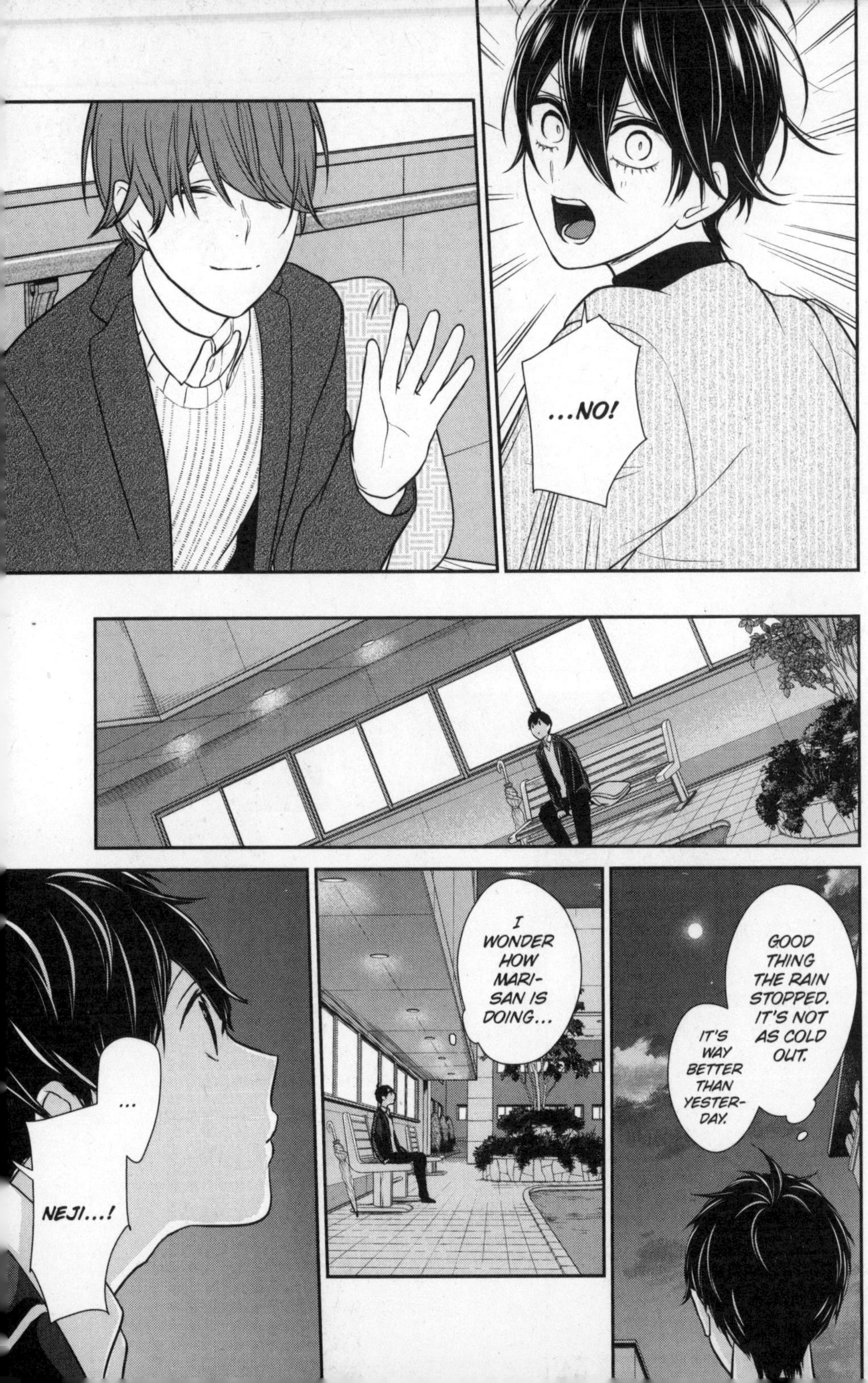
...NO!
GOOD THING THE RAIN STOPPED. IT'S NOT AS COLD OUT.
IT'S WAY BETTER THAN YESTER-DAY.
I WONDER HOW MARI-SAN IS DOING...
...
NEJI...!

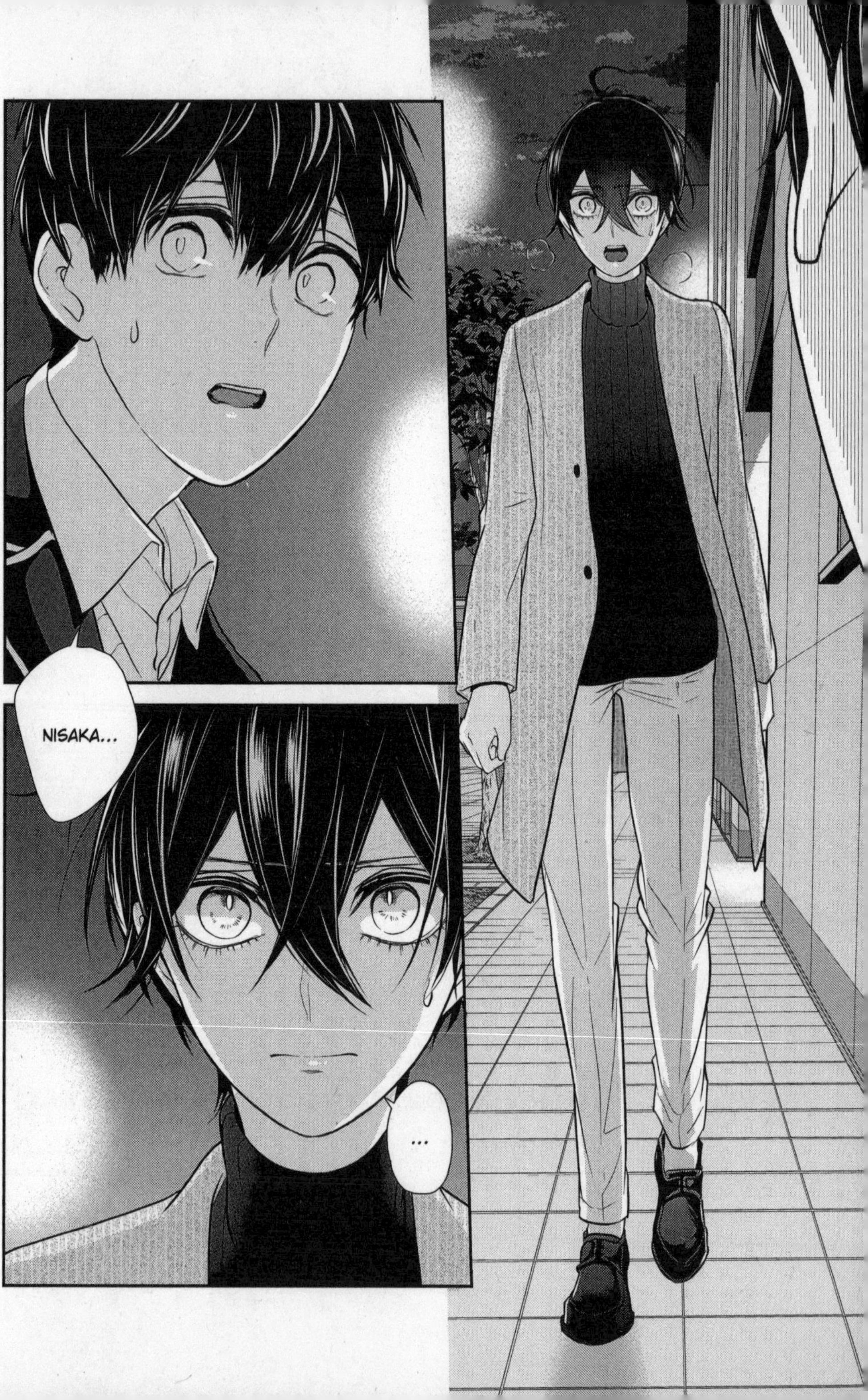
NISAKA...
...

★ SPECIAL THANKS ★

OGIWARA-SAMA
YOSHIMURA-SAMA
TANAKA-SAMA
TAKANAGA-SAMA
SUNAO-SAMA

MANARU AMAGAWA-SAMA
FUKU-SAMA
KAGUYA-SAMA
KOUSUKE KOMATSU-SAMA
YUTAKA TACHIBANA-SAMA
YAYOI HASEGAWA-SAMA
KANNA SUDOU-SAMA
FU YAMAGUCHI-SAMA

COVER & SPECIAL EDITION DESIGN
HIVE-SAMA

EVERYONE IN MY FAMILY

☆ AND ☆

ALL OF MY READERS

**THE TWO BOYS FINALLY FACE EACH OTHER—
AND THEY BOTH HAVE SOMETHING THEY WANT TO SAY.**

Love & Lies · Volume 10 coming soon!

A Kodansha Comics Trade Paperback Original
Love and Lies 9 copyright © 2019 Musawo
English translation copyright © 2020 Musawo

All rights reserved.

Published in the United States by Kodansha Comics, an imprint of Kodansha USA Publishing, LLC, New York.

Publication rights for this English edition arranged through Kodansha Ltd., Tokyo.

First published in Japan in 2019 by Kodansha Ltd., Tokyo as *Koi to uso*, volume 9.

ISBN 978-1-63236-676-4

Original cover design by Tadashi Hisamochi (hive & co., Ltd.)

Printed in the United States of America.

www.kodanshacomics.com

9 8 7 6 5 4 3 2 1
Translation: Jennifer Ward
Lettering: Daniel CY
Editing: Tiff Ferentini
Kodansha Comics edition cover design by Phil Balsman

Publisher: Kiichiro Sugawara

Director of publishing services: Ben Applegate
Associate director of operations: Stephen Pakula
Publishing services managing editor: Noelle Webster
Assistant production manager: Emi Lotto, Angela Zurlo